CELEBRATION

Studies in Festivity and Ritual

Victor Turner
Editor

Smithsonian Institution Press
Washington, D.C.
1982

Library of Congress Cataloging in Publication Data
Main entry under title:

Celebration, studies in festivity and ritual.

Published on the occasion of an exhibition organized by the Office of Folklife Programs of the Smithsonian Institution at the Renwick Gallery, spring, 1982.
Includes index.
1. Festivals—Addresses, essays, lectures. 2. Rites and ceremonies—Addresses, essays, lectures. 3. Ritual—Addresses, essays, lectures. I. Turner, Victor. II. Smithsonian Institution. Office of Folklife Programs. III. Renwick Gallery.
GT3930.C44   394   81–607102

ISBN 0–87474–920–4 (cloth)   AACR2
ISBN 0–87474–919–0 (pbk.)

Cover:
Men from the Marlboro Morris and Sword dance "Castle Ring" around a hobbyhorse (in this case a hobbydeer, held by the man in the center).

The paper in this book meets the guidelines for permanence and durability of the Committee on Production Guidelines for Book Longevity of the Council on Library Resources.

Contents

Preface

Wherever the human spirit is free, people celebrate. All cultures commemorate what makes them distinctive and worthy in their own eyes. Periodically, a common humanity in us all sets aside the work and worry of everyday life and blossoms into festivity, sometimes even in the face of cultural domination and economic deprivation. We are pleased to have the Office of Folklife Programs participate in the ancient and rich discourse of celebration and ceremony. When the Smithsonian's Assistant Secretary for History and Art, Charles Blitzer, suggested that an exhibition be mounted to show the extent of Smithsonian holdings in the area of folklife, and Lloyd Herman, the Director of the Renwick Gallery, offered the Gallery's elegant and ample exhibit space for a year, we deliberated only briefly before opting for celebration as theme. We have never looked back.

Central to the exhibition are specimens, gleaned from the Smithsonian museum collections, that were fashioned by their makers for use in ceremonies and celebrations. In the course of their construction and use, these objects have been imbued with layers upon layers of symbolic meanings, which can be read and felt by those who understand them. Ceremonial objects are the metaphoric maps and tools and social chronicles that people carry with them when they step out of secular space and time and explore the world of heightened celebratory consciousness. They can help a people look back on everyday life and criticize it and look forward to the processes that can re-make it.

Ceremonial objects, rich in meaning, draw our attention to themselves and then through themselves to the celebrations which gave them life; and through the celebrations to the religious, political, and economic systems of which they are a part; and through these systems to the actual communities whose ceremonial objects, celebrations, and social systems bespeak particular places, epochs, and struggles in the history of mankind.

Neophytes in producing object-oriented museum exhibitions, we chose a topic at once familiar to us in the fifteen years of producing the Festival of American Folklife, and problematical in its ability to be explored in a museum setting. Reviewing the three years' work of Victor Turner, Elaine Eff, Kristie Miller, and a host of researchers, writers, designers, and object preparers with many occupational specializations, we are confident that the unexpectedly large, lavishly rich, and somewhat overwhelming exhibition will perform its perhaps unusual mission of exploring the nature of evanescent events through the medium of material objects. For the exhibition is about the celebratory process itself—not (as is usual in museum exhibits) about the collection of a particular person, or of a particular region, era, or construction medium, or even of objects with a very specific function, like musical instruments or farm implements.

We ask nothing less than that the observer see through the objects to the celebrations of which they were part, to the celebrants and their historical situation and symbolic universe, to the phenomenon of celebration itself. We hope that the exhibit speaks to questions such as the behavioral modes that seem universally to mark celebratory events, the nature of points in the social field that occasion celebrations, and the magic that imbues material objects with spiritual meanings. Perhaps the constellations of objects, grouped for the most part by the events they were part of, are somewhat like folktales: evocative pieces that often entertain and sometimes strike resonances that impel insight to deeper levels or broader horizons. As for narratives, not every object or constellation of objects can effect this transcendence in every observer, but almost all objects, with their concatenation of symbols and meanings, arrest the attention, entertain, and invite reflection.

This collection of essays had its inception in the creative interaction of Victor Turner's theoretical intellect, knowledge, energy, and spirit with celebratory objects from Smithsonian collections. The essays both complement the exhibition and speak in their own clear, strong, and wonderfully rich discourse. The breadth of vision reflected herein is that of the Celtic demiurge who willed and inspired others to will the book's existence and the existence of the exhibition as a whole. It has been enlightening.

Ralph Rinzler
Peter Seitel
Office of Folklife Programs
Smithsonian Institution

Acknowledgments

Many have labored long and well behind the scenes to bring this book to completion, most of them being deeply involved in the *Celebration* exhibition as well. Mr. Charles Blitzer, Assistant Secretary for History and Art at the Smithsonian Institution, was the first to suggest that the Folklife Program should mount an exhibition on the theme of human celebration, viewed cross-culturally, drawing on the Smithsonian's rich resources. The Program's Director, Ralph Rinzler, and Peter Seitel, a leading folklorist and Africanist in the Program, enthusiastically endorsed the notion. They received the inevitably imaginative encouragement of the Smithsonian's Secretary, S. Dillon Ripley, and the "show was on the road." Ralph and Peter contributed at all times immeasurably to the dual enterprise of exhibition and book. I was invited to be Guest Curator and soon found myself associated with a lively and capable team of organizers and research workers. Elaine Eff, as Exhibition Coordinator, brought her formidable energy to bear in the selection and assembling of objects and the organization of research into their significant cultural contexts. Kristie Miller, Project Manager, overcame a thousand obstacles to ensure that exhibition and book were smoothly and efficiently coordinated, with the invaluable help of Elizabeth Hantzes, her Exhibition Assistant. A first-rate team of researchers, Leon Siroto, David Penney, Elizabeth Stockton, Chang-Su Houchins, Priscilla Rachun Linn, and Ira Jacknis (the last two, coincidentally, former students of mine at Cornell and the University of Chicago, respectively), and my colleagues in the Department of Anthropology at the University of Virginia, Professors Christopher Crocker and Stanley Walens, and Marianne George, just returned from fieldwork in New Ireland, gave contextual and exegetical meaning and hence human interest to the beautiful or striking objects gleaned from the Smithsonian's many museums. Kim Nielsen and Jeff Ploskonka worked sensitively and patiently to secure for us the most accurate and pleasing photographic record of the five hundred or so objects displayed. Since the National Museum of Natural History provided us with the majority of our objects, it was a matter of course that we should turn to its curators for permission and advice on the borrowing of treasured items from their collections. We are particularly indebted to William Crocker, whose responsibilities include South American Indian artifacts, and who has contributed an article on the Canela of Brazil to this volume; William Sturtevant, the famed editor for the definitive series of volumes on the North American Indians; and Gordon Gibson, in charge of the African collections. The exhibition was housed in the Renwick Gallery of the National Museum of American Art. Lloyd E. Herman, Director of the Renwick, has invariably given us sound advice on the aesthetics of our presentation, translated and elaborated by the consummate craftsmanship of the Renwick's Michael Monroe, who designed the exhibition. Their approaches have been transliterated into many aspects of this book. Sadly, Joshua C. Taylor, Director of the Smithsonian's National Museum of American Art, and a preeminent American art scholar, my former colleague at the University of Chicago, and a staunch supporter of our endeavors at the Renwick, died suddenly in his prime as this book was going to press. He was a great scholar and a teacher without parallel. Many more have contributed, both directly and indirectly, to both book and exhibition. One can scarcely forbear to mention Martha Breidenbach, who compiled film materials; Claudine Weatherford and Vince Wilcox, of the National Museum of Natural History, who took care of the physical existence of the objects entrusted to them; and Richard Derbyshire, Photographic Archivist of the Folklore/Folklife Program. Finally, Felix Lowe, the Director of the Smithsonian Institution Press, and his lieutenant, Managing Editor Maureen Jacoby, worked hard to make this complex study a publishable reality, as did Press editor John Harris.

V.T.

Introduction

Victor Turner

T his book is the twin of an exhibition entitled *Celebration: A World of Art and Ritual*, organized and mounted by the Folklife Program of the Smithsonian Institution at the Renwick Gallery in the spring of 1982. It is not, however, an identical twin, although its arrangement into sections corresponds closely with the exhibition's division into galleries. It is, rather, a fraternal twin having a similar parentage and background: folklife and anthropology. It is not a mirror image; it has its own distinctive features. Whereas the exhibition necessarily directs attention to objects, to material things, to what can be immediately seized by the senses, the book focuses on the meanings behind the forms, the inner significance of the objects, whose eloquent silences "cry out" for interpretation. The book, too, reflects the design governing the celebratory process, the scenario interlinking its events.

Washington, home of the Smithsonian, has, of course, been the scene and stage for many a celebration. America's ceremonies of respect, festivity, and rejoicing—our Independence Days, presidential inaugurations, state funerals, our national triumphs and tragedies—have been most signally celebrated at the capital. The Smithsonian's numerous exhibitions of art, technology, science, history, and anthropology represent a kind of perennial celebration of America's past and present achievements. But more than America is celebrated in its museums. Scientific and military expeditions, private collectors, missionaries, administrators, and foreign allies have loaded the Smithsonian's stores with objects of every kind, practical, quaint, precious, beautiful, massive, filigree, acquired from thousands of cultural sources as gifts, purchases, and sometimes, alas, booty. Among these objects are many which owe their very existence to those "high tides," "peak experiences" in social life which mark an occasion or an event with ceremony, ritual, or festivity. People in all cultures recognize the need to set aside certain times and spaces for celebratory use, in which the possibility of personal and communal creativity may arise. Celebrations may and do spring up spontaneously in response to unlooked-for good fortune, but they are generally connected with expectable culturally shared events, such as life experiences (birth, puberty, marriage), work (planting and harvesting of crops, quilting bees), seasons of the year (Christmas), religious beliefs (Jagannath processions, the Ghost Dance), upward shifts in social status (African staff ornaments and potlatch feasts and valuables), and shared community celebrations (Thanksgiving and Seder). Some of these events are tied in with the individual life-cycle; others are located in the family, the neighborhood, the village, the city, or the nation. Although the span and range of celebration are highly variable, events are framed by it in such a way as to draw on the innovative potential of participants. Each kind of ritual, ceremony, or festival comes to be coupled with special types of attire, music, dance, food and drink, "properties," modes of staging and presentation, physical and cultural environment, and, often, masks, body-painting, headgear, furniture, and shrines.

Abundant opportunities are offered for personal inventiveness within the culturally defined celebratory frame, for example, in musical composition, choreography, costume design, the use of ceremonial space, iconography (pictorial illustration, stylization of art forms used), enactment of ritual or dramatic roles, and so forth. Group stylistic traditions, sometimes of great power and beauty, may develop in ritual or festive frameworks, for example, the calypso music of Trinidadian carnival with its ironical improvised lyrics on topical subjects, or bridal dress in Muslim North Africa.

The Folklife Program at the Smithsonian has for thirteen years organized an impressive Festival of American Folklife, which has attracted millions of visitors to the Mall in Washington to enjoy its presentation of live performances of folk music, drama, carnival, and puppetry, as well as demonstrations of traditional American arts and crafts, regional, ethnic, and occupational. Ralph Rinzler, the Program's Director, was not alone in being impressed by the creative initiatives of many of the participants recruited from across the nation. Leading scholars of the Smithsonian, notably the anthropologist Peter Seitel of the Folklife Program, were convinced that among the resources of the Institution's many museums would be found a sufficient number of objects to form the basis of a major exhibition on the theme of celebration. Each object would be a product of the celebratory process, a precipitate from its eventful flow. The exhibition would retain the character of this process by the insertion of craft demonstrations, films, slides, music and other audiovisual aids, and a monthly presentation of actual ethnic celebrations at appropriate points in time and space. More than five hundred objects were eventually selected by qualified folklorists, art historians, and anthropologists from ten Smithsonian museums, representing sixty-two world cultures, requiring for their display the entire floorspace of the Renwick Gallery.

As we scanned the Smithsonian collections, my fellow researchers and I made several interesting discoveries. We found, for example, that by comparison with both the folk and high cultures of Asia and Africa and the preindustrial ("tribal") cultures of both Americas, of Australia, and of Oceania, the United

States was only sparsely represented by objects originating in religious celebrations. The exception to this finding consisted of images, icons, religious furniture, altars and their equipment, sacramentals, vestments, and other religious articles and adornments characteristic of the religious culture of immigrant minority groups now permanently residing in the United States: European and Latin American Catholics, Eastern Orthodox Christians, Jews, Chinese, Muslims, Vietnamese, and so on. Moreover, Europe was surprisingly underrepresented by celebratory objects of all types.

How may we account for such an apparently capricious and certainly uneven distribution? Let me hazard a few hypotheses. The New England Puritans in the seventeenth century, and after them many other religiously radical colonists, undoubtedly regarded Europe, especially in its religious aspect, as the Great Babylon or idolatrous Egypt, and their westward flight across the ocean as a new Exodus. An unsullied democracy, conceived as Christ's government in church and state (which were to be separate) was to be carved out of the wilderness. Obedience to God, not to earthly rulers, was man's supreme duty; the individual, dependent on his own conscience and finally responsible to God alone, was the ethical unit, and government was a compact between free individuals. Such a world-view was clearly opposed to postfeudal hierarchical political governance and to ecclesiastical hierocracy. The early Americans turned their backs on the Europe of kings, nobles, and priests. Similarly they rejected the visible symbolic system which gave expression to the political and religious *anciens régimes*. Sacredness was interiorized; human beings were made in the "express image and likeness of God"; the individual rather than the corporate group was the basic unit of worship. The Word was to be heard, not the icon or image seen. The naturalistic and individualistic tendencies of the eighteenth-century Enlightenment reinforced this rejection of perceptible sacred symbols. In the cyclical rituals of preindustrial and agriculturally based cultures, the past, mythical and quasihistorical, is "carried" by certain key or dominant sacred symbols. The unchangeable character of the cosmic and cultural orders and the notion of life as a repetition of structures are expressed by *sacra* ("holy things"), objects and activities believed to be charged with supernatural power, which are presented for worshipful attention in religious celebrations. In American culture there has been a general desacralization of objects, and celebrations focus on the immediacies of joy in human achievement, represented by such means as brisk or rhythmical bodily action, dancing or marching, and the music of marching bands. In museums this rational, naturalistic approach to the individual and culture has led to an emphasis on the collection of objects which have technological, artistic, political, scientific, historical, and economic significance, at the expense of objects held to have perennial sacredness or holiness. At least such a view holds true for things American. The *sacra* of other cultures, often including the most beautiful and striking articles in museum holdings, have always fascinated the Western public. Perhaps this is because they make visible what Westerners have thrust from conscious awareness in order to effect their rational conquest of the material world. Just as the capacity to dream and fantasize, though not immoderately, is considered by psychologists to be indispensable for mental health, so, likewise, exposure to those objectified dreams and fantasies which are thrown up by celebratory enthusiasm may be necessary for social health. Perhaps, paradoxically, we confront our own personal, singular depths more fully in these collective forms than we do through introspection, for they arise from a heightened sense of our shared humanity, even if they clothe themselves in the guises of a thousand different cultures. Whether laid down or crystallized in durable images and structures or expressed in the immediacy of social "peak experience," a celebratory performance rejoices in the key values and virtues of the society that produces it, and in a history whose high points of success and conquest (or even noble failure) exemplify qualities of moral and aesthetic excellence. The Smithsonian exhibition attempts to express the North American celebratory type by enlarged photographic prints ("blow-ups"), audiovisuals (sound filmstrips), and similar devices which stress the "processual," "becoming" character of this restlessly linear industrial civilization.

As we worked our way steadily through the Smithsonian collections—that world of storage drawers secluded from the viewing public—in fourteen museums, it became clear to us that an exhibition premised upon aesthetic "form"

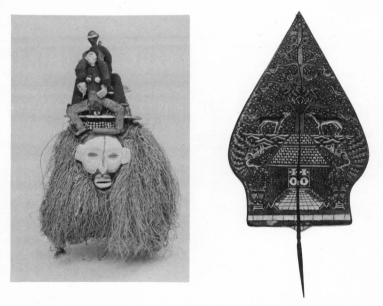

Figure 1 *Mask, Yaka People, southwestern Zaire. Mbala is the most important mask in the Yaka initiation rites. Often the masks depict a surprising scene: this one shows a woman in childbirth assisted by a midwife.*

Figure 2 *Shadow-play signal, Java, Indonesia. In Javanese shadow-puppet play, this figure signals the beginning and end of a performance. The translucent leather figure represents a mythical mountain where the tree of life grows.*

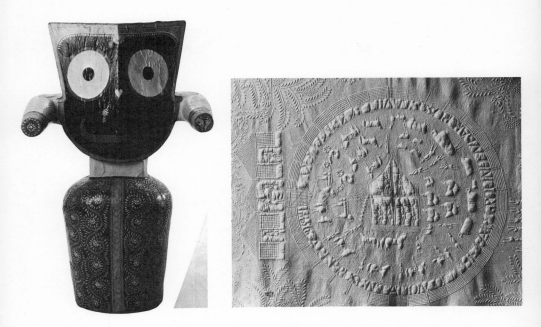

Figure 3 *This image of Jagannātha, Lord of the Universe, is worshiped at the shrine of Puri in Orissa, India. The most famous festival in which Jagannātha appears is the* Ratha Jātrā *or huge Car Festival.*

Figure 4 *Detail of trapunto quilt depicting horses, riders, carriages, livestock, and visitors to the Logan County Fair near Russellville, Kentucky.*

alone would conceal as much as it revealed about the nature of celebration. "Meaning" had to be taken equally into account. We had decided that the first hall entered by the public should be designated "Objects Speak," but it was obvious that some translation was required. The objects, unexplained, remained mute, though clearly charged with repressed eloquence. Those chosen by researchers were vehemently held by them to be the most beautiful or striking in the collection. Their selection was perhaps arbitrary and even sometimes ethnocentric, but it produced some lovely, bizarre, and suggestive pieces, including: facial masks used in boys' initiation rituals among the Yaka of Zaire (fig. 1); a shadow-puppet figure from the Javanese *Wayang* shadow plays (fig. 2); a bull-roarer from Bororo initiation rites in Brazil; an awesome image of the Jagannātha deity from Puri, Orissa, in India (fig. 3); and, from North America, a Tlingit "totem pole" and a Russellville County, Kentucky, "white work" quilt, representing the Logan County Fair of 1856, a celebration re-created from memory by Miss Virginia M. Ivey in a quilted representation containing 1,200,600 stitches (fig. 4). Objects certainly "speak," that is, they directly communicate a message through visible and tangible qualities such as form, color, texture, size, and so forth; but the "message" is greatly enhanced and expanded when the objects are recognized as being culturally specific symbols to be decoded and set in their proper celebratory context. A symbol is something that represents something else by association, resemblance, or convention. Spoken or printed words, for example, are symbols. But celebratory objects are, first and foremost, material objects, though they represent ideas, objects, events, relationships, "truths" not immediately present to the observer, or even intangible or invisible thoughts and conceptions. Such celebratory symbols, moreover, usually stand for many things and thoughts at once. Technical terms for this capacity are: *multivocal* (literally "many voiced"), "speaking" in many ways at once; *multivalent,* having various meanings or values; and *polysemous,* having or being open to several or many meanings. When a social group, whether it be a family, clan, village, nation, congregation, or church, celebrates a particular event or occasion, such as birth, harvest, or national independence, it also "celebrates itself." In other words, it attempts to manifest, in symbolic form, what it conceives to be its essential life, at once the distillation and typification of its corporate experience. The word *celebration* is derived from the Latin *celeber,* "numerous, much frequented," and relates to the vivacity—akin to what the great French sociologist Durkheim called "effervescence"—generated by a crowd of people with shared purposes and common values. When artists, craftsmen, songsmiths, and musicians are invited or commissioned to "make" something for a celebration, their work is inevitably informed by lively memories of that effervescence and equally lively anticipations of its next embodiment. In a way such "makers" become the articulators of the otherwise inchoate celebratory "spirit," and the ephemeral events they choreograph, or the permanent artworks—altars, statues, masks, totem poles, paintings, temples—they shape or construct, become a kind of shining language in which a society formulates its conception of the universe and its cultural philosophy. It is this heightened awareness and moral earnestness—in the midst often of tumultuous joy—that gives the best of celebratory objects a capacity to compel attention, even when they are products of a culture hitherto unknown to the observer.

When we see objects in an exhibition or a museum collection, we see them detached from the resonant ambiance of celebration. We see them in ingenious settings of background or lighting designed to restore in some measure the effervescence of their social matrix. But we are also able to some degree to trace the path back from object to meaning thanks to the labors in many cultures of a generation of symbolic anthropologists. In the first place, the external form and observable characteristics of the object give preliminary clues to its significance. The natural material from which it is made is seldom accidental: if an image or a throne is made of wood, for example, it will not be found arbitrary that a hardwood is chosen over a softwood or vice versa, or that the chosen wood is white, black, red, or mottled in hue. What kind of color or material is chosen will depend on a culture's system of classification: in Chinese culture, brides wear red, in European Christian culture, white; white garments are typically worn at Chinese funerals, black at European obsequies. The name given an object may also open a way to its meaning. Among the Ndembu people of Zambia in Central Africa, the root *kishi* stands for "ancestor" or "ancestral power": with the prefix *i-,* the term *ikishi* stands for a fiber-and-gum mask representing a remote tribal ancestor; with the prefix *mu-, mukishi* designates a wooden figurine representing a recently deceased relative. The meaning of an object may be partly inferred from features and attributes imparted to the original material by the artist. Here cultural convention plays a major role: the image of a water deity may be represented with a fishtail, a hunter deity may hold a bow and arrow. Several articles in this book—for example, Barbara Babcock's chapter on a Pueblo potter—discuss how the personal style of a gifted artist can powerfully affect the tradition within which he or she works. These bases of meaning, substantial, linguistic, and artifactual, pertain to the sensorily perceptible form of the symbolic object—what De Saussure called the *signifiant*. They may or may not be directly connected to the "invisible content" of the symbol, its *signifié,* the set of mental images, concepts, ideas denoted and connoted by the *signifiant*. Usually, there is a link between a symbol's perceptible features and aspects of its meaning: red often means blood, white a state of unblemished purity (though it may also represent semen, sunlight, milk, or blankness!); black may stand for the implicit fertility of black rain clouds, or it may mean death or feces. "Natural" resemblances are culturally selected. When the connections just listed are explained to us, they seem reasonable and familiar, facts of general human experience, but it is by no means easy to predict the precise association a culture will choose to make between "signifier" and "signified."

Further work is needed to discover the "field" of meaning in which a celebratory object has its potential for arousing thought, emotion, and desire. It is,

Figure 5 *Drums of peace* (kanko), *Japan. Traditionally beaten in an appeal for redress, these* kanko *now connote good government and peaceful society. The circular gold design was an emblem of creation, and the gilt cocks represented peace and prosperity.*

of course, important to know what the society which engenders and uses it says about it, if indeed it says anything at all. For not infrequently a key symbol, particularly one used in religious celebration, may be refractory to standardized verbal interpretation. It may be compared in this respect with a poem, which is its own interpretation and special kind of language. Here paraphrase and individual guessing at meaning may be possible, even frequent and fashionable. Local "theologians" and ritual specialists may declare the symbol to be what Western divines would call a "mystery," something beyond human knowledge or understanding, part of an undergirding structure of being (like Kant's "categories" or Jung's archetypes) that is impenetrable to total rational understanding. But in many cultures, persons will be found who are generally regarded as "exegetes," experts in the explanation of symbols. Often, the "explanation" of a celebratory or ritual symbol will be assigned by exegetes to its role or place within a religious myth or heroic tale. Analysis thus stops at myth, which replaces a representational mystery by a verbal mystery. In the exhibition, for example, images of Jagannātha (see fig. 3) are related to myths involving the Hindu god Vishnu, especially in his Krishna incarnation, while the decorative iconography of Northwest Coast Indian "potlatch chests" is connected with myths in which Raven and Bear are transformed into humans and vice versa. By "myths" I designate the creative deeds of gods, heroes, and ancestors who established the cosmic and social orders, often in struggle with powers of chaos. Myth and morality vary independently; indeed, some divine and heroic exploits violate what a society normally considers its standards of goodness or righteousness in conduct or character. Deities commit incest and parricide, tempt and deceive mortals, practice cannibalism. Great heroes have fatal flaws of character. Myth portrays generative power as transrational and transethical. Quite often, celebrations have mythical "plots," and are based on narratives of divine intervention in human affairs. Celebratory objects may remind participants of those myths, and of the primal energies they *re*-present (that is, make present again to the senses, changing the symbol into what is symbolized).

However, by no means all symbolic objects are explained by myths. There is also a form of interpretation which may be termed "piecemeal exegesis." Here the native interpreter can assign standardized meanings to certain qualities or characteristics of objects taken to be or formed into celebratory symbols. For example, the Ndembu of Zambia find significance in the color of an object, in its texture, in its slenderness or thickness, its hardness or softness, its rareness or typicality; in its location in water or on land, in cultivated land or in the bush; in its form as an animal, bird, reptile, vegetable, or mineral, or a plant bearing much fruit or a single fruit; in conventional designs incised as cicatrices on the human body; in marks carved in wood; or in paintings made on masks and walls. Naturally, exegetical knowledge is not shared equally by all, nor is the capacity to offer verbal interpretation. A ritual specialist, who knows how to conduct a complex sequence of rites involving many symbolic objects, may have difficulty in explaining their meaning in words. He has operational knowledge akin to a carpenter's who "knows the feel of the wood" even if he is no dendrologist, no tree botanist. The exegetical problem may also be compounded by secrecy: the "true" or "inner" meaning of a symbolic object may be known or shared only by the initiated few. In many secret societies, for example in West and Central Africa and Papua-New Guinea, as well as among the guilds of Western Masonry, there is a system of grades through which initiates pass. In some societies, the same objects may be differently interpreted as the novice moves from a lower to a higher level. The esoteric knowledge imparted at the highest level is held to be the "real truth," the final *gnosis,* annulling all previous interpretations. However, the exegesis of objects used in public celebrations is seldom dominated by a group of privileged specialists. Such objects are the product, center, and soul of a social group's self-manifestation. They are created to "speak" to at least the members of the culture they embody and manifest. And if they speak they are also "heard," for they have been brought forth from experiences shared with those of their "receivers." The fabricators of these celebratory objects share "social being" with all other members of the celebrating society, its history, traditions, religion, contemporary triumphs and tragedies, its hopes and fears for the future. There is perhaps no need to render into words what the symbols "say," for they transmit their messages in a number of sensory codes simultaneously. Moreover, we are seldom dealing with separate symbols but with clusters made up of objects, actions, sounds, states, odors, contacts, each unit, act, or thing, at once itself and standing for more than itself, the ensemble making up more than the sum of its parts. In the celebratory process we cannot detach the participants from what they participate in, the subject from the object. From the subject's sensorium, his "withinside," such clusters are no longer experienced as detached from him, held at arm's length, merely cognized. They invade him, alter his mode of perceiving, daze or dazzle him. He is made vulnerable to imprintment by whatever message is being conveyed by the symbolic cluster. In celebration, private space is thus socialized, enculturated; social space is correspondingly made private.

Yet celebrations end, and in most human groups certain people try to put into words, however lamely, what they have experienced in the "meta-experience" of culturally stimulated action. I call it "meta-experience" because celebration distills all other kinds of experience to draw out the part that is essential to each of them. Language is, no doubt, only the tip of the intersubjective iceberg, the dead husk of the living celebratory fruit, but it remains the most efficient means of expressing and communicating thoughts and feelings among members of a human community. Perhaps only celebration can adequately understand celebration, but language can give an approximate rendering of it and some semantic perspective on its products, the symbols it uses and leaves behind. Eugene d'Aquili and Charles Laughlin (1979:169) have argued that humankind has a "need for order as a cognitive imperative." There is clearly an equal need for the repetitive, motor, visual, or auditory driving stimuli, combined with the cadence of words and chanting which many kinds of celebration provide, producing arousal, heightened activity, and emotional responsiveness. The anchoring or "dominant" symbols of celebration, when these can be interpreted by native cognitive specialists, often betray this bipolarity. Even in the case of language we can see a migration of verbal meanings to opposite poles.

At what may be described as the "normative" pole we find that an anchoring celebratory symbol "stands for" or "signifies" a number of aspects of the moral, social, and political orders. At the opposite pole, the attributed meanings or "senses" point to physiological processes, such as sexuality or lactation, or metabolism. Sometimes, they designate aspects of human anatomy. Often, as in the case of blood symbolism, they represent violence and its sublimated equivalent, sacrifice. Earlier we saw that important celebratory symbols are multivocal, "saying" many things at once. They say many things about the social and moral order and many things about the natural and physical order *at the same time*. The natural-physical pole may be called the *orectic* pole of meaning, since this term in philosophy and psychology characterizes appetite and desire, wishing and feeling. Perhaps this duality or antinomianism in meaning is connected to the complementary functions of the two hemispheres of the human brain, as J. Bogen, S. Dimond, R. Ornstein, and D. Kimura have suggested; the left hemisphere being the domain of logic (and by extension social structuring) and the right hemisphere that of emotion, pattern recognition, and holistic, synthetic thought, but with limited linguistic capability and no sense of linear time. It might be suggested that the normative pole is left hemispheric (verbal, linear, time-binding), while the orectic pole is right hemispheric and also possibly connected with biological rhythms controlled by the autonomic nervous system. When symbols are "fed" into a celebratory process, the semantic poles are transformed from clusters of abstract "meanings" into agencies and indicators of social arousal. It is perhaps in this process that complementary interaction between the components of the central nervous system is at its maximum. The oppositions work/play, cognition/orexis, duty/pleasure, individual/group are overcome, or they mutually tincture/impregnate one another to produce a third, heightened state conducive to public creativity.

But interpretations offered by specialists and laypersons are not enough to give us an adequate understanding of celebratory symbols. We have to view them in action, in movement, in becoming, as essentially involved in process. Much of an object's "meaning" is equated with its use: we must observe what a celebrating group does, not merely what it says. We must find out how they act toward an object, what attitudes group members publicly display when they use it, handle it, venerate it, destroy it, dance around it, or otherwise orientate themselves toward it. Is their behavior defined as sad, penitent, joyful, derisive, aggressive, respectful? Furthermore, we must ascertain what kinds of persons compose the group: males, females, old, young, or all together? Persons of high rank or social status in everyday life, or low status, or both? Members of a family or kin group, neighbors, or total strangers? Members of a single caste or a multicaste group? We should also inquire why certain persons and groups are absent on given occasions, and if absent, whether and why they have been formally excluded from the presence of the important celebratory symbol. I would call this level or field of "meaning" the *operational meaning*. Social structure, social organization, and social psychology are all involved here. Unlike *exegetical* meaning, operational meaning is largely discovered by trained observation. It is the province of the social scientist. For example, when an anthropologist studies a celebration in a preindustrial society, he has usually already derived from his empirical data (censuses, genealogies, budgets, land tenure surveys, legal case histories, investigations of political and administrative structures, and the like) a set of models of constant and consistent social relationships, the sum of which approximates a hypothetical representation of the social structure as it exists at the time of investigation. He has also ascertained the forms taken by social conflict in the social field articulated by that structure: what types of persons are likely to have antagonistic interests, what groups are likely to collide over political issues or economic goals. Any major celebration, since it brings many members of a society into a single sociocultural space for a limited period of time, brings into proximity persons and groups with either endemic or transitory antagonisms. Celebration may be said partly to bring about a temporary reconciliation among conflicting members of a single community. Conflict is held in abeyance during the period of ritualized action. Perhaps the euphoria associated with the stimulation of "right-hemisphere" capacities and functions leads to that perception of shared emotional states I have called communitas. This might also involve a deemphasizing of "left-hemisphere" control over logical, linear, and classifying functions associated with social structuring, and the conflicts arising from structural oppositions.

A celebratory object may also be interpreted on a third level, its *positional* meaning. The positional meaning of such an object derives from its relationship to other symbols in a configuration, a Gestalt, having properties that cannot be derived from its parts or be considered simply as their sum. The object may be part of a cluster of similar or different objects; it may occupy a central or a marginal position. It may be strikingly contrasted with another object. Position has to do with time as well as space. Thus an object may form part of a series successively exhibited in a celebratory process. These spatial and temporal relationships modify an object's meaning. They may do this by selecting only one of the object's many possible designations as appropriate to a given situation. Anthropologists who follow the noted French structuralist Lévi-Strauss regard the positional dimension as providing the true key—through structure and positioning rather than through exegetical content—to the interpretation of symbols. Such writers also tend to find the key to meaning in the relations between the vehicles or *signifiants* (the objects of sensory perception) rather than between the systems of *signifiés,* the "senses" or "designations" assigned to them by the people, or directly inferable by an investigator thoroughly familiar with the themes and idioms of the culture. Those who stress the importance of looking for pairs of symbols, regarding them as "binary oppositions," then looking for a third symbol to serve as a "mediator" between them, as *the* key to the scientific analysis of symbol systems, are almost compelled to direct attention to their "vehicular" or "*signifiant*" aspect or to regard the symbols as "univocal," having a single, sharply defined sense, "meaning," *signifié,* or "nature." This is because it is difficult to make sharp antitheses between complex bundles of designations, many of them associated with emotions and desires. What we are confronted with here, it would seem, is a kind of cognitive chauvinism. Symbols are probably products, markers, and registers of behavior motivated by both cere-

bral hemispheres in conjunction with the autonomic nervous system, all trig-
gered and fired into action by selective cultural stimuli, themselves the creation
of centuries of cultural and ecological experience. As such they bear traces of
their complex neurophysiological sources both in their "appearance" (how they
impinge upon the senses) and in their semantics (the notions or conceptions
the group using them holds about them, whether stereotyped or legitimately
speculative). To reduce this wealth of "objectivized" mentality to the merely
cognitive is to wantonly impoverish one's capacity for scientific explanation of
the most human of human phenomena: symbol-making.

To be sure, if one looks at ethnographic accounts of ritual (constituting a sort
of retrospective "score," "script," or "scenario"), one cannot escape the fact that
many symbol-vehicles or "objects" are arrayed in antithetical pairs (red objects
against white, left against right, "male" things against "female" things, hard
against soft, and so on) during certain episodes or phases in a ritual or celebratory process. Here the objects' *relationships* (of opposition or complementarity)
may decisively influence the *meanings* they *situationally* possess. But the same
symbol-vehicles may be arrayed in threes, fours, or other plural formations, in
company with other symbol-vehicles in other phases or in other types of ritual
in the same culture—or may appear alone, opposed, or qualified by no other
symbol even by implication. Again, wherever in ritual or secular celebration
symbolic objects appear in clusters, they may or may not be arrayed and organized as a hierarchy, that is, with one object dominating or focal to the others,
or with a graded array into symbols with more or less prominence or semantic
importance. Looked at successively, whether from left to right, right to left, top
to bottom, bottom to top, as units in space, or in linear order through time,
symbol-vehicles, like words, may be grouped to form complex "messages" in
what one might call "sentences" of symbols. The "positional" dimension of symbol interpretation might also include consideration of asymmetrical pairs of
symbols, where the meanings of one are subordinated to those of another. Ethnographic experience in several cultures has shown me that where one has
managed to obtain reliable information about the "exegetical" and/or "operational" meanings of a given symbol-vehicle or "object," it is demonstrable that
even though only a single designation of that symbol is situationally manifest or
emphasized (perhaps by opposing it patently to another symbol in "binary"
terms), the "penumbra" (the vague, indefinite, or borderline area) of latent senses (to be manifest in other "positional" combinations) is nevertheless present.
I have shown, for example, in various studies of the Ndembu of Zambia
(1967:41–42; 1968:80–82) that latent senses of symbol A may be "projected"
upon symbols B, C, and D, which are present in the same "symbolic field."
Thus a symbol should be anticipated to be "dense with meaning"—what Edward Sapir called a "condensation symbol"—even when only a portion of this
richness (like the tip of an iceberg) is situationally emphasized or "visible"
through such tactical devices as its (surface) structural relations with another
contrapuntal symbol or set of symbols. Structural analysis reduces or simplifies
the overt "meaning" of a symbol-vehicle, or, better, is a "grammatical" tactic for
specifying which of its multiple meanings is situationally relevant at a given mo-

ment in the unfolding of a ritual or the staging of a celebration, hence actualizing or pinpointing that purport out of the vast semantic potential or latent wealth possessed by the communicative means we call "a symbol."

It must now be clear that museums have, traditionally, been at a great disadvantage in terms of conveying to the public the meanings of the objects they exhibit. For objects have been collected, in the main, as single items, divorced from their operational and positional contexts. In actuality, as we have seen, they are registers of complex processes, dependent upon one another for their meaning at a given time, and when they are quiescent, hoarded up, so to speak, in temples or shrines, they can be seen as storage jars or cells of multiple cultural and religious meanings (*signifiés*) that we can only gain access to, when lucky, through written accounts. Yet we must attempt to reanimate these silent, often lovely forms, whether in imagination or by means of the techniques available to us today—ethnographic documentaries, taped music, adorned plexiglas mannequins, dioramas, blow-ups, live performances (necessarily simulated or fabricated when done out of cultural context)—the whole range of audiovisual techniques. Alas, without time machines, we cannot use these means to capture the spirit of celebrations no longer celebrated. Here we do have to rely on sensitive and scientifically painstaking re-creation of forever-vanished events by inference from literary, archaeological, and historical sources.

Yet the endeavor has seemed to us worthwhile. The silent products of celebration or for celebration are more than utilitarian goods and chattels. Each of our lead essayists knows that though men, women, and children celebrate many achievements and many pinnacles of life or heroic death, one constant experience threads through and occasionally surfaces from all modes of celebration, solemn or festive: a transcendent ecstasy rooted in deep physiological passions and charged-up autonomic awareness but burgeoning and ramifying beyond them into transient imaginative apprehensions of the meanings inherent in self and society. The divine detritus, the holy or beautiful images and artifacts bequeathed to us by celebration, whether exalted or frenetic, testify to these moments when members of our species, scattered through every continent and clime, have exceeded their daily limits and left traces, culture by culture, age after age, to encourage the rest of us.

Richard Dorson, in his essay on "Material Components in Celebration," summarizes seven celebrations performed in cultures as widely dispersed as Peru, Trinidad, Louisiana, Africa, India, China, and Japan, paying particular heed to "the material culture props and properties . . . which might find their way into museum exhibits." He points out that "the term *celebration* can encompass festivals, rituals, ceremonies, spectacles, pageants, fetes, holidays, extravaganzas, and partakes of all these elements." His chapter is the literary analogue of the exhibition hall in the Renwick Gallery containing material components of celebration regarded cross-culturally. He finds that, in addition to the costumes, masks, musical instruments, serving bowls for festive food, and so forth, that we might expect to find, there are other objects charged with "religio-magical power." These include *images,* "key symbolic objects which represent the message and motive of the occasion," such as the image of the Virgen de la Puerta in the Otuzco Festival in Peru, and images of Lord Jagannātha, Lord Balabhadra, and Goddess Subhadrā in the Car Festival observed in the month of Asadha during the rainy season ("on the second day of the bright fortnight") in the coastal city of Puri in the Indian state of Orissa. Each of these, Christian and Hindu, is the object both of sophisticated, theological exegesis and of explanation in terms of folk mythology. And each is charged with the experiential power of mass devotion on a celebratory occasion that is both solemn and festive, devout and, at times, playful. Dorson also mentions "revered ritual *vehicles*" such as the "towering chariot in which rides Lord Jagannātha and the fierce dragon boat paddled by the Yangtse Valley fishermen" in the *King Tu* festival on the Hupeh-Hunan Plain in Central China. Images and vehicles are more than merely representational or functional: they are multivocal symbols, "condensation symbols" as Edward Sapir called them (1933:492–93). Dorson shows us how ephemeral costumes and masks and perishable food and drink also possess multiple meanings. On the other hand, it seems to be typical of carnival and fiesta that many symbols possess what Barbara Babcock has called "an excess of floating signifiers" (1978:291–302). Fireworks, exuberantly fantastic clothing, patchwork colors, the multiplication of apparently irrelevant masks and costumes "to the point of indeterminate nonsense," suspend customary meanings. Babcock follows Jacques Derrida in arguing that "a surplus of signifiers ["vehicles"] . . . creates a self-transgressive discourse which mocks and subverts the monological arrogance of 'official' systems of signification" (p.296). She continues: "The bantering *anti*-signified of carnivalesque discourse is an insult both to the complimentarity of ordinary speech and to the multi-signified of serious ritual communciation. It is also a statement in praise and a demonstration of the creative potential of human signification as opposed to its instrumental and representative use" (p.296). Dorson's chapter gives some examples of this. He mentions "the almost limitless variety of costumes seen at (the Trinidadian) Carnival" and "the trait of playful aggression that marks the behavior of carnival-type celebrants." However, he also points to "the humility that characterizes religious-festival behavior [in which symbols are multivocal]. Slave figures protect the Virgin; the Swazi mourn their king; the rajah sweeps the platform of the chariots. When the gods are present, men supplicate." It would seem that both structure and antistructure are present, in varying proportions, in different kinds of celebration, and that both act, in opposition or conjunction, to enhance the understanding a society has of its own essential nature, its plural reflexivity, so to speak. As Babcock concludes: "In ritual, society takes cognizance of itself and communicates its major classifications and categories both through ordering them and through disordering them—by overdetermining *and* by rendering indeterminate customary processes of signification" (1978:296).

Babcock's view that celebrations provide frames in which groups can scan, critique, and enjoy themselves, through construction and deconstruction of self-images ideal or realistic, is shared and developed by Barbara Myerhoff in her essay "Rites of Passage: Process and Paradox." Her discussion also duplicates and comments on a segment of the exhibition—a long gallery allocated to the display of objects drawn cross-culturally from such passage rites as birth, baptism, circumcision, puberty, marriage, initiation into membership-restricted associations, funerary and other celebrations of the passage of individuals and groups from one culturally defined stage of life to another in linear succession. Like the Turners in their essay on "Religious Celebrations," Myerhoff accepts van Gennep's formulation of rites of passage. These occur in three main stages of varying length and importance within and between cultures: (1) *separation* of the novices or "initiands" from everyday life, often by means of dramatic symbolic action; (2) *instruction* of novices by practice and precept in a secluded, "marginal," or *"liminal"* place; and (3) *reincorporation* of the now-initiated persons into the quotidian community.

Myerhoff laments the virtual absence of reliable data in anthropologists' accounts of the subjective experiences of those undergoing passage. Detailed descriptions of behavior and symbolism abound, but few have thought fit to inquire into the initiands' feelings about the transformation of their circumstances, often involving ordeals and always drastic breaks with comfortable routine. Thus, in premodern, preindustrial societies, we have a good idea of the public forms and standardized interpretations of symbols and ceremonies marking life-crises but little in the way of private reports from the participants. On the other hand, she argues, we have an abundance of reports in complex, modern societies, particularly from psychoanalysts, psychologists, and psychiatrists, on the private "rituals" of "alienated," isolated individuals, who have reacted to life-crises with neuroses or psychoses. But, as all know, there is a paucity of public rites of passage in Western industrialized societies. Christian baptism and confirmation, Jewish circumsion and Bar(Bat) Mitzvah, refer to symbolic progress through relatively restricted religious communities, not to public transformations of status-roles on the scale of the widest (plural) society. There are no communal, pan-American puberty celebrations, though commencement exercises and graduations have a rather weak functional equivalence.

On the other hand, with the increase in scale and complexity, with urbanization, specialization, professionalization, job mobility, labor migration, stress on individualism, the omnipresence of the cash economy, and so on, the occasions of personal crisis multiply exceedingly as compared with "tribal" or rurally based societies. Barbara Myerhoff makes a sound case for the "construction" of rituals and other kinds of celebration to handle such crises—those typical of our epoch and social condition. Her work during the past decade with the aged in Los Angeles, resulting in the widely read book *Number Our Days* (1978) and a short documentary film of the same title which won an Academy Award (made in collaboration with Lynn Litman) in 1977, has alerted Barbara Myerhoff to the lively possibility of a new kind of "applied anthropology." Such a program would include the "construction of performances" which would involve groups of modern individuals in assigning communal meaning to specifically modern and recurrent crises. She argues that the comparative study of celebrations on a global basis compels us to admit their "constructed" character. If our society does not provide them for us, why cannot we provide them for ourselves? For there is clearly a profound therapeutic value in the recognition and ritualization of recurrent problems involved in the maintenance and repair of human relationships and in assigning meaning to what subjectively may seem to be merely pain and loss. "What is required," she writes, "is a small community of friends or family, some symbolic and traditional resources for inspiration, a clear formulation of the change involved and its significance—and courage." She notes that in "our own society . . . in times of rapid individual mobility and social change, ceremonies of separation and disconnection are surely important." She shows how celebrations may represent an *overcoming* of difficulty, an affirmation of life in the teeth of affliction. As examples she cites "menopause, surgery, 'empty nests,' retirement. . . . a fiftieth birthday, a woman shedding her married name." All these, she writes, "can be opportunities for rites of passage, transformed from traumatic experiences or disorienting lonely episodes into commemorations that acknowledge change. The spontaneous ritual acts that we so often do alone—burning an unfaithful lover's photograph or returning gifts from one no longer cherished, the cutting of hair or cleaning house to announce to oneself that a new phase of life is beginning—all these are nascent rites of passage that can be enlarged, formalized, made to include important other people, memorialized with objects, notes, or records that are kept in recognition that the transition was successfully accomplished." Myerhoff's call is that we should be what I call more "liminoid" than "liminal," that is, take our crises and transitions into our own hands, ritualize them, make them meaningful, and pass through and beyond them in a spirit of celebration, to begin a new uncluttered phase of our lives, having learned from some of the world's oldest and most tenacious cultures a portion of their wisdom, their understanding of the human condition. As Myerhoff concludes: "Freedom is the other side of loneliness and isolation. When we take our lives into our own hands, we make ourselves author of our own stories." Her point is that we might create our own celebrations in communities of "intimately concerned individuals," instead of merely grieving over the lack of such institutionalized means in our depersonalized, industrial societies.

Roger Abrahams, in his essay "The Language of Festivals," focuses on those festivals which mark or once marked the passage of the seasons: planting, first-fruits, harvest, summer and winter solstice, May Day, vernal or autumnal equinox, New Year. He calls attention to the essential transitoriness of celebratory phenomena, for the seasonal rituals—from which festivals and carnivals derive—draw their energy and vitality from the very changes and transformations wrought by time's passage itself, the powers of the spinning year. To translate objects which are "made for the day, out of natural ingredients, and carted off to wither and die after the event (like Christmas trees and the petalled floats of the Rose Parade)," into objects of museum display, is surely to deprive them of their necessary ephemerality. No one can keep the almond blossom forever flowering in the town square or eternalize the all-but-flowering spring. Thus, for the Japanese, the cherry blossom symbolizes the heroic mutability of the warrior, for it falls in the prime of the flower, unwithered and ungathered. Ultimately, it embodies the perennial tension between Buddhism, which seeks release through Enlightenment from the pain in all changefulness, and Shinto, which affirms the fertility and sacrality of life-and-death as a cycle of eternal return. Seasonal rituals and festivals do not therefore owe their persistence to the durability of their material expressions but to their connection with recurrent communal experiences and needs. Abrahams contrasts "the languages of festive celebrations," interestingly, with those of the arts, as follows: "We memorialize creative acts by exalting permanence, by valuing the created object and keeping it in as clean and enduring a condition as possible." Museum and private collections and displays attest to this. Yet the Smithsonian exhibition of celebratory objects demonstrates that such objects often attain the status of "art," for they do embody a creativity of a particular kind. It is not the creativity of the solitary individual of the Western tradition but that of talented representatives of a raised communal consciousness, proceeding from and returning to the intersubjective ambiance of popular arousal.

Abrahams makes an important distinction between rites of passage and seasonal/calendrical festivals. Whereas transitional rites are often genuine crises of identity or respond to the social crises associated with marriage or death, seasonal feasts may occur "on the plateaus of the year when in fact nothing important occurs." There may, indeed, frequently be "a lull in the cycle of production and reproduction of the resources on which the ongoing constitution and characters of continuity of the community have been built." Since life-crisis rituals emerge in situations of already heightened emotion and energy, the task of ritual is to "provide an organizing set of principles, traditional ways of binding for the moment the opposing forces within the community and tying together the past with the present." But festivals have, on the contrary, to generate their own energies. They often begin, literally, "with a bang," using pyrotechnic and percussive means. Then there is the "surplus of signifiers" and extravagance of costume, masks, and cosmetics mentioned earlier. Abrahams calls attention to the "playful distortion" of the performing self characteristic of festive celebration, the "overextension of self," often expressed in gross overeating and excessive drinking. But, he cautions, the "language of celebrations of increase emerges from everyday ways of doing things," though such ways are hypertrophied, skewed, overstated, often to the point of caricature. In *The Ritual Process* (1969:chap.5) I showed how in many calendrical or seasonal celebrations of the economic yield, there was a marked component of symbolic status-reversal; the normally poor and powerless dressed in the clothes and insignia of upper-class power and often controlled the course of the ritual or carnivalesque events (like the slum-dwelling leadership of Rio de Janeiro's world-famous "Samba Schools"), while the habitually wealthy and powerful played the roles of bystanders or subordinates. Sometimes the rich were even lampooned, hazed, or subjected to mocking songs or satirical verses to which they were forbidden by custom to reply in self-defense. In ritual celebrations in preindustrial societies, such mockery is usually confined within limits, and, indeed, the celebrations are seen as saturnalian "sacralizations" of the social order. But in those festivals and carnivals which have succeeded them—sometimes in the same calendrical slots—as major forms of metasocial commentary or deep play (to use Geertz's terms), such genres of cultural performance can be "subversive" as well as merely "reversive." They may contain, in their multitudinous scenarios, scripts, and clown-acts, ludic models of a "protostructural" character (in Sutton-Smith's formulation), an independent critique of the society that brought them into being, and hence a possible font of alternative ideas, values, motivations, and designs (rough sketches rather!) for living. A detailed comparative study of carnival as it has developed over time in Europe and in Hispanic and Lusitanian America, as well as the civic *matsuri*-system in Japan, would reveal how individualistic and egalitarian cultural ideals and a sense of ethnic and class identity—as well as civic pride and nationalist fervor—come to be articulated and manipulated (politically and economically) in the verbal and many nonverbal (imagery, gesture, choreography, and so on) languages of festival. Such a study is overdue.

John MacAloon's essay "Sociation and Sociability in Political Celebrations" pays particular heed to "political and other rites that instrumentally maintain and regenerate social systems." He cites Simmel to show how such celebrations contain frequent episodes of play as well as solemnity and relates this regular feature to Simmel's distinction between "sociation" and "sociability." Sociation is "being with and for others in that construction of society out of contending interests, duties, and purposes," while "sociability" is "the autonomous or play-form of sociation," "the feeling . . . and satisfaction . . . of being sociated." Political and civic rites are, therefore, not merely "supreme acts of sociation, of differentiated rules, roles, and ranks answering to sober, ineluctable material interests." Their efficacy depends equally "on the generation of sociability which is, according to Simmel, ludic and democratic in character." Celebratory behavior is "framed" behavior. Anthropologists have used this concept of "frame" and "framing" in recent years to identify demarcated times and places for a particular use, such as ritual or play, by enclosing them literally or figuratively in a border (a temple, theater, playground, or court) and so creating a set of expectations about the kind of behavior or conduct that should fill the encased space-time. Different types of frames also involve different emotional moods or "atmospheres." They are also selective, including and excluding defined persons, relational styles, perceptions, values, sentiments, and social and symbolic types. Celebrations contain both ritual and play frames. Broadly speaking, ritual frames are based on the premise that "within this border what we do and say and think and feel is governed by the premise 'let us believe,' that is, trust in the truth, reality, or goodness of supernatural, transhuman beings, persons or powers regarded as the first and final causes of phenomena." Play frames, to the contrary, depend on the formula "let's make believe" or "let's pretend." While ritual frames depend upon traditional, immemorial authority (scriptures, prophecies, divinations performed by legitimate oracles, utterances by authorized shamans and visionaries, liturgies held to be transmitted from hallowed antiquity), play frames allow participants to escape from the "should" and "ought" character of ritual—more compelling than the very "laws of nature" in the view of some religions—and see themselves as free to fabricate a range of alternative possibilities of behaving, thinking, and feeling that is wider than that current or admissable in either the mundane world or the ritual frame.

Where religious systems are still "going concerns," commanding the assent of most social members, their rituals are believed to be instrumentally potent, to have effects on the natural and social orders. The messages communicated in play frames, on the other hand, are held to be disengaged from "reality" and free from the constraints of mundane existence. Play, within its privileged context, is "freewheeling," able to sound off. But in this very capacity inheres its social value. For ritual is bound by the sanctity of its frame to censor the commentaries on human life and society that it generates. Play in the guise of drollery and folly and in the ephemerality of its presence is licensed to comment on a great range of issues. Play thus becomes paradoxical, for it is revealed to have a serious function, a curious objectivity. Seemingly amoral, its moralism may cleave more sincerely and closely to the facts of contemporary life than the moralism of ritual, which can "cover up" distasteful social and political facts, that is, become hypocritical. Play's flexibility contains within it the possibility of *exploring* new ways of doing things. MacAloon, as we have seen, shows how Simmel relates "sociability" to "play," by calling it the "play form of sociation." Sociation, disengaged from the "business" of survival, production, and profit, appears in celebration as sociability—which, so says Simmel, "creates an ideal sociological world in which the pleasure of the individual is closely tied up with the pleasure of the others" (1950:47–48). The pure spirit of sociability can sometimes be seen in carnival, but it appears melded with ritual seriousness in the hybrid contexts of political and civic ceremonies, as MacAloon shows in some detail and depth in his discussion of the political rites of democratic peoples and the performative structure of the transnational Olympic games.

In celebration, then, much of what has been bound by social structure is liberated, notably the sense of comradeship and communion, in brief, of communitas; on the other hand, much of what has been dispersed over many domains of culture and social structure is now bound or cathected in the complex semantic systems of pivotal, multivocal symbols and myths which achieve great conjunctiveness. The objects selected for the exhibition are, in the main, just such many-layered symbols. And they emerge from and vitally emblemize the communitas, the joyous shared flow or solemn communion released by passing into the liminal, "betwixt-and-between" state intervening between the "safe" but dull domains of routinized and classified life. Several of our authors have indicated that celebrations have their perilous side, for they expose the chaos and indeterminacy that lie around the lighted areas of culture. Grimes, for example, actually defines a public celebration as "a rope bridge of knotted symbols strung across an abyss. We make our crossings hoping the chasm will echo our festive sounds for a moment, as the bridge begins to sway from the rhythms of our dance." But even as they expose our demons and chaos-dragons, celebrations also affirm our vitality and resolve to continue. They proclaim that our society has rich meaning and has experienced glories and triumphs which it insists upon reliving, sometimes as play, sometimes as ritual drama. The incredibly diverse forms of the celebratory objects exhibited manifest the lineaments of fear and glory, communitas and structure, faith and skepticism, masked and muted in the trivia of the everyday but given their proper entrancing shape in the world of art and ritual which is celebration.

Bibliography

Babcock, Barbara
    1978   "Too Many, Too Few: Ritual Modes of Signification." *Semiotica* 23:291–302.
Bogen, J. E.
    1969   "The Other Side of the Brain, II." *Bulletin of the Los Angeles Neurological Association* 34:134–62.
D'Aquili, E., and Laughlin, C.
    1979   "The Neurobiology of Myth and Ritual." In *The Spectrum of Ritual*, edited by E. d'Aquili, C. Laughlin, and J. McManus. New York: Columbia University Press.
Dimond, S.
    1972   *The Double Brain*. London: Churchill Livinston.
Kimura, D.
    1973   "The Asymmetry of the Human Brain." *Scientific American* 299:70–78.
Myerhoff, Barbara
    1978   *Number Our Days*. New York: Dutton.
Ornstein, R.
    1972   *The Psychology of Consciousness*. San Francisco: Freeman.
Sapir, E.
    1933   "Symbols." In *Encyclopedia of the Social Sciences* XIV:492–93. New York: Macmillan.
Simmel, Georg
    1950   *The Sociology of Georg Simmel*. Translated and edited by Kurt H. Wolff. New York: Free Press.
Turner, Victor
    1967   *The Forest of Symbols*. Ithaca, N.Y.: Cornell University Press.
    1968   *The Drums of Affliction*. Oxford: Clarendon Press.
    1969   *The Ritual Process*. Chicago: Aldine.

See *Figure 11*.

Material Components in Celebration

Richard M. Dorson

In celebrations people often affirm the joyous outpouring of their spirit and the creative play of their imagination in a variety of the performing and decorative arts. The term *celebration* can encompass festivals, rituals, ceremonies, spectacles, pageants, fetes, holidays, and extravaganzas, and partakes of all these elements. A celebration, in our sense, should fall at a fixed period and should involve, or at one time should have involved, sacred and symbolic elements. Our purpose here is to suggest the nature of the artifacts, the material culture props and properties, which contribute to the complex phenomena of a celebration, and which might find their way into museum exhibits. Museum curators cannot exhibit the song, music, dance, perishable foods, theatricals, gaiety, and exuberance that accompany celebrations, save through film showings, but they can display the physical objects—if they can acquire them—that play a part in celebrations. We may at once think of such objects as costumes, masks, musical instruments, and serving bowls, but, as we shall see in the following accounts, other kinds of objects will enter prominently into and even dominate the celebrations.

My intention here is to summarize seven celebrations, and then indicate their major material components. Almost any celebration could be selected for this exercise. My selection has been governed by the availability of usable ethnographic accounts, and a desire to suggest the diversity of celebratory events. Such events do not easily lend themselves to ethnography, in view of the multiple and varying elements in such events. Folklorists in the United States have only recently begun to report on celebrations and festivals, and a work such as Robert J. Smith's illuminating portrayal of the Peruvian fete devoted to La Virgen de la Puerta practically stands alone. In addition we must reckon with the deplorable lack of festive occasions in the United States, a point eloquently stated by Harvey Cox in *The Feast of Fools* (1969). The industrial work ethic has blighted the impulse for communal festivals that enlivens much of the rest of the world.

At any rate I here outline festive events that have given joy and pleasure, spiritual and sensory, to peoples in Peru, Trinidad, Louisiana, Africa, India, China, and Japan. The three festivals in the New World all owe their point of origin to European prototypes, although they have undergone considerable transformation in their changed setting. To the scholars of these celebrations synopsized below I express acknowledgment and appreciation.

The Fiesta to the Patroness of Otuzco: La Virgen de la Puerta

An American folklorist, Robert J. Smith, undertook an intensive field foray to Peru in 1966 to observe and interpret a patronal festival held annually in the city of Otuzco in the mountains of northern Peru, over eleven thousand feet above sea level. The book he subsequently published (1975) is the fullest report, from the perspective of a folklorist trained in the United States, of a community celebration.

For at least three hundred years the people of Otuzco have annually celebrated the fiesta of La Virgen de la Puerta. The celebration falls into two parts: the devotional observances to the Virgin, and the funmaking, the *alegria* or joyful activities, that surround and accompany the liturgical acts. The one is the official program sponsored by the community as a whole, the other consists of private celebrations of feasting, drinking, dancing, buying goods at the market, listening to the folkloric bands, watching the fireworks, socializing, playing games of chance, and cheering at sports contests. Rapt veneration of the Virgin and drunken revelry coexist in the public and private celebrations. Evon Vogt (1955:820–39) has characterized fiesta as (1) a religious ceremonial, (2) a vast native market, and (3) a carnival.

The key devotions occupy four days—December 13 to 16, in 1976—keyed to the lowering of the Virgin from the church balcony to the ground and her procession through the streets of the city. The event of the lowering, known as the *bajada,* has acquired a special, momentous character in Otuzco. It occurs at 2:00 P.M. on the second day, the day of Alba, and leads into the Great Central Day highlighted in the afternoon by the triumphal procession of the image of the Virgin. The first day, the Antevísperas, is a warm-up, with the reception of visitors and bands, and at 5:00 P.M. the turning of the sacred image on the church balcony from facing the altar to gazing at the worshipful throng in the plaza. The fourth day, the Day of Adoration, is a reversal, on which the Virgin of the Door is raised back onto her throne on the balcony.

Only for the fiesta do the people of Otuzco attend mass in force and pay homage to their Virgin. Otherwise church attendance is very low. But the allegiance and adoration felt by the Otuzcans for the Virgin of the Door (the origin of the name has been lost) cannot be gainsaid. When their priest agreed to ship the sacred image to Lima at the request of the archbishop, to allow her to appear in a procession featuring the most celebrated Virgins of Peru, the citizens rose up in wrath, stationed a body of women within the church for a round-the-clock vigil, blocked the van that came to transport the image, and compelled the priest to rescind his approval to let the Virgin depart. Word had reached the Otuzcans that the Virgen de la Puerta would be kept in Lima and a substitute image returned in her place.

On the morning of the Alba a steady stream of cars and trucks and pilgrims on foot and muleback course down the mountains to converge on the church and revere the Virgin. In the streets around the market, vendors, merchants, musicians, dancers, and folkloric bands beguile the countrywomen in their shawls, the countrymen in their ponchos, and the uniformed schoolchildren skittering about. By noon the crowds in the market streets have thinned and the plaza is now filled with three to four thousand people, awaiting the high moment scheduled for 2:00 P.M. and announced in the program as "Emotion-Filled Lowering of the Virgin of the Door." A folkloric group known as the "Negritos," whose special mission is to guard the Virgin, now raises up to the balcony a large pole attached to a platform by a steel cable. The sacred image is removed from her urn, placed on the platform, and very slowly lowered down the pole (fig. 6). All the costumed folkloric groups now dance, the church bells peal, the Negritos begin singing and rattling their chains, and worshippers on the balcony throw confetti and *estampas* (pieces of paper bearing verses in praise of the Virgin) onto the plaza. The roar in the plaza rises to a crescendo, while skyrockets and firecrackers light the sky above the mountains. As the Virgin reaches the ground, people in the vicinity strain to touch her. The Negritos transfer her to a small litter beside the pole and carry the litter, with a mighty heave, into the church to a throne beside the altar.

Figure 6 *Otuzco: The Virgin descending to the people, marking the end of the* bajada.

For the next hour folkloric groups dance and sing before the Virgin. Through the night, people file past in order to touch the sacred image, then join worshipers sitting on the church floor with large, lit, decorated candles, facing the Virgin in silent adoration. Late at night fireworks are set off and paper balloons six feet in diameter shaped like birds and animals are let loose into the air. So ends the day of Alba.

Next day, the Great Central Day, at 3:00 P.M., two men lift the Virgin from her throne and place her on a handsomely decorated litter. The program announces that she is "adorned with her royal crown and her finest jewels." As she emerges through the portals of the church, in a blaze of ornaments, the crowd gazes eagerly at their patroness to see if she is satisfied with the fiesta. For the next two and a half hours, the litter bearers, who continually rotate, carry the Virgin on a route covering twelve blocks. Folkloric bands, costumed dancers, devotees carrying candles, and bystanders who join in, form the procession. The priest accompanying the Virgin stops every block to recite a rosary.

On Adoration Day, on the following noon, the program highlights *"Raising of the Queen to her Throne*. Electrifying farewell, the venerated Virgin of the Door ascends slowly, carrying with her the heart of the town and of all her faithful devotees." The Virgin is raised to the church balcony and replaced in her urn facing into the church, where she will remain until the next fiesta. A desolate air hangs over the plaza, which is covered with litter and debris. The fiesta has ended.

Material objects. Central to the fiesta of La Virgen de La Puerta is the sacred image (*see* fig. 6). A photograph displays "La Immaculata Virgen de la Puerta de Otuzco" in a richly decorated flowing robe, embroidered with flowers. Her heavily lidded, pursed-lipped doll's face of striking beauty looks severely ahead. Three long dark ringlets lie on each shoulder. A sizable but delicate crown seems to grow from her head, spreading outward. She wears a thick necklace and long earrings. Her arms are drawn across her chest with her hands outstretched in a simple gesture of benediction. From the arms hang ex-votos—a silver bus, a trunk, an airplane—placed there by devotees. A semicircular throne with flowered upholstery is seen behind her, with a circular dais, also emblazoned with flowers, three-quarters visible on the wall behind the throne. The whole effect is one of regal splendor tempered with restraint and spiritual calm. Belief in the power of the Virgin to perform miracles, attested to by numerous oral accounts, motivates the fiesta, which provides the occasion for prayers, petitions, promises, gifts in the form of ex-votos, and devotional exercises in the form of music, song, and dance to the Virgin. Hence the sacred image takes on a living character, as the patroness of Otuzco and the dispenser of cures and blessings.

Costumes of the folkloric groups that both entertain the assemblage and pay homage to the Virgin also form a key part of the fiesta's material culture. The Negritos, guardians of the sacred image, who sing boisterously to a simple tune a devotional song of more than a hundred verses, dress down rather than dress up, in rough sackcloth and chains around their necks, with faces and hands blackened, wearing old hats turned up in front and sporting a red cross. By contrast, the Gitanos (Gypsies), a dancing ensemble of young couples, highly disciplined, who dance an intricate Contradanza from morning till night, wear gay white costumes, the men in white pants, white shirt, and red vest, with a large kerchief wrapped across the forehead to form a band sparkling with mirrors and sequins, the women in ankle-length flowered skirts, white blouses, large silk shawls, and similar sequined headdresses. Mothers dress their children in Gitano style for the festival. Yet another mode of costume is seen in the attire of the Pieles Rojas, or Redskins, modeled on North American Indians, and perhaps influenced by the movies. This dancing, nonsinging group of eight young men with a flute and drum player display a crown of feathers on their heads, a pelt flapping over their rear, and bells tinkling on their legs as they hop in pairs to the music of a *huayno* (traditional couple dance with each partner holding a handkerchief with both hands). Still another folkloric group from the rival town of Usquil, known as the Canasteros, or Basket Makers (although they do nothing with baskets), pride themselves on headdresses of two-foot-long turkey feathers, along with handwoven dark trousers tied below the knee above long white stockings, complete with blue shirts and vests and small bells on their arms and legs. Unlike other dancing groups throughout Latin America, they wear no masks of animals and devils.

The flute and drum players accompanying the folkloric groups perform the music for their singing and dancing on folk musical instruments that comprise another material component of the celebration. These are not professional musicians but farmers clad in ponchos and wide-brimmed straw hats. They play on a drum made from a hollowed-out tree trunk a foot and a half in diameter, over which cowhide, and on one side a resonating string, are stretched. The musician beats the drum with his right hand and holds in his left a long flute, two feet long, hollowed out from a young poplar, on which he plays a shrill tune by covering and uncovering four holes in the end. Once in a while a musician substitutes for the flute a pan-pipe (*traversa*) made of up to twenty reeds of varying length, on which he also plays *huaynos* with his left hand.

Feasting and snacking on festival foods also contributes to the spirit of celebration. On Central Day the families and official groups attending the fiesta gather ceremonially to dine on special dishes. These feature *cuy* (guinea pig fried or stewed), along with *patasca* (a preparation of peeled corn and sheep's intestines, liberally spiced, particularly with *aji,* a hot pepper sauce). Vast quantities of *chicha,* a fermented cornmeal drink known since Inca times, wash down the viands.

Trinidad Carnival

Called the "greatest annual theatrical spectacle of all time" (Errol Hill, 1972), the two-day Trinidad Carnival enlists one-tenth of its one million population. Since the time when carnival was inherited from Europe, it has metamorphosed into a native product of Trinidad that features calypso singing; the music of steel bands; street processions of masquerade bands, with masked dancers and characters in brilliant costumes; performance of skits and pageants in mime and dialogue; and feasting and revelry. Carnival may best be described as street masquerade, the folk community's counterpart to the masquerade balls held in mansions of the wealthy. At one time the contests between bands signified the struggle between the New Year and Old Year, Summer and Winter, Life and Death, Good and Evil. The Roman Catholic Church adapted the pagan ritual as a pre-Lenten festival, and the Spanish brought it to the New World. But today, with African, Asian, European, Middle Eastern, and North and South American peoples in Trinidad (an independent nation since 1962), carnival represents an exhilarating affirmation of national spirit and creativity.

The steel band that so distinguishes Trinidadian music and carnival evolved after 1883, when the drum, favored by African and East Indian cultures on the island but grating to the ears of the English ruling class, was banned. To replace the drum the laboring classes developed a percussion orchestra from bamboo stems. Sometime in the 1930s, bamboo gave way to metal. One account, with a folkloric quality, sets the moment in 1936 just before carnival time, when the boys had gathered in Tanty Willie's yard to beat bamboo. One casually picked up a dustbin and flailed at it, another struck at the gas tank of an old auto sitting in the yard. Liking the sound, the others threw away the bamboo and picked up a paint pan and a piece of iron scrap and cut down a cement drum for a kettle. They formed the first steel band just in time for carnival. Whether or not this story is true, the steel-band movement caught on, in spite of derogation from members of the educated colored class. With the acceptance in 1948 of the fifty-five-gallon oil drum, used in Trinidad in connection with oil producing and refining, the steel band came of age. Since then steel bands have performed concerts in the world's capitals, winning plaudits from such master musicians as Pablo Casals. But the chief location for the steel bands remains the backyard of the carnival tent. Each year some five thousand bandsmen associated with some two hundred orchestras rehearse before carnival, vying for victory in the national steel-band competition and hoping to astound their competitors during the street masquerade.

Another special feature of the Trinidad Carnival is the calypsonian, singing the improvisational satirical folksong now known worldwide; for several decades he has been part of a masquerade band. In the street procession he dresses as a principal character second only to the king and sings songs in character, or he might even be king of the band and lead his subjects against rival bands. From 1919 on, carnival competitions were organized around calypso singing by masquerade bands. Gradually attaining the status of an independent professional entertainer, the calypsonian during carnival led his band on the streets, singing rehearsed choruses and improvising songs of praise and criticism. By the 1930s the calypso singers had separated from the bands to form competitive singing teams. With the advent of the steel band, they tailored melodies to the new music.

A once flourishing game-dance that formed a prominent element in the Trinidad Carnival until the restrictive legislation in 1884, and that still survives in attenuated form, is the calinda or stick-dance. The dancers thrust and parry with sticks two and a half feet long, a custom that is perhaps a survival of slavery days, when slaves were allowed to carry sticks to beat off snakes. Described as both a dance and a combat, the calinda influenced not only dance but also folk-song and folk language. The dancers have to perform intricate and elaborate dance steps leading directly into an attacking or defensive posture. One stick-man is said to have practiced his stickmanship by breaking stones hurled at him in rapid succession by two or three throwers fifteen or twenty yards distant. At carnival, rival batonniers challenge each other with boasts and hyperbole as well as sticks: "I come to measure your grave," a stickman might announce to his adversary, eying his weapon. Calinda chants sung by the stickman glorifying battling troubadours of the past later entered the repertoire of calypso singers.

Material objects.   The instruments in the steel bands, the sticks in the stick-dance, and the dazzling costumes and masks of the masqueraders immediately come to mind as tangible components of Trinidad Carnival. Early instruments included various kinds of metal containers thrown in the garbage dump: biscuit tins, paint cans, dustbins, cement drums. To keep the band together during the noise of the street masquerade, a metal rod was struck against a piece of iron from an old automobile chassis as a rhythmic timer. Today, fifty-five-gallon oil drums have replaced all previous pans.

Masks transform not only the physical appearance but also the psychic per-sonality of the masquerader. One masker who played Lucifer in the Devil Band thus described his sensations at the moment of altering his visage: "When the moment comes for me to take up that mask, and I take the mask and put it on, I become a different being entirely. I never feel as if I'm human at all. All I see in front of me is devils! Real!" His oversized head mask portrayed a gloating mien, sported small horns, was encircled by a bearded ruff fanning out from the shoulders, and was topped by a crown, while he carried a fork and flapped wings six feet in length. Associated with him in the Devil Band was the Beast, whose dragon's head mask exhibited movable ears, eyes, and tongue, and emit-ted flames and smoke through its mouth, until the burning of a masquerader's face brought that display to an end. A 1930 newspaper described the Beast's costume as made of papier-mâché scales, painted in metallic green sprinkled with amethyst, gold, and crimson. Several lengths of chain wrapped around his waist were held taut by Imps, who prodded him with axes, causing the Beast to lunge at them in a frightening step-dance. The Imps themselves wore close-fit-ting tights sprouting wings and tails, and they covered their faces with horned half-masks. While dancing with sliding, swaying, darting motions they carried and shook axes, scrolls, horns, bells, dice, and face cards. On the competition stage Lucifer engaged the Beast, stabbed him with his pitchfork, and trampled on him.

Of the almost limitless variety of costumes seen at carnival we may single out three more for illustration. The old European carnival masked character, the Pierrot, a harmless clown, changed in Trinidad to a garrulous fighter with whips or sticks, for he had merged with the stickman, appearing as an individual masker, with an attendant to carry his long multicolored train and stick. His knee-length satin gown was covered with three-inch satin triangles colored white and gold or red and mauve, alternately placed and overlapping each other. Bells hung from points on the triangles, from the cuffs on the broad sleeves, from the base of the gown, and from his light canvas shoes, so that he jingled vibrantly as he moved with stately steps. A heart-shaped velvet breastpiece, red or green, bordered with swansdown and sparkling with sequins, spangles, and tiny mirrors, adorned the gown. Colored ribbons cross-gathered the stockinged feet. An upturned iron pot rested on the head concealed by a floppy velvet beret. Thus elegantly attired, the Pierrot boasted about his prowess and lineage in grand speeches, challenges, and insults that might culminate in a stick-fight with a rival Pierrot or a general free-for-all involving the bystanders. Because of such melees, Pierrots were banned, and they disappeared from Trinidad around 1820.

The costume of a calypso singer, king of the White Rose Band, merited this depiction in a Port-of-Spain newspaper of 1903. Dressed as an Elizabethan courtier, the calypsonian sported a cutaway jacket and tight-fitting knickers of white flowered silk trimmed with imitation ermine and gimp. The breast of the jacket shone with sequins sewn on a ground of gold and silver braid, parted down the center with a double row of silver buttons. A cloak of Japan silk bordered with imitation ermine was draped over the shoulders. Thus bedecked, the calypsonian sang his satires and diatribes.

Beloved among masquerade characters is the Midnight Robber, evolved from a cowboy into a fearsome braggart in Elizabethan doublet and breeches, beaded and braided, underneath a towering hat with fringed brim molded into animal shape and shoes resembling a creature with moving eyes. A flowering cape bearing painted symbols of death further awes the spectators. The Robber fingers guns and a cartridge belt at his waist and blows insistently upon a whistle. From his lips pour forth a constant stream of threats and braggadocio until his intended victims pay him ransom. As he recites his medley, he gestures and dances in rhythm with his tirade and whistle-tooting. He brags: "Don't be surprised of the beautiful costume that I wear, for I am quest by the unknown, I am the symbol of manage. I struggled to master the earth. I braved the sea, I pierce the jungle. I scale the mountain. I conquered the desert, and the last thing on earth I am going to do is to rob the last breath of life that was place in you."

A whole museum could be filled, in a blaze of splendor, with costumes and masks of Trinidad Carnival.

Grape-Harvest Festival of Arpádhon, Louisiana

"The largest rural Hungarian settlement in the United States" is the self-awarded label of the town of Arpádhon in southeastern Louisiana (Linda Dégh, 1977–78:114–31). Save for its name, derived from a tenth-century Hungarian chieftain, Arpád, little trace remains of Hungarian ethnic features, in language, culture, or Old World loyalty. The one link between this community of less than five hundred persons and the mother country is an annual Harvest Dance, consisting of a set of nine to eleven dances. These Louisiana Hungarians consider this grape-harvest festival to emanate in pure and unaltered form from their homeland, although analysis shows it to be a strange hybrid.

Arpádhon owes its origins to the enterprise of three men from Hungary who placed an advertisement in Hungarian-language newspapers in the east and midwest, inviting jaded industrial workers to purchase farmland in a mild climate where they could grow two crops a year. A number responded from northern mining towns and industrial cities and moved to Louisiana early in the present century. The last family to join the settlement came in 1941 from West Virginia. Arpádhon became especially known for its strawberry crop.

Throughout Hungary in grape-growing districts an October ritual procession celebrated the grape harvest. A parade of costumed grape-pickers, led by horseback riders and followed afoot by mummers and gypsy musicians, marched through the vineyards and streets to mark the closing of one growing season and the safeguarding of another through the winter. A feast of roast calf, pig, or lamb, and new wine capped the dancing, and play-party games followed, underneath bunches of grapes suspended from the ceiling. Transplanted to America, the custom became standardized as a festive dance in a community hall, though the procession was abandoned, since the grapes were purchased by miners and factory workers rather than grown. The Arpádhon festival evolved from this general pattern but has acquired its own patina.

For some seventy years the people of Arpádhon have held their festival days on two Sundays in October, scheduled to avoid conflict with football games in New Orleans or Baton Rouge. Festivities begin with an ethnic luncheon of meat noodle soup, stuffed cabbage, and walnut roll. Then follows a dance program of ten or twelve couples. One Harvest Dance is held in the Presbyterian Hall, the other in the Catholic Hall, with the same dancers, band, and audience. The dancers practice twice a week for two months before the event, coached by four dance teachers, who arrange the dances into a neat choreography. Everyone in Arpádhon, young and old, knows the steps and the tunes. After the luncheon the dance floor is cleared and the young dancers, boys and girls, march in from opposite sides and meet in the middle. Red, white, and green ribbons—the colors of the Hungarian flag—hang from the ceiling, along with bunches of grapes, apples, and oranges. After the formal staged dance, the band plays on, alternating Hungarian *csárdás* (a modern national dance for couples) with American jazz, while the dancers and audience join in on the floor. All the dancers sing, jump, clap, and tap while they dance.

Comparison of Old World Hungarian music and dance with the Arpádhon performance reveals a wide deviation from the European model to which the Louisiana Hungarians believe they are strictly adhering. Only the violin among the Arpádhon band's instruments—saxophone, piano, drum, accordion—also appears in Hungarian orchestras. The saxophone drowns out the violin and alters the rhythm from Hungarian-gypsy to potpourri American. So too the dances reveal a medley of styles and influences, with the exaggerated syncopation shifting the form from the csárdás toward the square dance, as the dancers form arches and circles, break up in pairs, hug and twirl, clap and stamp, then perform the csárdás in a big circle and yank the fruit from the rafters in a grand coda, ending the formal program. In spite of its idiosyncratic character, the Arpádhon dance troupe was chosen to represent the Hungarian ethnic tradition in the United States at the Bicentennial Festival of American Folklife held in Washington, D.C., in 1976. The festival's organizers saw fit to announce that the Arpádhon event was a spring festival celebrating the strawberry harvest!

Material objects. Costumes comprise the chief material-culture component of the grape-harvest festival. As with the music and the dances, they do not reflect a folk-regional tradition. Rather, they represent an idealized Hungarian national tradition. The male dancers wear white drawers with matching white, wide-sleeved shirts, trimmed with red, white, and green ribbons, a black bow tie, black boots, a black vest with tricolor ribbon running diagonally across front and back, and a black English derby hat, also adorned with the tricolor ribbon. The female dancers dress themselves in a full-pleated white skirt and tiny white apron trimmed with red, white, and green, a tight red velvet bodice embroidered with gold beads and ribbons, and a blouse with short puffed sleeves and a round collar with a ruff (fig. 7). A beaded velvet headdress, a red kerchief, and black shoes or boots complete the costume. Band members emulate the worldwide costume of Hungarian Gypsy orchestras, of white shirt, red vest, black bow tie, and black trousers.

Incwala in Swaziland: Ceremony of Kingship

The South African kingdom of the Swazi celebrates an annual ceremony of kingship known as Incwala (fig. 8). For three weeks, from the Little Incwala, a two-day observance initiated when the sun reaches its southern summer solstice and the moon is dark, to the Big Incwala, lasting six days from the night of the full moon, the inhabitants of Swaziland set aside the routine preoccupations of daily life and ritually honor their king with songs, dances, and sacred acts. According to Hilda Kuper, the chief ethnographer of Incwala, observers have interpreted the occasion "as a first-fruit ceremony, a pageant of Swazi history, a drama of kingship, and a ritual of rebellion" (1964:68; for primary ethnography, 1947:chap. 13, "The Drama of Kingship," 147–225; 1968:57–59, 90). An independent reading by T. O. Beidelman contends that Incwala symbolizes the separation of the king from the groups within his nation, to free him for the responsibility of assuming supernatural powers consonant with his office (1966:372–405).

At the onset of Little Incwala, the king's councilors inquire about discreetly to locate a black ox belonging to a clan member other than Dlamini, the king's clan. They then steal the ox, whose parts will decorate sacred vessels and the king's ritual costume in the course of the celebration. Between the Little Incwala and the Big Incwala, groups at selected villages practice songs and dances they will perform ceremonially. The Big Incwala occupies four days, building to the Great Day. On the first day, pure youths go forth from the central village to cut from a magic tree the branches they will use to enclose the king's sanctuary. They return on the morning of the second day bearing wands and chanting a

Figure 7 *Arpádhon: Women dancers in woods.*

Figure 8 *Left to right: New priest of the Mkatshwa clan; old governor of the royal village of Zombodze, who opens the singing of the sacred songs; the Mkatshwa instructor who will go to the ocean to fill the sacred gourd with sea water.*

lullaby. The third day brings the killing of the black bull, which is thrown to the ground by young warriors and slaughtered with a special spear. They dismember the beast and carry the hide and tail into the sacred enclosure. Priests cut the hide into strips and twine them around two calabashes kept in the sacred store hut in the harem, and tie the tail around one, to be used by the "people of the sea." Then they pour the contents of the gallbladder over the mouths of both calabashes, which by this act become sacred vessels, named for a heavenly deity. The gallbladder, inflated, will rest on the king's costume, and the bull's fatty tissue will be tied crosswise on the king's chest.

During these days the Swazi performers sing mournful songs expressing their hatred and rejection of the king, to the accompaniment of dances miming the rituals. These hostile songs provide Beidelman with evidence for his interpretation of Incwala as dismissal of the king by his people and subsequent reunion with them after achieving his reincarnation.

The fourth day, the Great Day, belongs to the king. He begins the morning by biting into green foods. At midday the people are commanded to dress in Incwala regalia and assemble at the cattle byre, where the king in his Incwala dress dances under the sun in their midst and all sing Incwala. At sunset he leaves them. Foreigners are ordered to depart from the cattle byre. The climactic moment has come. Suddenly the king reemerges, unrecognizable in monstrous guise. A cap of black feathers and a partly visible headband of lion's skin cover his face; a mantle of green grass and evergreen shoots drapes his body; a belt of silver-monkey skin clasps the mantle. His left hand holds a black shield smeared with fat from the sacred herd. On top of the costume bobs the bull's gallbladder. The monster dances in a demonic frenzy, said by the Swazi to be instinctual to kings. Reaching a crescendo, he hurls the sacred bright-green calabash—known as the Gourd of the North, whence comes the clan of Dlamini—onto the horizontal black shield of an age-mate, who must catch it without its touching the ground. Incwala has completed its cycle. According to Kuper, the throwing of the calabash signifies the discarding of the old year; according to Beidelman it represents the king-priest's decision to rejoin his people and submit to the social order, after the lawless period in which he has charged up his supernatural powers.

Material objects. The two sacred calabashes, one tended by the Belwandle (people of the sea) and the other by the Bemanti (people of the water) play key roles, as has been noted, in the Incwala. They are physically and ritually connected with the sacred bull and the king at different stages of the ceremonies. Throwing of the Calabash of the North by the dancing demon to an age-mate signifies the transition from the unfamiliar monster-figure back to the known and beneficent king. Subsequently the Bemanti set out with the sacred vessels to fetch water, and they behave arrogantly to any Swazi they meet on the way, demanding payment of a fine before the others may proceed. The same calabashes are used over and over until they crack, when the decorative hide is removed and burned on a sacred pyre at the ceremony's end.

On the Great Day, handsome costumes worn by all the people mark the high

Figure 9 *Four of the king's age mates. Note the similarities of their shields and other items of costume.*

point of Incwala. The queen mother wears a leopard-skin cloak. Males of each age-class place on their heads a crown of animal skin topped by an ostrich-feather cap (fig. 9). But it is the king's demon dress, described above, that is invested with the greatest degree of ritual meanings. The razor-sharp grass in which he is clothed, used to make mats kept in the shrine hut from one reign to the next, symbolizes the continuous life of the Swazi people. So too the silver monkey, from whose skin a belt has been made, symbolizes a life-force. From the sacred herd (*mfukwane*), dedicated to the kingship and said to give red milk and to possess human emotions, comes animal fat with which the king smears himself and his shield. If a drop of the fat touches the body of a person eating meat, it causes madness.

The Car Festival of Jagannātha, India

In India in the state of Orissa in the coastal city of Puri on the Bay of Bengal, a famous temple honors Lord Jagannātha (see fig. 3), regarded by Hindu worshipers as the protecting deity of the world. (All facts taken from K. C. Mishra, 1971.) Pilgrims and visitors throughout India and from many countries come to Puri to worship the images there. Twelve festivals throughout the year celebrate Jagannātha, and the best known of these is the Car Festival (*Ratha Jātrā*) observed on the second day of the bright fortnight in the month of Aṣādha (June) during the rainy season. With its alternating periods of heat and cold, the rainy season symbolizes the calendar round of summer and winter, and rain heralds hilarity and humanity. A legend of the origin of Jagannātha's car states that Indra, king of heaven and lord of rains and thunder, hurled a lightning bolt at the demon *Brutrāsura*. The lightning weapon splintered into four parts, and the third part assumed the shape of a chariot or Ratha.

Three cars (chariots) take part in this festival. Besides the car of Lord Jagannātha, the people also draw the car of Lord Balabhadra, incarnation of the holy
serpent on whom Lord Visnu rests. The banner of this car displays the outline
of a mirror, recalling the mirror of wisdom placed on Balabhadra's altar and
through which he receives a view of the entire universe. In the Lord are seen
the pure and transparent qualities of the mirror. Goddess Subhadrā, goddess of
the lotus, symbolizing wealth, prosperity, and grace, possesses the third car, on
whose banner appears a lotus profile. On the festival's eve, the people worship
the cars and invoke the deity of the wind and other deities who, in popular
belief, descend from the heavens into the cars and protect them for the next
nine days. During this period the cars are considered divine. The worshipers
regard the protection given to the cars and to the clothes, decorations, and
weapons placed within them over the nine days, as of greater importance even
than their veneration of the deities.

The day before the ceremony commences, the three chariots are lined up
before the lion's gate of the temple, facing north (fig. 10). Balabhadra's car
comes first, then Subhadrā's, and finally Jagannātha's. Flower crowns are placed
on the heads of their images inside the temple, an offering is made to them,
then one by one they are carried out and installed in their chariots. Before the
chariots can proceed on their way, the Rājā of Puri, a descendant of the builder
of the Jagannātha Temple, arrives in a palanquin, pays homage to the deities,

Figure 10 *Painting,
Puri, Orissa, India. Made
by a group of hereditary
artists for pilgrims to buy as
souvenirs, this painting of
the temple of Jagannātha
portrays worshipers, priests,
gods, and the mythology
surrounding the worship of
the god Visnu.*

Figure 11 Wooden model, sold as a remembrance of a pilgrimage to the temple of Jagannātha in Puri, India. Guardians painted on the doors watch over the deities who stare out from within the miniature shrine.

and sweeps the platform of each car one after another, in the ceremony known as *cherā panharā*, "sweeping the chariot floor."

Now all is in readiness. On the festival morn, thousands of people gather in the temple courtyard, and at the priests' signal they surge forth, seize the thick ropes attached to the chariots, and pull joyously and exuberantly. But they must not pull too speedily, and a hymn cautions them to restrain their high spirits and pride of strength:

> The car ought to be
> Dragged very slowly
> And the Holy wheels
> Shall move slowly
> And with sounds
> Of universal love.

The reason for this decorum in pulling the cars is to allow the gods to seat themselves comfortably and rest themselves during the journey. Sudden lurches or jolts might disturb them, and any damage to the cars would be regarded as a national calamity. So with sedate movements the worshipers pull the cars along the main road, until at the road's end they reach Gundicā Maṇdir, Lord Jagannātha's garden house, a richly sculpted building, entered through an archway guarded by two stone lions. There the gods repose for a week. On the eighth day they make the return trip to Puri. The same ritual offerings of cooked food are tendered the deities in the garden house as in the temple of Jagannātha, but in the cars they are offered uncooked foods such as milk and ghee. Everyone regardless of caste, creed, or religion, may see, touch, and worship the Lords placed on the cars. No restrictions on untouchables limit this ceremony.

Material objects. The central objects of the Car Festival are the three cars in which the deities ride. They are splendid and imposing structures for which the English translation *cars* or *chariots* is inadequate; the Sanscrit word *Ratha* might best be retained. Jagannātha's Ratha stands forty-five feet high, a foot higher than Balabhadra's and two feet higher than Subhadrā's. They are painted respectively bright yellow, blue, and dark red, and covered with cloth of the same color, which also corresponds to the color of the garments worn by the deities. Jagannātha is thought by some to be equivalent to Kṛṣṇa, who customarily wears yellow robes. The deities themselves within the Rathas are attired in golden garments.

Every phase of the construction, christening, and consecration of the Rathas bears ritualistic significance. They are made only of Sāla wood, formerly supplied by the Rājā of Dasapallā and currently by the government of Orissa. Lord Jagannātha's Ratha rests on sixteen wheels, indicating as many divine principles, divided into five subtle elements and eleven organs. Balabhadra's Ratha is supported on fourteen wheels representing the fourteen worlds in the lifetime of Brahma, while Subhadrā's Ratha has twelve wheels corresponding to the twelve months. On the festival day the Rathas tower above the multitude in the street and the adjacent buildings, looming like huge ornamental bells capped by a spire and surmounting a raised platform on which dignitaries and attendants stand.

The Dragon Boat Festival on the Hupeh-Hunan Plain, Central China

Known in the Western world as the dragon boat festival, this ceremony is called by the Chinese "To fight and cross over" (*King Tu*). (All information from Göran Aijmer, 1964.) Long narrow boats bearing a dragon head at the stem and a dragon tail at the stern are launched in a race that also involves violent struggles between the boatmen. The commonly accepted tradition ascribes the ceremony's origin to the suicide of the minister and celebrated poet K'ü Yüan, who in the fourth century B.C. fell into disfavor with the king of Ch'u, a feudal state, and drowned himself in a river in northeastern Hunan. "To fight and cross over" represents a ceremonial search for and mourning of K'ü Yüan. Widely performed all over China and neighboring countries, the dragon boat festival is most intensely observed in the southern provinces and particularly on the great well-watered plain of the Central Yangtse Valley in the provinces of Hupeh and Hunan. Various interpreters have explained "To fight and cross over" as a summer solstice festival to produce rain through a struggle between dragons in heaven and to ensure a good harvest; as a pre-Chinese agricultural rite centering on the notion of a dying god and the return of the growing season; and as a rice-bread festival to propitiate malevolent river demons. In these readings the figure of K'ü Yüan has dropped out or is regarded as a beneficent force of nature.

The dragon ceremonies very likely take place after the heavy work of transplanting rice plants, which occurs from mid-April to the beginning of June. All the people involved in the ceremony are born into and belong to one or another boat region. Forty to eighty men man the boats, according to the length of the vessels. These crews are recruited from fishing families, and the paddlers are selected by *chan* divination and tests to determine the strongest men. A headman (*t'ou*) of social standing is chosen to stand in the boat's stem. Before the actual ceremony, the boats visit officials of the town (Ch'ang te fu), whom the *t'ou* greet with bows. Other crew members beat a drum and clap boards to furnish rhythm for the paddlers, and one guides the boat with flag signals, while a fifth in the stern holds a steering oar. These five could be associated with the principles of wood, fire, earth, metal, and water.

The night preceding the ceremony the headman invites a potent sorcerer from up in the mountains to perform his arts. On his part, the headman gives this *wu* sorcerer (named for a sorcerer mentioned in K'ü Yüan's poetry anthology) wine and sacrificial animals. The sorcerer scatters buckwheat from stem to stern of the dragon boat, lights a fire "to illuminate the boat," and gives lucky seals to the crew, while drums beat steadily through the night. All these rituals serve to counteract the spells of hostile sorcerers. The *wu* sorcerer is dressed in red and exhibits a demon face, either painted or masked.

On the morning of the dragon boat race, the *wu* sorcerer lights an oil fire to start the craft on its way. By the color and height of the flames, he predicts the race's outcome: high red flames (a symbol of good luck in the *yang-yin* system) signifies victory; low black flames (a symbol of bad luck), defeat. Barefooted, with rolled-up trousers, the sorcerer jumps seven steps, throws some object into the fire, causing it to flame, and recites these words: "The fire of heaven is burning the sun. The fire is burning the fire regions. Lightning, master of the principles, is burning to death everything that is not auspicious. The dragon boat goes down the Jo water to the five lakes and the four seas and is permitted to float and to be propelled." Meanwhile the outsides of the dragon boats have been swept with *po mao* grass from stem to stern to ensure that hostile persons have not attached destructive objects to the craft.

As the flames of the oil fire lit by the *wu* sorcerer shoot upward, the dragon boat sets off. In the Chinese conception of the world, Jo shuei (Weak Water) is a cosmic river whose source springs from the foot of the Jo tree, the tree of sunset. Thus the launching of the dragon boat may be interpreted to symbolize a voyage down the cosmic Jo water from the region of the setting sun to the world of man.

The festival here described takes place in the town of Ch'ang te fu in northeastern Hunan, the capital of an underprefecture. "To fight and cross over" is staged in the middle of the district, at a point in the river ten *li* in width, although the distance between the banks changes with the rise and fall of the river. On the south bank a white sandy beach fronts thick grass and dense woods. On the north bank stand tall buildings three stories high with painted balustrades, flanked by the old thick crenelated town wall. Spectators crowd the buildings, gather on the south bank, and watch from the boats on the river. Town officials take up their positions in a special building set off by colorful decorations and bamboo mats. All the boats taking part in the ceremonial contest approach this building, muffle their drums, and ply their paddles rapidly until they reach the beach. Then the headman steps ashore, enters the building, and salutes the officials by knocking his head on the floor. The crew throws peach amulets and soldier pots filled with rice and beans into the river to drive away demons. All preliminaries are now concluded.

Two or three boats paddling side by side strive with mighty exertions to cross the river from north to south. But this is no simple boat race. By various maneuvers, tricks, and stratagems, and outright force, the crews seek to beat each other. They will advance suddenly, stop suddenly, drift while preparing for an encounter, lie crosswise in each other's path, change directions. One boat might inveigle the other two into a combat, then return to attack the victor. A strong boat might drive off and pursue a weaker one. Sometimes the struggle takes the form of direct combat, with the crews striking each other with bamboo canes and goose-egg stones. Boats are sunk, fights occur, crew members drown or are mortally wounded.

Meanwhile the spectators cheer the boat from their region, and when it passes by them they light fireworks, wave fans, and throw pieces of red and green silk to the crews. But when a boat from a rival region enters their area, they shout angrily and hurl stones at the boatsmen, who in retaliation hold aloft their paddles horizontally and shake their hands to simulate the act of fighting another boat. Small boats decorated with muticolored scrolls and two trees on which are hung yellow money, and carrying drummers and flutists, stand by to provide the dragon boats with food and wine. The paddlers must consume every last crumb and drink every last drop, no matter how drunk or sated, and throw the bowls and chopsticks into the river.

The race is ended, and the victorious boat paddles backward, stern first. When it passes a losing boat, the triumphant crew holds its paddles on high, dances for joy, beats gongs, and plays wind instruments, while the defeated crew half-heartedly emulates the victors and then retreats into silence. That evening and all next day, relatives, friends, and neighbors feast the winners, tie colored ribbons over their doorways, even enact plays to honor the crew, and write scrolls praising them which are hung over the town gates. Dogs, tortoises, plants, and fruit are hung to mock the losers, or are sent to them in the mail. People from the losing regions hang their heads on seeing the defeated crew, and slink away.

On the eighteenth day of the fifth month the dragon boats are paddled swiftly downstream. Sacrificial animals, wine, and yellow paper money carried on the boats are burned and poured out, to allow evil influences to drift away with the current. Then the dragon boats return secretly, without drums or flags, to be pulled up on the beach, propped up, and covered over till next summer. The festival is over.

Material objects. The dragon boats are clearly the center piece of "To fight and cross over." In Ch'ang te fu, six dragon boats are recorded, each mounted with dragon heads and tails and painted in different colors. The largest was 130 feet long. Each boat possessed its own temple spirit, its own flags, and its own uniforms for its personnel. Two of these fighting boats were painted in five colors, presumably green, red, yellow, white, and black, a third was painted purple, a fourth white, a fifth black, and a sixth red. A yellow dragon boat had once been built, with realistic head, horns, scales, claws, and body, but it sank with a hundred men on board, and the reason given was that it resembled too closely an actual dragon. These boats were made of conifer wood, prized for its seaworthiness.

   Mention should be made of the dragons, which give their name and appearance to the boats, and their likeness to the flags on the five-colored boats. The dragons are said to inhabit ponds and springs, rivers and brooks, lakes and rice fields. They also haunt caves and ravines. In the symbolism of the boats, the dragons appear as vessels in disguise and represent the *yin* principle in their underground habitat and death-dealing force.

Namahage in Iinomori: Japanese Masquerade

In the last week of December, young men in the village of Iinomori on the Oga Peninsula in northeast Japan, fourteen hours by train from Tokyo, begin preparations for the Namahage Festival. (All information from Yoshiko Yamamoto, 1978.) Outsiders, especially women and children, are not permitted to see the men prepare the wooden masks and costumes of plaited straw (fig. 12). On December 30, the eve of the festival, the young men gather at Inari Shrine, light candles, and build a huge bonfire. People purify themselves ritually before the

Figure 12 *Wooden masks and costumes of plaited straw fashioned for the Namahage festival.*

fire and toast rice cakes on bamboo branches. On the night of December 31, households in the village make ready for the Namahage. Good luck scrolls are hung in the guest room, offerings of rice cakes and other food are placed on a desk before the scrolls and the household altar. Square trays are set around the *Io* (a fireplace on the floor) in the guest room, and here the family members seat themselves in assigned places. Meanwhile at the community center the young men ritually offer seven candles and two large bottles of *sake* to eight masks lined up at the altar, clap their hands twice, and bow three times. Then the worshipers drink the *sake* out of a large cup, don the masks and straw shirts, and screaming like animals, "W-a-aw, wa-aw," rush outside down the hill to commence their visits.

In the houses every room is lit, doors are opened, food and *sake* are left out. No children, young brides, or single girls are to be seen, for they have hidden from the Namahage, in the granary, the closet, in other houses. Now the eight Namahage, chosen for their strength and loud voices, rush into the house, after removing their straw shoes, followed by uncostumed young men, shouting and banging on the door. The straw shirts of the Namahage swish as they prowl about the house searching for children, girls, and brides, and keeping up a running patter of questions: "Are there naughty boys and girls in this house? Do they listen to their parents? Does the new bride get up early in the morning or not? If she sleeps late in the morning, we'll do magic to her! [i.e., they will pinch her]. Where did you hide Yukiko [a single girl]?" The adults in the hamlet have instructed the Namahage in advance on some of these matters to teach the children a lesson. But much of the conversation is impromptu and gives the Namahage opportunity to respond wittily to questions from the head of the household.

"What is your name, Mr. Namahage?"
"My name is Lid and Handle of Pan. Wa-aw."
"I understand that the ice on Hachiro Lagoon is thinner this year. You must have had trouble crossing it."
"Wa-aw, wa-aw. Yes. It was so difficult that we had to come by helicopter."

If the Namahage find children and brides they pinch them. Then they assemble in the guest room, shouting and moving continuously, while the wife offers each visitor a tray and the host beseeches them to drink *sake*. This they do, lifting their masks, but they spurn the food. With a final outburst and last-minute search they depart, repeating their warnings to children and brides. A follower collects money and rice cakes in a paper bag. Each visit to a house lasts about ten minutes. By 11:00 P.M., the Namahage have concluded their rounds and, like the rest of the villagers, they watch the New Year's Eve program on television. Sometimes household members will play tricks on the Namahage, such as putting pepper in the *sake* to sober them up or tying the straw shirts of two Namahage together while they sit on a cushion, so that when they stand up they topple over.

After the festival the members of the household sweep up the bits of straw left from the Namahage's costumes. It is believed that tying the straw shreds around one's head cures a headache, or an ache in any part of the body where they are tied. The rice cakes collected by the Namahage protect them from misfortune when they leave town for outside work.

Attitudes of the inhabitants of Iinomori toward the Namahage Festival vary. Some resent the boisterousness, drunkenness, and violence of the masqueraders and the idea of youths drinking unlimited amounts of *sake* and begging. Children fear the Namahage as *oni* or demons, and new brides fear them because of their appearance and behavior. Older villagers see virtue in the Namahage for representing the discipline they themselves approve of. Also they recognize religious aspects of the festival, seeing the Namahage as messengers of *kami* (spirit deities) who seek to remove misfortunes and insure abundant crops in the coming year. The young men relish the occasion to shed their customary reserved behavior and let loose with the sanction of their elders. For the inhabitants of the hamlet, the festival serves to bring them together when the winter snows have driven them apart.

Various legends explain the origin of the Namahage. In one account, Emperor Fu of the Han Dynasty brought five *oni* to the Oga Peninsula and worked them relentlessly. Finally he gave them a day off to do as they wished in the village, and they ran beserk, crying "Wa-aw," demanding *sake* and roast chickens, threatening children and idlers, abducting girls. Finally the villagers struck a bargain with them: if the *oni* could build a thousand steps overnight up the hill toward Goshado Shrine, the people would offer them a girl each year; if they did not complete the task they must leave. The *oni* built 999 steps, when a mimic hired by the villagers crowed like a rooster. Thinking the morning had come, the *oni* fled to the mountains in anger, never to return, save in the form of the Namahage. In European tales the Devil is similarly tricked.

Japanese folklore scholars have interpreted the Namahage as belonging to a cycle of mysterious visitors at the New Year who represent spirits of the dead, ancestors, or deities, who come from distant lands beyond the sea to confer blessings. In old folk-belief, *kami* in the form of a man-god wear straw coats and hats in their earthly appearances when they visit villagers in their homes. The main functions of the religious visitors are to guarantee a rich harvest, to drive out evil demons, and to control the spirits of the land.

Material objects. Costumes and masks play the central role in the artifacts associated with the Namahage festival. The masqueraders drape themselves almost completely in their straw skirt and coat (*kende*), so that only their masked heads and hands and feet appear out of the straw mass, while bunches flare out sideways from their necks. Each Namahage wears at least three *kende*. Strands of straw are plaited together on a straw rope that encircles the neck to form the *kende*. The straw man looks merely grotesque, but the mask gives him his frightening appearance (fig. 13). Masks are almost twice the size of a face, with exaggerated eyes, nose, and mouth, two fangs and two horns. The masker looks out through two small holes pierced in the eyes. No two masks are alike, but most are colored red or green. Silver and gold paper cover the horns and fangs, and hair from horses' tails dangles from the head over the face. The jut-

Figure 13 *Almost twice the size of a human face, this Namahage mask, with its exaggerated eyes, nose, mouth, and gold and silver paper-covered fangs and horns, projects a fearful countenance.*

ting horns and fangs cut from branches replicate each other. Sometimes paint rather than colored paper is used on the surface of the mask, and grasses painted black, gold, and red replace the horsehair. The youths in the young men's association who play the part of Namahage also make and repair the masks, which are fashioned from willow or paulownia trees. With hand axes, chisels, and other tools the maskers cut the logs into lengths of ten to thirteen inches and split them into halves, one for each mask, and then fashion features from the blocks. The young men take turns working on each mask, not following a particular model but striving for fearsomeness. In painting, one person takes charge of each of the four basic colors, gold, silver, red, and green. With the gluing of the horsehair or grasses on the head, the mask is completed. Villagers reuse the same masks for many years and repair them with parts from other damaged masks. Masqueraders say, and villagers agree, that wearing the masks and costumes makes them seem larger than life and gives them a new sense of potency.

Some expected and unexpected objects emerge from this review of these diverse celebrations. The costumes and masks cause us no surprise, nor does the sacred image of the Virgin of the Door. But the towering chariot in which rides Lord Jagganātha and the fierce dragon boat paddled by the Yangtse Valley fishermen belong in a special class of revered ritual vehicles. The sacred gourd or calabash hurled by the king onto a shield at the height of the Incwala ceremony has acquired its own mystique. And discarded gasoline drums provide a now-famous music in the steel bands of the Trinidad Carnival. In physical appurtenances such as these we see tangible markers of the celebratory impulse shared by all peoples.

Our seven celebrations, somewhat randomly chosen, display a number of common elements. In all of them we can perceive key symbolic figures or objects which represent the message and motive of the occasion. With the Otuzco festival the image of the Virgen de la Puerta dominates all the proceedings. The image takes on a living character as the patroness and protectress of the community, the mother of Jesus in a special incarnation devoted to this mountain corner of Peru. People revere the Virgin on her throne in the church and as she is paraded through the streets. Giant chariots house the deities in the Jagannā-tha festival and become their surrogates, honored ritually by the throngs of worshipers. The king-deity garbed as a demon in the Incwala ceremony is anticipated by the sacred gourd and the sacred bull, whose hide decorates the gourd and the royal costume; in the flinging of the gourd the king throws off his demon self. The Incwala contains both divinity and deviltry in his being and so stands between the god-figures in the Otuzco and Jagannātha festivals and the devil-figures in the Dragon-boat and Namahage festivals. The boats propelled by muscular oarsmen represent the dragons and the yin female principle of underground powers of darkness, as opposed to the yang male principle of sunshine and positive forces. So too the straw-cloaked and wooden-masked Namahage impersonate the oni who according to legend once threatened the villagers of Iinomori.

In the other two celebrations the central symbols do not relate to supernatural beings. At the strawberry farmers' festival in Arpádhon the grapes hung from the ceiling and the traditional csárdás dance recall the original grape-harvest ceremony in Hungary, which perhaps at one time contained its own symbolic references to a life-renewing deity of the seasons. Pieces of scrap iron fashioned into musical instruments symbolized Trinidad's carnival with its famous steel bands; carnival itself symbolizes a triumph of slaves over masters, colonials over imperials, coloreds over whites, as the Trinidadians re-create their music from tin cans and oil drums.

Another theme that binds together these celebrations is their ritual re-creation of a legendary past. Costumes especially recapture days of yore: those of gypsies and redskins among the folkloric bands in Otuzco; of clownish gallants and Elizabethan cowboys at carnival; of Hungarian peasants in Arpádhon; of straw-jacketed ogres from the Han Dynasty in the Japanese New Year festival; of a forest demon in Incwala, when the king cloaks himself in a green-grass mantle. In the festival of Jagannātha, the construction of the chariots contains symbolic elements from a mythical time, associated with legends and attributes of the three deities: Jagannātha's chariot was fashioned from a splinter of a lightning bolt the god threw at a demon. The design of the dragon-boats and the ritual offerings to them in "To fight and cross over" recall the search for a fugitive court poet over two thousand years before.

All the festivals save that at Arpádhon display the presence of religio-magical power. It is manifest in the image of the Virgen de la Puerta, which confers blessings and healings on the people of Otuzco; in the Namahage masks that alter respectful youths into ogres, a transformation also remarked on by the Trinidad masqueraders, who allege they feel themselves different and powerful beings when they put on their masks; in the sharp-grass mantle symbolizing the life of the Swazi people worn by the Incwala; in the boats disguising dragons in the Central Yangtse Valley; and in the chariots in which gods are seated in Orissa. In every case the people treat these figures and objects respectfully and deferentially.

At the same time the festival participants transcend the customary barriers that separate them from higher authorities and display a familiarity and even license unthinkable under ordinary circumstances. The Otuzcans welcome the image of the Virgin when it descends to the plaza, surround it, and transport it through the streets. Pulling the chariots of Jagannātha along the sacred route, worshipers mingle irrespective of caste to revere the gods seated inside. But familiarity also breeds contempt; calypsonians sing songs critical of the civil authorities; Incwala performers express hatred of the king in song, dance, and mime; polite Japanese youths turn noisy and aggressive toward their elders when in their Namahage personae.

These actions are related to the trait of playful aggression that marks the behavior of carnival-type celebrants. Stick-fighters at carnival and boat crews in "To fight and cross over" do battle with each other, sometimes causing injury and even death. Bemanti clansmen carrying the king's sacred gourd harass and fine tribesmen who cross their path. The Namahage, drunk with *sake,* intimidate households. Drunken revelry and turbulence resulting from high-spirited crowds cause problems in all the festivals, at Otuzco, Arpádhon, and Jagannātha as well, so that the aggression approved within the ritual blends with the lawless violence of the throng.

But humility characterizes religious-festival behavior. Slave figures protect the Virgin; the Swazi mourn their king; the rājā sweeps the platform of the chariots. When the gods are present, men supplicate.

Comparable in some respects, differing in others, our seven celebrations all illustrate the power of symbolic action and the continuing force of the festive spirit in the contemporary world.

Bibliography

Aijmer, Göran
   1964   *The Dragon Boat Festival on the Hupeh-Hunan Plain, Central China: A Study in the Ceremonialism of the Transplantation of Rice.* Stockholm: Ethnographic Museum of Sweden, Monograph Series, No. 9.

Beidelman, T. O.
   1966   "Swazi Royal Ritual." *Africa,* vol. 3, no. 6, pp. 372–405.

Cox, Harvey
   1969   *Feast of Fools.* New York: Harper and Row.

Dégh, Linda
   1977–78 "Grape-Harvest Festival of Strawberry Farmers: Folklore or Fake?" *Ethnologia Europaea,* vol. 10, no. 2, pp. 114–31.

Hill, Errol
   1972   *The Trinidad Carnival.* Austin and London: University of Texas Press.

Kuper, Hilda
  1947   *An African Aristocracy: Rank Among the Swazi.* London: Oxford University
          Press. (Reprinted with new preface, 1961 and 1965.)
  1964   *The Swazi, A South African Kingdom.* New York: Holt, Rinehart, and Win-
          ston.
  1968   "Celebration of Growth and Kingship: Incwala in Swaziland." *African Arts/
          Arts d'Afrique,* vol. 1, no. 3, pp. 57–59, 90.
Mishra, K. C.
  1971   *The Cult of Jagannātha.* Calcutta: Firma K.L. Mukhopadhyay.
Smith, Robert J.
  1975   *The Arts of the Festival As Exemplified by the Fiesta to the Patroness of
          Otuzco: La Virgen de la Puerta.* Lawrence, Kansas: University of Kansas Pub-
          lications in Anthropology, No. 6.
Vogt, Evon A.
  1955   "A Study of the Southwestern Fiesta System as Exemplified by the Laguna
          Fiesta." *American Anthropologist* 57:820–39.
Yamamoto, Yoshiko
  1978   *The Namahage, A Festival in the Northeast of Japan.* Philadelphia: Institute
          for the Study of Human Issues.

Clay Voices: Invoking, Mocking, Celebrating

Barbara A. Babcock

> ... these things made or born into
> special forms by the hands of man also
> have life and function variously,
> according to their various forms.
>
> *Frank Hamilton Cushing*
>
> They're singing. Can't you hear them?
>
> *Helen Cordero*

I n the logic of Western rationalism, things do not speak except metaphorically. In another worldview, that of the Pueblo Indian, they do: both natural phenomena and those of human manufacture have life and voice and spirit.[1] Recognizing that molded clay is an informed substance, archaeologists talk a great deal about what ceramic fragments and design sequences can "tell" us about prehistoric Pueblo cultures. Less frequently do they acknowledge that in the belief systems of these peoples, *every* piece of clay sings, whether shaped into a bowl with geometric design for daily use or into the image of a man. Unless a specific ceremonial use can be ascribed, matter and spirit are usually separated and opposed in analytic discussions of Pueblo pottery in a way they never have been in the life that produced it. This distinction, like its close relatives utilitarian vs. nonutilitarian and mundane vs. sacred, is counterproductive to any understanding of Pueblo art and virtually assures a sort of deafness with regard to hearing and attempting to translate clay voices.[2] Unfortunately, as Merleau-Ponty once remarked, "science manipulates things and gives up living in them" (1964: 159).

For over 2,000 years, Puebloan peoples of the southwestern United States have shaped the flesh of Mother Earth into useful, playful, and ceremonial forms.[3] For the past 100 years, archaeologists have been reconstructing much of the story of prehistoric Pueblo life from these ceramic remains. Despite the fact that figurative pottery is widely distributed in both time and space in early Pueblo cultures,[4] scholars have, with few exceptions, looked away from this form of self-portraiture. Because they are difficult to classify and define, and because they inevitably raise questions of meaning and use, representative zoomorphic and anthropomorphic forms have become a marginal category such as "miscellaneous shapes" in discussions and exhibitions of both prehistoric and historic Pueblo ceramics.

The representative impulse in Pueblo pottery takes several forms: fetish, figurine or effigy, effigy vessel, and both appliquéd and painted design on nonfigurative shapes as well as figurative ones.[5] While it is comparatively easy—excepting the early historic period—to document and verify these figurative forms, accurate interpretation is considerably more difficult. The best that can and has been done is to conjecture meaning and use on the basis of scattered ethnographic remarks from the late nineteenth and twentieth centuries. The relevant generalizations, my own and others, are several. First, there is no description of any Pueblo ceremony—curing, hunting, rain, fertility, etc.—or any altar that does not include both ceramic vessels containing water and sacred meal *and* effigies, ceramic and otherwise. It has been suggested that these objects, like the ceremonies and dances with which they are associated, function to maintain an equilibrium among the natural, supernatural, and social orders of things.[6] Second, both two- and three-dimensional figurative designs may be described as both embodiments of and prayers to ancestors, gods, or spirits for rain, for crops, for hunting, and for human and animal procreation.[7] That they are still so regarded is evidenced by the fact that at Santo Domingo, the most conservative of the Keresan Pueblos, both painted and molded figures are prohibited in pottery made for sale. Third, every recorded Pueblo origin myth either includes a description of how the people came to make pottery or, more significant still, describes creation itself as occurring in part through the process of potterymaking. This is notably the case in the Keresan origin stories recorded or referred to by Parsons, Stirling, White, and others in which Iyatiku ("bringing to life") and her sister, Nautsiti ("more of everything in the basket") are sent up into the light, to this earth, with baskets crammed full of images and seeds from which they create all forms of life. Several of these seeds and "little images" actually enable the two sisters to reach their goal: the pine tree which they climb up, the badger who makes the hole in the earth big enough for them to climb through, and the locust who smooths the hole by plastering.[8] Fourth, both Keresan and Hopi townspeople have been represented collectively by male and female clay images. At Santo Domingo, for example, the *cacique* (religious leader of the pueblo) "takes care of his people by looking after 'his children' just as the Mother (Iyatiku) whom he represents looked after the images in her basket. When the chief of Awatobi invited the Oraibi chief to destroy Awatobi, he displayed two clay figurines, representing one, the townsmen, the other the townswomen. 'Here I have brought you my people,' calmly he said" (Parsons 1939: 336).[9] Fifth, small figurines, which are frequently unbaked and unpainted and which are made of cornmeal or clay, are central to rites and prayers of increase, particularly those associated with the winter solstice and/or Christmas. Images of domestic animals are placed on the respective altars and thereafter buried in the corral, "so that there will be more of them" (Parsons 1929–30: 279). Similarly, a woman wanting children will make a clay "baby" and take it to the altar; alternatively, the kachina may give a woman a clay or wooden baby in a miniature cradle which she then cares for and regards as "the heart of the child" (Dumarest 1918: 141). Such clay figures are taken to be "the seed from which the real objects will grow" (Parsons 1939: 574).[10] Finally, with regard to small animal figures in particular, it has been suggested that they are nothing more than children's toys. Even if they are, such "idle playthings" as clay horses or wooden kachina dolls are regarded by the elders who make and give them as educational, as embodiments of supernatural personages or animal spirits, and as expressive of a ceremonial system as complex and as powerful as any ever known.[11]

Modern scholars may debate the religious significance of Pueblo figurative pottery; the Spanish clergy who arrived in the sixteenth and seventeenth centuries did not. Their zeal in smashing and burning "the idols" and discouraging further manufacture was protracted and intense.[12] We may wish to gain more knowledge of change and continuity in the figurative tradition, but there is much that must remain unavailable. Between the many prehistoric figures and those collected and described in the last quarter of the nineteenth century, there are at least 500 years of silence.

Despite the efforts of Spanish and then Anglo missionaries to stamp out Pueblo religion and idolatry, the ceremonial system survived, together with its figurative painting, carving, and pottery traditions.[13] When the railroads began to bring tourists to the Southwest in the 1880s, Pueblo potters sold them "odd and attractive pieces" as well as "utility pieces." While Anglos bought and sold these "curiosities" and even used images of them to advertise their wares,[14] they did not regard them highly. The prevailing attitude is summed up in Thomas S. Dozier's "Statement to the Trade for 1907" in which he says regarding pottery figures:

> No attempt will be made to describe these as it would necessarily lead to a discussion of the ceremonies themselves. . . . There is no doubt that children have been amused with pottery shaped to represent the human form, wholly or in part, or to represent the forms of the lower animals; perhaps, the makers themselves have learned to make new or strange forms from idle dallying in lazy moments; and it may be that many pieces considered ceremonial are but the results of these idle moments, or they may have been made simply to amuse. To this trait of character, not uncommon to more enlightened races, may be ascribed the reason for much of the pottery being made up and sold to the tourists, since the Indians derive some revenue from the sale of odd and attractive pieces, as well as from the utility pieces. . . . Education and a consequent learning of new duties will yet make an end of her pottery days . . . in this utilitarian age, she cannot always go on making toys. (6,9–10)

Fortunately, "she" did go on making "toys." Unfortunately, something of this attitude has remained among scholars and collectors, so there is much that we do not know about the figurative pottery that we have from the last 100 years.

For reasons that we may never discover, the most sizeable, various, and continuous production of figurative shapes and designs during the past century has occurred and continues to occur in the Rio Grande Keresan Pueblo of Cochiti, New Mexico. Notwithstanding this variety of painted and modeled figurative designs, there is a distinctive Cochiti style,[15] which has been repeatedly described as "crude," "haphazard," "spidery," and "grotesque." While the style has been continuous, the primary context for Cochiti pottery has changed from a domestic or ceremonial one within the pueblo to that of other people's shelves, and with it there have been modifications in both form and function. The voices of the Cochiti figures obtained by and later made for white men during the last 100 years have shifted from invoking to mocking to celebrating and remembering. If it is difficult to hear and understand these voices, we can at least look, with some effort, at countless Cochiti figurative potteries gathering dust on museum shelves and see that "from all these things a shape in time emerges. A visible portrait of the collective identity . . . .This self-image reflected in things is a guide and a point of reference to the group for the future, and it eventually becomes the portrait given to posterity" (Kubler 1962: 9). The remainder of this essay describes and illustrates these modulations in voice and changes in shape of Cochiti's ceramic self-portrait.

The earliest known figures, particularly those collected by Colonel Stevenson and Reverend Jackson in the late 1870s and early 1880s, are predominantly polychrome (buff, black, and red) effigy vessels in human, animal, or bird form, which are frequently painted with figurative designs as well. The majority of the smaller figurines included in these collections are undecorated and bear a distinct resemblance to (a) Keresan human altar figures which represent supernatural beings and which have been described and illustrated by several generations of ethnographers;[16] (b) the Koshare and Kwerana, the Keres' sacred clowns; and (c) animal fetishes and figurines used notably in curing and in rites of increase. I would guess that if such forms were not themselves used ceremonially, they were at least reproductions of ceremonial shapes and designs. What is certain is that as the presence of an alien market increased, the production of these types of figures declined. Figurative pottery continued to be made in abundance, and Cochiti potters continued to decorate bowls and jars with figurative designs prohibited in other pueblos except on ceremonial pieces, but within a decade the shapes and the voices had changed.

Museum data suggest that except for an occasional bird pitcher, effigy vessels ceased to be produced for sale after ca. 1885. Animal and bird figurines became smaller and cruder and simpler but were otherwise unchanged. The shape of man, however, was dramatically transformed into a much larger, standing figure. The earliest of these are, like the effigy vessels, painted with figurative designs— birds, leaves, rainclouds, etc. In what may be a transitional phase, some of these figures are dressed biculturally in both Cochiti designs and white-man's garb. By 1880, their painted dress is almost entirely Anglo, and an unmistakable note of caricature and mockery has crept into their stances as well as their voices (fig. 14).[17] Whether the white man realized it or not, what he purchased and termed "grotesques" were in fact portraits of himself (fig. 15). The impetus for these humorous imitations was two-fold: along with tourists and assorted white professionals, the railroad brought carnival, circus, and vaudeville to New Mexico; in turn, it took Cochiti men to Washington and New York where, among other things they were introduced to the opera. Their mimings of countless versions of the white man in stereotypical operatic poses were re-presented in clay, as were the two-headed, no-legged, armless freaks and dancing bears of the car-

Figure 14 *Cowboy with vest and chaps, ca. 1890. Height: 15¾".*

nival and circus (fig. 16). These figures were called *monos* (Spanish meaning "monkey, silly fool, mimic, mere doll"), the same term which was used for figures that were knocked over or broken in carnival ball games.[18]

Given this shift in both subject and intent of many of the figurines of this period, it is tempting to argue, as students of the "arts of acculturation" frequently have, that such an obvious intrusion of the white man marks not only a commercialization but also a secularization of traditional religious art—in this

Figure 15 *Mrs. George H. Pepper packing pottery at Cochiti, 1903. Monos in foreground.*

case, ceramic human effigies. As with other traditional Pueblo arts made for an external market and/or incorporating Anglo themes, the Cochiti case is not so simple as that. To begin with, there is nothing secular about clowning, which is at the center of all Pueblo mythology and ritual. Sacred clowns are among the most powerful of ritual persons, and burlesque and caricature of that which is seen as "other" is a recurrent mode of behavior.[19] What the clowns did on the plaza, Cochiti potters re-created and fixed in clay: all but one of the makers of these *monos* whom I have been able to identify were themselves members of one of the two Cochiti clown societies.

Figure 16 *Two-headed strongman with bandolier and decorated tights, 1875–80. Height: 25".*

In the years between 1915 and 1960, there was a marked decline in both the quantity and the quality of Cochiti's figurative production. Human forms are considerably smaller and are more frequently portraits of Indians rather than white men: a drummer, a dancer, a woman with a bowl of bread or a child. The last, a "singing mother" or "madonna,"[20] was the most common, but only a few women at Cochiti made them and "for a long time pottery was silent in the pueblo."[21] The silence was broken in the late 1950s when Helen Cordero and her husband's cousin, Juanita Arquero, "started up again," making pottery as an alternative to leather and beadwork. Juanita was already an accomplished potter and, in comparison, Helen's bowls and jars "never looked right."[22] Juanita suggested that she try figures instead and "it was like a flower blooming"—countless tiny birds, animals, amphibians, and eventually people came to life. The first time Helen "showed them out," Alexander Girard, a prominent folk art collector, bought all her "little people," encouraged her to make more and larger figures, and commissioned a 250-piece Nativity set. Recalling a "singing mother" of which Helen had already made several, Girard then asked her to make a larger seated figure with children. In Helen's mind, his suggestion became an image of her grandfather, Santiago Quintana, a gifted storyteller who was always surrounded by children.[23] When Helen Cordero shaped that first Storyteller in 1964, she modified the Cochiti figurative tradition which she had inherited in two important respects. First, the primary figure became male rather than female; second, the attached small children exceeded a realistic number—the first Storyteller had five children; subsequent ones have had as many as thirty.[24]

Helen Cordero's Storytellers brought immediate acclaim and success, and with each year since both her reputation and the demand for her work have grown. In addition to widespread professional recognition and substantial material rewards, other significant changes have occurred because of what she has created. In her own work, there have been both technical refinements and the invention of new forms—in addition to Singing Mothers, Nativities, and Storytellers, she now makes a Drummer, a Water Carrier, a Pueblo Father, a Nightcrier, an Owl, a Turtle carrying children on his back, and a Children's Hour in which the youngsters are grouped around rather than on the storyteller (figs. 17 and 18).[25] This list does not exhaust her repertoire, but these are the figures that she repeatedly makes. The Storyteller remains her favorite and most requested figure. More important, Helen's clay people have initiated a remarkable

Figure 17 Turtle "taking children for a ride to learn the old ways," 1980. Height: 6½"; length: 11".

Figure 18   "Children's Hour," 1980. Height of Storyteller: 9"; height of children: 2¼" to 3½".

revival of figurative pottery both in her own and other Rio Grande pueblos, which in turn has resulted in figurative pottery being taken more seriously than ever before. Perhaps for the first time, Pueblo ceramic figurines are regarded as "art" by dealers throughout the United States and Europe. Pottery is anything but silent in Cochiti pueblo today—at least thirty other potters are presently making figurines—and the voice of the Storyteller can be heard in distinctive accents from Taos to Acoma.[26]

For Helen Cordero, however, the Storyteller will always speak in a personal voice: "It's my grandfather. He's giving me these. His eyes are closed because he's thinking. His mouth is open because he's singing." In addition to being a family portrait and *memorate*, her Storyteller, as well as its ceramic cousins and descendants, is also a remarkable form of cultural self-portraiture and a significant new statement of Pueblo identity.[27] The Storyteller is not used in any ceremonial or storytelling context and his voice, if it is heard, is heard and intended to be heard far beyond Cochiti Pueblo. Nonetheless, these clay images are celebrations of the life and the culture as well as the earth from which they are shaped. More specifically, they are reenactments of the life-giving event of storytelling.

Stories are regarded as "life for the people," and this figure, alive with children, is itself a story of generations, procreations, and the power of the word. As Laguna novelist and poet Leslie Silko has emphasized, Pueblo storytelling involves a vital dynamic of "bringing and keeping people together," of maintain-

Figure 19   Helen Cordero shaping a Storyteller and telling several young visitors about her work at Bandelier National Monument, June 28, 1980.

ing a continuity between past and present, and of endless creation, for each story is the beginning of many stories—"a seed of seeds."[28] The very structure of the Storyteller re-creates this dynamic; its proportions are indeed social proportions.[29] Helen Cordero's first Storyteller was the beginning of many Storytellers because, among other things, it speaks in terms of cultural constants—stories, generations, and the persistent problems of community organization and survival.[30] And like their subjects, Storytellers themselves have become a means of bringing and keeping Pueblo people together.

Implicitly, all art is "forever bound ... to man's most mysterious power, and his most precious one: the power of creation" (Rosenberg, 1975: 218). This connection—likely to be denied or made into an analogy in Western conceptions of art—is at the very center of Pueblo aesthetics. Like its clay ancestors, the Storyteller as conceived by Helen Cordero is both the celebration and the embodiment of this creative force: "When God took away my babies, he gave me my little people to keep me going. If I hadn't had my potteries, I would have just gone down myself. I don't know why people go for my work the way they do. Maybe it's because they're not just pretty things that I make for money. They come from my heart and they're singing."[31] And so, indeed, they are (fig.19). These clay people "materialize a way of experiencing" and "bring a particular cast of mind out into the world of objects, where men can look at it" (Geertz,1976: 1478).

Notes

1. There are numerous discussions of the centrality of this belief in Pueblo religion, but see especially Cushing (1883, 1886, 1896, 1920), Bunzel (1932), and Parsons (1933, 1939).

2. To discuss Pueblo pottery from a materialistic, utilitarian, or purely aesthetic perspective is to misunderstand both its place and its meaning in Pueblo culture. Pueblo religion is an all-pervasive metaphysic and aesthetic: even the once routine and simple act of shaping a cooking pot is surrounded with ceremony, and sacredness is not an attribute conferred only by religious use. Perhaps the best response to the interpretive dilemma created by these Anglo dichotomies is that of John Sloan and Oliver LaFarge: "In Pueblo pictures and in pottery, one is faced by the problem of symbolism, how much is meant to be interpreted, how much pure aesthetic design. *The answer probably is that it's all one*. Potter and artist draw their spiritual sustenance from their tribal life, and that life is all a design, a dance and a ceremonial, from birth to death, and through all the ramifications of daily life; it is a whole, individuals are part of the pattern. The deer and the rain design and the unit derived from a butterfly, are used on jars and pictures, they are set deep in the life of the dances. Of course they are conscious of their symbols, but their whole life is charged with symbols, from them, inevitably they draw their aesthetic patterns" (in Spinden 1931: 31). And, in an early museum guide to Pueblo pottery, Mary Austin similarly remarks: "Design is for them a language which relates itself to the processes they conceive of as going on in all nature and all created things" (1934: 2–3). Regrettably, these insights of poets, painters, and novelists rarely inform the studies of ceramic scholars. Even Ruth Bunzel, when she turns from Zuñi ceremonialism to her classic study of Pueblo pottery-making, eschews discussing the ceremonial and spiritual aspects of the latter. For further discussion of the impossibility of separating matter and spirit, art and religion, see Parsons (1939) and Koenig (1976).

3. Archaeological evidence suggests that pottery-making came into the American southwest ca. 500 B.C. from northern Mexico. The earliest pottery found in the Southwest dates from 500–300 B.C. and occurs in the Hohokam and Mogollon cultures of south and south-central Arizona and New Mexico. By A.D. 200–300, pottery technology had spread to the Anasazi culture of the Four Corners area. The Mogollon and Anasazi were very probably the ancestors of present-day Pueblo peoples.

4. Figurative pottery dates from at least A.D. 300 to the end of the prehistoric period and is found in all prehistoric Southwestern cultures. For discussion and illustration of prehistoric figurines and their temporal and spatial distribution, see Tanner (1976) and Morss (1954). For discussion of prehistoric effigy vessels, see Hammack (1974).

5. The term *fetish* can refer to any object used for a religious or ceremonial purpose; in Pueblo studies, however, it is used primarily to designate very small zoomorphic figures carved from stone or molded from clay. Generally, the term implies the former method of manufacture, and unpainted clay creatures even when used ceremonially tend not to be called fetishes. For detailed discussion of fetishes, see Cushing (1883) and Kirk (1943). *Figurine* or *effigy* refers to a free-standing, three-dimensional animal or human figure, which may be solid or hollow depending on size. Effigy, of course, connotes religious use. The term *effigy vessel,* and sometimes just *effigy,* is used to describe a vessel such as a bowl, jar, or pitcher wholly or partially shaped to form a

three-dimensional representation of a human, animal, or bird. Frequently this involves nothing more, e.g., than the shaping of a ladle handle into human or animal form. Finally, both two- and three-dimensional figures are used for decorative purposes on bowls, jars, etc., as well as on figurines and effigy vessels. Painted figurative design reached its highest form in prehistoric times in Mimbres pottery. For discussion and illustration, see Brody (1977). In the historic period, both painted and appliquéd figurative designs are most common and most highly elaborated in the Keres Pueblo of Cochiti, N.M. Archaeological evidence suggests that figurative forms in particular are Meso-American in origin. For illustrations of prehistoric figurative forms, see Morss (1954), Kidder (1932), Parsons (1919), Hammack (1974).

6. In addition to the references previously cited in fn. 1, see Stevenson (1894), Curtis (1926: vol. 16), and White (1932a, 1932b, 1935, 1942). There is abundant archaeological evidence that figurative pottery, especially miniatures, is also associated with mortuary rituals and is buried with the deceased. The Spanish clergy discouraged these practices, but various ethnographic remarks attest to their persistence in the historic period. See especially Dumarest (1918) and Parsons (1939). For discussion of ceramic miniatures associated with the spirits of the dead and their general use as prayer images, see Parsons (ibid.: 316–18) and Nequatewa (1936).

7. For discussion of the meanings of various figurative designs and/or objects, see Parsons (1919, 1939), Cushing (1883, 1886, 1920), Spinden (1931: 3–18), Bunzel (1932, 1972), Austin in Spinden (1931: 3–5), and Coolidge (1929: 106–14). In her introduction to *Pueblo Indian Religion* (1939: xi), Parsons remarks that all forms of Pueblo art "whatever else they are, also are measures to invoke and coerce, to gratify or pay, the Spirits." And, in his classic essay on post-Spanish Pueblo pottery (1950: 6), Kenneth Chapman observes that "through the three centuries that have passed, the designs of Pueblo pottery have had one dominant theme, a prayer for rain for the maturing crops, a matter of gravest concern in this semi-arid region where the menace of drought is ever in mind. So in endless profusion of combinations appear the symbols of mountains and clouds, lightning and rain; and leaves, flowers, and seed pods as emblems of growth and maturity. With these frequently appear fantastic forms of birds or the feathers of birds, both of which serve to bear their prayers aloft."

8. In addition to the summary statements of Pueblo origin myths made by Parsons (1939), see Cushing (1896, 1920), Stirling (1942), White (1932a, 1932b, 1935, 1942, 1962), Boas (1928), and Benedict (1931). The motif of creation through the molding of meal, dust, or clay is not limited to origin myths but is widely found throughout Pueblo narratives.

9. For further discussion of the *cacique's* "children" and associated beliefs and practices among the Keresan Pueblos, see White (1932b, 1935, 1962), Lange (1968: 241–48), and vols. I and III of Bandelier's *Journals*, ed. by Lange and Riley (1966, 1975).

10. For further discussion of objects for increase, see Parsons (1918, 1919, 1920, 1929–30), Dumarest (1918), and White (1935, 1932b, 1942). Because of their similarity to Catholic practices, associated both with Christmas and All Saints' Day, and because these rituals of increase as observed earlier in this century involved *santu* worship, Parsons and others have questioned whether or not they are of Spanish provenience. There is no doubt that there was and is Catholic influence and that Pueblo religious practices are characterized by what Robin Fox has rightly described as "accretion"; there is also

considerable and widespread archaeological evidence of similar figurines and practices in pre-Spanish times.

11. Both Morss (1954) and Bullen (1948) discuss the "toy vs. fetish" controversy among archaeologists and anthropologists.

12. A favorite tactic of the missionaries was to denounce native religion as the work of the devil and to decry the making and using of images as witchcraft. One consequence was the patterns of secrecy that developed in the seventeenth century and that persist in the Pueblos today. Another possible consequence may have been the association of dolls with witchcraft and the curing thereof, which both Bandelier (Lange and Riley, 1966) and Dumarest (1918) report at Cochiti in the late nineteenth century and which several scholars suggest is of Spanish origin. For discussion of the Spanish reaction to the Pueblos' "*muchos idolos,*" see Bandelier (1890–92: 146 ff.).

13. For further discussion of the dynamics of Pueblo survival and the importance therein of both the ceremonial system and aesthetic traditions, see Ortiz (1976).

14. Several dealers in Indian "curios" in Denver, Los Angeles, and Santa Fe used logos based upon either Tesuque or Cochiti figurines on letterhead stationery by 1899. Most notable was the engraving for Jake Gold's Old Curiosity Shop based upon a Ben Wittick photo taken between 1878 and 1881.

15. I use the word *style* here in Meyer Schapiro's sense to refer to "the constant form— and sometimes the constant elements, qualities, and expression—in the art of an individual or a group" (1953: 287). As he notes and as the Cochiti case demonstrates, "it is easy to imagine a decided change in material, technique, or subject matter accompanied by little change in the basic form. . . . A style is like a language, with an internal order and expressiveness, admitting a varied intensity or delicacy of statement" (289, 291).

16. Most of the altar figures described and illustrated by Bandelier (1887–88), Stevenson (1894), Dumarest (1918), White (1932b, 1942, 1962), and Lange (1968) are of carved stone rather than clay.

17. As the studies of Lips (1937), Burland (1969), and Blackburn (1979) demonstrate, one response of native peoples everywhere to the incursion of the white man has been parody and caricature. Since the coming of the railroad, if not the conquistadores, the Indians of the Southwest have done verbal, dramatic, and graphic imitations of the white man. To this day, Rio Grande potters continue to shape tourists, Hopis carve caricature kachinas, Navajos draw, weave, and sandpaint cartoons, and Western Apaches verbally reenact Anglo doctors, schoolteachers, and VISTA workers. For a sensitive description and analysis of the latter, see Basso (1979); for discussion of this aspect of Pueblo clown performances, see Ortiz (1972, 1976).

18. When I initially asked Helen Cordero what pottery figurines, particularly the older ones, were called, she replied "*monos,*" but added that she did not use that word for her dolls because of the negative connotations. When I used *mono* in a later conversation in reference to these early figures, I was told that "we" don't call them that, "they" (the Spanish and Anglo traders) did. "We call them raingods, like the Tesuques."

19. For recent discussions of Pueblo clowning, see in addition to Ortiz (1972, 1976), Hieb (1972a, 1972b), and Babcock (1980, 1983). The "raingod" appellation suggests that what we have in these ceramic caricatures are not simply portraits of white men, but portraits of portraits of white men—i.e., representations of sacred clowns (who do indeed control rainmaking) imitating white men. Babcock (1980) provides a discussion, with quotations from Bandelier's journalistic and novelistic descriptions, of Cochiti clowning during the same decade (1880–90) in which many of these ceramic "grotesques" were shaped.

20. Again, it is tempting to argue that this figure is of Spanish Catholic derivation, but that is to ignore the fact that figures of mothers with children are widespread not only in the American Southwest but throughout Meso-America long before the Franciscans introduced the Virgin and the Christ Child.

21. This statement and those which follow in quotation marks regarding Cochiti pottery were made by Helen Cordero in conversations with me between 1978 and the present.

22. Like the majority of Pueblo potters, Juanita Arquero learned the art as a child from maternal relatives. Helen Cordero is atypical in not learning until she was over forty years old and in learning from her husband's kinswoman.

23. In addition to telling stories to his many grandchildren and being known in the pueblo both as a gifted storyteller and a leading member of the Koshare society, Santiago Quintana was the valued informant for several generations of anthropologists: Bandelier, Curtis, and Benedict. The last describes him as follows: "Informant 4 was a very different individual from the others, as can be seen in the material recorded from him. He spoke Spanish fairly, and had been an adventurer all his life. He is very old now, but a leading member of the principales, in great demand in those acculturated Mexican ceremonies in which repartee must be carried on in what is considered to be Spanish [a description of a Koshare performance at a matachine dance]. He liked best to give true stories ... and his tales of the mythological heroes always emphasized their success in turning the mockery that had been directed against them against those who had mocked them" (Benedict 1931: ix).

24. Given the obvious female connotations and interpretive schema we bring to this type of figure, it is easy to misread Helen Cordero's Storyteller as many Anglos (notably Girard and Lange) as well as Pueblo imitators have. Many Storytellers made by other potters in the last decade are indeed female figures and are not, as far as Helen Cordero is concerned, "real" Storytellers: "They call them Storytellers but they don't even know it's after my grandfather"; "at home, no womens are storytellers."

25. Regrettably, there is not time and space here to illustrate all of these other creations or to discuss in detail their personal and cultural significance. Like the Storyteller, each of these other figures is both a family and a pueblo portrait, representing actions and/or individuals of social, ceremonial, or mythological significance.

26. Helen Cordero has initiated a revolution in Pueblo pottery style comparable to those begun earlier in this century by Maria at San Ildefonso and Nampeyo at Hopi. Figurative pottery has been rediscovered and reinvented by both producers and consumers. In addition to the revival of figurative pottery at Cochiti, at least fifty other Rio Grande

potters are presently making Storytellers, each in the clays, paints, and designs characteristic of her pueblo. Figurative pottery ranges in price from $30 to $3,000 and is sold to both the tourist and the fine-art market. One-half- to two-inch miniatures have appeared in the past two years, and other subjects have been adapted to the Storyteller form—frogs, racoons, bears, clowns, etc. Sotheby's has recently auctioned old Cochiti figures for thousands, galleries have shows devoted entirely to figurative pottery, and competitive shows and fairs such as the Santa Fe Indian Market not only award prizes to pottery figures but even have categories for them other than "miscellaneous." It is something of an understatement to say, as Helen once did, "I guess I really started something." I should add that Pueblo Indians are not the only imitators—in addition to Anglo craftspeople making similar ceramic figurines, the image of the Storyteller is appearing in a wide variety of media, the latest being a needlepoint kit.

27. For discussion of Pueblo art as a statement of personal and cultural identity and as a mode of cultural survival, particularly in the twentieth century, see Brody (1976, 1979) and Ortiz (1976). Like Ortiz, Brody underlines the importance of Anglo patronage in the survival and revival of Pueblo ceramics, but he concludes by saying that "in a very real way, the survival of the craft symbolizes the survival of the people—an involvement with tradition far more basic than 'patrons' interest in archaic patterns" (1976: 76). It is indeed, as I hope my remarks have demonstrated.

28. Leslie Silko has made these statements and others about the power and importance of Pueblo stories and storytelling in several recent contexts: in a panel discussion at the English Institute, September 1979; in *Running on the Edge of the Rainbow: Laguna Stories and Poems,* a videotape in the series *Words and Place* documenting Native American storytellers and artists; and most importantly in her novel *Ceremony,* which, among other things, is a story about the power of traditional stories. The storyteller who speaks in the title poem is described as follows: "He rubbed his belly./I keep them here/[he said]/Here, put your hand on it/See, it is moving./There is life here/for the people.//And in the belly of this story/the rituals and the ceremony/are still growing" (1977: 2).

29. I am endebted to Raymond Firth both for this phrasing and the very relevant ideas behind it: "In general, primitive figure sculpture is concerned to bring out certain social attributes of the figure or to express through it certain sentiments which are of importance in the culture of the people . . . What the primitive artist does in many cases is to select and represent what may be termed the social proportions of a subject—that is, its relation to the rest of a social structure. One of the most obvious examples of this kind of treatment is the making of some human figures in a sculptured or painted scene larger than others. This is done not in accord with the rules of perspective, nor with their relative physical size in life, but with their social importance" (1963: 174–75). Arguing against simple utilitarian and instrumental views of art, James C. Faris similarly asserts that "cultural symbols such as manifested in an art tradition symbolise social relations and people's ideas about social relations" (in Greenhalgh and Megaw, 1978: 319). The fullest and finest discussion of "the meaning of things for the life that surrounds them" is Geertz's "Art as a Cultural System" (1976).

30. This point is made by John Szwed in discussing "the social basis of persistence of given forms of communication" in his discussion of a Newfoundland song-maker (Glassie, Ives, and Szwed, 1970: 150). Prestige, novelty, and economic factors are ob-

viously important variables in the widespread imitation of Helen Cordero's work among Pueblo potters, but they do not, I would argue, tell the whole story nor are they the deepest reasons for the Storyteller's popularity.

31. I am endebted beyond saying to Helen Cordero for sharing these and other words with me and to Keith Basso for helping me gather them together.

Bibliography

Anderson, Richard L.
　　1979　　*Art in Primitive Societies.* Englewood Cliffs, N.J.: Prentice-Hall.
Austin, Mary
　　1931　　"Indian Poetry." In Spinden, ed., *Introduction to American Indian Art.* N.Y.:
　　　　　　The Exposition of Indian Tribal Arts, Inc.
　　1934　　*Indian Pottery of the Rio Grande.* Pasadena: Esto Publishing Co.
Babcock, Barbara
　　1980　　"Ritual Undress and the Comedy of Self and Other: Bandelier's *The Delight
　　　　　　Makers." Discovery,* 53–71.
　　1983　　" 'Arrange Me Into Disorder': Fragments and Reflections on Ritual Clown-
　　　　　　ing." In John J. MacAloon, ed., *Rite, Drama, Festival, Spectacle: Rehearsals
　　　　　　Toward a Theory of Cultural Performances.* Philadelphia: ISHI Publishing
　　　　　　(in press).
Bandelier, Adolph F.
　　1887–88　*Histoire de la Colonisation et des Missions de Sonora, Chihuahua, Noveau
　　　　　　Mexique, et Arizona: Jusqu'à l'année 1700.* Vatican Library.
　　1890–92　*Final Report of Investigations among the Indians of the Southwestern United
　　　　　　States, Carried on mainly in the years from 1880–1885,* Pt. I. Papers of the
　　　　　　Archaeological Institute of America, American Series III & IV. Cambridge,
　　　　　　Mass.
　　　　　　　　For Journals, see Lange and Riley, eds.
Basso, Keith H.
　　1979　　*Portraits of "The White Man": Linguistic Play and Cultural Symbols among
　　　　　　the Western Apache.* New York: Cambridge University Press.
Baylor, Byrd, and Bahti, Tom
　　1972　　*When Clay Sings.* N.Y.: Charles Scribner's Sons.
Benedict, Ruth
　　1931　　*Tales of the Cochiti Indians.* Bulletin of the BAE, No.98.
　　1935　　*Zuñi Mythology.* 2 vols. Columbia University Contributions to Anthropology,
　　　　　　vol. 21.
Biebuyck, Daniel, ed.
　　1969　　*Tradition and Creativity in Tribal Art.* Berkeley: University of California
　　　　　　Press.
Blackburn, Julia
　　1979　　*The White Men: The First Response of Aboriginal Peoples to the White Man.*
　　　　　　N.Y.: Times Books.
Boas, Franz
　　1928　　*Keresan Texts.* Publications of the AES, vol. 8.
　　1955　　*Primitive Art.* N.Y.: Dover Publications, Inc.

Brody, J. J.
   1976   "The Creative Consumer: Survival, Revival, and Invention in Southwest In-
             dian Arts." In Nelson Graburn, ed., *Ethnic and Tourist Arts.* Berkeley: Uni-
             versity of California Press, pp. 70–84.
   1977   *Mimbres Painted Pottery.* Albuquerque: University of New Mexico Press.
   1979   Pueblo Fine Arts. In Ortiz, ed. *Handbook of North American Indians,* vol. 9.
             Washington, D.C.: Smithsonian Institution Press.
Bullen, Adelaide Kendall
   1948   "Archaeological Theory and Anthropological Fact." *American Antiquity* 13:3,
             128–34.
Bunzel, Ruth
   1932   *Introduction to Zuñi Ceremonialism.* 47th Annual Report of the BAE, 467–
             544.
   1972   *The Pueblo Potter: A Study of Creative Imagination in Primitive Art.* N.Y.:
             Dover Publications, Inc.
Burland, Cottie A.
   1969   *The Exotic White Man: An Alien in Asian and African Art.* N.Y.: McGraw-Hill.
Chapman, Kenneth M.
   1931   "Indian Pottery." In Spinden, ed., *Introduction to American Art.* N.Y.: The
             Exposition of Indian Tribal Arts, Inc., pp. 3–11.
   1950   *Pueblo Indian Pottery of the Post-Spanish Period.* Santa Fe: School of Ameri-
             can Research.
   1977   *The Pottery of Santo Domingo: A Detailed Study of Its Decoration.* Albu-
             querque: University of New Mexico Press.
Coolidge, Mary Roberts
   1929   *The Rain-Makers: Indians of Arizona and New Mexico.* Boston: Houghton
             Mifflin Co.
Curtis, Edward S.
   1976   *The North American Indian,* vol. 16. 1926. Reprint. N.Y.: Johnson Reprint
             Corporation.
Cushing, Frank Hamilton
   1883   *Zuñi Fetiches.* 2d Annual Report of the BAE, 2–45.
   1886   *A Study of Pueblo Pottery as Illustrative of Zuñi Culture Growth.* 4th Annual
             Report of the BAE, 437–521.
   1896   *Outlines of Zuñi Creation Myths.* 13th Annual Report of the BAE, 321–447.
   1920   *Zuñi Breadstuff.* Indian Notes and Monographs, vol. 8. New York: Museum
             of the American Indian.
Dozier, Thomas, S.
   1907   "About Indian Pottery." *Statement to the Trade for 1907.* Santa Fe.
Dumarest, Noël, Fr.
   1918   *Notes on Cochiti, New Mexico.* Memoirs of the AAA, no. 23, 135–236.
Firth, Raymond
   1963   *Elements of Social Organization.* Boston: Beacon Press.
Focillon, Henri
   1948   *The Life of Forms in Art.* N.Y.: Wittenborn, Schultz, Inc.
Fox, Robin
   1967   *The Keresan Bridge.* N.Y.: Humanities Press, Inc.
   1973   *Encounter with Anthropology.* N.Y.: Harcourt Brace Jovanovich.
Geertz, Clifford
   1976   "Art as a Cultural System." *Modern Language Notes* 91:6, 1473–99.
Gerbrands, A. A.
   1957   *Arts as an Element of Culture, Especially in Negro-Africa.* Leiden: E. J. Brill.

Glassie, Henry
  1973   "Structure and Function, Folklore and the Artifact." *Semiotica* 7:4, 313–51.
Glassie, Henry, Ives, Edward D., and Szwed, John F.
  1970   *Folksongs and Their Makers.* Bowling Green, Ohio: Bowling Green University Popular Press.
Goldfrank, Esther Schiff
  1927   *The Social and Ceremonial Organization of Cochiti.* Memoirs of the AAA, No. 33.
Greenhalgh, Michael, and Megaw, Vincent, eds.
  1978   *Art in Society: Studies in Style, Culture and Aesthetics.* N.Y.: St. Martin's Press.
Haeberlin, H. K.
  1916   *The Idea of Fertilization in the Culture of the Pueblo Indians.* Memoirs of the AAA 3:13, 1–55.
Hammack, Laurens C.
  1974   "Effigy Vessels in the Prehistoric American Southwest." *Arizona Highways* 50:2, 33–34.
Harlow, Frank, and Frank, Larry
  1974   *Historic Pottery of the Pueblo Indians 1600–1800.* Boston: N.Y. Graphic Society.
Hieb, Louis A.
  1972a   *The Hopi Ritual Clown: Life as It Should Not Be.* Ph.D. dissertation, Princeton University.
  1972b   "Meaning and Mismeaning: Toward an Understanding of the Ritual Clown." In Ortiz, ed. *New Perspectives on the Pueblos.* Albuquerque: University of New Mexico Press, pp. 163–96.
Holmes, William H.
  1886a   *Pottery of the Ancient Pueblos.* 4th Annual Report of the BAE, 257–360.
  1886b   *Origin and Development of Form and Ornament in Ceramic Art.* 4th Annual Report of the BAE, 437–65.
Kandinsky, Wassily
  1977   *Concerning the Spiritual in Art.* N.Y.: Dover Publications, Inc.
Kidder, Alfred V.
  1932   *The Artifacts of Pecos.* New Haven: Yale University Press.
Kirk, Ruth F.
  1943   *Introduction of Zuñi Fetishism.* Santa Fe: Papers of the School of American Research.
Koenig, Seymour, ed.
  1976   *Hopi Clay, Hopi Ceremony.* Katonah, N.Y.: The Katonah Gallery.
Kubler, George
  1962   *The Shape of Time.* New Haven: Yale University Press.
Lambert, Marjorie F.
  1966   *Pueblo Indian Pottery: Materials, Tools, Techniques.* Santa Fe: Museum of New Mexico Press.
Lange, Charles H.
  1968   *Cochiti: A New Mexico Pueblo, Past and Present.* Carbondale: Southern Illinois University Press.
Lange, Charles H., and Riley, Carroll L., eds.
  1966   *The Southwestern Journals of Adolph F. Bandelier, 1880–1882.* Albuquerque: University of New Mexico Press.
———, and Lange, Elizabeth M., eds.
  1975   *The Southwestern Journals of Adolph F. Bandelier, 1885–1888.* Albuquerque: University of New Mexico Press.

Lips, Julius
    1937   *The Savage Hits Back.* New Haven: Yale University Press.
Matson, Frederick R.
    1965   *Ceramics and Man.* Viking Fund Publications in Anthropology, No. 41. N.Y.:
                Wenner-Gren Foundation.
Merleau-Ponty, Maurice
    1964   *The Primacy of Perception and Other Essays.* Edited by James M. Edie. Ev-
                anston: Northwestern University Press.
Mitchell, W. J. T., ed.
    1980   *The Language of Images.* Critical Inquiry 6: 3. Chicago: University of Chi-
                cago Press.
Morss, Noel
    1954   *Clay Figurines of the American Southwest.* Papers of the Peabody Museum
                49:1.
Nequatewa, Edmund
    1936   *Truth of a Hopi* ... Edited by Mary-Russell F. Colton. Flagstaff: Northern Ari-
                zona Society of Science and Art.
Ortiz, Alfonso
    1976   "The Dynamics of Pueblo Cultural Survival." Paper presented at the AAA An-
                nual Meetings.
————, ed.
    1972   *New Perspectives on the Pueblos.* Albuquerque: University of New Mexico
                Press.
    1979   *Handbook of North American Indians: Southwest,* vol. 9. Washington, D.C.:
                Smithsonian Institution Press.
Parsons, Elsie Clews
    1918   "Nativity Myth at Laguna and Zuñi." *Journal of American Folklore* 31:120,
                256–63.
    1919   "Increase by Magic: A Zuñi Pattern." *American Anthropologist,* n.s. 21, 279–
                86.
    1920   *Notes on Ceremonialism at Laguna.* Anthropological Papers of the American
                Museum of Natural History 19:4.
    1929–30   *Isleta, New Mexico.* 47th Annual Report of the BAE.
    1933   *Hopi and Zuñi Ceremonialism.* Memoirs of the AAA, No. 39.
    1939   *Pueblo Indian Religion.* 4 vols. Chicago: University of Chicago Press.
Pilles, Peter J., Jr., and Danson, Edward B.
    1974   "The Prehistoric Pottery of Arizona." *Arizona Highways* 50:2.
Rosenberg, Harold
    1975   "Metaphysical Feelings in Modern Art." *Critical Inquiry* 2:2, 217–32.
Schapiro, Meyer
    1953   "Style." In A. L. Kroeber, ed., *Anthropology Today,* pp. 287–312. Chicago:
                University of Chicago Press.
Shepard, Anna O.
    1965   *Ceramics for the Archaeologist.* Carnegie Institute of Washington, Publication
                #609.
Silko, Leslie
    1977   *Ceremony.* New York: Viking.
Silver, Harry R.
    1979   "Ethnoart." *Annual Review of Anthropology* 8, 267–307.
Spinden, Herbert J., ed.
    1931   *Introduction to American Indian Art.* N.Y.: The Exposition of Indian Tribal
                Arts, Inc.

Spivey, Richard L.
    1976   "Pottery." In Clara Lee Tanner, ed., *Indian Arts and Crafts,* pp. 100–131. Phoenix: Arizona Highways.

Stevenson, James
    1883   *Illustrated Catalog of Collections Obtained from the Indians of New Mexico and Arizona in 1879.* 2d Annual Report of the BAE.
    1884   *Illustrated Catalog of Collections Obtained from the Pueblos of Zuñi, N.M. and Walpi, Az. in 1881.* 3d Annual Report of the BAE.

Stevenson, Matilda Coxe
    1894   *The Sia.* 11th Annual Report of the BAE, 3–157.

Stirling, Matthew
    1942   *Origin Myth of Acoma and Other Records.* BAE Bulletin, No. 135.

Tanner, Clara Lee
    1968   *Southwest Indian Craft Arts.* Tucson: University of Arizona Press.
    1976   *Prehistoric Southwestern Craft Arts.* Tucson: University of Arizona Press.

White, Leslie A.
    1932a   *The Acoma Indians.* 47th Annual Report of the BAE, 17–192.
    1932b   *The Pueblo of San Felipe.* Memoirs of the AAA, No. 38.
    1935   *The Pueblo of Santo Domingo.* Memoirs of the AAA, No. 43.
    1942   *The Pueblo of Santa Ana.* Memoirs of the AAA, No. 60.
    1962   *The Pueblo of Sia.* Bulletin of the BAE, No. 184.

Ceremonial Masks

J. C. Crocker

Almost twenty years ago, during my short introduction to anthropological fieldwork, I saw my first masked ceremony in Zuñi Pueblo, found in northeastern New Mexico. We fledgling anthropologists arrived early at four or so in the morning, to find the darkness punctured by lanterns and flashlights as people hurried about various mysterious tasks. The entire place seemed to be vibrantly alive: children and women dashed about with pots of steaming food while men passed with misshapen bundles of cloth and straw. We Anglos were contemptuously ignored and several times roughly shouldered aside. I tried to melt into a doorway, overwhelmed by my sense of incomprehension, of being excluded by my skin, my dress, my language—my whole, dumbfounded "selfness." As that western sky slowly grew illuminated in the alien cold, an endless file of personages rounded a street corner and lined up across one end of the large central plaza. They wore huge masks which completely enveloped their heads, masks whose exaggerated noses, eyes, and mouths, protuberances and hollows, were dramatically stressed by the light and shadow cast by the flickering oil lamps. Low drums started to beat in time to my pulse, and then the masks sang. Such noise I had never heard before: the dirt walls and the very earth seemed to vibrate to its harmonies. With no understanding whatsover of the words or the masks' heraldry, I was drawn into a moment of high elation in which the manifest barriers between myself and the other spectators were swept away.

It felt, I thought, just like another celebration I had attended half the world away: the New Year's masquerade in Basle, Switzerland. There, people dressed in elaborate, oversized papier-mâché masks and carried smaller masks at the end of poles, all lit from within by candles. Again, the public festivities began in the black predawn cold, spilling over into the streets from earlier private parties in homes and restaurants. There were two remarkable similarities in these experiences: first, while the Swiss were enjoying an entirely secular moment and the Zuñi were enacting a basic testimony to their traditional faith, both the means and the moods of these occasions were nearly the same. Secondly, my outsider's responses were similarly intense, though I knew nothing in either case of the community or of the elaborate iconography of the masks. These responses seem to be awe, social embarrassment, and intellectual puzzlement. Since masks and the ceremonies in which they are employed seem to elicit just these confused impressions in most non-native witnesses, I address this paper to the issue of why this should be so.

Masking involves by simplistic definition a disguise of personal identity, primarily by concealing the face,[1] and we can begin by wondering about the meaning of the human face. Oddly enough, this topic has not been explored as extensively by anthropologists as its importance in human conduct might warrant, probably because its apparently subjective character (ranging from the inchoate private associations of infancy to the received cultural judgments of "beauty") removes it from the legitimate domain of scholarly inquiry. Yet the face remains central to our behavior: look at a series of photographs of yourself, a child or a parent, any loved one, over as many years as possible. To what extent can you attribute the physical transformations to the interplay of character (however one understands that) and the curious flux of historical event, in the particular or on the larger scale? Most of us ignore the object in the mirror we shave or pluck or tattoo: we do not catch ourselves in the historical, physical round. But by donning masks—by hiding ourselves—we find our identity.

Just how this happens remains mysterious. But in all cultures that traditionally disguise themselves, masks are credited with supernatural powers. This is true even when masking is highly "secular," as in the masquerades which accompany Mardi Gras. It persists even when the particular meaning of a masked costume has been mostly or entirely forgotten. Contrary to the usual doctrine of functionalism, which claims that social customs must contribute to the integrated functioning of society and be meaningful to its members, certain kinds of masked celebrations have persisted in our own industrialized Western culture, even though the performers and spectators appear to have no knowledge of the celebrations' meaning, nor could they explain why the celebrations should be continued.

A good example of the masked celebration is the English custom known as the "hobbyhorse" (fig. 20.). Although the details vary greatly from one place to another, it usually features at least three performers: one dons the costume mimicking a horse, the next carries a symbolic club (the "Teaser"), and the last is a male transvestite with a broom (the "Old Woman" or "Shemale").[2] The horse costume is distinctive to the locality, with a unique name ("Ol' Hoss," "Old Tup"), and it is regarded as very old. Often a distinctive song with many verses accompanies the performance, together with drums, accordions, whistles, or fiddles. Traditionally the song makes references to local gossip and scandal, complete with names and juicy details. Usually the hobby is followed by pairs of dancers, and it is sometimes preceded by costumed and masked figures, for ex-

Figure 20 *Men from the Marlboro Morris and Sword dance "Castle Ring" around a hobbyhorse (in this case a hobbydeer, held by the man in the center).*

ample a Fool in motley, a "Maid Marion," a boy with bow and arrows, or men wearing deer horns. Many hobbies appear around Christmas or New Year's Day, some at All Souls' Day (November 1), and a few around Easter. Some also appear at weddings or other communal celebrations. But in nearly all well-recorded instances (Cawte: 1978) their intrusions, scheduled or not, are by no means entirely welcome. Masks, as shall be seen, are not just mysterious; they are also threatening to conventional social order.

Invariably the hobbies and their companies parade around the village, visiting both business places and residences. They demand food, money, or drink, make obscene remarks, and disrupt any gathering they can. But the custom is more than a revelrous precursor of our contemporary Halloween or New Year's Eve celebrations, in two ways. First, the hobby itself occasionally charges into the crowd and tries to envelop a young woman with the folds of its costume, or, if the audience is seated, to sit on a pretty girl's lap. In a few locales, such as Padstow, Cornwall, the meaning of this behavior is still locally understood: if the horse succeeds in his capture, the woman will deliver a baby within the year (Cawte 1978:162). Secondly, in some places, at a certain verse in the song the Teaser lightly strikes the Horse with the symbolic club. The Horse falls "dead" but is revived upon the singing of the next verse.

Although modern representations of the hobbyhorse may be little more than self-conscious revivals of local folklore, they were certainly common throughout Britain up to the beginning of the present century. Cawte lists over three hundred documented cases from that period and notes that descriptions of remarkably similar festivities began in Celtic in the fourteenth century and became frequent in the sixteenth century (1978: 230–49). Alford records both the presence of animal disguises generally and hobbies particularly throughout Europe up to present times, ecclesiastical opposition to them dating from the fourth century A.D. (1978: *passim*). Finally, the hobby even appears in North America, in Newfoundland, and the Outer Banks of North America, though apparently lacking the songs, behavior, and accompanying personages found in Europe. But perhaps the most startling aspect of all this is the frequent appearance in the famous Upper Paleolithic cave paintings of men wearing deer antlers or costumed as bears and horses. These paintings were done around 20,000 B.C., in south central France. Not much later than this, horse skulls began to appear in graves (presumably of chiefs) in Russia, Poland, and Germany. Thus it may well be possible that the hobby is a very ancient custom indeed, with an extraordinary persistence through time.

The historical meanings of this masquerade are topics of considerable debate (Dumézil, 1929: Cawte, 1978: 222–27), but they are not at issue here.[3] The point I wish to stress is that a masking tradition can survive even when its original symbolism and relation to social context have been completely lost. Nor is the hobby the only example. The late Donald Cordry, to whose scholarly dedication we owe the splendid Mexican masks in this exhibit, found that in the vast majority of Mexican masquerades, neither performers nor audience understood much at all of the costumes' significance (1980: 23–31). Should we then conclude that such masked celebrations are empty charades or romantic anachronisms? Quite the contrary; I think that they demonstrate two things: the power of masked disguise in and of itself, and its vital importance to the social community even in the absence of specific meaning. How much more powerful masks must be when they are comprehended!

All human societies ground personal identity in the physical self, first in its characteristics of sex and age, its organic connections to other selves and to locality (although every society has different notions about the nature of these connections). Since such aspects of identity as rank or group affiliation are seldom mirrored by body differences,[4] they must be represented by symbolic additions either worn or graven in some way into human flesh. The "ornamented" body is a mode, then, of communicating at once to society and to the self a specific identity. Simmel revealed that the latter of these processes may be more significant than the former, because our self-depiction determines our behavior and so, in appearance and manner, the responding confirmation of others of what we consider ourselves to be. So when identity is changed or transformed, the material body must be altered; and the face is, for many reasons, the most frequent subject of these cosmetic modifications. Their simplest form, as van Gennep pointed out many years ago, is concealing the face during a rite of passage: brides in many societies wear veils, and social death is often marked by covering the face of the deceased. Frequently a change of status is literally inscribed on the face, as when initiation into adulthood involves tattooing, scarification, piercing of the nose or lips, and so forth.

But masks are more than a painless way of changing personal identity: just because they completely hide the wearers they *transform*. By donning a mask one becomes what otherwise one could never be. Men into women, old into young, human into animal, mortals into gods, dead into living (and vice versa): masks mediate the fundamental oppositions of social and conceptual life. In-

deed, they sometimes even personify these dualities. The Eskimo mask in this
exhibit does this: the smaller face in the mask's left eye represents the *inua* of
the larger creature (fig. 21). The *inua* was thought to be the single spiritual
essence of an entire species, something like a Platonic idea. The Haida "double-
face" mask allows the wearer to transform himself from one spiritual being into
another, perhaps its conceptual opposite (unfortunately, we know little about
Haida masks). When the hidden strings are pulled, the two halves of the outer
masks dramatically fly open to show the other spirit.

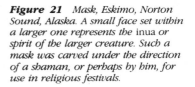

Figure 21 *Mask, Eskimo, Norton
Sound, Alaska. A small face set within
a larger one represents the* inua *or
spirit of the larger creature. Such a
mask was carved under the direction
of a shaman, or perhaps by him, for
use in religious festivals.*

There are, of course, many varieties of masking, and it would be very mis-
leading to reduce them to some kind of ur-mask both in form and in social
function. Even in a single cultural tradition, masks (broadly defined as some
form of social "disguise" of the normal self) appear in many different situations
and are used for quite diverse social ends, including those of a most antisocial
nature. The concealment of identity seems almost to generate challenges to culture's rules about law, order, and etiquette. Sennett hints that "freedom" became a compelling European gospel during the eighteenth century just because
masquerades and masking had become such common things in everyday life
(1976). Masks had become popular in Italian, French, and English courtly circles
during the early seventeenth century, ostensibly for practical reasons: they preserved the fair complexion then considered essential to beauty and protected

against the inhalation of foul, pathogenic odors. But commentators of the era cynically rejected such motives for masking: "In a dissolute court like that of James I, the mask was an essential, and was worn upon all public occasions, even in the chase ... Sir John Harrington, in 1606, says: 'the great ladies do go well masked, and indeed it be the only show of their modesty, to conceal their countenance' " (Ashdown 1968: 274). Reforming moralists eventually brought about laws banning the daily wearing of masks as leading to moral corruption. Even later festive masquerades were condemned. In 1869, the *New York World* described the Artist's Ball: "At the end of the evening the masqueraders were revealed: the panting women in the delirium of excitement; their eyes, flashing with the sudden abnormal light of physical elation, bound and lead like tigresses; they have lost the sense of prudence and safety" (McCabe, 1970: 604).

The masquerades of Saturnalia feature not just sexual licence but inversion of the usual social hierarchy. In Brazil's carnival, the slum-dwellers traditionally wear the costumes of the eighteenth-century Portuguese court, while the elite appear in such antiestablishment roles as pirates, bandits, Indians, and prostitutes. Such experiences seem to be truly liberating. In Europe at various times, carnival used to attack the established order, at first through jest and the mocking of pompous bourgeois officials, but then by open rebellion. In many cultures occupations which use physical violence in the "normal" accomplishment of their professional skills, must wear masks: bandits, surgeons, executioners. Even sporadic practitioners of violence, such as initiators and investors into high office, are often concealed by masks. The victim of socially sanctioned execution must have his or her face disguised. All such occasions only have in common the physical transformation of the existing physical and social world, in the accomplishment of which masks are a facilitating if not indispensable instrument.

Such things, as potent in human lives as a nuclear reactor or magical fetish, are guarded by elaborate rules. The mask itself, even if publicly viewed once a year or even less often, may be the object of a cult and personified as an existential being. In Mexico, only adult persons in a "pure" state can view a mask in its hidden place, where it may manifest its power by blinking or weeping. In West Africa, the accidental breaking of a mask obliges the perpetrator to undergo the elaborate, onerous ritual procedures prescribed for the purification of a homicide. The mask-maker himself, most often an ordinary member of the community with some technical competence, comparable to that of a potter or leather-worker, is obliged to follow numerous "magical" techniques in executing his craft. He can use only certain woods, themselves gathered by holy techniques at certain times of the year, and then only when he has abstained from corrupting behavior, as consuming "bad" food or doing "wrong" things, such as copulation. The technology of mask-making often involves elaborate mystical techniques as well as materials, errors in the execution of which are held accountable for any failure of the disguise to perform its designated function.

Once again I have allowed the physical means of disguise and its human repercussions to deflect examination of the mask's symbolism. This vast topic is, I think, best approached through the Turners' insight that the iconography of masks rests upon a didactic synthesis of moral ideas, and that the effectiveness of a mask lies in its physical emblematizing of verbal metaphor. "Much of the grotesqueness and monstrosity of liminal *sacra* may be seen to be aimed not so much at terrorizing or bemusing neophytes into submission or out of their wits as at making them vividly and rapidly aware of what may be called the 'factors' of their culture. I have myself seen Ndembu and Luvale masks that combine features of both sexes, have both animal and human attributes, and unite in a single representation human characteristics with those of the natural landscape ... Elements are withdrawn from their usual settings and combined with one another in a totally unique configuration, the monster or dragon. Monsters startle neophytes into thinking about objects, persons, relationships, and features of their environment they have hitherto taken for granted" (Turner 1967: 105).

Clearly the complex meanings shown forth in any one mask are amplified, negated, and generally culturally debated through other masks, both those appearing simultaneously with it and those in other ceremonials. Furthermore, the mask's symbolisms are obviously enhanced by those meanings conveyed through other material objects used in the ceremony—the songs, lyrics, dance movements, special foods and drinks and drugs consumed only or mainly on such celebratory occasions. Finally, Lévi-Strauss argues that a society's iconography must be comprehended in terms of the symbolic and social modes of neighboring human cultures. The problem here is that documenting and analyzing all this encyclopedic meaning needs many costly pages. Lévi-Strauss himself requires two books just to sketch the main symbolic features of two kinds of masks used by American Indians of the Northwest Coast (1975), and many anthropologists have devoted the equivalent of entire books to deciphering the significance of a single masked celebration (to cite only outstanding instances: Bateson, 1935; Turner, 1967; Hugh-Jones, 1979). Therefore I have hesitated to confront the topic with just a paragraph.

But one mask here seems to detach itself from its ethnographic context, from the richly complex imaginings and frozen iconographic meanings of the culture that produced it. This is the mask of Malinche (fig. 22). "Malinche was the Indian woman who served as Cortés's interpreter and who became his mistress. She is viewed as the betrayer of her country and as a woman whose uncontrollable sexual passion destroyed the Indian nations. However, when all is said and done, the Indians of Mexico have a certain amount of respect for Malinche because of the power she had with the Spaniards" (Cordry, 1980: 34). The projections with circles in their centers and ribbons at their ends are stylized representations of butterflies, a pre-Columbian symbol of warriors' souls. The horns connote Malinche's satanic character as traitor and seductress. The mask of Rangda, from Bali, represents some of the same ideas, but is even more intimately associated with evil, anger, and fear (fig. 23). In her annual festival she is confronted and overcome by Barong (a lion-dragon danced by two men), a beast that symbolizes the beneficent forces which sustain Balinese moral order and prosperity. The contrasts between the portrayals of Malinche and Barong suggest just how crucial traditional iconographies can be in understanding local expressions of a similar human theme.

They also suggest how ceremonial masks, while sometimes permitting a chal-

Figure 22 *Malinche dance mask, region of Altamirano, Guerrero, Mexico. This carnival dance mask represents Malinche, an Indian woman who served as Hernando Cortés's interpreter. Although Malinche is regarded by some as a traitor, many express their grudging admiration for her power over the Spaniards.*

Figure 23 *Mask of Rangda, Bali, Indonesia. Rangda, a witch who cannot be killed, embodies evil, anger, and fear. In an annual temple festival, she confronts another masked figure, Barong, who represents good.*

lenge to the cultural establishment, most often end by supporting it, and this in a subtle variety of ways. I do not believe in a catharsis theory of masked celebrations: they are too stylized, too sporadic, or too scheduled. For similar reasons, masks lie outside the liminal sphere of communitas, though with their dramatic protuberances and whirlpool holes they can pierce through and bring down the artificial conventions of daily life. As Leach suggests (1961:135), they are modes of entrance and exit, not conditions of the liminal state. Masking is simply too potent a symbolic mode to permit the free expression of the liminal state: its institutionalized removal is perhaps more crucial than its obligatory assumption. Society is most careful to harness the power of masking for its own ends, in a variety of ways. First, it stipulates just who can wear what kind of mask. While disguise transforms and mediates opposition, there are established limits to this alchemy: only members of a certain lineage, of a specified age, with an attested esoteric speciality, may don a particular mask. Or the privilege of mask rests upon subtler notions of appropriateness and style: in carnival, the lowly don the apparel of aristocrats three hundred years dead, not emulating contemporary signs of "authentic" class membership. (We actually know very little about these covert but absolutist restrictions on the alternatives to historical self which regulate masking. You might assist by reflecting on the costumes which you felt "appropriate" for the last masquerade you attended [fig. 24] or the dime-store devices your children wore for their annual neighborhood Halloween hold-up.)

A second function of mask is dramatically shown in two exhibits here, those made by the Mende and the Bakuba (fig. 25), used respectively in female and male initiation rites. Here disguise presents, in those richly symbolic manners already outlined, the principles of social order, either as conjunctions of natural forces or as personified in historical personages or "gods." This sort of mask can also appear in celebrations accompanying passage from one time of the secular year to another, during which prior statuses and relations of authority must be sustained so that they carry over into the new conditions of social life. Sometimes masks accomplish this by at once representing the "beauty" of accomplishing a role into which one is born, and by attacking (in the manner of the hobbyhorses) those who have denigrated or corrupted this role. The Mende mask was so used in female initiation in the bush and also in town, where the masker (unusually for Africa, always a woman) could force men to trial for wrongs done to women (Richards, 1970; Hommel, 1974). Even the clowning mockery of a role deemed fundamental to social continuity, such as an ancestral chief, can be easily changed through masked costumes from a critique of the inherited status to a bitter challenge to its incumbent's abilities. Now, something of this function seems to be accomplished by the personless media, perhaps too by the courts, but there seems an aching need for a more subjective mode of reaffirming values and finding punishments for their violations.

Figure 24 *Frances Benjamin Johnston's birthday party, ca. 1895.*

Figure 25 *Helmet mask, Kuba People, Zaire. During initiation ceremonies for Kuba youths, their maskers perform a dance acting out a love triangle. They represent three of the main figures in Kuba mythology: mwaash a mbooy, an idealized king and son of a Kuba culture hero; ngaady a mwaash, his sister and incestuous wife; and bwoom, a pygmy and common villager. The dance of the three masks dramatizes the rivalry between king and commoner for the love of the king's sister.*

So, thirdly, we use masks to cure: we as a species seem to wear them in confronting our most horrible, self-eroding moments: disease, disaster, death. The majority of the masking objects in this exhibition were used, or were meant to be used, in the locally prescribed response to the end of a human life. All our intellectual unraveling of signs' meanings, of the ways objects reinforce power, fall away before this final mystery. Masking is its own function, its own meaning. The song of the Shalakos celebrates the unity of opposites; the oneness of all things; the excellence of this earth and its beings, both material and immaterial; the power of social memory. The mask of the ancestors does not clamp the present into the modes of the past: it frees us to negate the present, and accomplish past dreams in the future.

Notes

1. Such disguise is entirely a matter of cultural definition. Some societies consider a person masked when only the area around the eyes is hidden, as with the domino masks of the European seventeenth century, while others insist on completely hiding all aspects of the "normal" self. And to a large extent, all cosmetic modifications of the face, hair, and body are efforts to present a "different" self.

2. In rural England, traditionally, a broom outside its usual context represented illicit, unfettered female sexuality.

3. Generally the issues involve the extent to which the horse was considered a sacred animal, associated with kingship and fertility, to be sacrificed at such socially dangerous times as temporal rites of passage (such as the winter solstice), kingly installations, or epidemics and wars.

4. This is most definitely not the case in ethnically plural societies, in which the most minute aspects of physical appearance are used as a code expressing class and group memberships. But even these "natural signs" are liable to considerable symbolic modifications (hair straightening and dyeing, skin bleaching, plastic surgery, and so on).

Bibliography

Alford, Violet
 1978 *The Hobby Horse, and Other Animal Masks*. London: Merlin Press.
Ashdown, E. J.
 1968 *British Costume During XIX Centuries*. New York: Nelson.
Bateson, Gregory
 1935 *Naven*. Stanford: Stanford University Press.
Buran, George
 1948 *Les Masques*. Paris: Editions du Seuil.
Cawte, E. C.
 1978 *Ritual Animal Disguise*. Cambridge and Ottawa: D. S. Brewer; Rowman and Littlefield.
Cordry, Donald
 1980 *Mexican Masks*. Austin and London: University of Texas Press.
Dumézil, Georges
 1929 *Le Problème des Cauntaures*. Paris: Paul Géuthner.
Glotz, Samuel
 1975 *La Masque dans la Tradition Européenne*. Paris: La Roue à Livres.
Hommel, W. L.
 1974 *Art of the Mende*. Catalogue. College Park, Md.
Hugh-Jones, Stephen
 1979 *The Palm and the Pleiades*. Cambridge: Cambridge University Press.
Leach, Edmund
 1961 *Rethinking Anthropology*. London: Athlone Press.
Lévi-Strauss, Claude
 1975 *La Voie des Masques*. Paris: Plon.

McCabe, James D.
    1970   *Lights and Shadows of New York Life.* New York: Facsimile Editions.
Paulme, Denise
    1962   *African Sculpture.* New York: Viking Press.
Richards, J. V. O.
    1970   "Factors of Limitation in the Art Forms of the Bundu Society of the Mende
                in Sierra Leone." Ph.D. dissertation, Northwestern University.
Sennett, Richard
    1976   *The Fall of Public Man.* New York: Harper and Row.
Shalleck, Jamie
    1973   *Masks.* New York: Viking Press.
Turner, Victor
    1962   *Chihamba, the White Spirit.* Manchester: Manchester University Press.
    1967   *The Forest of Symbols.* Ithaca, N.Y.: Cornell University Press.
Valentine, C.
    1961   *Masks and Men in a Melanesian Society.* Lawrence: University of Kansas
                Publications.

Ramlila of Ramnagar and America's Oberammergau: Two Celebratory Ritual Dramas

Richard Schechner

amnagar is a town hunched around a maharaja's fort, across the great Ganga from Benares (also called Varanasi and Kashi), the holy city dating back at least 3,000 years: a holy river, a holy city, a town dedicated to the god Rama—yet also a place of commerce, learning, industry, art, entertainment. Ramnagar literally means "town of Rama." And Rama, like his fellow avatar, Krishna, is a great culture hero to hundreds of millions in India and beyond, throughout Southeast Asia. Rama, whose face is slate blue like the underbelly of the thundercloud; whose arms are so long they reach to his knees. His story—told in the first *Ramayana* (Valmiki's Sanskrit version of the epic) and told again and again in many modern languages: Bengali, Malayalam, Tamil, Hindi—each version as classic as the English King James Bible, but no version really a translation. Rather all are refractions through the lenses of divergent histories and cultures, of a story so powerful that it cannot be lost; refracted through different genres ranging from temple devotions to literature to pop postcards and posters showing Rama dallying with his bride Sita, or showing Hanuman, the giant monkey, carrying a whole Himalayan mountain on whose slope grows the plant whose juice will restore wounded Laksman to life. Everywhere in today's Benares you will find them: Rama, Laksman, Hanuman, Dasaratha, Sita, Ravana, Sugriva, Bharat: the cast of the epic drama.

But nowhere are they more thoroughly incarnated, incorporated in both the theatrical and theological senses, than in the Ramlila of Ramnagar, a thirty-day cycle play performed just as the rainy season ends and the glorious clear dry days of early fall begin; a celebration clustered around Dassarah, the tenth day of the lunar month, the day Ravana's twenty arms and ten heads are cut off by Rama, and this demon king's effigy burns across the land: not to celebrate Ravana's defeat, but Rama's victory and Ravana's release through cremation. To be killed by Rama is to achieve *moksa,* ultimate release. That moment is performed in Ramlila by the ascent of a hot-air balloon, a fiery basket like a golden candle rising higher and higher until the sky swallows the fire, and the crowd of 100,000 or more knows that Ravana has been accepted into the mouth of the heavens. And the moment happens earlier, too, when the performer playing Ravana takes off his mask and prostrates himself, kissing Rama's feet: Rama, played by a boy of fifteen, his voice still high-pitched, light, and very musical. When this boy—and those other boys playing Sita, Rama's bride, and Laksman and Satrughna, his brothers—wear their golden crowns, they are thought to be one with the divine roles, but when the crowns are removed they are just boys. But "just" does not do justice to the dynamics of a religion that is built on reincarnation, on the transmigration of essence from person to person; for the boys may indeed have a touch of the divine in them, as every person does. So a drama representing Rama's story also to a high degree manifests it: brings it into actuality here and now, during all those thirty afternoons and evenings.

There are at least 10,000 Ramlilas performed across the Hindi-speaking belt of North India each Dassarah season. Some are of only a few days' duration; some are mostly for children. But all bite into the bread of the divine and make that communion actual. All base their acts on Tulsidas's *Ramcaritmanas,* the sixteenth-century Hindi version of the Ramayana. And if Valmiki is a legendary figure, a Homer among the Vedic Aryans, Tulsi is an actual man whose slippers I have touched, whose manuscript of *Ramcaritmanas,* copied in his own hand on palm-leaf, I have seen, whose room in Tulsi Mandir, hard against the Ganga, I have sat in. So, with Tulsi, the divine touches real human ground. Yet his version of Rama's story leads its listeners to a deeper experience of the divine than even the Valmiki. For Tulsi tells a story he knows everyone knows, even Rama himself. Thus the emphasis is on the quality with which events are lived, not on the raw action.

Yet plenty of action there is: Rama's breaking of Siva's great bow—performed in Ramnagar in the flaring light of fireworks, to the roar of the maharaja's cannon signifying the world-thunderous shattering of Siva's cosmic weapon; the wedding feast of Rama and Sita; the weeping of King Dasaratha as he recognizes he must live up to his vow to Kaikeyi, his youngest wife, and grant her a wish that will send Rama into exile for fourteen years; the procession out of Ayodhya-Ramnagar led by Rama, Sita, and Laksman, and followed by thousands of spectators; Sita's kidnapping by Ravana while Rama is away stalking the Golden Deer, itself a masquerade since it is, in fact, a form of the demon-magician Marich; Hanuman diminishing himself to the size of a fly and then zipping into the mouth and out the other end of a giant demoness guarding the seaway to Ravana's island kingdom, Lanka; Hanuman's burning of Lanka by thrashing his blazing tail; the great battles between Ravana's army of demons and Rama's army of men, monkeys, and bears; the reunion after fourteen years of the four brothers; Rama and Laksman returning, Bharat and Satrughna greeting; the coronation of Rama and the adoration of the crowd; the feasting in the maharaja's fort, where Vibhuti Narain Singh, king of Benares, entertains Rama, king of Ayodhya—a supper party transcending and linking realms of time, space, and reality (figs. 26–29).

Figure 26   Ramlila, 1978: Ravana sits on his throne.
Figure 27   Ramlila, 1978: Hanuman and Ravana fight.

Figure 28   Lanka, Dassarah Day, ca. 1825. From Benares Illustrated by James Prinsep. Printed in Calcutta, 1830.

Figure 29 *Ramlila, 1978: Ravana's
effigy is cremated on the night of Dassarah.*

Each Ramlila is different. But none has more drama, importance, attraction, joy, celebration, complexity, and participation than that of Ramnagar. It was begun in the nineteenth century by the maharaja of Benares (whose official residence is in Ramnagar) and is sponsored to this day by the maharajas, with some financial help from the government. In the Ramlila, the people celebrate the maharaja as reigning king, even though the princely states were abolished with Independence in 1949 and the privy purses extinguished some few years later. In talking to Vibhuti, reigning since the late thirties and thereby participant in the great changes as India emerged from colonialism to world-state status, I was aware both of his devotion to the Ramlila and to the difficulty of maintaining such a show in these money-poor times. It's not a problem or a devotion I am a stranger to, having tried to keep an experimental theater going in New York from 1967 to 1980.

When the maharaja appears each day, the crowds chant "Hara Hara, Mahadev." The maharaja, dressed as a king (he does not always, in private, dress this way), gestures royally to the adoring multitudes as he passes by on his elephant, or in his horse-drawn carriage (fig. 30), or sometimes seated comfortably in the back seat of his 1927 Cadillac. He told me he prefers the carriage or elephant. There the people can see him, and they have a right to. The chant is that traditionally offered to Siva, another great Hindu god and sometimes thought of as a balance to Visnu and his avatars, among whom is Rama. So at the heart of Ramnagar Ramlila is a dialectic:

World of Rama	World of Ramnagar/Benares
Visnu	Siva
Rama	Maharaja
Ayodhya, Janakpur, Lanka, etc.	Ramnagar

I shall take up this subject of correspondences again later. Enough to know now that the drama unfolds, bringing thousands of spectator-participants into a celebratory time-space: a time-space in which the mythic rulers of legendary days, played by ordinary people, contain the actual rulers of today. A boy who is a king who is a god rules over a man who is a king who is a worshiper of this same god. But because living is not schematic there is a twist. The maharaja is no longer "real"—he no longer rules over a realm but is himself a symbolic figure. So the people of Benares and Ramnagar temporarily reinstall their former ruler, proclaiming him king so that the ancient drama may be reenacted in its full dimension.

Halfway around the world in Union City, New Jersey, there is another play celebrated yearly, telling a story equal in power to Rama's—that of Christ's Passion. This play, advertised by its sponsors (the Holy Family Parish, a Roman Catholic church) as the "American Oberammergau," is performed eight times each Easter season. I have seen the performance but have not studied it in detail. Most of my information is drawn from the master's thesis of Peter Wynne (New York University, Department of Performance Studies, 1979). The Union

Figure 30   *Ramlila, 1978: Maharaja Vibhuti Narain Singh.*

City Passion Play began in 1916 in a German section of town. There were reasons why these German-American Catholics wanted to focus in on themselves. The war had made the new immigrants frightened, and some felt divided loyalties because America was siding with Britain and France against their old country, Germany. The Reverend Joseph N. Grieff, from Luxembourg, pastor of Holy Family, wanted to produce a play that would bind his congregation together and get them through hard times, just as the Oberammergau play of Bavaria, first done in 1643 and repeated every ten years since, had been staged as fulfillment of a vow when the village was spared from the plague.

But other concerns were there, too. As Wynne notes: "Father Grieff no doubt had in mind as well the remarkable success [in June 1915] of the New Passion Play, *Veronica's Veil*, presented by the parishioners of Saint Joseph's Church in the nearby West Hoboken section of the city." In fact, Father Grieff had founded Saint Joseph's in 1887, but by 1915 it had long been independent.

The Union City play has no great text as its source, other than the New Testament. Father Grieff asked the Reverend Emile Juville, a young Alsatian, to compose the play; his manuscript, on nearly fifty legal-sized pages, still exists. Father Juville's play was in German. It was translated by James White, a public school principal in nearby Union Hill. So the first peformance of the play was not only a turning in by the German community, and a hope for peace—a wish to be spared the plague of war—but also a definite entrance into this new, English-speaking country. The Ramlila of Ramnagar, first done in the teens or twenties of the nineteenth century (it is hard to document the precise first performance, though drawings by an English traveler definitely establish a performance in 1829), also served a political function. This was a time of growing Hindu-consciousness—against both the English as colonial rulers and the older Muslim rule that had set the style for so many of the maharajas. In identifying with Rama—legendary uniter of all India, founder of the Raghu line of kings, leader of the great Hindu army—the maharaja of Benares clearly declared his Hindu-Indian allegiance, but in a way that the British could hardly object to since Ramlila was a purely religious exercise. There are several episodes in the Ramnagar Ramlila that support this interpretation. On one day the maharaja celebrates a "weapons Puja," a ceremony special to this Ramnagar Ramlila, where representative weapons of the maharaja are laid out and displayed, then worshipped. Also in a popular episode in the nineteenth and early twentieth centuries, the maharaja marches out with his army to the very limits of his domain, establishing, at least symbolically, his realm's boundaries. In both these ceremonies the maharaja is identifying with the militant aspect of Rama.

Just as the Union City Germans wanted to show both their American loyalties and their German roots, so the celebrants of Ramlila wanted to look back to the days of Rama's all-India rule, and forward to a new period of "Ram-raj," when Rama would be king of a united, Hindu India. Westerners forget that along with Gandhi's *ahimsa* (nonviolence) there was, and is, a strong militant strain in Indian politics. Even today India has the fourth largest army in the world. Also it is interesting to know that in some parts of India, the south especially, where Hindu-speaking northerners are suspect, the demon Ravana is sometimes the hero of the epic and of its derivative dramas. These Dravidians look behind the British, Muslim, and Aryan Hindus to the Harrapan civilization. There is no such depth operating in Union City. But both plays draw into their theatrical net feelings that are political, historical, and ethnic as well as religious, aesthetic, and immediately social.

In the early years the Passion Play was staged in the Holy Family School Auditorium. This space was remodeled and enlarged around 1922. In 1931–32, a theater was especially built for the Passion Play. It was modeled on a Broadway theater, with a big proscenium forty feet wide and eighteen feet high, a fly loft and grid, the newest in lighting controls, a raked orchestra floor, orchestra pit, and balcony. The theater seats 1,450. The play is staged there still, with much of the original scenery in use.

The play itself tells the story of Jesus from the time he enters Jerusalem on Palm Sunday, through his betrayal by Judas, to the Crucifixion and the Resurrection. These episodes are told both in dramatic scenes of dialogue—such as the meeting of the Sanhedrin and the decision to arrest Jesus; the Palace of King Herod, where the king is entertained by a belly-dancing Salome (fig. 31); the Courtyard of Pontius Pilate, where Pilate washes his hands of the whole affair—and in eight tableaux, such as "The Last Supper," "Jesus is Laden With the Cross," "Veronica Wipes the Face of Jesus," "The Crucifixion" (fig. 32), "Jesus,

Figure 31 *Madeline Stahl as Salome, who dances at the Court of Herod in Act II, Scene 2, of Union City's Passion Play, ca. 1916.*

Figure 32 *Epilogue, Tableau 5, "The Crucifixion," shown in rehearsal on March 11, 1979. John V. Amberg, as Christus, is on the center cross.*

Taken Down from the Cross, is Laid in the Arms of His Mother." These tableaux are often modeled after classic artworks such as Leonardo's *Last Supper* and Michelangelo's *Pietà*.

The acting style, even today, is very much like turn-of-the-century melodrama. Sentences are proclaimed, the pacing is slow and exaggerated. Many persons play the same role year after year. Because of this, rehearsals are different from those in either amateur or professional theater. Father Carl Young, curate at Holy Family from 1953 to 1972, recalls: "At the first rehearsal, early in January, most of the principals would show up without scripts. They'd start talking, and this one would remind that one that he had a line, and within an hour they'd have all the lines back. It was really quite amazing." An actor would work his way up in the play, beginning with walk-on parts and ending playing principal roles. Albert G. Frech began performing in the Passion Play in 1922, and for the next fifty-six years he played every major role and was the play's unofficial director from 1945 to 1955, and its official director from 1955 to 1977. He says:

> Three of us entered the play at the same time—Edward Wetzel, Robert Fertig, and I. That was in 1922, and the three of us were in the sixth grade at Holy Family School. We started out playing minor parts—attendants, soldiers, and so on. Eddie went on to become Judas, which he played for thirty-five years. I played an attendant, a Jewish soldier, a Roman soldier, Peter, Nicodemus, Pontius Pilate, you name it. As director, I played any number of parts. If anybody got sick and we didn't have an understudy, I'd step in and do the performance that day.

The current director, David Corso, tells how parts get assigned: "You play one part for a couple of years, and one day you find that just by listening you've memorized another. Then one night, somebody doesn't show up and you go on in that part and it becomes yours."

But Corso also tells how the play has changed. The change is not in the text itself, or the staging, though there have been some additions, cuts, and re-arrangements. But the context of the play is altogether different from what it was during the first decades of its performance. Most of the original German-speaking population is dead, and their descendants no longer live in the neigh-borhood. Union City is today largely a Cuban community—the largest and most active in America outside Miami. Even more significant is the fact that during the period of the Second Vatican Council, many Catholics rejected the play as old-fashioned. Corso says: "Today Catholics are beginning to see the play as a period piece, but our audience now is mostly Baptist." Much of that audience arrives by bus—most of each night's audience of more than a thousand comes in groups. "If we get a hundred people off the street at a typical performance, we're doing very well." Still, the performers report that something keeps them doing the play, year after year, with hundreds of hours of rehearsal put in. And participation in the play is frequently a family affair. Fathers bring their sons, aunts their nephews and nieces—roles are shared among families.

Some get deeply involved in their roles. John V. Amberg has played Christ for sixteen years. He began as a Roman soldier—"That first performance as a sol-dier made me more nervous than I've ever been since, including the first time I played Christ." Amberg is a professor of philosophy at Saint Peter's College in nearby Jersey City. His interest in the role of Christ is scholarly, attentive to de-tail:

> Pierre Barbet's *A Doctor at Calvary* [published in French in 1950] has pro-vided a great deal of material for my interpretation of the role—for exam-ple, the way the nerve spasms caused by the nails would have forced the thumbs inward toward the palms. That's the way I hold my hands during the Crucifixion tableau. When I started playing Christ, I did it very strongly, with great firmness in the words. This was a Christ going about the busi-ness of accomplishing the Redemption. But then about ten years ago, I be-gan trying to emphasize the personal torment that Christ suffered—torment that made him sweat blood during the Agony in the Garden. But now I'm beginning to feel that that's playing too much to the emotions of the audi-ence, and I want to go back to a stronger Christ. I want to restress the strength and mute the torment.

> But the play is more than a performance to me. It's living a part of Scrip-ture, not merely reading it. It's a way of concretizing the words. And I get a feeling of accomplishment, of fulfillment out of the knowledge that I have been able to reach people with my work.

> And you can't ignore the camaraderie. You work very closely with the peo-ple in the play for several months each year. I think that is as strong a motive for me as any. The whole thing got started out as a parish play, but then people began to move away. Still, the people keep coming back to Union City for the play, and now it's a way to keep in touch with our roots.

There in a nutshell is the heart of the Passion Play: teaching Scripture by theatrically living it; cameraderie among the performers; a way of keeping in touch with a community's roots when the branches have diverged. But the negative input is there, too: the actual community surrounding Holy Family Church is Cuban-American. Their situation is analogous to that of the German-Americans of seventy years ago. Americans are somewhat distrustful of foreigners who come from a country toward which America is hostile. It is unlikely that these newcomers will be integrated into the Passion Play. For in Union City between the time of the Germans of the 1910s and the Cubans of the 1970s, there were the Irish and Italians: Catholics all, but the Passion Play remains German-American.

This way of slicing up the ethnic pie is not the Indian style. There, the division is more likely to be among castes, all sharing the same locality. In America each successive group moves away; in India everyone remains in place but lives according to still-strict rules of touch and avoidance.

The contrast between the two performances can be most clearly focused by examining what spaces are used, and how. Space, in modern Western theater—and the Union City play must be seen in this context—is neutral, empty, a "black box." Theaters are not animated except when in use. And rehearsals traditionally proceed from empty rooms, to stages marked with tape and indications of the scenery-yet-to-appear, to a finished set. Meaning is given to space by the set, the text, the acting, the presence of the audience. A certain bias still exists in Western theater that illustrates the Lockean *tabula rasa;* the empty stage is our best metaphor for such a blank tablet. Also, were I to be Freudian about it, the empty stage may be likened to the "dream screen" onto which fantasies are projected: first by the author and his interpreters, and then by the spectators. Such a theater is, indeed, dominated by "spectators," and not by "audiences," by visions seen, not texts and music heard. Even such a musical theater as Wagner's—which actually is scenographically related to the Union City play, not by direct influence but through a general "word-tone" approach, a kind of staging that transforms action into iconic scenes and tableaux—even Wagner's music is fundamentally "visual," that is, synchronic, highly patterned. But in Asia space is not empty, dark, void: it is pregnant, full of particular potentiality even before the first performer sets foot on it. This is most clearly expressed in the Japanese *Nō* theater stage with its polished wood floor, its symbolic Nara pine painted behind, its three living pines demarcating points of a progression from the backstage, that other world down across the *hashi-gakari* (literally, bridge), onto a place of complete manifestation. Such a space brings to every performance an already detailed cosmographic program. Each performance, though different from every other, also shares with every other a relationship to this cosmography. That is, nothing can be done on a *Nō* stage without coming to terms with that stage's own definite meanings—meanings which exist separately from any peformance happening thereon. This sense that space has an inherent significance is true also, and most powerfully, of sacred trees, caves, hills, and rivers. These are marked by the erection of shrines, many of which integrate the natural object or growth into their very bodies, as I have seen in the case of a *Teyyam* shrine in southern India which is situated within and around the trunk of a very old tree. This is also what occurs when performances are staged in temples, churches, or other sanctified places. What happens often is a three-part process. A place is sacred; upon it a shrine is built; in, on, or near that shrine a performance is given. The performance, as when *Nō* is staged in Nara near the sacred pine, sometimes is itself a mark of the original special natural place. I might go so far as to say that sacred geography is analogous to circumcision, tattooing, or body painting: one signals a transformation of the world, the other of the person.

What has happened at Ramnagar is a version of this experience of sacred space. The Ramayana itself is an epic drenched by spatial themes. At one level, Rama's exile and flight southward, his gathering of a native army of bears and monkeys, and his domination of the demon Ravana are all representative of the Sanksritization of the subcontinent. Wherever Rama moves he is recognized as an avatar; he is worshipped, and his places of rest achieve status as shrines: Ayodhya, Panchavati, Ramaswaram. At another level Rama's journey is itself a pilgrimage. And many Indians wish, at some point in their lives, to touch the bases of Rama's geography. Most of those attending Ramlila will never leave their areas of birth, but through participation in the performance they vicariously go with Rama and share in a national religious unity. These various levels are theatricalized in the Ramnagar Ramlila. Many Ramlilas include some degree of multiplace staging and pilgrimage. But Ramnagar has actually changed a whole town into the various stages of Rama's progress. The maharajas of the nineteenth century who first sponsored the Ramnagar Ramlila built copious environmental theaters for Ayodhya, Janekpur, Rambagh (Rama's pleasure garden), the Kir Sagar (the ocean of milk on which Visnu floats before Rama is incarnated), the Ganga and Jamuna rivers (both represented by very spacious ponds), Citrakut, Panchavati, and Lanka. Each of these places is connected to the other and linked to the maharaja's own lands. Ayodhya, Rama's capital, is hard by the fort, the maharaja's palace; Rambagh, the Kir Sagar, and Citrakut are near an old Druga temple that predates Ramnagar Ramlila by hundreds of years—a place renowned for harboring powerful goddess energies, and connected to birth; Lanka, several miles outside of town, is a vast open field dominated by the earthworks of Ravana's Fort: opposed to the maharaja's architecturally as well as geographically. And some of the most impressive scenes in Ramlila occur when Rama and his entourage move from one spot to another.

Then many thousands of spectators follow, so that as participants they get directly involved in Rama's journeys, exiles, marches: all of which become subsumed under the sense of pilgrimage with Rama. The entire thirty days constitute a circular journey, or, better, a spiral. The first days are staged outside the walls of Rambagh, on the surface of the great tank (manmade lake) of the Durga temple, where it all starts. Then the performance moves to Ayodhya and Janekpur, both close to the center of Ramnagar. When Rama is exiled, he and the crowd move through back alleys and across rice paddies and cornfields, only to end up at Citrakut, which is again outside the walls of Rambagh. But then Rama goes deeper in exile, at Panchavati, which is in an empty field truly on the out-

skirts of town. After Sita is kidnapped and taken to Lanka, about two miles further out of town, Rama and his party take several days to reach her. During this
time, two centers of action appear: Lanka, where Ravana and Sita are, and the
Road where Rama and his army are on the march. During one night at Lanka,
when Laksman is wounded, Hanuman is sent all the way to the Himalayas—back
to the center of Ramnagar—to fetch the herb that will cure Laksman. On the
way back to Lanka, Hanuman, who is flying through the air, is shot down by
Bharat, who mistakes him for a demon. Hanuman's journey takes place at the
same time as Rama laments for his wounded brother. Part of the audience goes
with Hanuman on his three-hour journey (fig. 33); most stay around Rama and
Laksman. But all deeply participate in the story as they celebrate its movement
through time/space and the transformation of Ramnagar into its mythic counterpart.

Surrounding this mythopoetic action all the while are thriving businesses sell-
ing snacks, tea, trinkets. And in Ramnagar itself two groups of outsiders—*sadhus*
(holy men) and *nemis* (people devoted to Ramlila)—have moved in for the
month. The *nemis* rent rooms and arrange their vacations and work schedules
so that they can be present from 4:00 P.M. each day. The *sadhus* arrive by the
hundreds (fig. 35) for free lodging and food at the maharaja's *dharamsalas*
(dormitories). There is a mixture of devotion and opportunism. The more *sadhus* present, the more effective the performance; the more generous the maharaja's largesse, the greater the attendance by *sadhus*. There is nothing cynical
about this relationship; it is a traditional arrangement that does not reflect badly
either on the *sadhus'* religiosity or the maharaja's generosity.

Figure 33 *Ramlila, ca. 1960:
Hanuman and others crossing the sea at
Runeswaram.*

Figure 34 *The day of the contest for Sita's hand. After all the princes have failed to lift Sita's bow, Rama lifts and breaks it, thus winning the contest. Here we see the moment when Sita comes to meet Rama as the winner and accept him as her future husband. They are decorated with flower garlands and at their feet is the broken bow. Tomorrow they will wed.*

Figure 35 *Ramlila, 1978:* Sadhu *dancing and singing. Note how the energy of performing has produced sweat that stains the* sadhu's *shirt.*

In a word, there are circles of audiences ranging from the keepers of snack stalls, who see very little of the Ramlila but who attend each performance year in, year out; to spectators who come for the big nights only—Rama's breaking

of Siva's bow, the kidnapping of Sita, the death of Ravana, the reunion of the
four brothers, the coronation of Rama; to spectators who attend all performances, those faithful *nemis;* to the *sadhus,* for whom attendance at the Ramlila is
almost a professional obligation.

Then there is the maharaja. He is there for each performance, punctuating it:
when he arrives it starts, when he goes off for evening prayers it stops, when he
returns after dark it begins again. He sees it all, except for the death of Ravana.
"It is not proper for one king to witness the death of another," he told me.
Often the maharaja is too far away from the performers to hear much of the
dialogue or see very carefully what is going on. But close to him are the *ramay-
anis,* a group of men led by the maharaja's own temple priest, who chant the
text of Tulsides's *Ramcaritmanas.* This recital is always in the marahaja's ear: it
is the essence of the performance. The dialogue spoken by the actors is in
modern Hindi. This text was assembled 150 years ago and combines fragments
from Tulsidas, classic poetry, and lines composed by the scholars and poets
convened by the maharaja to construct the *samvads,* the nightly dialogues. Thus
occurs another set of correspondences: the maharaja, Tulsidas, *Ramcaritmanas,*
and *sadhus* correspond to the people, *samvads,* the refreshment stalls (while
the maharaja prays, the audience eats), and the *nemis.* These do not represent
fixed oppositions, but poles of attention: to the Tulsidas text or the drama, to
prayers or food, to the intense *bhajans* (devotional songs) of the *sadhus,* or the
fixed attention of the *nemis* on the performance.

Of the acting both of Ramlila and the Union City Passion Play, little can be
said here. It is not "good acting" judged against the dominant artistic standards
of either culture. The Passion Play is highly melodramatic—even its participants
recognize that. The play's director, David Corso, has likened it to a Gay Nineties
"mellerdrammer." He adds:

> What's sad is that the intellectuals, the theater-goers who could appreciate
> the show as a period piece, have mocked this sort of production for a long
> time. But if they were willing to see it for what it is, they'd realize the
> play's quality. Also, though my own personal religion is more contempo-
> rary, more people-oriented, the play is an important part of many people's
> religion and has to be seen as such. We play to more than 10,000 people
> each year, so we must be reaching someone.

Lines are proclaimed, emotion is forced, gestures are wooden. Much of the play
is too loud sonically and visually. But all this may work for the play. After all,
the play is not meant to compete with Broadway just a mile across the Hudson
River from Union City. Nor is it an experimental theater production introducing
new techniques or ideas. Its very origin as well as its current *raison d'être* is
conservative: to keep in touch with the Old Country ("America's Oberammergau"), the Old Values, the Old Church (before Vatican II). A theatrical style that
is old-fashioned is chosen. Of course this style once was current, but even in
1916 it was outmoded. The high points of the play are the tableaux, which call
up associations of aesthetic-religious artworks of the confirmatory kind—not Hi-

eronymus Bosch but the Italian Renaissance. Christ's life is seen as Leonardo and Michelangelo depicted it. So we have the pale, bearded Chirst, the steel-helmeted Roman soldiers, the noisy, quarrelsome Sanhedrin, the lascivious, corpulent Herod, the ascetic yet motherly Mary, the voluptuous Salome. The Passion Play is one with the movie *The Robe,* a piece of American pop art. The acting also is iconographic: Great Figures presented as visions of visions. Maybe this is as it should be, the "historic Christ" being forever beyond our grasp. Ritual confirms myth, creates it processually and continuously, and certain performances are designed only to actualize these images of images.

The same is true of Ramlila, which in this regard is strikingly like the Union City Passion Play. Ramnagar is also across the river from a great metropolis. The producer of the Ramlila, the maharaja, is both absorbed into the production as performer (he plays himself) and separate from it as he reveals himself in private conversation. His attitude is not so different from Corso's.

Schechner: The people call you Mahadev [a name for Siva].

Maharaja: It's not personally for me. It's for my whole family. My ancestor who started the dynasty also began a renaissance of Hinduism.

Schechner: The Ramlila is part of this renaissance?

Maharaja: The Ramlila was started by Tulsidas. My family gave it a push.

Schechner: For the people, the eternal realm of Rama is mirrored in the role of your family?

Maharaja: Not quite.

Schechner: But Ramlila is the only drama I know of that can't begin until a certain spectator arrives. What happens if you are sick?

Maharaja: Some member of my family must represent me. Someone must be in control. From the audience point of view, my presence does give some prestige. Someone has to take the lead. It is also spiritual: in the *Ramayana*, Siva tells the story to Parvati [Siva's wife]. So the representative of Siva must be there.

Schechner: Do you believe that the boys are gods?

Maharaja: If you see a Christian picture, like *The Robe,* what do you feel?

Schechner: I feel it's a representation, done with devotion maybe, but still a great distance from being god.

Maharaja: The same, I feel the same.

But the vast crowds watching and participating in Ramlila feel differently, especially at the end of each night's performance when the Hindu temple service of *arati* is performed: the boys who are Rama, Sita, and the others serve as temple *murtis* (images, icons), while the performer playing Hanuman gently waves the fly-whisk to protect Rama and Sita. At this time, as great glaring flares burn first red and then white, the crowd surges to get an actual glimpse of the actual gods who are manifest at that moment. For the *nemis* there are two levels of god-head present in Ramlila. When the boys do not have their headdresses on, their "crowns," they are "just boys"—although they are treated very specially during the month of performances, fed a diet rich with milk and ghee, nuts and fruit. When they wear their crowns it is thought that the gods have descended into them. And during *arati* it is assumed that the gods have descended. This presence of the power of the original Rama and his family is felt for the whole night of the Coronation of Rama on the twenty-ninth day. Then thousands of people come to where Rama and the others sit on their thrones in Ayodhya and press their hands on the feet of the boys. When I questioned the boy playing Rama what he felt during this night, he said—"Nothing." It was not an empty, void nothing, but one full of unspeakable feelings.

The acting in Ramlila is iconographic. Most scenes are static pictures. Lines are recited in singsong fashion. The boys rehearse for two months before Ramlila begins, from mid-July. And they rehearse the day of each performance for two hours or so. Putting on their ornate costumes and making up their faces take another couple of hours. All this helps them sink into their roles or, if you prefer, allows the roles to possess them. But they are not in trance. Standing behind the boys—and the other characters, too—are two *vyases,* priests who serve as directors of the Ramlila. One *vyas* works with the *swarups* (the divine family) only, the other *vyas* with all the other characters. The *vyases* stand there with open promptbooks, whispering the dialogue into the performers' ears, moving them around the stage in case they forget their blocking or make an error. The men who play the main roles have inherited them. Some roles are traded around among a few families who dominate the Ramnagar Ramlila. The acting is loud, and the speaking voices are rough. But this amateurishness has a pinch of power in it: the people are behind their roles not as psychological entities but as figures the performers believe in. The distance separating performers from their roles does not dissolve; there is no attempt at a Stanislavskian identification. Both spectators and performers are aware of the power residing within the great roles—Hanuman, Ravana, Narad, Angad, Sugriva. Frequently these are approached from a great distance, gingerly handled, their inherent powers treated with respect, as one warms the fingers not too close to an intense fire. Yet some performers, over many years of doing their roles, harmonize with them to an astonishing degree. The man who plays Narad, a semi-divine sage who sings to Rama and counsels him, has become known far and wide as Narad. He has grown to be a rich and powerful priest in Mirzapur, a city fifty miles from Ramnagar. Ravana has been in the same family since the midnineteenth century. When I went to Ravana's village to interview the father and son who play the role, I was told again and again that "Ravan-raj [King Ravana] lives over there." The villagers respect the family as the Ravana family; they are the richest in the village because with the role came land given by the maharaja of the time. Ravana, after kissing Rama's feet, leaves the Ramlila ground. He does not linger around for the last five days of the performance. The role of Ravana is shared by father and son: the old man plays the less vigorous portions. Someday he will retire, or die. Old Brahma, most ancient of the gods, is portrayed by a ninety-six-year-old man who barely has breath left, let alone voice. He is coached in his lines. His entrance into the spectacle is appropriate, and moving.

The boys who have been picked by the maharaja to play the five *swarups* chant their lines in high, singsong voices. The maharaja selects them from candidates brought before him in June. He makes his choice on the basis of religious and family background, speaking voice, appearance, and deportment. It is no easy task these days to get boys to take four months from their school year. School authorities, in these secular times, refuse to grant them anything but "medical leaves," and these mar their records. Pay for performing the *swarups* is about 440 rupees, which used to add up to much more in buying power than it does today. Others are also paid, though much less, and surely not enough to justify their participation on economic grounds. Even though some complained bitterly how inflation has made their honorariums meaningless, I was convinced that no one would allow lack of money to keep him from participating in the Ramlila. And many people—from a Benares man who takes five hours a day to buy flowers and then weave them into garlands for the *swarups,* to "old Hanuman," the man who played the role for decades and who now attends the *swarups* offstage, continuing in life the traditional duties of Hanuman—many people donate their full being to Ramlila.

The boys who play the *swarups* command great attention and affection. Their acting style is strange to one educated in Western theater. Rama, the great hero, conqueror of tribes, demons, and warriors—an Achilles among soldiers—is played by a slim boy whose voice has not yet deepened; Laksman, Rama's impetuous, always-ready-for-a-fight brother, by an even younger boy. And the four brothers who are twins are played by actors who range in size from Rama, the tallest, about fifteen years old, to Satrughna, the smallest, about eight years old. Size represents not chronology but the proportion of the divine within them, and their relative importance theatrically. When Rama and Laksman meet Ravana and his army of demons—some of whom are represented by great forty-foot-high papier-mâché figures—it indeed looks like a battle pitting babies against giants. But the Indians, like the Balinese, believe that prepubescence is a time of life when the divine can most easily descend into the human body. Just before sexuality blossoms, persons are full of potentiality, yet they retain a childish innocence. This innocence is the basis of their strength, both as characters and as performers. The tendentious sermons of Rama on loyalty, marital duties, and religion, all take on a certain sweetness when coming from a mouth too young to have invented these aphorisms. And when he laments over his wounded brother, Laksman, lying limp and bloody in his lap, tears fill many eyes, including mine. It's a kind of Brechtian acting—not surprising, since Brecht stole many of his best ideas from Asian theater.

The performers of Ramlila, like the audience, are of mixed motive, background, and experience. For this is a celebratory time of the year, just as the rains are ending, before the brisk winter season, which is brief—when the highest and lowest, the most venal and the most inspired, share a single space that is both local (Ramnagar) and cosmic (Rama's space). So little of this kind of sharing happens at Union City. Actually, the opposite has occurred as the neighborhood has gone Latin. Buses import the audience just as cars bring the performers. At Union City the motives are "purer." No one gets paid. No one will launch a Broadway career. Everybody knows that taking part in the Passion Play is a kind of charity. Some participants in Ramlila have gone on to careers in journalism and theater, using their Ramlila experiences as a jumping-off ground. In Union City a club keeps a tradition going that is meaningful to members at the social level, and perhaps to a few at a religious level. Theatrically, Union City is nowhere, and being across the Hudson from Manhattan does not help. Ramnagar is across the Ganga from Benares, and thousands row or ferry across that sacred river each day to attend Ramlila: the performance in Ramnagar definitely enhances the pilgrimage aspect of Ramlila. And Ramnagar is the official residence of the maharaja.

Sitting in the balcony in Union City, watching Christ hanging from his Cross and a group of teenagers next to me munching popcorn, I realize that at Ramnagar, too, local snacks are munched—but why is this not a contradiction there? Because under all the secular treats of the Ramlila season—and it is a whole season, a month off, a celebratory period leading from the sticky, unpredictable flood-laden monsoon to the glorious dry days of October—under it all is religious bedrock. For its month of performances, the Ramlila absorbs so much of the available energy of Ramanagar and even of Benares (although there are plenty of local Ramlilas being played there too): the eminences and the untouchables, the holy and the profane, the performers and the spectators, the *walas* (shopkeepers) and the consumers. At Union City a version of the aesthetic is striving toward the religious, or maybe to hold onto a thread of the Robe. Striving but not achieving. Busloads of Baptists seeing a German-Catholic performance in the middle of a Cuban neighborhood—something was not fitting together. The Passion Play was no pan-Christian ecumenical event but the leavings of fifty-five years of American social change.

However, it is all too easy to disparage one's own culture, for one knows so much about it, experiencing it daily, using its nonverbal as well as verbal languages, wishing it to be what it is not. What I felt at heart about the Union City Passion Play was the players' authentic desire to make leaves send down roots, instead of the opposite. This tendency to create from the top down, to have theater create roots instead of presenting or actualizing them, may be one of the great curses of our American situation. We truly have been uprooted, and we float like cut flowers in a vase. So many of our efforts to make "it" happen "at bottom" are, pardon the metaphor, fruitless, sterile. But still those efforts must be made: for if only one in a thousand takes root, it is enough.

It will take another essay, and more, to expound the ideologies set forth by Ramlila and the Passion Play. My point here has not been to evaluate their utility as ideologies in the postmodern world, but their ambitions and achievements as celebrations. There is today a wholesome need to sing hallelujah. The cleanliness of the divine ears that hear those hosannas—well, that's another story.

2

See *Figure 43*.

Rites of Passage: Process and Paradox

Barbara Myerhoff

Rites of passage are a category of rituals that mark the passages of an individual through the life cycle, from one stage to another over time, from one role or social position to another, integrating the human and cultural experiences with biological destiny: birth, reproduction, and death. These ceremonies make the basic distinctions observed in all groups, between young and old, male and female, living and dead. As Claude Lévi-Strauss has pointed out, we live at the edge of a paradox: we belong both to Nature and Culture, and we perpetually struggle to announce and renounce that ambivalent condition, to emphasize that we are at once human and animal, that though we are born, mate, and die as part of our mortal heritage, we manipulate that condition endlessly, so that biology with all its imperatives and universals is often only faintly distinguishable beneath the template of symbolic and ritual understandings we lay over it.

The interplay of biology and culture is the subtext of all rites of passage, and often the play is fast and loose. The "inevitable facts" of human experience— what T. S. Eliot calls "the brass tacks—birth and copulation and death"—are acknowledged everywhere by ceremonies, to be sure, but the variation in form and content of the rites of passage is staggering. For ultimately, birth and copulation and death are social events as much as natural ones. An infant bride cannot mate or procreate; many years separate puberty from the ceremony of betrothal. And in many places, simple biological death is no death at all. Ceremonies must transform the corpse into a properly deceased person; death is only the necessary condition for departure from the world of the living. Neither are men and women simply born: they are "made" by ceremonies (fig. 36); nor are they truly sexual, adult beings until certain social conditions have been fulfilled: sometimes a man must hunt successfully or otherwise prove his male-

Figure 36 *Girl's initiation costume, Mandalay, Burma. After their initiation and ear-piercing ceremony, which is usually held at puberty, Burmese girls are able to act as women. They wear a costume like this one for the ceremony.*

ness before he may mate. A woman may be "initiated" into fertility (fig. 37) by her society before she is allowed to mate, her social definition as "woman" provided by ceremony, whether she has or has not begun to menstruate.

We are inclined to think of the ages of a life likewise as given by nature. But Philipe Ariès (1962) has shown that "childhood," as a distinctive, universally recognized condition, was only discovered (or more accurately, "invented") in Western Europe after the Renaissance. Before that a child was treated, dressed, and regarded as a miniature adult, without special needs or privileges. Adolescence is also a recent invention, having been established as a distinctive phase in the human life cycle in America by Stanley G. Hall in 1904. Since then, the physiological and social tensions accompanying puberty have been seen as inevitable and natural, definitive of that stage of growth. Experts, technical writings, and practitioners have grown up around that conception; legislators, educators, psychologists and physicians, reformers, social agencies, and all manner of commercial enterprises specialize in understanding and serving a category of people: "adolescents"; we quite forget there was ever a time when people passed from childhood to adulthood without being "teenagers." Margaret Mead reminds us that "Sturm und Drang" are not universal to this life stage in her classic study of puberty in Samoa (1928). Adolescent girls there had never experienced the menstrual cramps and discomforts we consider a natural part of puberty. That physiological symptoms may be caused by disruptive, conflicting social conditions is a lesson we lose sight of at our peril, for it recalls to our mind most vividly the paradox with which we began—that we belong to culture as much as to nature.

Figure 37 *Coming-out dance in girl's puberty ceremony of Ndembu of Zambia. Note the fly-switch of male authority which the dancer holds in one hand, and the cloth representing female fertility in the other.*

The point is made for us in many ways. For example, old age is a conspicuously socially determined life stage in our society. We are retired at a specific, legal cut-off point, and separated from the "useful" members of society, without regard for individual capacity or physiological function. Here nature and culture stand at a great distance from each other. Among the Eskimo, retirement was much more tightly tied to an individual's capacity to work: an old woman's task was chewing frozen garments into softness. When her teeth wore down and she could not perform this job, she usually withdrew and "retired" by committing suicide.

The life course is for the most part unmarked by nature, with the exception of birth, sexual maturation, and death. Separations are socially imposed upon its natural continuity, divisions established, cut-off points provided, distinctions made. The experience of sameness and continuity over the life span is deliberately destroyed by rites of passage, though one of their persistent functions is to symbolically state the fact of continuity despite the appearance of change and disruption. This is another of the paradoxes of the life course.

Rites of passage straddle yet a third paradox: that the subject, the initiate, in these rituals is at once alone and yet never entirely independent. For biological reasons, we are creatures achingly vulnerable to the emotions, opinions, and physical care of others. We cannot endure the experience of living in an incomprehensible world, so, as often as not, we trade our freedom and creativity for the assurance that life is meaningful. We are born and die alone, ultimately unique and separate, yet we are unable to survive without our fellows and the web of symbols and activities that bind us one to another.

Rites of passage take advantage of this paradox: inevitably they are moments of teaching, when the society seeks to make the individual most fully its own, weaving group values and understandings into the private psyche so that internally provided individual motivation replaces external controls.

In accomplishing this, societies may be quite literal, inscribing their designs and modifications upon the bodies of the initiates. The procrustean bed of culture may manifest itself by modifying or obliterating the neophyte's "animal" traits. Thus before a young Balinese may marry, he or she undergoes a tooth-filing ceremony, during which the canine tooth, the mark of the beast in humanity's heritage, is smoothed, so that the smile is less reminiscent of an animal's snarl. And continuity is expressed most concretely in some African societies, where, according to Victor Turner, a youth being initiated into manhood may ingest a powder made of the foreskins of previous initiates, incorporating and sustaining in his body the vitality and power of his forebears. James Fernandez (1980) describes an initiation ceremony in which a neophyte stares into a looking-glass until the face of an ancestor appears and merges with his own. The identification between the ancestor behind the glass and the living descendant in front of it literally presents a picture of genealogical continuity between the living and dead, and allows the initiate to pass into a new state of being. In such instances, and the examples are many, the human body itself serves as a symbolic message, at once presenting to society and to its owner the statement that the individual and the group are one, inseparable, vehicles for each other. The fundamental, recurrent theme that appears in so many of the symbolic and substantive teachings of rites of passage is often reducible to that: the interdependence of the collective and the single, the group and the separate people who make it up and carry its purposes forward.

Rites of passage are often merged with messages and occasions that go beyond the change of status of an individual or age cohort. When the initiate is thought to embody messages about the cosmos, is considered a microcosm or miniature version of the largest concerns of the natural and the supernatural order, then what happens to the individual may transform the collectivity at the same time. Rites of transition performed for divine royalty—birth, marriage, procreation, and death—are rites performed for the perpetuity of the kingdom as a whole. The well-being of the group and its representative is literally rather than symbolically identified. The land, perhaps, cannot rejuvenate or continue to yield crops if the king is barren, and in some cases a king has been annually killed to allow the land to be reborn seasonally. Rites of passage may serve to resolve social problems and perpetuate the social order directly as well as indirectly, through promoting the integration and socialization of its members. This occurs, too, when seasonal rituals are contained within or coordinated with rites of passage for an individual or age set. Then the individual initiate is presented with a paradigm for his or her future; collective tensions and disorders are overcome, and the calendar by which the society understands its long and short history is articulated, with the transitions being marked for the individual. This occurs in some Mesoamerican cargo systems, described by 'Alexander Moore (1979).

Because rites of passage occur at moments of great anxiety, they are dramatic occasions, naturally or socially provided crises, when the person is most teachable. Tension is heightened by rites, and resolution is eagerly sought. The society is then most urgently pressing itself upon the subject of the ceremony, making him or her into its own creature. Yet in the midst of such rituals, individuals are most often aroused to self-consciousness or brought to the edge of profound self-questioning by the play with forms—the use of mirrors, masks, costumes, novelty. Borders are crossed; identity symbols stripped away, familiar roles and customs suspended (figs. 38–41). These conditions make it likely that one may experience that sense of radical privacy, uniqueness, and freedom, the irreversible moment of reflexive awareness, amidst the efforts of the group to

Figure 38 *Aungsaing village, near Thanton, Burma, 1964: Procession of initiates on horseback.*

Figure 39 Rangoon, Burma, 1964: Head-shaving. Parents hold a cloth to catch the hair.

Figure 40 Rangoon, Burma, 1964: The four newly initiated monks, after being robed, recite scriptures before the initiating monk.

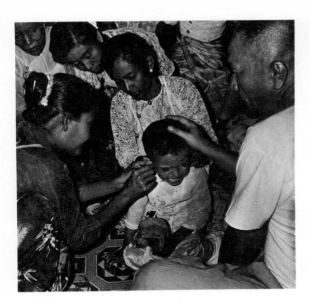

Figure 41 Rangoon, Burma, 1964: Ear-boring.

impose itself and its interpretations most irresistibly upon the person. Rites of passage invite and forbid independent consciousness at the same moment.

This, then, is part of the third paradox: that rites of passage announce our separateness and individuality to us and at the same time remind us most firmly and vividly that we belong to our group and cannot conceive of an existence apart from it. These paradoxical elements express some basic truths of the human condition: that while all societies attempt to absorb the individual and shape the creature into a bona fide, self-regulating member, they never wholly succeed in doing so. Even in the most highly integrated, small, stable, tribal societies, there are distinguishable individuals: outstanding men and women whose traits and thoughts go beyond those required by their offices, roles, and circumstances. No society has failed to generate a few people who are innovators, poets, madmen, deviants, skeptics, and intellectuals. Thus, rites of passage present us with a set of paradoxes that document our peculiar nature. In rituals we may *enact* these contradictions, which is the most appropriate response possible. Because they are genuinely paradoxical, these contradictions may not be resolved, and there is little point in struggling with them cognitively. They defy understanding and are often inarticulable, yet we experience their truth in the safety, predictability, and virtual magic that ritual provides. Then we are allowed to discover the intractable parameters of our fate as humans.

"Rites of passage" was the term first used in 1907 by Arnold van Gennep to refer to those rituals that mark the passage of the individual through various stages in the life cycle. From the bewildering variety of examples of such rituals, he discerned a fundamental tripartite structure determined by the necessity for functionally separating the person from one status before incorporating him or her into a new one. In between the departure from the old position and the incorporation into the new one was a transitional or liminal period, now known as liminality.

Van Gennep's theories appeared at a time when anthropology was dominated by the passion for the classification of "customs," often without regard for the context in which items appeared. Before him, Victorian anthropology was quite ethnocentric, valuing its own usages as the measure of all things, and it was busily seeking the origins of customs in the interest of establishing evolutionary phases. Though van Gennep was concerned with classification of social categories, he was strikingly modern in his respect for context and his interest in process and change. Like modern structuralists, he recognized that a distinction is most easily made by citing its opposite, that is, by binary opposition. This leads to a scheme of two opposing categories defined in three stages. Huntington and Metcalf (1979) suggest the following diagram, using the distinctions of "Death" and "Marriage" as examples:

Distinction:	death	marriage
Binary categories:	alive/dead	single/married
Tripartite stages:	living→dying→dead	single →engaged→married

Some anthropologists have suggested that in discussing rites of passage we treat as subsets, "rites of separation," "rites of transitions," "rites of reincorporation." Often one phase of the total ritual process will be dominant and obscure the others, but most often logic requires that all three rites are present to some degree. Thus rites of separation may be expected to be predominant in funerary ritual, but most often there will also be some ceremony to separate the dying from the living and to announce the transitional phase between life and death.

In illuminating the underlying structure and function of rites of passage, van Gennep did much to make otherwise exotic and puzzling ceremonies of non-Western societies understandable.

> Elements of ceremonial behavior were no longer the relics of former superstitious eras, but keys to a universal logic of human social life. Mock battles in marriage rituals were dramatic representations of the function of separation, not left-overs of a rude past. (Huntington and Metcalf, 1979:11)

By identifying the logic underlying rites of passage and pointing out their universal form (tripartite) and function (clarifying and separating people's movements through status positions in a social system) van Gennep laid much of the groundwork for the modern interest in symbolic and ritual studies. But one of the implications of his work has never been fully explored, that of the integration of the individual in society, a point to which we will return. Van Gennep's concept of liminality, his emphasis on process and the alternation of movements between the fixed and fluid in social structure, has been more fully developed by anthropologists who followed. Most important by far is the work of Victor Turner (1969, 1974), who has expanded "liminality" beyond its original use as an intermediate stage in rites of passage to an exceptionally rich and generative approach. Building on van Gennep's ideas that stress the importance of transitions, Turner develops an interpretation of the liminal or marginal phase as existing autonomously, an independent and sometimes enduring category of people who are "betwixt and between." All manner of possibilities occur: tricksters, clowns, poets, shamans, court jesters, monks, "dharma bums," holy mendicants; even social movements such as millenarian cults, or social principles such as matrilaterality in patrilineal systems, qualify for examination as liminal phenomena. They are astonishingly diverse but share some of the characteristics of neophytes in the liminal phase of a ritual of transition: the symbols used for them are similar, emphasizing innocence, rebirth, vulnerability, fertility, change, emotion, paradox, disorder, anomaly, opposition, and the like. Underlying all these traits are a lurking sacrality and power that accompany movement toward the borders of the uncharted and unpredicted. The edges of our categories, as Mary Douglas (1966) has also stated, are charged with power and mystery. The people, objects, or events that touch those margins may be taboo or polluted because they are out of place. They are sources of danger, a threat to our orderly conceptualizations and desire for form and predictability, but also, as Turner shows, they are sources of renewal, possibility, innovation, and creativity.

Turner elaborates his theory of liminality into an exploration of "communitas," the state of oneness and total unity that neophytes living outside the norms and fixed categories of a social system share during liminal periods. Equality, undifferentiated humanness, androgyny, and humility are some of the characteristics of this condition. Neophytes are symbolically represented as a kind of *tabula rasa,* pure undetermined possibility, the very opposite of social structure with its emphasis on differentiation, hierarchy, and separation. The liminal person comes to stand for the sentiment of undifferentiated humankind: all that is universal, innate, whole, and unified.

Continuing along these lines, Turner describes liminality as occurring during transitional periods of history "when the past has lost its grip and the future has not yet taken definite shape" (1980:1). At such transitional times the "subjunctive mood of culture" may prevail. Play, imagination, and paradox with all its possibilities come to the fore, and along with them, an attitude of mind that is interpretive, self-reflexive, self-conscious. Criticism and awareness are almost inevitable in liminal circumstances. When an initiate is stripped of all that he/she knows and understands—the sources of knowledge of self and society—he/she is likely to develop a freer, deeper understanding of the system from which he/she has been removed. Then the moral order is seen from a different perspective and the result may be alienation, social change, and/or individual self-awareness. Moral choice, creativity, and innovation are possibilities that emerge from the agony of isolation and the joy of communitas which may accompany the liminal stage in rites of passage.

Does a rite of passage always cause its participants to think about their condition? Some anthropologists argue that rituals make individuals less likely to do so. By keeping them busy in the obsessive, formal, repetitive activity that rituals

Figure 42 *In an Eastern Orthodox ceremony, a memorial feast is held on the graves of recently deceased family members* (daca)—*village of Topolovnik, East Serbia.*

require, consciousness and questioning may be inhibited rather than encouraged. In discussing a Balinese funeral, Clifford Geertz remarks: "Funeral ceremonies consist largely of a host of detailed little busy work routines, and whatever concern with first and last things death may stimulate is well submerged in a bustling ritualism" (1973:183; *see* fig. 42). A funeral ceremony, he suggests, stifles one's view of mortality and distracts one from seeing oneself in the corpse and its destiny.

This viewpoint calls our attention to the need for a theory about the kind of experience that rites of passage in particular, and rituals in general, provide. Surely one does not "think" about a corpse as oneself with the usual direct, daytime, orderly consciousness that characterizes and accompanies mundane and logical activities. But on another, deeper, less verbal, less cognitive level, we understand something about our own death in contemplating and enacting rituals involving a corpse (figs. 43–46). Symbolic experience—whether in dreams, poetry, myth, the arts, or trance—holds forth its particular kind of information, eluding words but nonetheless significant and real. The failure of anthropology to deal with the experiences of ritual participants—private, subjective, psychological, conscious, and unconscious—is an enormous barrier to our understanding of the subject.

The rite of passage calls for a psychological anthropology. It is a moment of conspicuous teaching. Central to nearly all such rituals, particularly rites of initiation, is the integration of the person into the society. These are occasions when most often the formal teaching of the culture is transmitted to those who are to become full members. How does this learning take place? How is culture

Figure 43 *Figure of a woman with child, Kongo People, Zaire. Installed in a shed constructed on a grave, this wooden figure depicts people associated with the deceased. This woman and child probably refer to a deceased man's role as husband and father.*

Figure 44 *Portrait skull, possibly Iatmul, Sepik River, Papua, New Guinea. A portrait likeness, modeled with clay over the skull of the deceased, is placed by the Iatmul in the men's house in a lavishly ornamented display that honors the dead. During a nighttime mortuary ceremony, men sing ancestral songs of the deceased and play ancestral flutes. Later the skull is buried.*

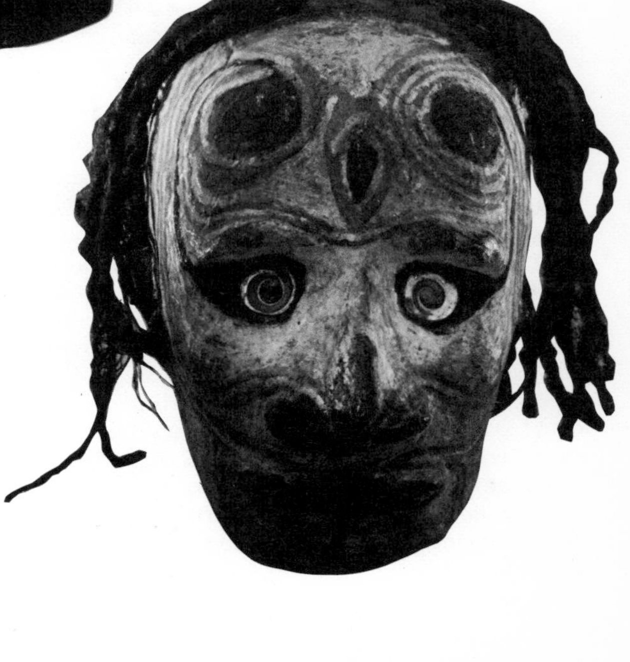

Figure 45 *Mask with flaring horns, Dogon, south-central Mali. This mythical or extinct animal carved by Dogon master craftsmen corresponds to no known animal in the region. A dancer wearing this mask carries a baton, with which he pretends to cultivate and weed the ground.*

Figure 46 *Poster of a cow's face, Patan, Nepal. On the day of the cow festival in Patan, a cow may push open the gates of heaven with her horns, allowing waiting souls to enter. In households where someone has recently died, families send a member out, usually a young boy, to make sure that a cow stands ready at the gate. The boy parades through the town wearing the disguise displayed here—a colorful printed-paper cow's face, two bamboo "horns" decorated with paper rosettes, and a small paper poster depicting Ganesh, the elephant-headed god.*

communicated, not simply as an external, neutral set of principles, but as a motivational, internalized system, so that one's duty, as Turner puts it, becomes one's desire? Thomas Scheff (1979) raises this question in complaining about anthropologists' failure to consider the role of catharsis in ritual. Bruce Kapferer (1975) has examined the role of emotion in ritual, but not at great length. Psychological learning theories have not been applied to this subject with any consistency or rigor. There are many useful theories. One conspicuous example comes to mind: rites of passage are often strikingly painful, particularly rites of initiation at adolescence. Tattooing, mutilation, circumcision, and various ordeals are standard features, culturally induced suffering that dramatizes what might otherwise be a mundane physiological change. Cognitive dissonance theory is clearly pertinent, stating as it does that the degree to which individuals have suffered for an experience is directly related to the value they place on that experience (Festinger, 1957). The higher the price paid, the more likely are subjects to insist that it was worthwhile. The implications are clear for the understanding of rites of passage, but they have not been explored systematically.

Anthony Wallace (1966) has outlined what he calls a "Ritual Learning Process," which describes a set of activities whereby the neophyte in a rite of passage is radically removed from past knowledge and presented with much new information while in a state of semantic dissociation that allows for the acquisition of much new knowledge, in paradigmatic and symbolic form. This follows what he calls the law of dissociation:

> This is the principle that any given set of cognitive and affective elements can be restructured more rapidly and more extensively the more of the perceptual clues from the environment associated with miscellaneous previous learning of other matters are excluded from conscious awareness, and the more of those clues which are immediately relevant to the elements to be reorganized are presented. (1966:240)

Cognitive and affective restructuring occur through dissociation, and newly acquired information is then maintained, in part, by the operation of reinforcement in the conventional learning sense. The stages of this kind of learning are: prelearning or anticipation; separation (through sensory deprivation, monotonous stimuli, extreme physical stress, and the like); suggestion (high suggestibility associated with trance or dissociation, sometimes thought of as conversion or possession); execution (achievement of a new cognitive structure); and maintenance (through repetition or reinforcement), occasionally involving a resynthesis.

Jerome Frank (1961), in his study of brainwashing, religious conversion, and magical cures, employs a similar paradigm. It is clear that a complex theory is necessary to explain ritual learning, involving several kinds of learning, and Wallace's scheme is, on the face of it, up to the task. Unfortunately, it does not seem to have been applied rigorously or consistently by studies of ritual that have ensued, in American anthropology or elsewhere, for reasons not at all evident.

In her review of the study of the socialization process in anthropology, A. I. Richards points out that at one time British social anthropologists regarded socialization as an important part of their ethnographic work (1970). But since the fifties and sixties, interest in that area has been lacking. Less and less information on child-rearing is contained in monographs, and less on the communication of values and the integration of the individual into culture.

Some anthropologists, Max Gluckman (1964) most conspicuously, have urged that disciplinary distinctiveness be preserved, that anthropologists respect their own naiveté, leaving psychology to the psychologists. Richards and Fortes (in Mayer, 1970) among others, point out that the best interdisciplinary study occurs when all the disciplines are contained within one person's head. Anthropology cannot hope to comprehend rites of passage, the transmission of culture, socialization, or the maintenance of values without expanding its conceptions of learning theory and symbolic processes, unconscious and conscious.

Psychologists, too, have not mined the rich ethnographic literature on rites of passage, despite their interest in learning theory and in individual lives. The only exception to this is the work done by some psychoanalytically oriented theorists concerning puberty ceremonies; this constitutes a sizable literature which we will examine briefly here.

Freudians have turned to the often florid and dramatic adolescent initiation ceremonies in tribal societies for evidence that supports their interpretation of society's origins as based on an original act of patricide. In *Totem and Taboo* (1914), Freud used evidence from aboriginal societies to support his theory that civilization began when an ancestral patriarch was slain by his jealous sons because of his monopolization of the females of the group. This act was subsequently commemorated by totemic rites, including taboos that expressed awe of the patriarch and prevented the recurrence of patricide. In guilt and grief, the sons forbade that any of them should take the women of their group as mates, and this led to the establishment of the incest taboo, or exogamic regulations. In adolescent rites, particularly those that involve genital mutilation of neophytes, Freudians claim to find proof for their theory. The rites are viewed as a reenactment of the fathers punishing their sons for their incestuous yearning toward their mothers and for the sons' desire to overthrow the authority of their elders. The threat of castration of the boys by the men is regarded as a warning and a miniature expression of what will befall those who transgress the boundaries of taboos (see Kimball, 1960:15).

This view was modified by Bruno Bettelheim (1954), who interpreted circumcision as indicating males' envy of females' power of procreation. When boys are "reborn," moving through the legs of older men, when the penis is cut and bleeds, they are emulating women, emulating menstruation, giving birth to new life, and, in extreme cases of subincision, making their genitals superficially similar to those of women. Thus male initiation ceremonies express male procreation envy.

Other psychoanalytically oriented psychologists have seen male initiation rites at puberty as aimed at establishing masculine identity, particularly in societies where the mother-child bond is especially strong (Young, 1965). When the father is often absent, the son sleeps in his mother's house; since he does not have a strong masculine figure in his life, the argument goes, a sharp, shocking break of his identification with the mother is necessary to allow him to resolve a severe Oedipal conflict. Initiation rites firmly separate the boy from maternal figures, sever his identity with the mother, and place him psychologically and socially within the father's group. A male is, in these conditions, twice-born, once into the world of mother and female society, then at puberty he symbolically dies and is reborn into manhood and the world of men.

Discussions of female initiation ceremonies are fewer by far in the literature, though some recent writings have stressed the importance of the female bonding that may accompany them. Often their function is clear: a severe suppression of female sexuality and symbolic expression of female inferiority.

Mircea Eliade (1958) reads a religious impulse into initiation ceremonies. Men and women are fascinated with special attributes that are opposite to their own. Each envies the other because of the reciprocal attraction to their missing half, so to speak. Penis envy on the part of women, womb envy on the part of men, are expressions of the "antagonism and attraction between two types of sacralities—feminine and masculine—(expressing) strong and essential religious desire to transcend an apparently irreducible existential situation and attain to a total mode of being" (figs. 47–50). Initiation ceremonies abound in sexual symbolism, he notes, and often each sex dresses like the opposite. The novice thus symbolically becomes a totality, the androgyne being superior to both sexes because it incarnates totality, hence perfection.

Mary Douglas (1966) has a structuralist interpretation of these rites and finds that ceremonies such as those Bettelheim interprets as signifying womb envy

Figure 47 *Catholic first-communion procession, village of Lumbarda, Adriatic island of Korcula.*

Figure 48 *Crowning of the bride and groom in an Eastern Orthodox wedding in the village of Donja Borina, western Serbia.*

Figure 49 *Baptism in Eastern Orthodox church: priest with baby and baptismal godfather* (kršteni dum), *village of Donja Borina, western Serbia.*

Figure 50   *Ramon Medina Silva, Huichol shaman, initiates the pilgrims who are making their first trip to Wirikuta, Huichol sacred land of the ancestors. The pilgrims who come here for the first time are blindfolded at the edge of the sacred country, then baptized with water from springs associated with eternal life. The blindfold is then removed to allow them their first sight of their destination.*

are in fact expressive of a condition in the social order, mirrored by the person. The imitation of women by boys is perhaps an imitation of symmetry, a structural principle of great importance in a society in which two groups exchange wives and must regard each group as equal and symmetrical. In tribal societies differences between male and female are used to indicate features of the social order; this is an expression and enforcement of a common vision of the society. Thus in such societies even what we would regard as the most intimate personal experiences are mediated through ritual and mythological conceptions.

What can we conclude from this little survey of initiation ceremonies? Only that we lack sufficient critical knowledge to make any firm conclusion save this: males and females are as much made as born. The most fundamental distinction with which we enter the world—as male or female—is only further material for a culture to work with in organizing and endowing our individual experiences with its characteristic stamp.

Some nonpsychoanalytically oriented discussions of initiation ceremonies can be briefly mentioned. Schlegel and Barry (1980) in a recent article take an evolutionary approach to the subject. They regard initiation ceremonies as celebrations of gender status and find that gender status has different consequences in different levels of social complexity. Ceremonies for girls are predominant in simple societies where female participation in food production may be more important; in middle-range societies where same-sex groupings may be important economically, ceremonies appear and are important for boys and girls, but boys' ceremonies predominate since here most communal activities are carried on by men. In modern complex societies practicing intensive agriculture, other types of social marking are more important than categories of maleness or femaleness. As societies grow more complex, gender as a classificatory principle recedes in importance, and fewer initiation ceremonies are found altogether. Here, adolescence does not lead to particular kinds of socially important affiliations. The interpretation throughout this approach is that the presence of sexual initiation serves to underscore the importance of the group or sex which is its subject.

A survey of the vast, intricately detailed descriptions of rites of passage in tribal societies sooner or later leads one to the questions: what do these rites have to tell us about ourselves living in a modern world? Where did all that ceremony go? How do we solve the problems taken up by these rites, of clearly and safely moving from one life stage to another? Even more ambitiously, we may ask, how do we pass through such changes in the company of important others with whom we will henceforth live in our new condition? How is change codified into a sustaining set of understandings, a social order, a body of commonly held beliefs, not only for ourselves but for the communities in which we dwell? How can stability and order be recaptured and reaffirmed, our cherished ideals and relationships renewed and invigorated, following the chaos and contradictions that, inevitably, ritual handles? We may sigh with relief that we never need to face the prospect of circumcision or tattooing, but we also dread the next Bar Mitzvah in which everyone, even the boy about to become a man, is bored and psychologically absent, or worse, manifests interest only in the gifts he will receive. And we may become desolate in contemplating the funeral of someone we love, conducted by strangers, devoid of personal significance and the power to help us celebrate the deceased and mourn our loss. There is, as Solon Kimball (1960) indicates, no reason to think that rites of passage are less important in modern secular societies than they were in simpler ones. Ceremonialism alone, practiced without sacred or significant shared meanings, cannot provide us with a sense of integration, but, he suggests, the way societies deal with individual life changes adds up to their ability to assist people in adjusting to transitions. Modern secular societies may still be of some assistance, though they fall far short of offering the totality of expression and significance found in genuinely sacred contexts. We have had to develop rituals and employ symbols in increasingly private contexts, living as we do in a diffuse, fragmented world with shattered or shallow consensual structures. This privacy leaves individuals nearly completely on their own when dealing with the subjects previously taken up by rituals:

> Ritual has become so completely individualistic that it is now found for many only in the privacy of the psychoanalyst's couch. But it seems much more likely that one dimension of mental illness may arise because an increasing number of individuals are forced to accomplish their transitions alone and with private symbols. (Kimball, 1960, xviii)

Lately some attention has been given to the dearth of literature on the adult life cycle in our society. Sheehy (1974) and Gould (1978) have written in some detail on the necessity for conceptualizing the phases of maturity in terms of predictable, normal, adult crises. They conceive of adult life along the lines followed by many developmental psychologists, regarding each stage as presenting the individual with a particular psychosocial task that must be mastered on the way to maturity. Neugarten has suggested some refinement in our approach to the phases of adult life, emphasizing the crudeness of our view of aging. We do not usually make any distinctions among the old; those between ages sixty-five and ninety are treated as a single category. She suggests at the very least we make a distinction between the young-old and old-old. The former have much to offer society, and our task as a group is to find ways they may make a meaningful contribution, though they may be occupationally retired. The old-old are frail and in need of care. The problems they present are entirely different.

Helpful as such theories are in suggesting a less simplistic approach to the life cycle, none of them draws our attention to ritual. The authors provide some guidance in making clear the characteristics of each age, and, implicitly, the nature and meaning of a change from one to another. But they do not help us in identifying ceremonies that define and accentuate the changes. But then psychologists should perhaps not be expected to cast their studies in the form of rituals, which are, ultimately, social matters, even though they are enacted individually. It seems more appropriate to look to anthropologists for insights as to how ceremony and ritual might be usefully considered as part of the life cycle; but even anthropologists do not agree on the importance of rites of passage. A recent book by the Frieds (1980) casts doubts on the utility of these rites. The Frieds examine four critical transitions: birth, puberty, marriage, and death, in cultures deliberately selected to provide variation in terms of geographical distribution and technological and social complexity. All the societies they examine celebrate some transition points in the life cycle, and all place a symbolic template over the facts of biology, treating it as socially manipulable. It is often thought, they note, that societies without profound rituals, particularly adolescent rites, are "asking for trouble." But in their survey they find no association between the absence of ritual and the presence of social problems, as indicated by high rates of delinquency or suicide. They remark:

> It is possible, then, for cultures to survive with relatively small attention to ritual and also with extraordinarily rich preoccupation with ritual, including life transition ceremonies. We cannot say for sure that a culture cannot exist unless it has a bare minimum of such rituals. (1980:268)

"But," they add, "we have no record of societies up to the present that have existed without ritual, hence if such existed they did not survive." From this they assume rituals play some adaptive role in the process of cultural evolution. They claim that human, that is, cultural life came into existence considerably in advance of the first clear evidence of ritual. The latter is dated by the Frieds at roughly 40,000 B.C.,

... in the flower-strewn remains of Neanderthals who used flowers to acknowledge and celebrate death. Since culture is now regarded as definitely manifested by the appearance of tools, two million years ago, it may be that rites of passage have existed for only two percent of the history of culture—a relatively recent, hence optional development, as things go. (1980:269)

Rites of passage may be functionally adaptive at the social level but probably are not necessary for the survival of individuals, the Frieds conclude.

But can we be so certain that individual and social evolution are as separable as the Frieds maintain? Surely the ability of individuals to cope with increasing complexity, conflict, and isolation contributes to the evolution of society. Human beings are the carriers of culture, and they may do this more or less successfully, in confusion and disarray or with a sense of coherence and well-being. The well-being of the units of a society, the living people, surely cannot be so sharply severed from the success of the society, even in terms of mere survival and evolution. Durkheim's classic study, *Suicide* (1897), long ago indicated how social anomie may be expressed by the individual in the form of suicide. Rites of passage certainly do not *cause* social integration, rather they reflect and enhance it.

The relationships between rituals and various indicators of social disorganization are surely attenuated and blurred by the presence of countless intervening variables. Nevertheless, we need not conclude, with Max Gluckman (1962) and other anthropologists, that modern secular societies cannot sustain genuine rites of passage because of the narrow, segregated nature of social relations within them. Gluckman reserves the terms "ritual" and "rites of passage" for ceremonies that address themselves to mystical forces, that is, are basically sacred. This cannot happen in modern urban situations where social relations do not serve multiple purposes and are not charged with moral valuations. Since religion occupies a smaller place in urban settings, it is no longer true that everything social is also religious, as in the case of simpler societies.

But though Gluckman may be correct when he states that religion has shrunk in modern society, does it necessarily follow that rituals, too, are inevitably less important? Rituals have some distinctive attributes that suggest that it may not be so. First of all, they are performed. Problems of doubt, subtle inner states, and motivation may be less troublesome in ritual than in religion; rituals are innately rhetorical. Doing is believing, and as Mircea Eliade puts it so well, one may become what one performs. Rituals call for belief, but not through the cognitive mechanisms that allow critical thinking to interfere with conviction. Secondly, rituals deal with paradox and conflict, as we indicated earlier. Problems of codification and consistency, for example within religious systems, and between religious interpretations and the social order, need not be managed directly in ritual. Ambiguity may be glossed, even celebrated, then transcended in ritual performances, more readily than in the often cerebral, more systematic tenets of religion. Through ritual we organize our understandings and dramatize our fundamental conceptions, as Sherry Ortner (1978) puts it, rearranging our fundamental assumptions in the course of rituals themselves. Rituals begin with a cultural problem, stated or unstated, and then work various operations upon it, arriving at "solutions"—reorganizations and reinterpretations of the elements that produce a newly meaningful whole. Achieving the appropriate shift in consciousness is the work of ritual. Ortner concludes:

> The re-shaping of consciousness or experience that takes place in ritual is by definition a reorganization of the *relationship* between the subject and what may for convenience be called reality. Ritual symbolism always operates on both elements, reorganizing (representations of) "reality," and at the same time reorganizing (representations of) self. (1978:9)

A view of reality and a corresponding view of self are thus established through ritual, creating a subjective psychological state that restructures meaning. This is the work of ritual and the way it provides solutions to problems.

Ortner's approach does not suggest that there is any reason for rituals in general or rites of passage in particular to differ or subside in modern circumstances in contrast to tribal societies. We still need their work, may still use them for a reorganization of meaning, a change in consciousness; the absence of unifying, axiomatic common symbols does not alter the possibility of our use of rites to provide and state meanings of life changes on a smaller scale. There are groups, communities, kin, and friendship networks that are more inclusive than Kimball's individual on the psychoanalytic couch, but less inclusive than total societies.

There is every reason to believe that rites of passage are as important now as they have always been, for our social and psychological well-being. Indeed, given the fragmented, confusing, complex, and disorderly nature of modern experience, perhaps they are more important: to orient and motivate us in the predictable and unique life crises that present themselves. But now we are left to devise for ourselves the myths, rituals, and symbols needed to endow life with clarity and significance; we do so alone, often in ignorance and always in uncertainty. Our needs have not changed, though the gods, demons, heroes, and spirits that once animated our ceremonies have fallen into disuse. Joseph Campbell puts this well:

> The problem of mankind today, therefore, is precisely the opposite to that of men in the comparatively stable periods of those great co-ordinating mythologies which now are known as lies. Then all meaning was in the group, in the group's anonymous forms, none in the self-expressive individual; today no meaning is in the group—none in the world: all is in the individual. . . . One does not know toward what one moves. One does not know by what one is propelled. . . .
> The hero-deed to be wrought is not today what it was in the century of Galileo. Where then there was darkness, now there is light; but also, where light was, there now is darkness. The modern hero-deed must be that of questing to bring to light again the lost Atlantis of the co-ordinated soul. (1956:388)

The language is not too strong for the dilemma: it is heroic to assemble meanings, find the symbolic expressions for them, gather a small society of one's choice, then enact one's story in a ritual. To be sure, there are some guidelines, for as conventional religion and secular ceremonies seem to be drained of the possibilities for renewing the individual life crises with significance, other, smaller, more idiosyncratic and inevitably less conventional, therefore more personal paradigms and models are appearing. An instructive example is found in a volume entitled *The Second Jewish Catalog* published in 1976. It reflects a desire to give modern young people access to the vocabulary and underlying axioms of the Jewish religion, suggesting ways of personalizing and adapting it to special times and circumstances, while being faithful to Jewish law. The implicit message it carries is that the established institution of the Synagogue does not (perhaps should not) provide the person and family with all its requirements for rituals. In this book, the life cycle is cut up into units that reflect modern conditions; for example, there is a ceremony "On Leaving Home: A New Rite of Passage." Say the authors:

> At one time, not long ago, the institution of marriage acknowledged the transition from adolescence to adulthood. Young people lived with their families until they were ready to marry, and they were encouraged to wed while still young. . . . Of course that era no longer exists. We are living in an age when geographical mobility is the norm and when adolescence is extended by postponing one's career and marriage into the mid and late twenties.

> One can argue that the ceremonies and parties revolving around high school graduation could provide a meaningful transition from high school to college. . . . (But) the overwhelming emphasis at the graduation ceremony is on academic achievement. Other factors, such as a sense of separation and transition, are alluded to in passing if at all. And the personal element is practically lost in the routinized, mass-oriented production of graduation. (Strassfeld, 1976: 88–89)

The authors then ask "What can be done about it?" How can this disorienting phase be made into a meaningful rite of passage? They suggest using a Jewish idiom to give the crisis shape and form, pointing out that Judaism has appropriate ceremonies for dealing with separation and reincorporation that may be readily adapted. The Havdalah ceremony, a ritual that separates the sabbath from the rest of the week, can be used, with its associated prayer, foods, candles, wine, and song. The traditional element can punctuate the introduction of situationally specific and individual motifs. The alternation between sacred and personal or secular elements in rituals is profoundly useful and common, endowing the particular nonrecurrent features with a transcendent quality, traditionalizing that which is new and revivifying the timeless and collective elements by endowing them with deeply felt personal experiences.

Any religion can be mined and explored for symbols and rituals to adapt to personal use in life-crisis ceremonies. What is critical here is the *active* relation to ritual. Instead of having rites performed on us, we do them to and for ourselves, and immediately we are involved in a form of self-creation that is potentially community-building, providing what van Gennep would call regeneration by revitalizing old symbols from the perspective of the present. If our rituals do not fully succeed in convincing us, we will at least have thought through the messages we wish to state, made an attempt at formulating a transitional moment in a particular problem, and this in itself is a major accomplishment, a movement in the direction of clarification and resolution. Transformation is the ultimate goal in life-crisis ceremonies, but it is not the necessary condition for success in ritual. The change in attitude, the realization that one can and should begin to play with ritual symbols and enact their truths, is the first and hardest step. This requires a delicate balance, the clear existential recognition that one is constructing a message for oneself, then performing it. It requires some suspension of the knowledge that ritual has been made rather than given, and along with it, the realization that we are dealing with interpretations, not mutable, externally provided truths. But given the times in which we live, perhaps it is easier to maintain this paradox than hold out for unqualified, sacred axioms which may so easily slip into someone else's totalitarian program. An approach which maintains belief alongside critical consciousness is ultimately more imaginative, more responsible. As Clifford Geertz (1972) put it so felicitously, these rituals and symbols are stories we tell ourselves about ourselves, in the realm of art rather than objective reality.

What may we conclude from this examination of life crises and the ceremonial celebration of change? Simply this: after studying one's own and other people's rituals, it is possible to decide that since these are all constructed performances, if they are not provided for us, we may provide them for ourselves. They may never be the magical affairs that Gluckman calls genuine rituals, but neither will they be the stultifying routines that professionals impose on us in a vacuum. What is required is a small community of friends or family, some symbolic and traditional sources of inspiration, a clear formulation of the change involved and its significance—and courage. The first step, the actual doing of a ritual for oneself or for another, is often quite frightening, then exhilarating.

When we examine the occasions that call for rites of passage in our own society, we are likely to be struck by the absence of ceremonies that undo relationships or divest people of statuses. But in times of rapid individual mobility and social change, ceremonies of separation and disconnection are surely important. Erving Goffman (1964) has studied some ceremonies of this kind, but in quite negative terms, examining how societies make former citizens into non-persons, through status and role-stripping rituals and degradation ceremonies. Becoming a soldier, a prisoner, or mental patient usually involves ceremonies of undoing prior statuses. But positive aspects of some losses and disconnections could also be occasions for ritual and ceremony.

It is above all to be hoped that the study of celebrations is more than interesting and amusing: it should also provide examples. A person who is approaching a fiftieth birthday in terror can contrive to mark the transitional moment by including a ritual that makes some personal statement *within* the secular, impersonal trappings of cake and candles. A woman shedding her married name can feel she is made new by including friends, and ritually burning some item associated with the past she is leaving behind, or inscribing her new name in some significant place or on a symbolic object. A divorced man can be ceremonially reintroduced and reincorporated into his group of friends as single, eligible, newly defined apart from his spouse, welcomed as a potential companion and mate by marriageable women. A girl at the onset of menarche can become one of the group of older women, her mother, female relatives, and friends, who may ritually pass on examples to the girl from their lives, or give gifts signifying some aspect of womanhood.

Menopause, surgery, "empty nests," retirement, are all regular occasions in life that go largely uncelebrated. All those can be opportunities for rites of passage, transformed from traumatic experiences or disorienting lonely episodes into commemorations that acknowledge change. The spontaneous ritual acts that we so often do alone—burning an unfaithful lover's photograph or returning gifts from one no longer cherished, the cutting of hair or cleaning house to announce to oneself that a new phase of life is beginning—all these are nascent rites of passage that can be enlarged, formalized, made to include important people, memorialized with objects, notes, or records that are kept in recognition that the transition was successfully accomplished.

The society in which we live leaves us in the hands of "experts" and anonymous agencies or individuals who care for only a small part of our human needs. We are born, for the most part, in hospitals, and we usually die there. Birth and death, the irreducible entrance and exit, are often utterly secular affairs, matters of the most profound emotional significance that are left uncelebrated. Instead of being the center of a ceremony at such a critical moment, the person is "processed," a mere body that must be categorized socially, statistically, physically dealt with, then moved on. In reaction against this, there are some attempts to relocate birth and death in the home, or at least in the hands of a community of intimately concerned individuals. The hospice movement and the nascent movement encouraging the use of midwives and home births are encouraging. They are instructive examples of people who take matters into their own hands on a small scale and encourage others to do the same. It is wasteful and fatuous to lament the paucity of society's arrangements or its insensitivity in such matters. In our times, society deals with other concerns than the dispensation of meaning or the attentiveness to the needs of the soul. These matters, now, we must take into our own hands. And the chances are that individually, in our own communities, we may do a decent job. Freedom is the other side of loneliness and isolation. When we take our own lives into our own hands, we make ourselves, author our own stories. To whom else should we commend ourselves, or look to for a better spirit, a deeper vested interest, fuller understanding, or an attitude of genuine celebration?

Grateful acknowledgment is made to Alexander Moore of the University of Southern California, Department of Anthropology, for his critical reading and for pointing out the relevance of Kimball's and Wallace's writings to my topic.

Bibliography

Ariès, Philippe
1962   *Centuries of Childhood: A Social History of Family Life.* Translated by R. Baldick. New York: Alfred A. Knopf.

Bettelheim, Bruno
1954   *Symbolic Wounds.* New York: Free Press.

Brown, Judith K.
1963   "A Cross-Cultural Study of Female Initiation Rites." *American Anthropologist* 65:837–53.

Burton, Rover V., and Whiting, John W. M.
1961   "The Absent Father and Cross-Sex Identity." *Merrill-Palmer Quarterly of Behavior and Development,* vol. 7, no. 2.

Campbell, Joseph
1956   *The Hero with a Thousand Faces.* New York: Meridian.

Chapple, Eliot D., and Coon, Charleton S.
1966   *Purity and Danger: An Analysis of Concepts of Pollution and Taboo.* London: Routledge and Kegan Paul.

Durkheim, Emile
1952   *Suicide: A Study in Sociology.* Translated by John A. Spaulding and George Simpson. London: Routledge and Kegan Paul. (First published 1897.)

Eliade, Mircea
1958   *Rites and Symbols of Initiation: The Mysteries of Birth and Rebirth.* New York: Harper Torchbook.

Fernandez, James
1980   "Reflections on Looking into Mirrors." *Semiotica* 30 1/2:27–39.

Festinger, Leon
1957   *A Theory of Cognitive Dissonance.* Evanston, Ill.: Row, Peterson.

Frank, Jerome
1961   *Persuasion and Healing: A Comprehensive Study of Psychotherapy.* Baltimore: Johns Hopkins University Press.

Freud, Sigmund
1950   *Totem and Taboo.* 1914. Reprint edition. London: Routledge and Kegan Paul.

Fried, Martha N. and Morton H.
1980   *Transitions: Four Rituals in Eight Cultures.* New York: W. W. Norton.

Geertz, Clifford
1972   "Deep Play: Notes on the Balinese Cockfight." *Daedalus* (Winter):1–37.

Gluckman, Max
1962   *Essays on the Rituals of Social Relations.* Manchester: Manchester University Press.
1964   *Closed Systems and Open Minds.* Chicago: Aldine.

Goffman, Erving
1964   *Stigma: Notes on the Management of Spoiled Identity.* Englewood Cliffs, N.J.: Prentice-Hall, Inc.

Gould, Roger L.
1978   *Transformation: Growth and Change in Adult Life.* Louisville, Ken.: Touchstone.

Hall, Stanley G.
1904   *Adolescence: Its Psychology and its Relations to Physiology, Anthropology, Sociology, Sex, Crime, and Education.* New York: Appleton.

Huntington, Richard, and Metcalf, Peter
    1979   *Celebrations of Death: The Anthropology of Mortuary Ritual.* Cambridge: Cambridge University Press.

Kapferer, Bruce
    1975   "Form and Transformation in Ritual Performance: The Organization of Emotion and Feeling in Sinhalese Healing Rites." Paper presented at the 74th annual meeting of the American Anthropological Association, San Francisco, Cal.

Kimball, Solon T.
    1960   Introduction to *The Rites of Passage,* by Arnold van Gennep. 1908. Reprint edition. Translated by M. B. Vizedom and G. L. Caffee. Chicago: University of Chicago Press.

La Fontaine, J. S.
    1972   *The Interpretation of Ritual: Essays in Honour of A. I. Richards.* Kennebunkport, Me.: Tavistock.

Lewis, Gilbert
    1980   *Day of Shining Red: An Essay in Understanding Ritual.* Cambridge: Cambridge University Press.

Mayer, Philip, ed.
    1970   *Socialization: The Approach from Social Anthropology.* Kennebunkport, Me.: Tavistock.

Mead, Margaret
    1928   *Coming of Age in Samoa.* New York: American Museum of Natural History.

Middleton, John
    1970   *From Adult to Child: Studies in the Anthropology of Education.* New York: American Museum of Natural History.

Moore, Alexander
    1979   "Initiation Rites in a Mesoamerican Cargo System: Men, Boys, Judas and the Bull." *Journal of Latin American Lore,* vol. 5, no. 1, pp. 55–81.

Moore, Sally Falk, and Myerhoff, Barbara G.
    1977   *Secular Ritual.* Amsterdam: Van Gorcum.

Ortner, Sherry B.
    1978   *Sherpas Through Their Rituals.* Cambridge: Cambridge University Press.

Richards, Audrey I.
    1970   "Socialization in Contemporary British Anthropology." In *Socialization: The Approach from Social Anthropology,* edited by Philip Mayer. Kennebunkport, Me.: Tavistock.

Sanday, Peggy R.
    1973   "Toward a Theory of the Status of Women." *American Anthropologist* 75:1682–1700.

Sargent, William
    1957   *Battle for the Mind: A Physiology of Conversion and Brainwashing.* New York: William S. Heinman.

Scheff, T. J.
    1979   *Catharsis in Healing, Ritual, and Drama.* Cambridge: Cambridge University Press.

Schlegel, Alice, and Barry, Herbert
    1980   "The Evolutionary Significance of Adolescent Initiation Ceremonies." *American Ethnologist* 7(4):6996–715.

Sheehy, Gail
    1974   *Passages: Predictable Crises of Adult Life.* New York: E. P. Dutton.

Silverman, Sydel F.
    1967   "The Life Crisis as a Clue to Social Functions." *Anthropological Quarterly* 40:127–38.

Strassfeld, Sharon and Michael
    1976   *The Second Jewish Catalog.* Philadelphia: The Jewish Publication Society of America.

Turner, Victor
    1969   *The Ritual Process.* Chicago: Aldine.
    1974   *Dramas, Fields, and Metaphors: Symbolic Action in Human Society.* Ithaca: Cornell University Press.
    1980   "Liminality and Morality." Firestone Lecture, delivered at the University of Southern California.

Van Gennep, Arnold
    1960   *The Rites of Passage.* 1908. Reprint edition. Translated by M. B. Vizedom and G. L. Caffee; introduction by Solon T. Kimball. Chicago: University of Chicago Press.

Wallace, Anthony F. C.
    1966   *Religion: An Anthropological View.* New York: Random House.

Whiting, John W.; Kluckhorn, Richard M.; and Anthony, Albert S.
    1958   "The Function of Male Initiation Ceremonies at Puberty." In *Readings in Social Psychology,* edited by E. E. Maccoby, T. M. Newcomb, and E. L. Hartley. New York: Holt, Rinehart and Winston.

Young, Frank
    1965   *Initiation Ceremonies: A Cross-Cultural Study of Status Dramatization.* New York: Bobbs-Merrill.

The Cut That Binds: The Western Ashkenazic Torah Binder as Nexus between Circumcision and Torah

Barbara Kirshenblatt-Gimblett

The Torah is the central text in Jewish religious life. In a narrow sense, Torah refers to the Pentateuch; in a broader sense, to Jewish tradition. The kernel of the Torah is the Ten Commandments, which were given to Moses by God on Mount Sinai. According to Philo, all the precepts of the Torah were noted down between the separate commandments, although the tablets were not more than six handbreadths in length and as much in width. Throughout the millennia, highly trained scribes have faithfully inscribed these precepts on a parchment scroll. So great is their responsibility that should they so much as add or eliminate one letter, they would precipitate the destruction of the world. It is from this scroll that the Torah is read publicly three days each week.[1]

The interior of the synagogue is focused upon the Torah scroll, the ark where it is stored on the eastern wall facing Jerusalem, and the desk where it is read aloud. Like a human, the scroll is "dressed" in its finery, and when it is beyond repair, it is buried in a cemetery. Like a queen, the scroll wears a regal mantle and bears a precious crown and sceptre-like pointer, which is used for reading. Further accessories include finials and a shield. The scroll is treated with the decorum befitting a sovereign power. A new scroll is brought to the synagogue by procession. All must stand in the presence of the scroll. Should the scroll be dropped, the community must fast. The "naked" scroll is not to be touched with bare hands. The scroll must always be covered except when it is being read.[2]

To be a Jew is to live a life governed by the precepts of the Torah. For a male, initiation into that life is made by a cut that binds.

The Cut That Binds

When a Jewish male infant is eight days old, he is circumcised, just as Abraham circumcised his son Isaac, when he was eight days old. With this cut, the child is brought into the convenant between God and Israel. He is bound to the Torah and to the community of Torah. The permanent sign upon his flesh serves as a constant reminder of his entry.[3]

Traditionally, the ceremony of *berit milah* (covenant of circumcision) is held in the synagogue at the end of the morning services. Though the basic components of the liturgy and ceremony are the same in the many Jewish communities around the world, there are important differences. One variation, the making of a binder for the Torah scroll from a cloth used during the circumcision, is specific to Western Ashkenazim—Jews who lived in Germany, Alsace, Switzerland, Denmark, Holland, Bohemia, Moravia, and neighboring areas.[4]

The Performed Object

For at least four hundred years, Western Ashkenazim have forged a powerful nexus between two central convenants in Jewish sacred history—the convenant of Abraham, marked by circumcision, and the covenant of Moses, marked by the giving of the Torah. They have concretized this link by means of a long strip of cloth.[5]

A rectangle of unbleached linen is still used by some Western Ashkenazim today to provide a clean surface on which the infant lies during the circumcision. After the circumcision, this cloth is torn into four strips which are sewn end to end to form one long band about twelve feet long and six inches high. Someone with a good hand, possibly the local teacher, cantor, or circumcisor, draws the inscription and images, which are either embroidered by the mother or another female relative, or painted. The inscription carries the child's name, birthdate and zodiac sign, and a wish drawn from the circumcision liturgy that he grow up to a life of Torah, marriage, and good deeds.

After one to three years, when the child first visits the synagogue, he presents the binder as his first gift to the synagogue. At the end of the public reading, the scroll is ritually raised so the congregation can witness the text, and it is then tightly rolled shut. The child then offers his binder, which is used to wrap and bind the scroll so that it holds firm. His father lifts him so that he may grab hold of one of the two wooden staves of the scroll, known as "trees of life," as the congregation says "Torah is a tree of life to them that lay hold of it" (fig. 51).[6] The binder is left on the scroll until the next time the scroll is used, at which point it is put away. When the child reaches the age of thirteen, he reads publicly from the sacred text as part of his bar mitzvah, his initiation into the ritual responsibilities of adulthood; the scroll used on this occasion may be bound with his binder.

Circumcision is known as *berit milah* (covenant of circumcision), and the etymology for *berit* (convenant) is believed to be "binding." Thus the cloth used during the circumcision ceremony that symbolically binds the child into the convenant is later transformed into a physical binder for the "terms" of that convenant, the Torah. Carrying the child's name and birthdate, and even the blood of circumcision, the binder symbolically binds the child around the law each time it is used to secure the Torah scroll.

Made after the circumcision, the binder provides an opportunity to reflect on

Figure 51 The First Visit to the Synagogue, *M. Oppenheim, 1869. The rolled binder rests on the balustrade as the father lifts the child up so that he may grasp the stave of the Torah on his first trip to the synagogue.*

the promise of new life and to express hopes and wishes for that new life. The very act of expression helps to bring about the realization of what is expressed, so powerful are language and ritual and the objects associated with them.

Spatial Metaphors of Temporal Passage

Only a fraction of the total length of a Torah binder is actually wound around the Torah scroll. The remaining two-thirds or more of the binder is wound on itself to form a tight coil and is tucked under the previous windings between the two rolled portions of the scroll. The coil is tucked in from above, in communities where tradition has it that the gesture symbolizes God's giving of the Torah from on high; it is also tucked in from below, where the tradition dictates that we should always aspire upward and, hence, tuck the coil in that direction. Young boys in the men's section of the synagogue are expected to roll the binder tight in readiness for the end of the reading, when the scroll needs to be fastened.[7] The question arises—why is this object so much longer than is required to do the job?

Clues may be found in the format, iconography, and inscription. The binders are read from right to left, as the line of text extends, generally in a single row, down the center of the long band, without doubling back on itself. The text begins by announcing the birth of the child and then expresses the wish that he should grow up to a life of Torah, marriage, and good deeds. According to tradition, premature death may be averted by good deeds, devotion in prayer, and the zealous study of Torah. And continuity beyond death may be had through one's children, the realization of the injunction to be fruitful and multiply.[8]

In the visual exegesis of the text, there are multiple images of beginnings and endings, within the life of the individual, the community, and the universe. At the far right of the binder, we might find a stork delivering a swaddled infant, a toddler in a walker, a corsage bearing a congratulatory greeting, or a clock set at the hour of birth. At the far left, we might find eyeglasses, suggesting the dimming vision of old age, or, in at least one case, a swaddled baby above and a dead man below, suggesting the full course of life; or we might find an alms box, alluding to the dictum that "charity delivereth from death."[9] Throughout, the buds, twigs, fruits, and flowers associated with new life provide natural analogues for the onset of the biological life of the individual and concretize the metaphor that appears in references to the circumcised infant as "der neue Sprots am Baum der jüdischen Gemeinschaft."[10] Key points in the life of the child as a social and cultural being are marked by the presence, on occasion, of the circumcision knife and an image of the bar mitzvah, and almost always of the wedding ceremony. In sum, the lifetime of an individual is extended, displayed, and secured by words and images proceeding the length of the binder.

Interlaced with the passage of biological and social time is the movement of sacred history—the onset point for the purposes of the binder being the giving of the law to Moses and the terminal point being an eschatological vision of the coming of the Messiah. Thus the word *Torah* may be accompanied by an image of Moses holding the Tablets of the Law, and the mythological animals associated with the coming of the Messiah—the Leviathan, for example—may appear toward the end of the inscription.

By its physical, textual, and iconographic nature, the binder thus provides a spatial metaphor for temporal passage and for the paradox of temporal limit and extension. Simultaneously the binder attests to what is hoped will be the long, though finite, life span of the individual; the recurrent life cycle of many individuals; the continuity of the community; and the eternal time of God's creation.

The Expandable Text: Opening the Gates of Interpretation

The product of a literate (manuscript and early print) culture with a long and elaborate tradition of hermeneutics, Torah binders exemplify in the extreme the "interplay of text, commentary, symbolism, and style of representation in the wordbound image" (Schapiro, 1973:17). They do what they are about.

A distinction is made between the "written Torah" and the "oral Torah," both of which are essential. Whereas the written Torah is fixed on the page, the oral Torah maintains the openness of the written Torah to interpretation. As Scholem (1969:47ff.) points out:

> According to the exoteric usage of the Talmudic sources, the written Torah is the text of the Pentateuch. The oral Torah is the sum total of everything that has been said by scholars or sages in explanation of this written corpus, by the Talmudic commentators on the Law and all others who have interpreted the text. The oral Torah is the tradition of the Congregation of Israel, it performs the necessary role of completing the written Torah and making it more concrete. According to Rabbinical tradition, Moses received both Torahs at once on Mount Sinai, and everything that any subsequent scholar finds in the Torah or legitimately derives from it, was already included in this oral tradition given to Moses. Thus in Rabbinical Judaism the two Torahs are one. The oral tradition and written word complete one another, neither is conceivable without the other.

Furthermore, no aspect of the sacred text is arbitrary—neither the shape, choice, combination, and sequence of letters and words, nor their number and numerical values. And there are many ways that a text may be approached in the quest for its meanings.

The text of the Torah scroll is written in accordance with precise rules, which dictate that it may never be decorated or illustrated. In contrast, accouterments such as the Torah binders are often dense with iconography. The beautification of the Torah by means of accessories fulfills the Talmudic dictim to enhance the performance of precepts through aesthetic elaboration, and specifically to clothe the Torah itself in beautiful silks.[11] The proliferation of visual imagery on the walls and ceilings of synagogues, on the ark that holds the scroll, on the ark curtain, and on the metal and textile accouterments for the scroll itself, thus constitutes a kind of oral Torah, a visual exegesis and concretization of the often metaphorical readings of the unadorned text.

Letters

The unadorned text provides visual markings, or letters, that enable us to convert speech into writing and writing into speech. Both modes are at work in the ritual and artifacts of circumcision. Thus, the formula "May he grow up to a life of Torah, marriage, and good deeds, amen selah" is *written* in the prayerbook and on the binder and *spoken* aloud during the circumcision event. At one level, then, letters are simply visual markings for the spoken language and constitute the basic building blocks of texts.

The letters of the Hebrew alphabet also have assigned numerical values and are used to indicate the child's birthdate on the binders. For example, the year is indicated by a series of three or four letters whose numerical values total the year of the child's birth. Since the same total can be achieved using different combinations of numbers arranged in various orders (though some orders are preferred), people sometimes compose the year from letters that spell an appropriate word or form an abbreviation or acronym for a relevant biblical passage or postbiblical quotation. Thus, in one instance, the date spells the word *zaddik,* which means a pious or saintly man. In this way, not even the form of the number is arbitrary; it carries in addition to information about the date the expression of the desire that the child aspire to the wisdom and piety of a *zaddik*.

Nor need the name of a letter be treated as arbitrary. Thus, we sometimes find the letter *nun sofit* (final "n") in the form of a fish, because *nun* is both the name of the letter and the generic Biblical Hebrew term for fish. The association of the fish with fertility makes this animal highly appropriate for a binder celebrating new life.

However, letters also acquire a life of their own, independent of their relation to speech. A favorite method of teaching the Hebrew alphabet from Talmudic to modern times has been to treat each letter as a representation of a familiar object or person in the child's environment.[12] The *alef* א is a water-carrier with two pails suspended from a yoke; the *bet* ב is an open mouth; the *khet* ח is the entrance to the *kheyder* (Jewish primary school). The *lamed* ל is a stork. These visualizations of letters are concretized strategically on binders where the *lamed* in the word *nolad* (born) appears as a stork and even carries a swaddled baby in its beak. The shape of a letter and its resemblance to an animal thus provide a basis for expanding the meaning of the text by means of a witty pun—the letter takes the explicit shape of the expanded meaning of the word in which it appears.

Letters on the binders are also areas to be filled with plants, animals, houses, faces, abstract designs, and texts (fig. 53). The presence of faces inside letters is reminiscent of a statement about the meaning of Torah found in late commentators and in the Zohar, the central text in Jewish mystical thought. The "thesis put forward is that every word, indeed every letter, has seventy aspects, or literally, 'faces' " (Scholem, 1969:62). The openness of the text to interpretation is thus exemplified by a visual concretization of the literal reading of a metaphor.

Figure 52   *Torah. Inscription date: 1843. Secondary texts written in cursive are in Western Yiddish and consist both of translations of Hebrew texts and of independent statements. "Torah" is illustrated by an open scroll, within which are found the tablets of the law, and above which is the "Crown of Torah." Khupe appears both in the form of the letter* khet *and as a wedding canopy filled with phrases from the wedding liturgy.*

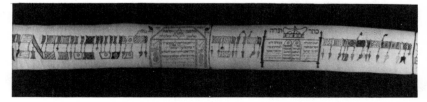

Figure 53   *Torah. Inscription date: 1924. Illustrations are substituted for the words* Torah *and* khupe, *to create a rebus effect. In the case of* Torah, *the illustration is a bar mitzvah scene, an occasion when this binder would be read. In the case of the* khupe, *the illustrations include the wedding canopy and the festive meal following the ceremony.*

The extraordinary variety of designs, plants, and animals found on the binders, and the tendency for no two letters to be decorated in the same way, make the Torah binder a tour de force of ingenuity, a virtual needlework sampler, folk bestiary, and affirmation of infinite variety.

When texts are written inside texts, other statements are being made. Thus, in the case of abbreviations, the full word may be spelled out inside the letters of the abbreviation, thereby affirming that the whole is present in each of its parts. Or when a gloss or explanation of the meaning of a word is written inside the letters of the word, the maker affirms that interpretation is an integral part of the text. Indeed, we have here a visualization that parallels the symbolism of the Torah as a nut in Jewish mystical thought and Hebrew manuscript illumination. The Zohar symbolizes the Torah as a nut consisting of a kernel, and of a hull that must be penetrated through study, interpretation, and obedience to the precepts (Scholem, 1969:57).

Images

As we have seen, the verbal text, which was recited during the circumcision event, is restated on the binder and subjected to visualizations that take as their point of departure some aspect of the text—the shape of the letter, the name of the letter, the numerical value of the letter, the combination of letters, and the interpretation of words and phrases—though not all images on the binders relate directly to the text. Two points in the text which are most often visualized are Torah and *huppah* (literally: wedding canopy; figuratively: marriage ceremony). By examining the visualizations of these two terms on binders drawn from various periods, we can see how the understandings of the text change through time. As Schapiro has pointed out: "It is such pictorial transformations of a single text in the course of time that give to iconographic studies their great interest as a revelation of changing ideas and ways of thought" (1973:13). Furthermore, the images reveal not only different interpretations of the meanings of words, but also different approaches to the reading of a text.

The power of images on the binders inheres in part in their ability to render the text simultaneously more concrete and more symbolic. So clear are the images in this regard that sometimes they even replace words, thereby giving the inscription on the binder the quality of a rebus. When most concrete, literal, and circumscribed in meaning, the words Torah and *huppah* are visualized as a scroll and canopy, respectively.

Other readings of the text make the scroll and canopy part of a larger whole, for example, the public reading of the Torah scroll in the synagogue and the wedding ceremony under the canopy, respectively (fig. 53). And one element such as the Torah scroll may form part of several different and expanded wholes. Thus, the scroll appears on one binder together with the Tablets of the Law, the crown of Torah, and a solar image suggesting the light of Torah. In this case the scroll is a member of a set of visual synonyms for the idea of Torah as the law and ultimate authority. On another binder, the Torah appears in the hands of a man who holds it upright during the ceremonial raising up of the scroll at the end of the public reading (fig. 54). In this case, the scroll is presented as a ritual object just at the moment it is about to be rolled up and bound with a binder. A more modern binder presents a bar mitzvah scene near the word Torah, alluding to the point later in the boy's life when his reading

Figure 54 *Torah. Inscription date: 1812. Embroidered Torah is illustrated by the* hagbahat ha-torah *(raising up of the Torah) ceremony. The Torah is inscribed with the phrase recited during the ceremony: "And this is the law which Moses set before the children of Israel at the commandment of the Lord by the hand of Moses" (Deuteronomy 4:44 and Numbers 9:23).*

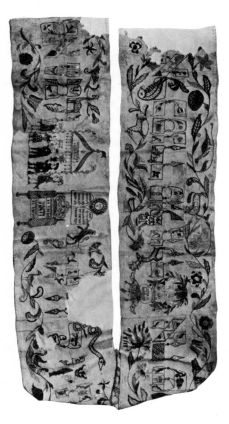

Figure 55 *Torah, 1750. "Torah" is illuminated by the open Torah scroll (on which is inscribed "and this is the Torah"), the crown (which bears the words "crown of Torah"), the tablets of the law (which bear the ten commandments), and a sun. A rampant lion emerges from the adjacent* lamed, *alluding to Temple and to the paired lions often found flanking these images on other ceremonial objects.*

publicly from the scroll will demonstrate his readiness to assume the ritual responsibilities of an adult.

Changing notions of marriage are expressed in the imagery associated with the word *huppah*. Most commonly, a wedding canopy appears; its place as part of the wedding ceremony is made even more explicit when the bridal pair and other members of the wedding party are present and the blessing that seals the bond is provided. On later binders, we find a couple standing in nature, suggesting the conjugal pair rather than the wedding ceremony proper; the wedding feast, pointing to the social rather than contractual nature of the event; and even flaming hearts, indicating romantic love.

Conclusion

Ritual acts and utterances may be experienced as ephemeral, even though their effects endure. Ritual objects, in contrast, provide a sustained physical presence, a constant, tangible reminder of the rituals of which they have formed and will again form a part. They serve not only as a reminder but also as a stimulus, focus, affirmation, guide, and resource for ritual activity. They are activated by ritual acts and utterances, at the same time that they possess a power of their own.

The long narrow binder provides a spatial metaphor of temporal passage, beginning with birth and the first initiation of circumcision and proceeding through subsequent initiations into ritual adulthood and marriage. By means of a long strip of cloth, a powerful link is forged between the sacred text of Jewish life, the Torah, and the act by which a new male is initiated into that life, circumcision. The act of binding the child to the Torah, through circumcision and through his binder, concretizes and personalizes an abstract concept of central importance in Jewish life.[13]

Notes

1. For Philo's legend regarding the Tablets of the Law, *see* Louis Ginzberg (1954, vol. 3:119). For attitudes toward the writing of the Torah scroll, *see* Gershom Scholem (1969:39).

2. Rules for the handling of the Torah scroll are provided in Solomon Ganzfried (1961:chap. 28).

3. The injunction for circumcision appears in Genesis 17:11–12.

4. Jewish communities around the world are generally distinguished on the basis of their historic connection to Spain and Portugal (Sephardim), Germanic lands and Eastern Europe (Ashkenazim), or the Middle and Far East. The Jewish vernacular of Ashkenazim is Yiddish, which varies regionally. In the Western Yiddish spoken by Jews in Germanic lands, the circumcision ceremony is generally known by the term *brismile* and the term for "to circumcise" is *tsu yidishn* (to make Jewish). The Western Ashkenazic Torah binder is known by a variety of terms, *vimpl, vindl, vikl,* and *mape* being the most common. Hebrew terms in this article are romanized in accordance with the *Encyclopedia Judaica* (Jerusalem, 1972).

5. On covenant in Jewish tradition, *see* Delbert R. Hillers (1969).

6. Proverbs 3:18.

7. This information was provided by Bruno Stern, who was raised in Neiderstetten, Bavaria, during the first half of this century. Personal communication, 1980.

8. *See* Ginzberg (1954, vol. 4:62).

9. Proverbs 1:2.

10. "The new sprout of the tree of the Jewish community" (S. Müller, 1934:44).

11. *See* the Talmud, *Shabbat* 133b.

12. *See* Diane Roskies (1978:21–53).

13. The research for this paper was supported in part by a grant from the Memorial Foundation for Jewish Culture. I am grateful to Nancy Berman of the Hebrew Union College Skirball Museum and Vivien Mann of the Jewish Museum of the Jewish Theological Seminary for making it possible for me to examine the binders in their collections. My work on this subject has benefited from the helpful suggestions of Alice Greenwald and Max Gimblett.

Bibliography

Ganzfried, Solomon
   1961   *Code of Jewish Law: Kitzur "Shulhan Arub."* Translated by Hyman E. Goldin. New York: Hebrew Publishing Co.
Ginzberg, Louis
   1954   *The Legends of the Jews,* vols. 3 and 4. Philadelphia: Jewish Publication Society of America.
Hillers, Delbert R.
   1969   *Covenant: The History of a Biblical Idea.* Baltimore: Johns Hopkins University Press.
Müller, S.
   1934   "The New Branch of the Tree of the Jewish Community." *Von jüdischen Bräuchen un jüdischen Gottesdienst.* Frankfurt-on-Main: J. Kauffmann Verlag.
Roskies, Diane
   1978   "Alphabet Instruction in the East European Heder: Some Comparative and Historical Notes." *Yivo Annual of Jewish Social Science* 17:21–53.
Roth, Cecil, ed,
   1972   *Encylopedia Judaica.* Jerusalem: Keter Publishing House.
Schapiro, Meyer
   1973   *Words and Pictures: On the Literal and Symbolic in the Illustration of a Text.* The Hague: Mouton.
Scholem, Gershom
   1969   *On the Kabbalah and Its Symbolism.* New York: Shocken Books.

Canela Initiation Festivals: "Helping Hands" through Life

William H. Crocker

Canela means "cinnamon" in Portuguese and Spanish, so let's call these Gê-speaking, South American Indians the "Cinnamon" people. They live in two villages in the high (1,000 feet/300 meters), "closed" savannas (*cerrados*)* of Central Brazil in the state of Maranhão and municipality of Barra do Corda, and they practice agriculture, although some of their food is still obtained by hunting and gathering (fig. 56). The Ramkókamekra-Canela (pop. 600) and the Apanyêkra-Canela (pop. 250) used to fight each other until they were "pacified" by pioneer fronts of settlers in the first quarter of the last century, but they share the same language and culture with some variations.**

The Cinnamon people celebrate life ceremonially and secularly during the whole yearly cycle, but most intensively in their summer festival season (*wë'të*). During this approximately three-month span, they usually carry out a minimal daily ritual act, but they often sing and dance in a secular manner as well. These celebrations—of the Canela nature itself—usually take place three times a day, in their round plaza at the center of their circular village, in the late afternoon, midevening, and from about three in the morning until the sun almost appears. This secular celebration of being Cinnamon people—joy-in-self (*amyi-'kin*),

---

* *Cerrado* or "closed" savannas are characteristic of the central Brazilian plateau and consist of grassy woodlands where the low trees are generally far enough apart so that a person can walk between them but not see more than twenty-five to fifty yards away unless from a hill.

** In describing the Cinnamon people I will be writing always about the Räm-kô-kãm-me-'kra (almecega-tree grove in [plural] Indian-people: tribe of the almecega [protium sp.] grove) unless I specifically refer to the Apän-yê-'kra (piranha [plural] Indian-people: the piranha [flesh-eating fish] tribe) for purposes of contrast.

Figure 56   *Canela, Brazil, 1975: View of the village from the air.*

generosity (*hä'cayren*), activity (*hä'kritkrit*), and following orders (*harkwa-kôt*)—is accompanied by ritual pageants, the various acts of which are drama-tized either daily or periodically, depending on the nature of the rite. The Cin-namon people cannot read or write, and therefore they communicate and pass on their culture through these festivals. Cosmological beliefs, relationships be-tween men/women and ghosts, the drama between men and wild game animals, the play among men and women, how parents should treat children, relations between kin and affines—all are portrayed and sanctioned in these traditional festival-pageants which are carried out in essentially the same way every time they are performed.

The Cinnamon people "own" a number of annual rituals as well as five great festivals, one of which is put on each summer (April-August). The "initiation fes-tivals" are two of these five summer pageants, and they must each be enacted twice over a period of about ten years in order to process and graduate an age class of boys into adulthood. A third one of these five summer festivals may be carried out once or twice during this ten-year period so that the older men can dramatize their adult roles and orientations in life, in contrast to the two earlier stages of the initiation process.

These three festivals parallel each other in many ways: the first (Kêêtúwayê) emphasizes prepubertal security relationships; the second (Pepyê) focuses on postpubertal life challenges; and the third (Pepcahäc) clarifies and sanctifies var-ious adult roles. All three festivals involve the internment and segregation of a male group (each with two ceremonial girls) in order to separate them from the villagers (*põõ-catêyê:* savanna people) so that these novices can grow and evolve more rapidly in their new and very special environment. While each of the three festivals begins with the acts of "catching" and secluding a group of internees, the middle sections of these pageants vary considerably, and each is specifically oriented toward the ceremonial's particular objectives. The terminal days of each of these three dramatic sequences are—like the initial parts—almost exactly the same. These three festivals not only bring meaning to each other but are also part of a continuing maturation process and therefore must be treated as one unit.

The Kêêtúwayê festival begins dramatically with the interruption of a late afternoon secular dance in the center of the plaza by an elder of the tribe who raises before the rank of singing women a curved staff (about 2½ feet long by 1½ inches in diameter) covered with falcon down and red urucu paint. The symbol has "spoken." Silence falls upon all immediately; the women stop singing, and the dancing youths freeze in place before the female rank. Immediately, two "catchers" (*me-hapën-catê*) spring into action. Having been appointed by the elders, they proceed with unchallengeable authority and begin to catch and group all the boys within a ten-year age span into two parallel ranks facing each other in the center of the plaza (fig. 57). These "novices" are promptly marched off, filing in opposite directions, to two family homes of internment, one in the east and the other in the west, where large rooms are being hastily prepared to house these boys for from two to four months (fig. 58).

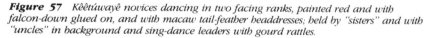

Figure 57 *Kêêtúwayê novices dancing in two facing ranks, painted red and with falcon-down glued on, and with macaw tail-feather headdresses; held by "sisters" and with "uncles" in background and sing-dance leaders with gourd rattles.*

Figure 58 *Kêêtúwayê internees in their room of seclusion.*

During the initial internment of an age class (ranging in age from one to ten), it is often the very first time such boys have spent a night away from their mothers. Of course the very young children are allowed to go home to their families since they are only required to perform according to their age and abilities. About five or six years later, this same age class will again experience the socializing effects of this same Kêêtúwayê pageant.

There are a number of scenes in a Kêêtúwayê pageant-festival drama. (The Canela [Cinnamon] festivals are theatrical dramas or many-act pageants, the various "scenes" of which take place in a traditional sequence over a period of days, weeks, or months, depending on the particular festival.) The two most important ones are the group singing in the plaza, where potential dangers from ghosts are encountered, and the activities in the two houses of seclusion, where the internees become imbued with a certain disciplinary style of life. The Kêêtúwayê boys may sing in the plaza in two ranks facing each other as many as six times a day, depending on how often they are called out by the leaders of the next oldest age class of the opposite faction—their "enemies." (The tribe is divided into halves, or moieties, each composed of alternately graduated age classes.) They may sing for ten minutes or for up to an hour, depending on how many songs are required of them according to the particular scheduling of the festival, the time of day, the desires of the opposing age class, or the energies of the great sing-dance leaders conducting the performance of the boys.

For every outing into the plaza, however, the sing-dancing formation can be described in the following manner: the boys (forty to sixty in number) face each other in two ranks, with sisters or more distant female relatives holding them from behind, with their hands firmly securing each boy around the chest. For any of the lengthier performances, the boys have to be colored red with greasy urucu paint and must wear a headband made of three to five macaw tail feathers attached and pointed skyward. Two older male sing-dance leaders with gourd rattles will take their places at the head of each rank, facing each other, and male relatives will group themselves well behind and on either side of the ranks of boys who are held by their female relatives.

At first, the boys just stand in ranks, facing each other while they chant a set of sad, ghost-attracting songs to the slow and precise rhythm of the gourd rattles. Soon, each boy begins to stamp his right foot in toward the other rank, in time with the two sing-dance leaders. Then they turn face out, stepping backward and opening the ranks in a ripple of unified motion. After about twenty minutes of this swaying in and out, the sing-dance leaders set a faster and faster pace, leaping six steps in before stamping and then swinging six steps out, singing heartily with great booming voices. Later the two ranks turn to file after their respective leaders, forming "S" curves and circles in a snakelike manner. Now they sing happily in rich choral harmony, the sisters and uncles chanting with operatic volume. The girls still hold their little brothers, following them as they can, in their leap-hopping motion around the circular village plaza. At the end of the rite, each boy is doused by his sister with several gallons of water poured onto his body from great gourds—"to give him strength and to help him grow," it is said.

The Kêêtúwayê set of songs were obtained from the ghosts themselves (dead Cinnamon people) in earlier times by a culture hero who had been away on a trip in the savanna. Although their choral music was freely given, the ghosts still long for their enthralling songs, it is believed, and so assemble in great numbers around the singers in the present village when their chants are being sung.

Ghosts love to snatch away the souls of little boys when they can, which usually results in death. Thus, precautions have to be taken to prevent soul loss, especially against those recently dead such as a mother longing for the company of her little son. This is their reason for the necessity of the presence of *living* female and male relatives. It is perceived as family solidarity against hostile forces, since ghosts are believed to be afraid of large groupings of living people. It is also believed that ghosts do not like the urucu paint and macaw tail feathers worn by the singing boys.

Beyond what the Canela say, the social ties being formed in these repeated theatrical dramas are quite important. The act of being held securely by a sister, while celebrating the strongest protection against soul snatching, certainly contributes to the development of what is probably the most serious interpersonal loyalty among the Cinnamon people—the brother-sister bond. These dramatic situations provide an excellent setting for teaching both family and age-class solidarity. Sisters help brothers, and uncles help nephews in their time of potential danger, and urucu paint and macaw feathers possess a defensive magic against ghosts. All these arrangements act as protections against the unknown.

Moreover, from other situations it is clear to the Canela that people who go about *alone* in the forests or savannas are likely to be harassed and bruised and even killed by ghosts, so it is quite important for uninitiated and undisciplined youths to travel in groups when they are away from the village. In this way, the Kêêtúwayê boys are learning to live for each other—to work and cooperate together, and for the tribe as a whole, rather than for just themselves—at quite an early age.

In their group internment rooms, the boys must adjust to and play with each other respectfully, speaking little and always obeying the orders of the assigned commandant (much older), his deputy (one of them), and the "corporals" who are young representatives of the next highest, opposing age class. It is important that the ceremonial "catcher" and commandant are not a Kêêtúwayê novice's relatives; having been appointed by the elders, they represent tribal authority. Thus they learn to take commands, and their behavior is molded by the group and its leaders. Certain elders come by to pass the time of day, telling stories about the ancestors, while the novices listen and learn their society's values.

Just two or three years after the original Kêêtúwayê "catching" and formation of this age class, its members are caught again, this time to be internees in a different festival, the Pepyê. On this occasion they are secluded in separate cells built in their mothers' houses. This Pepyê family home internment festival occurs again about ten years after the original "catching" of this age class and amounts to their final "initiation" or "graduation" into manhood and, in old times, into warrior status. (The word "pep" meant "warrior," though the new peaceful Cinnamon people do not know that these days.) Members of a graduating age class may range between approximately ten and twenty years of age in current times, but some 150 years ago or more, the age span of these graduated warriors is believed to have been between fifteen and twenty-three.

While the Kêêtúwayê pageant serves somewhat as a school away from home for inculcating group solidarity, the Pepyê festival, which takes place when the same boys who took part in this Kêêtúwayê are a few years older, serves to instill individual self-control, personal fortitude, and certain unique skills into its internees. Ultimately, however, this more individualistic training must be completed within the context of the age class and even more so by the youth himself by his special conduct in daily life. For a Pepyê festival, then, taking place a few years later, the same set of young people (an age class) are "caught" (fig. 59) by a special representative of the elders but interned this time in their mothers' houses, where a small round hut, about four to five feet high, is prepared by their families' sons-in-law for them to live in—to repose and think. Their own uncles then make a fenced-in yard extended behind the house from the hut to enclose a latrine. In theory, these separately interned youths are supposed to converse only very briefly with anyone, except with visiting uncles who lecture on traditions. These youths must never walk in the yard exposed to the sun or moon, except when they are well covered with mats or cloth. They must avoid stepping upon dry twigs or dead leaves when filing behind the houses at night to attend morality lectures at their commandant's house; they must avoid being seen by any village members possessing an "evil eye" (but no

Figure 59 *Pepyê novice in the act being "caught" for internment by the "catcher."*

Figure 60 *Pepyê novices, just out of internment, line up kneeling in the plaza, facing the women with whom they broke the internment restrictions regarding sexual intercourse.*

one knows just who these persons are); they must never talk with women who have just had sexual relations, even their relatives (*see* fig. 60); and they must eat only foods with little or no "poison" in them. For example most meat and some vegetable juices are polluting. Damage from any of these sources will prevent the youth from becoming a great hunter; he will be unable to bear up under the heat of the noonday sun or to develop the ability to talk with ghosts (i.e., become a shaman). And, in earlier times, eating these "poisonous" foods would have prevented him from acquiring the necessary skills and magical abilities required to be a great warrior.

To attain these cultural goals, it is necessary to enter into quite a different existence, one in which the individual becomes ultra-sensitive to the perils of life and therefore must take unusual precautions to avoid these dangers. At the same time, however, in this other existence, the individual, through his ultra-sensitivity, has the means to grow very rapidly in strength, ability, knowledge, and perception, aided by continual bathing, eating only "pure" foods, and listening to his uncles. In this condition of "purity," he may even be visited by ghosts and become a shaman.

The Cinnamon people firmly believe that it is *only* through carrying out extreme protective measures against these potential "pollutions" and through drinking herbal medicines daily to eliminate the poisons already accumulated in the body, that a youth can ever develop the expected strength of a respected adult. If a person happens to be weak and lazy, they usually say he must not have completed his postpubertal restrictions very well. If a hunter returns without game, they say he could not have undertaken sufficient restrictions and drunk sufficient medicines during the preceding days. If a shaman has difficulty curing a patient, they suspect this highly sensitive man must have failed to maintain his relative state of purity. All skills, except singing and dancing, are acquired through maintaining strict food and sex restrictions and through drinking certain purifying medicines.

Maintaining restrictions is, for the maturing of Canela individuals, the *great* "helping hand" (*i'te caypar tsä:* leg-supporting device, or in English, "a helping hand"). These procedures are learned in the setting of the Pepyê festival internment, but their practice must be maintained in daily life when the novice has returned from his special sheltering after the termination of the festival. In this existence, quite apart from daily life, it is possible for the youth to mature much more rapidly. Where the various pollutions can be far more damaging because of his sensitivity, the youth must be thoroughly impressed and possibly even scared by the perceived threats in the situation. Faced with this challenge, he learns he must control (i.e., apply restrictions to) his environment while he is gaining strength through avoiding certain foods, taking purifying medicines, and bathing continually with fresh water. (The association with water—bathing in it, or its consumption—is believed to enhance magical growth.)

One dramatic event occurs separately for all of the interned youths in succession around the village circle of houses at a time when they are nearly ready to come out of their circular cells as partially initiated young men. During the seclusion, sunlight has not touched their skin, and after an initial period of severe food restrictions, they have been allowed to eat well, though only foods relatively devoid of polluting substances. Consequently, these youths have grown light in color and heavy in weight, which the Cinnamon people associate with having grown big and strong, having ripened and matured. At various times during the internment, the uncles have come by the cells all together to see how well their nephews are developing. First, they peek through the thatch wall and on another occasion summon each youth to show his face at a window. At a certain time each lad must display his whole body in the entrance way so that the uncles can judge whether he is ready to emerge—to be born anew as a warrior. Accordingly, all the older men assemble to witness this rite for testing maturation, and each man calls forth his nephew in turn. But when a youth appears white and fat in the doorway, his uncle shouts at him in hostile hazing tones, demanding to know whether he is prepared to join the men and sally forth into the savanna to fight enemy warriors should they come to massacre his people. The youth, however, is not ready to answer affirmatively, and so is thrust back into his womblike cell for further gestation.

The cultural analyst would say that when put in danger, we, as well as the Canela, are more likely to develop the self-control and will power necessary to cope with and manipulate the environment, and that it is then possible for these learned behaviors to be transferred and applied to daily living. Thus, the individual internship of the Pepyê festival can be seen as a culturally "fabricated" challenging situation, in which a youth is given a chance to develop his will power to resist the "bad" and select the "good," while at the same time magically receiving, as a result of maintaining the necessary restrictions, great abilities to become superior in various life roles. This will come to pass for him only if he accepts the challenge seriously while in his cell of seclusion and only if he makes a great effort to maintain similar standards in daily life after the termination of the seclusion period.

While the Kêêtúwayê socialization experience partly furnishes the circumstances for the basic prepubertal learning of social solidarity, and the Pepyê training partly provides the setting for the individual's learning of the necessary postpubertal abilities to cope with his environment, there is still a perceived need for reexperiencing both the early acquired longing for living out group solidarity in its epitome—group internment—as well as the later learned ability to manipulate the world scene through self-imposed restrictions. Thus, the purposes of the Pepcahäc festival internment are to reinforce the society's need for group solidarity by giving individuals a chance to practice it again as well as providing them with a helpful environment in which to enhance their abilities to maintain strict food and sex restrictions through which most valued life accomplishments are to be attained.

Again in the Pepcahäc festival, as in the two earlier ones, the internees are "caught" by a representative of the elders, but this time they are selected from all the graduated age classes regardless of their tribal activities and are secluded in a hut which they themselves build about 150 yards outside the village. They are supposed to remain together as a unit, performing services for the community on orders from the elders. No commandant from a higher age class of the opposing side chastises them or maintains group discipline, nor can their uncles harass them if they do not maintain reasonably high food and sex restrictions. They are adults now, and therefore achievements are their own responsibility. The apparent dangers and the "helping hands" they utilize are, as they should be, consistent with the nature of adult life. Instead of supernatural threats to be neutralized (ghosts) or personal challenges to be overcome (pollutions), the Pepcahäc are "menaced" by wasps and opposing men's festival societies (both symbolizing enemy tribes), and also by the cold of the night in its literal sense. The "helping hands," instead of being relatives, urucu paint, macaw feathers, food and sex restrictions, physical enclosure, and herbal medicines, are now each person's "ceremonial friends" who are special nonrelatives, said to be like Brazilian *compadres,* who are supposed to protect a person from almost any wordly danger.

For instance, in the Pepcahäc festival, when a wasp nest planted near the Pepcahäc hut is broken by "enemies" of the Pepcahäc troop, it is the ceremonial friends who swat down and kill *all* the escaping wasps so that none can reach the Pepcahäc membership to sting them. When the Falcon society attacks the Pepcahäc troop, it is again the ceremonial friends of the Pepcahäc who ward them off with long staffs (fig. 61). When the Pepcahäc sing through the night during the terminal period of the festival, it is again their ceremonial friends, bearing large mats on their backs, who surround the Pepcahäc on all sides in order to keep out the cold of the early morning (fig. 62). While the other defenses are against artificially created dangers, this last protection offered by the ceremonial friends of the Pepcahäc alleviates a very real discomfort (cold) and is quite effective.

It happens in this way: in the center of the circular village plaza, an old singer of the Pepcahäc songs takes his place, sitting and leaning on a carved staff. Op-

Figure 61 *The Falcon troop coming to attack the Pepcahäc (1970).*

Figure 62 *The Ceremonial Friends of the Pepcahäc troop members bear mats on their backs and surround the singing Pepcahäc to keep them warm as they sing all night (1970).*

posite him sit two young girls, the Pepcahäc troop girl associates who share the associates of former Pepcahäc festivals that took place some five to ten years earlier. The Pepcahäc troop members, supporting themselves on their carved poles, sit around the old man and the women on all sides in several concentric circles.

The singing starts so softly that no one outside the plaza can hear it, but little by little it gains momentum and volume, with all participants rocking on their staffs in a circular motion to the accentuated rhythm of the choral chanting. Eventually, it is time to stand up, and then the singing becomes even louder, well punctuated and precise, the men very low and the girls high and harmonizing in several parts. The earlier anthropologist who lived with the Canela, Curt Nimuendajú, wrote that this Pepcahäc chanting sounds like a slowly accelerating train engine. This is true, and the shrill nasal voices of the girls sound as if the locomotive were gathering speed with its whistle modulating and continuously blowing. This ensemble can be heard a number of miles outside the village and is among the best series of songs the Canela possess. (These days the Pepcahäc songs are always sung on Good Friday evening to prevent God from dying before midnight, so they have become part of a folk Catholic rite that will surely outlast the aboriginal festivals.)

The cast of the Pepcahäc performers is completed around ten o'clock when the troop members' ceremonial friends, bearing human-size mats, form a circle around the Pepcahäc to sing with them and protect them from the cold with their own body heat, conserved and held in by the mats. They sing and sway in this communal manner until dawn, with few breaks, hanging on their white staffs and rocking in unison.

It would seem, from the analysis of the Pepcahäc festival, that an adult defends himself largely through his ceremonial friends, although he still continues to do so with the help of his relatives, magical devices, food and sex restrictions, self-discipline, and purifying medicines. It should also be noted that the goals of the three festivals change from the general and long-term to the actual and immediate, that is, from group solidarity and personal development to tribal defense and personal comfort.

At least for the Cinnamon people (the Canela) it appears to be psychologically beneficial to artificially remove young persons from ordinary daily living and place them in seemingly stressful situations in order to enhance their learning acuity and even their maturation. In other cultural situations and among other peoples, such rites may also be beneficial. Can we see football, final exams, and even graduation ceremonies in this perspective?

3

See *Figure 68*.

The Language of Festivals: Celebrating the Economy

Roger D. Abrahams

F estive celebrations: resounding times and elaborated places for excited exchange, for bringing out, passing around, for giving and receiving the most vital emblems of culture in an unashamed display of produce, of the plenitude the community may boast, precisely so that the community may boast (fig. 63). The emblems explode with meanings, for they are invested with the accumulated energies and experiences of past practice. They epitomize not only the seasonal passage but the history of the culture, a history spelled out in terms native to the group and appropriate to the place and the season. They are brilliant in their simplicity, simple in their energetic displays. Today these objects, these carefully stylized products arising out of the work of the community, are collected and put on the wall or in Plexiglas display cases. We call them pretty, striking, interesting, even beautiful, thus translating their spirit into our Western aesthetic notions.

As objects made and used with care and abandon, they will contain a vital spirit and a crafted integrity that encourage us to look at them, to appreciate them in and of themselves. But though they call attention to themselves, they were not made just to be looked at. Their power arises from being used and then put away, indeed often (like a Christmas tree) unceremoniously discarded. Like the floats in the Rose Parade, they are often made for the day, out of natural ingredients, and carted off to wither and die after the event. By preserving such festive objects and putting them on display away from the big occasion, we give up this quality of the transitory, a quality the objects share with the passage of the seasons. And in this translation, we lose some of the defining character of celebration, its sense of seizing life in process; for festivals encourage us to harmonize ourselves with the changes of the season, through an identification with the seasonal passage itself. By this process, we avail ourselves of the accumulated wisdom by which we sort out the formulaic from the novel expression.

Figure 63 *Consolidated Fireworks Advertisement, U.S.A. Taken from the inside front cover of* Confectioners' Journal *for December 1892, this advertisement relates that Consolidated Fireworks, Inc., put on a dazzling pyrotechnical display from the Brooklyn Bridge in commemoration of the 400th anniversary of Columbus's discovery of America.*

The languages of festive celebrations are, in this regard, in contrast to the languages of the arts. We memorialize creative acts by exalting permanence, by valuing the created object and keeping it in as clean and enduring a condition as possible. Thus, we do not regard festive creation as we do those works of art designed and carried out in the more enduring materials.

Which does not mean that we have devalued seasonal festivals. To the contrary: we have clung to them long after our close participation in the agricultural year has passed. However, precisely because we are no longer tied so firmly, both economically and psychologically, to the yearly passage, we have been able to translate festivals into special weekend events. The techniques of observance remain the same, but their messages are launched in different contexts, and therefore they come to mean something very different to us. We continue to draw on the same vocabularies of having fun and making fun festival style: by dancing; by moving together in procession or parade; by drawing on objects and actions which are heavily layered with cultural and historical meanings; by tearing elements of the everyday world apart and then piecing and stitching them together in new forms but using old techniques; by using the times as occasions when social and economic inequalities may be given up, when gifts are given and ties are renewed, and community of spirit becomes more important than social structure. Most of all, we enter into these fantasy worlds enthusiastically because they continue to offer times out of the ordinary, times when we can enter into our experience for its own sake, not for what it produces.

Where we differ from our ancestors and our less technologically oriented contemporaries is that these festivals have become detached from our work. Thus, when the festival carries its release from the need to produce, it means something very different than it does to those who live by working with the earth and its productivity on a day-to-day basis. For ultimately, festivals are celebrations of the capacity of increase of the earth, carried on as a way of maintaining that cycle of fertility by acknowledging the powers of nature and the place of humankind in enhancing that process, on seizing it and magnifying it. When natural "things" are enlarged or prolonged, magnified and amplified in the festival, or when they are miniaturized, made into toys, gifts, souvenirs, the creative ones of the community are honoring nature while giving humanity its place in the larger scheme of things. Fertility, in such a world, is a capacity of nature enhanced by humans acting together in serious play.

If these events continue to be sentimentally connected to notions of agricultural fecundity, we, nevertheless, have trouble really experiencing with our bodies and souls what this means for agricultural people who live so close to the process of nature. It is too easy today to adopt a sniggering tone when we discuss such notions as fertility and increase, because sexuality has been eroticized in our culture, connected in so many subtle ways to the cult of radical individualism. Sexual expression has become a facet of the ethos of "doing your own thing"; as the bumper sticker puts it, "If it feels good—do it." In our agrarian past, there was simply a common-sense connection made between the fruitfulness of the earth and human sexuality.

"Fertility ceremony"—what a verbal antique the term seems, how resonant with the old progressive arguments about civilization and its benefits. But there is no getting away from the connection of festivals and even holidays with the old seasonal calendar, with its emphasis on the cycle of natural increase. In spite of the growth of our cities and the technological sense of control over nature this entails, we continue to maintain our connection with the year's passage through festive engagements that still speak out in behalf of fertility. Moreover, one might reasonably ask how different is, for instance, the dancing of giant yams, resplendent in dressed-up human finery among the Abelam of Papua-New Guinea, and the ceremony of welcome to spring with the Cherry Blossom Festival among the natives of Washington, D.C., and environs (fig. 64).

Of course, there *are* major differences, not least of which is that Washingtonians do not rely upon the cherry and its blossom for the continuation of community and culture. Moreover, the cherry blossoms have little to do with any work done in Washington (especially as they are not, on the very face of things, "native" to the area, having been given by Japan in 1906), while the yam festival directly expresses the basic economic and social life of the Abelam.

Yet at a deeper, pan-human level, these differences are not so great; perhaps the more profound message of the cherry blossoms is that in a complex world economic system, symbols of renewal do not have to be indigenous to carry an important symbolic message. Indeed, Japan's gift of such a natural and renewing cultural item does, in fact, not only bear up under the symbolic load occasioned by the arrival of spring, but also corresponds to the most enduring work of those important members of the Washington community, the diplomat and the politician. At any rate, the subject of how man devises ways of celebrating the process of nature continues to be a compelling one. All over the world, objects and figures of great power, like the largest yam and the Great Pumpkin, the holy couple of Isar and Gauri of the Rajasthani (figs. 65 and 66) and the King and Queen of the May, still fascinate us.

To understand such objects, of course, we need to know where they come from and how they are used and given meanings. There is no problem for us in recognizing the launching point of their power, for they speak out of a larger loving care that goes into their making. But to hear all of the resonances by

Figure 64 *Cherry Blossom robe, U.S.A. This robe was worn and used by the Cherry Blossom queen in the 1972 Cherry Blossom Festival in Washington, D.C.*

Figures 65, 66 *Gan-Gauri figures, Rajasthan, India. These figures play an important role in the annual Gan-Gauri festival, celebrated with great levity shortly after the spring equinox throughout India. The pair represent the holy couple of Shiva (left) and Parvati (right) who are symbols of conjugal bliss.*

which the objects achieve meaning, one must somehow enter into the worlds which produce them. In this enterprise, we are limited in so many ways: one, because of the immense geographical and cultural differences between us; and two, because we have little self-conscious understanding of our own system of celebrations, and therefore often find it difficult to translate the practices of others into terms generally understandable by our general public.

To many of us, for instance, the dressing-up of the yam among the Abelam will seem exotic, an element of a nature religion that is uncivilized. But we see the very same motives of humanizing non-human objects and, in the process, magnifying and distorting them, in a great many of our own popular cultural expressions, especially those emerging in parades. Is the revered figure of Uncle Sam on stilts in a July Fourth parade all that different from the stilt-dancers in the West African cult observance (fig. 67); and is the spirit of the yam so very dissimilar in both form and meaning from what we see on floats and other giganticized displays in Thanksgiving or New Year's Day Parades? When it comes to festivities, our repertoire of devices is consistent throughout the world. We blow things up (both by enlarging and exploding them) even as we miniaturize them. The contrary impulses of expansion and contraction, of condensation and dispersion, are often invoked simultaneously, for in festivities we may make the most challenging contrasts and contractions, just for fun—though the play is often deeply serious, of course.

We can see just such techniques of contraction and distortion clearly, even in the festivities of peoples as different from us as the Abelam. It is not only the

Figure 67
Stilt dancer, West Africa.

yam that is subjected to such magnification by them; as in the harvest festivals found in so many places throughout the world, the principles of increase are directly celebrated through the dramatic display of male and female figures, ones whose postures and physiological distortions make it ever so clear why they are to be found at the center of the festivities. As with the living, these figures enter in many ways into the exchange process which is ceremonialized on this occasion: food offerings are given them in their place of repose in the back of the *Tamberam* spirit house, and in reply, scrapings from the paint of these figures are planted with the yams, explicitly to increase fecundity and growth.

The men identify themselves with the yam planting and growth process. Yams, like men, have a soul and must be treated as such. Just as a man will be known by the yield of his fields, so too will he be known through his display of the "dressed-up" yam, especially if it is a large one. To underscore this man-yam relationship, these representatives of their crop are given beautiful decorations in the form of masks, rings, shells, and plumes.

It is just this sense of identification between "the people" and their primary natural resources that marks festivals of increase throughout the world. These celebrations of significant spots in the yearly passage bring into high display the corn, the cow, the wheat, or the walrus—whatever bounties the earth provides for a group contending for continuity. Never held in the midst of the hunt or the planting, but rather at those important times which permit a joyous, if anxious, contemplation of the procession of nature, these festivities call the people together for nothing more complicated than celebration. But it is precisely at these points of repose that the accumulated repertoire of expressive devices can be brought forth so that the message of the occasion is epitomized in each move and magnified by the very evidence of the profusion of sounds and symbols.

No events come closer to the heart of the spirit of celebration than the festivities which emerge from the passage of the year. These are the times when participants dress up for the sake of feeling new, revived, and whole (at least for the moment). Because they employ many of the same means of bringing people together in rites of passage, calendared events such as festivals often have been regarded as simply a different kind of rite. In as much as they dig into the deepest repository of shared experience and objects and actions which have become endowed with power through their past use, such feasts, festivals, and fairs are appropriately classified with rituals. The experiences are very similar, for ritual and festival times share a different sense of time and space from the everyday world; they are all betwixt-and-between experiences, ones in which the usual passage of time is stopped and the larger life-rhythms are invoked as a means of measuring our days. But these festive times are also definitively different, for unlike rites, they are not responses to the crises of the transitional events of life like birth, death, marriage, initiations, or physically moving on. Rather, they arise out of states of feeling which are, in crucial dimensions, the very opposite of crisis, for they commonly take place on the plateaus of the year when in fact nothing important occurs. If there is a sense of life-passage involved, then, it is that of a lull in the cycle of production and reproduction of the resources on which the constitution and continuity of the community have been built.

The difference has great implications for the ways in which celebration is launched; when a ritual is celebrated at a point of life-transition, like a death or a marriage, the energies of the celebrants are already raised; the ritual, at that point, simply provides a focus for those energies, and a vocabulary of significant objects and actions which detail what the occasion means, or is supposed to mean. Ritual, in such a case, provides an organizing set of principles, traditional ways of momentarily binding the opposing forces within the community and tying together the past with the present.

Festivals, on the other hand, must initiate their own energies even while they organize the celebrants for mutual fun and profit. Thus, festivals begin with a bang, literally, with loud noises produced by drums, guns, firecrackers, and other attention-grabbers. The vocabulary of festival is the language of extreme experiences through contrasts—contrasts between everyday life and these high times, and, within the events themselves, between the different parts of the occasion. The body is made into an object by dressing up, costuming, and masking—but the costumes and masks are usually made of common materials torn apart and put back together in ways that remind us constantly of the process of recombination. This splicing together and this painting up and dressing up are at the center of the creativity of these expansive events. The everyday objects of work are changed by carrying them around as nonfunctional items for display, in the process stylizing them, blowing them up, distending or miniaturizing them. The performing self, too, is expected to be playfully distorted, for everyone involved is expected to eat or drink to excess. And, of course, singing and dancing and other kinds of play are part and parcel of festive celebrations, again with the idea of overextending the self. All of these motives underscore the spirit of increase, of stretching life to the fullest, that lies at the heart of festive celebrations.

The language of these celebrations of increase emerges from the everyday ways of doing things, then, but alters them severely as it puts them into play and display. Thus, connections are maintained between ordinary life and these extraordinary times; but the intensity of feeling and experiencing is greatly altered in tune with the changes made in these objects.

For instance, to many Eskimos, the hunting of walruses and seals provides them with their basic food resources. Thus, there is a deep identification with the walrus and seal as the sources of nourishment, and also with the great hunters, the masters of the seals. During the Eskimos' time of repose, at the season of ice pack when hunting is not possible, they stylize both the hunt, through dancing, and their prey, through making things out of walrus parts, then using them in play as well as drawing on them as objects for display. Among the Nashagak, for instance, the Bladder Festival occurs during ice pack, in which all kinds of extensions and distortions of the hunt are brought to bear: not only through feasting, but by entertainments and gift-giving of such symbolic objects as stuffed animals and the walrus ivory carvings so highly valued today by collectors. The very fact that such objects are made to be displayed and given underscores the fact that these beautiful artifacts are not created just for aesthetic effect but to enter into the system of exchange of the Nashagak.

Indeed, such festivities wherever they are encountered represent special renderings of the exchange system of the community. Just as we become conscious of those with whom we need to exchange gifts, for one reason or another, at Christmas, so important exchange relationships are brought to the surface in other cultures at these betwixt-and-between times. By such means, celebrating the benefit of nature provides the occasion for the redistribution of goods throughout the community; the products of nature and of human enterprise are used to create and re-create the bonds between human and human, humanity and the gods. In a number and range of cultures, indeed, one is able to achieve distinction by sponsoring a festival, for in so doing, one who is disproportionately blessed by worldly goods makes a symbolic egalitarian statement in which the individual is subordinated to community solidarity, even as he is elevated as a Big Man, or a Cargo-Holder (as he is called in many parts of Latin America), or a Pillar of the Community. The spirit of natural increase, in this way, serves a social as well as a cultural purpose.

All of this activity produces a sense that profound movement suffuses the festive event, movement being carried out in a great number of ways but bearing the same messages in which the seasonal passage itself is at the center, and the products and proceedings of the seasons provide the impulse for the moving experience. And we continue to be fascinated by these experiences as we en-

counter them, even when they are maintained in somewhat conservative opposition to our technologically inclined value-system. Such is the case, for instance,
in the fascination so many of us have felt for the ceremonies of indigenous
Americans in the Southwest.

Of all of the indigenous American festival complexes celebrated, perhaps the
best known are those associated with the planting and harvest of corn among
the Pueblo Indians, especially the Zuñi and the Hopi. These ceremonies are
widely known because of their connection with the "Kachina dolls" which depict some of the most important actors in this yearly drama. Kachinas, whether
in full-dress or doll form, sound out the call of festive celebration by the high-
intensity contrasting colors and shapes (fig. 68), which continue to spell out the
ways in which the world was constructed "in the beginning." Though their spe-

Figure 68 *Kachina doll, Hopi,
northeastern Arizona. The
Kachinas are spirits of ancestors.
They are sometimes represented by
dolls or by masked dancers who
perform at ceremonies petitioning
for rain and fertility.*

cific interpretation differs from one community to another among the Hopi, and
though this interpretation is known to change over relatively brief periods of
time, everything in the appearance and clothing of the Kachinas reminds the
viewer of the mythic importance of the process of interpretation. The Kachinas
call attention to themselves, both in the ways in which they articulate the visual
symbols of the culture and in the ways they appear and disappear, the movements they make as they bring their special power into the proceedings, and by
the way they interact with each other and with spectators.

Everything which is worn, in fact, may call for explanation to the uninitiated.
Even the ubiquitous sashes worn by most of the two hundred and more Kachina figures can be read as a mythical text in need of explication (fig. 69). To
the Hopi of the First Mesa, for instance, the front panel is a representation of a
Broadface Kachina mask, the white zigzag below being a stylized rendering of

Figure 69   *Blanket and sash, Hopi, northeastern Arizona.*

the teeth, the two diamonds the eyes, the white lines representing the facial markings associated with various warrior gods. On the other hand, members of the communities in the Second Mesa associate the white portion with the snow of barren winter and the brocaded part, in contrast, with summer fertility. Moreover, the outer bands of black and white are associated with storm clouds, the white zigzags with lightning, and the black areas with falling rain. The central green panel, then, relates to cultivated fields, the blue to the sky, the hooked white lines to the water courses in the fields, and the diamonds represent flowers, plants, upturned soil.

In a stable culture which has been connected with the land for centuries, perhaps millennia, the accumulation of such shared meanings is hardly surprising. Moreover, those from outside the community who have witnessed these festivities have never doubted the integrity of this vision and the depth of its meaning. For the Hopi, religion places harmony and balance as its highest values; the component elements of the symbolism put this value into practice within a world-order in which everything naturally has its place.

Which is not to argue that these festivals are placid and only depict a four-cornered world under control. To the contrary, in these ceremonies, disordering and even chaos-bearing devices are constantly being brought in, often in dramatic contrast to the most order-maintaining features. Clowns, in many forms, enter into the proceedings in the most hilarious and shocking fashion, in fact, to the point that they sometimes follow the most powerful priests, parodying their moves.

There are many and deep differences between such celebrations that emerge directly from the economy of a people and the seasonal festivals into which we joyously and freely throw ourselves. Perhaps most important, among the Abelam, Eskimo, and Hopi, there is a sense that community members must enter into the event for it to be successful; it is, after all, an epitome of everything which is important to the continuity of the community. Moreover, in the ways by which these people bring together the accumulated experiences of the past in the many-layered symbolic objects and movements, they are able to celebrate their very existence even while they remind themselves of their history and their values. What a magnificent world of harmonies, both internal and external, these festivals dance out and bespeak.

Next to the mighty yam and the dancing Kachinas, the Cherry Blossom Queen and the Rose Parade seem pale stuff indeed, even while such activities continue to amplify significant natural images. The difference lies in the fact that those involved in the American events celebrate with locally grown symbols our *national* values, among which we number our freedom from the inexorable dominion of natural forces. Thus, these are optional events, shorn of their awe-inspiring dimensions, filled with images which remind us only of the beneficence of nature and the joys of coming together on such an occasion solely because we want to. There is never any question in these American festivals as to where humanity stands in relation to natural forces, for everything—including the coming of the fruits and the flowers—always appears to be under control.

Celebrations represent a choice in how we allocate play and pleasure time. Thus, joy is disengaged from our deeper human anxieties, and in this move we simultaneously lose (in engagement with the deeper forces) and gain (in our recognition of our opportunities to choose). We register this double sense by the operation of nostalgia, a sentimental backward looking that capitalizes on the old festive vocabulary of intensification: now gigantism becomes a means of advertising and promotion; and miniaturization, often of the same symbolic object, produces the memento, the souvenir, the means by which one can recapture through memory the pleasure of the experience. Such a tying together of past and present is strongly bound now to the moving experiences of individuals, ones who have come together only for the historic moment.

But the vocabularies of celebration remain essentially the same, as do most of the motives. For when we gather together, we do so to bring out our best and to bring out our worst, sometimes simultaneously. Festivals have always been moments of high display, indeed, even times of crass materialism. In them we extend ourselves by dressing up or by wearing an unaccustomed costume; either way we get things purposely out of proportion. We overextend ourselves, expecting that everybody else will, too, and without exciting any sense of obligation beyond the event. We rewrite the rules, giving special permission to turn things over, for we gain a new power of action by wearing beggars' rags or regal robes. Either way, we win.

The image of the costume of rags is an especially useful one in understanding how the vocabulary of festival operates. For one of the most common ways we have of symbolizing shared life is to conceive of each community, each culture, as if it were a fabric, one with various strands woven together, therefore subject to being torn asunder or ripped apart by forces of adversity or progress. Festivals of increase seize on such an image and (in the spirit of self-conscious testing and reaffirmation) propose ways of tearing up the fabric and yet maintaining its integrity. Such is the implicit idea in flags, in fact, a point made explicitly in the old-fashioned Fourth of July speeches in which the "meaning" of Old Glory is explicitly discussed. The American flag, of course, is known also as "the stars and stripes" and "the red, white, and blue." These alternative names not only describe the salient features of the object but focus on the assigned meanings of these contrasts of color and shape, summarizing American history (in the progression from the thirteen colonies to the fifty assembled states), symbolizing our values (the colors), and epitomizing our highest national ideal (out of the many, the one). In such circumstances, the integrity of the objects speaks for itself and must be protected as the object is celebrated. The flag must not touch the ground, for instance, especially during the most ceremonial moments, and it must be handled with the greatest care.

But look how it can be torn apart and reassembled in other contexts on July Fourth, for use as bunting for the speakers' platforms, as the motif of car and bike decorations, and so on. Yet it took a countercultural festive environment to remind us of the subversive potential implicit in this process of display, when, in the nineteen sixties, the flag was put to other, profane uses—as when it was used to mend people's old clothes. Suddenly, the implications of its having been pieced together was brought to the fore, and under such new festival conditions it was reimagined as a rags-and-patches object.

Such a use of the flag created intense reactions because, among other things, the rags-and-patches approach to cloth and costume symbolizes the outcast and the outrageous festival characters, the wild man, the tramp, and, especially, the clown. Indeed, in a great many places throughout the world, the costume of *motley*—the one made up of such thrown-together, highly contrasted shapes, colors, and textures—characterizes the play as that of the madman, the fool, the bumpkin. The player, like his costume, appears to be always on the verge of coming apart, going crazy, going wild.

The flag, by speaking out with so many voices simultaneously, is a common material rendering of the idea of the fabric of community. As such it makes an interesting contrast with another pieced-together object within our culture, the quilt. No object is more redolent of the message of endurance through significant labor in harmony with nature, or is more at the center of our sentiments, than the quilt. It maintains this imaginative hold for a number of reasons: it is made for family use and is passed down within the family; it is a forcefully dynamic, ordered object that visually depicts the dance of life; and we associate the object with the process by which (we assume) it was made—that ideal cooperative community occasion, *the quilting bee* (fig. 70).

Such country objects and images maintain for us representations of exuberance in repose, portraying a sense of comfort in continuity, of vitality through a display of significant movement carried on within a circumscribed and compre-

Figure 70   *Neighborhood women gather for a quilting bee (1946).*

hended, visually rendered world. In our culture, there is no simpler and more elegant statement of this complex of motives than that geometric contradiction, the squared circle, the circled square, a figure we see rendered not only in the quilt but in the square dance, and, rendered larger, in the topical plan for the village commons and meeting houses in colonial New England, and its symbolic descendants, town squares and county courthouses. In this figure is reflected the simple ideal of the agrarian world order, one which seems to arise out of the interlocking passage of seasonal times, the seasons themselves marked out by the disposition of energies and the allocations of tasks on the farm and in the fields. This is a four-cornered world, one bounded spatially and temporally, in which one's place within the scheme is unquestioned, even in the moments of greatest upset.

The patchwork quilt is a simple but elegant rendering of this agrarian ideal. In the minds of those who make and use them, and of those who regard them simply as quaint relics of our country past, they are attached to the passage of life and of the seasons. They represent family and friends, reconstructions of the fragments of life as lived, pieced together by hand in the company of helpful others. That most quilts are not, in fact, put together at bees matters little—for the fiction of the homogeneous, cooperative community-in-practice is central to our structure of sentiments. If quilts are actually pieced and framed at home and in private, generally they still carry a public and ceremonial message that reads very much like the wedding vows and the baptismal service, a message of continuity in process. Each square of a patchwork quilt visually projects the life-enhancing endeavor, a patching together process that breaks previous orders only to restate them, now with the concentrated vigor of a personal undertaking in the service of kin and community. This is public work of the most private sort, a familiar object which is both useful and beautiful, which belongs in the home but which is also made "for show." In this capacity, quilts are entered into competition at county fairs and are sold at country stores, thus becoming counters on the country exchange.

The country images on quilts—their careful balance in symmetry—evoke the seasons and their four-cornered world. In a more moving rendition, we find the same kind of clean and balanced figure in square dances. Just as the quilt has its repeated pattern, the square dance *figures* actively circle the square. The *set* (four couples facing inward to each other) is put into motion by the assigned figures by the caller, who breaks the stability of the square, sending the males in one direction, the females another, only to find them both arriving back *home* at the end of each figure. What joy is contained in this balance, this breaking and reestablishing of the square!

A similar image is presented to us in the terms used in what was once called "The Great American Pastime:" baseball. Here the square is poised on its point to make a *diamond,* the four corners strongly marked as bases. The valued movement, of course, is to circle the bases, again ideally ending up at *home*.

Circling the square (or diamond), then, is our special, old-fashioned, playful way of testing boundaries, the orders of life, even while we affirm them.

But the fullest statement of these country ways in festive form surely is the *county fair*. Here each year the products and processes of farm work are cleaned up and transported to the fairground for purposes of display and competition. No occasion more fully projects images of increase and plenitude in their ideal forms. For here the animals, fruits, and vegetables are presented to us in cleaned-up and cooked-up form. Competitive show enters into the occasion by the judging of the biggest and the best, thus drawing our attention to the bounties of the harvest.

Americans were predominantly agrarian people until recently; our notions of festival and increase emanate from observances still carried out at those points in the agricultural year in which the work of the season has been translated, by tradition, into the work of the gods and maintained in the notion of *holiday*. And so it occurs throughout the world wherever an economy is based on the yield of the earth. With us, *custom* and *tradition* are translated into a sentimental backward look, which we call, ambivalently, *old-fashioned* ways. Almost by sentiment alone, certain practices and values are maintained long after the particulars of the agricultural economy have lost their hold on us. In fact, at the center of this sentiment is a simplified version of farming; no longer is work involved, but only the fairs, games, festivals, and of course, the holiday dinners and picnics that remain to remind us how to live by the seasons. Indeed, what does "season" mean to most Americans but, on the one hand, the time when those holiday feasts are served, and, on the other, the segment of the year when a specific sport is played?

Many of our most powerful holiday symbols continue to speak in terms of the processes of life, of death and rebirth, of maturing, reaping, and lying fallow. As a country made up of groups that come from a variety of traditions, so many of which have contributed to our symbolic repertoire, we often have to think about the connections of our most popular and powerful symbols and the messages they carry with the agrarian yearly round. It takes us a while, for instance, to recognize the Christmas symbols we hold in common: the Yule log, the candles, the star (light in the midst of the dark season) and the holly, the mistletoe, the poinsettia, the Christmas tree and wreath (enduring growth and even flowering and fructifying in the midst of winter). Indeed, having so many symbols derived from so many different traditions provides a stirring lesson in the organizing powers of festivities and our capacity for using them to bring diverse peoples together.

But to underscore only such homely traditions, our four-square observances, is to ignore other projections of ourselves in festive form. For though we do cling to many kinds of clean, old-fashioned observances, we also have innumerable ways of celebrating that face forward and emphasize the new. In fact, our holidays have two sides to them: the old practices that are commonly carried out in the home or some homelike place, and the emergent, the glittering new, which is, as often as not, a street affair. What could better embody and elicit the holiday spirit (no matter what holiday) than a parade? Here the self-made groups, the voluntary associations of the community, celebrate their sense of coming together just for the fun of it, by developing a costume theme and building a moving form of display that signals to the spectator what this theme and its message are. Here the emphasis is on the future, a fact made clear in the choice of themes and spelled out in the signs. As opposed to the enclosing moves of, say, the square-dance, or even one of the ancestors of the parade, the procession, the parade is open-ended, beginning in one place and ending up in another by design (fig. 71).

The parade is our most dramatic technique for announcing the beginning of some major form of celebration: the Christmas season, the New Year, the July Fourth ceremonies. But the increase it has come to celebrate often reflects the technological as much as the agricultural side of the economy. Parades have easily become advertisements for business, much as they did on the frontier, where they were hastily organized to show off the new goods that had just hit town. The pageant, then, becomes a symbolization of the forward march of commerce and industry. Festive intensification in such cases is rendered gigantically, with the immense floats, the amplified size and sounds of the marching band, and the skyscraping balloon representations of animals and comic characters.

The language of holiday and festival maintains, then, a repertoire of symbolic images and movements in which the power of the most typical kinds of things may be condensed and then exploded, or cut up and dispersed; it is not simple chance that makes not only the parade but the lowly firecracker and the bal-

Figure 71 New York City,
January 31, 1981: Tickertape
parade on Broadway to welcome
the hostages freed from Iran.

loon, the wrapped present, the cornucopia, the piñata, the stuffed turkey, and
Santa's stuffed bag the most powerful and pervasive images of our holidays.
These embody the essence of holiday wholeness on the one hand, then the
breaking, cutting, exploding that allow everyone to share the now-freed energies and resources. Feasts and festivals continue to be, perhaps above all else, a
technique of celebrating plenty by engaging in a spotlighted display and a sharing of goods and of energies with all of the community. They are the times in
which some statement of significant wholeness is made in large or in small, in
parade or on the family dinner table. Thus, we witness the continuing importance of "The Bird," the stuffed turkey at Thanksgiving or Christmas, a symbolic
object which is capable of being presented whole and then cut to pieces, then
shared and consumed by the family, each member of which must then become
stuffed individually to induce a state of body and mind shared by all.

To understand the festive behavior and seasonal celebrations of other peoples, then, we must recognize how our own festive occasions continue to draw
on these most archaic and basic motives and means of having fun seriously. For
though we are predominantly a highly mobile city people, we have maintained
innumerable occasions for celebration from our country past. To be sure, we

have changed them a great deal, and they fit into our lives very differently from the way they did in simpler times. Moreover, we have developed new forms of celebration, ones which reflect alternative ways of proclaiming and maintaining our relationships with others and with the world around us. But in certain respects, these festivities, and the spirit of life-enhancement that has always been their source of inspiration, are of ever-greater importance to us. Our calendar has become more rigid as we schedule in our weekends, holidays, and vacations; but the festival, the fair, and the other public celebrations that are reenacted each year have become the high points of our collective lives, events we plan for and look forward to. Moreover, we sneak all kinds of other festive occasions onto our calendars by making such a to-do about birthdays and anniversaries. If any cultural practice most strongly marks American life today, it must be the events that celebrate nothing less than the continuity and vitality of humans in groups. To be sure, the groups are as often as not brought together voluntarily and only for the celebration. In this we have departed greatly from our ancestral practices, and in many ways we feel a sense of loss in this. But with the growth in leisure time, we find new families, new communities of interest all the time, ones with which we can celebrate.

The Weight of My Name Is a Mountain of Blankets: Potlatch Ceremonies

Stanley Walens

T he peoples of the Northwest Coast lived along a stretch of rugged coast some 1,200 miles long, from Yakutat Bay in Alaska southward to the northwest corner of Washington state. Wherever the ceaseless action of the sea eroded a protected beach out of the cliffs which rise hundreds of feet above the water, or wherever the action of tide or torrent deposited a sheltered strip of sand, they built their villages, a thin wedge of humanity between the forces of the sea and the darkness of the forest (fig. 72). There they developed a unique culture whose beauty and vibrancy never cease to amaze those who learn about it.

The dramatic, powerful, and complex ceremonies—called potlatches—of these peoples are among the most spectacular in North America. Potlatches were involved with the maintenance and orderly transfer of rank and power and the distribution of wealth that was an essential part of the responsibilities of a person of rank. The amount of wealth that was distributed at a potlatch could be tremendous and might take years of hard work and judicious saving to amass. At one Kwakiutl potlatch the chief not only fed several hundred guests during the two-week-long ceremony but distributed to them 18,000 Hudson's Bay blankets (which cost $.50 each), 700 carved silver bracelets, a dozen canoes valued at 3,000 blankets each, sewing machines, outboard motors, pots and pans, clothing, hundreds of sacks of flour, sugar, fruit, and other food, a large amount of cash, and a copper worth 12,000 blankets. At some potlatches, chiefs gave away everything they owned, even the boards with which the walls and roofs of their houses were built.

It must be realized, however, that, whether a great amount or a small amount of wealth was distributed—and potlatches of the splendor just described were by far the exception—the peoples of the coast had a well-defined philosophy about the nature of wealth and the necessity of giving it away. Furthermore, if we look at potlatches in terms of profit and loss we miss the very basis on which they were predicated: it was the purpose of the potlatch, not to make a profit, but to lose wealth for the benefit of others, to obtain spiritual purity through philanthropy. It was not enough just to distribute wealth; it was important that it be distributed in the correct way. It was not extravagance that they admired, it was the ability to distribute great amounts of wealth to everyone according to their rank and station.

The distribution of wealth had its foundation in the cosmology of the Northwest Coast Indians. Like other North American Indian groups, they envisioned the world as a place of constant flux and motion, like a great river ceaselessly flowing. Those features of the world which seemed permanent—the mountains, the inlets and fjords, and the beaches—were created by Raven to give people a place from which to observe the world in motion. To distribute one's wealth was to be in harmony with the world's flux, to contribute to this cosmic motion.

Every Northwest Coast group had a myth about how the world as we know it came into existence, about how generosity, reciprocity, sacrifice, and moral responsibility were first created. Perhaps the most famous of these is the story (found in different versions) about how Raven stole the sun. At the beginning of

Figure 72   *The Haida village of Skidegate. Detail of a photograph taken at the end of the nineteenth century.*

time, the sun, like all the world's treasures, had been kept in a box by a man. Raven, through magical means, impregnated the daughter of this man and was born to the man as his grandson. The joy Raven brought to the old man was so great that when Raven asked for the man's possessions as playthings, they were given to him one by one. Finally Raven asked for the sun as a plaything, and as soon as he got it he changed from a boy into his true form and flew away with the sun in his beak. The sun was hot and burned Raven's feathers, turning them from their primal white into their present black; Raven dropped the sun in the sky, where it can be seen today, a great treasure for the entire world.

In this myth is encapsulated the entire moral basis of generosity and exchange in Northwest Coast society. Raven presents the first gift—he gives himself as a child, the greatest of all treasures. His grandfather reciprocates by giving Raven (though not altogether willingly) those treasures he had previously kept only for himself and which now benefit everyone. Raven gives himself as a sacrifice for the world, sacrificing his beauty for the benefit of the rest of the world. Raven's black feathers now remind us that we are part of that covenant, that we must give, must sacrifice. Nothing—not wealth, not beauty, not power, not status, not life itself—can be kept. Everything must be given away. Indeed, as in the myth, it is to one's descendants that everything a person owns must and will be given.

The pattern of food and wealth distribution at a potlatch was necessitated by the particular nature of the Northwest Coast environment. The Northwest Coast was a land uniquely rich in natural resources. The forests grew as densely and luxuriantly as those of the tropics, providing the Indians with the materials they needed for their homes, their canoes, the baskets and boxes in which they stored their food and material possessions, their clothing, and their sacred objects. The animals of the forest—bear, deer, elk, mountain goats, and so forth— were part of the Northwest Coast larder, but it was fishing and sea-mammal hunting which formed the basis of the Northwest Coast economy. Salmon could be found in virtually every stream along the coast and provided the staple food of the native diet, but cod, halibut, herring, candlefish, octopus, and a score of other varieties of fish, as well as sea mammals and shellfish, were also important.

However, though food was plentiful, the rugged topography of the Northwest Coast limited the number of places where human access to food was possible. There were only a limited number of places where a person might stand to spear passing fish, only a limited number of river mouths with geography that was conducive to effective fishing with nets, only a limited number of shallow spots along streams where it was possible to set up weirs. Furthermore, the abundance of any given animal varied from season to season, year to year, and area to area, although these fluctuations were somewhat offset by the methods of food preservation which allowed the Indians to stockpile large amounts of dried fish.

The limited number of spots where food could be collected required the Indians to develop an economic system which combined the most efficient gathering of food by a small number of people with a widespread distribution of the food. The division of the tribe into small units, which was necessary for efficient resource exploitation, was achieved by making the composite household an autonomous economic, political, and ceremonial unit. A household might consist of twenty to forty people, related by membership in a common lineage or clan; a village might consist of eight to ten households. The ownership of resources resided in a household head who was often the head of the lineage or clan as well, and under whose aegis the members of a household worked together to gather resources at places that belonged to their clan (fig. 73; *see also* fig. 111).

On the household heads—often called chiefs—fell the responsibility of organizing not only the collecting and distributing of food but a large number of ceremonial and religious responsibilities as well. As executor of his clan's estate, the chief had the responsibility of displaying the rituals of his clan and distributing its wealth. It was the chief who decided what dances must be performed and by whom, when to place a new totem pole (which by its images recapitulated an important myth of his clan's past), when new songs or prayers must be composed, a new mask carved, or a potlatch given. The chief stood as representative of his clan, as ambassador both to other human groups and to the animals as well.

A household's rights of access to resources were jealously guarded and formed an important part of the patrimony a chief passed down to his heirs. Indeed, a great deal of the public ceremony in Northwest Coast society centered

Figure 73 *Tlingit people in ceremonial potlatch costume, about 1900. The complexity of the symbolism of status and identity is immediately apparent.*

around the establishing or maintenance of the legitimacy of a chief's claims to resources, the acting out of his ritual and spiritual responsibilities toward both the animals being collected and the humans to whom they are being given as food, and the orderly succession of a chief's heirs to his rank and to the responsibilities attendant upon that rank.

It is not surprising, then, that the peoples of the coast saw their world as one where myriad forces were at work, all influencing food, and humans' ability to obtain food. Every animal, every human, every clan, had its own needs, its own demands, its own hunger. All these conflicting needs and demands needed to be balanced against one another, to be directed for the greatest mutual benefit. It was through ritual that this balance was obtained, that the competitive forces which could have brought about the destruction of the universe were tamed. It was a delicate balance; the slightest misweighing could send the world back into the chaos of selfishness and conflict from which Raven had delivered mankind. The judicious balancing of one's needs against one's obligations was a difficult and complex task.

Indeed mutual dependence—the idea that one's life was securely in the hands of others—was so important an idea that some tribes made a religious proscription against any clan's performing some of the most important rites of passage of its own members. Among the Tlingit and Haida, for example, members of each moiety (half the tribe) were solely responsible for the birth and funeral ceremonies, the housebuilding and pole raising, of the other moiety. Thus only through cooperation of the entire tribe could the proper succession to rank be accomplished, and the order of the world maintained.

Potlatches occurred at all points of social stress, wherever society might fall apart because of some change. At these times, the order and control of the ceremony, with its reassertion of mutual dependence, was meant to reestablish the order and control of the universe as a whole. Northwest Coast peoples were so aware of their central role in maintaining world order that their very names for themselves—"Providing Smoke for the World," "People of the Raven," "First People"—signify the centrality of ritual in their lives.

Perhaps the clearest demonstration of the Northwest Coast idea that human sociality and morality tame the potentially destructive forces of the universe can be found in the Hamatsa (Cannibal) ritual among the Kwakiutl. Here an initiate into the Hamatsa society returned to the world of humans after a sojourn in the world of the spirit-being, Man Eater. Man Eater was a symbol of the endpoint of time and the ultimate destruction of the universe; he was a black hole of hunger, the power of his desire pulling everything toward a final dissolution. The Hamatsa initiate threatened to bring this destruction to the human world to which he had returned. He was tamed only when his fellow humans pledged to uphold the covenants they had made with the animals and the spirit-beings and to provide these beings with the requisite sacrifices of their wealth and possessions. Indeed, since wealth was an agreement to sacrifice oneself during one's lifetime and to provide the spirit-beings with a properly treated body upon one's death, a person who owed his life to others also owed them his death.

The idea of death as sacrifice, and wealth as a symbol of death, lies at the basis of Northwest Coast religion. Like many other Native American peoples, the peoples of the Northwest Coast believed that success in hunting was achieved not only by technical mastery of hunting skills but by the maintenance of a ritual relationship between a hunter and his prey. This relationship placed humans and animals in a web of mutual dependency: humans survived only because animals sacrificed themselves for human welfare, in return for which humans treated animals' bodies with respect and performed rituals which insured the reincarnation of the animals. Knowledge of these rituals and possession of the songs, dances, prayers, and paraphernalia which comprised them were the most precious treasures of Northwest Coast culture. It was through performing these rituals and distributing to other people some of the food which one had obtained that the social and political status of a chief and his associates was legitimized. No event of importance in a person's life occurred without the accompaniment of a ceremonial in which a person displayed, performed, validated, and revitalized in a public display the all-important ritual links between himself and his animal benefactors.

It was in myth that these convenants between humans and animals were set forth. Myths are sacred narratives of how things became as they are, of how chaos became cosmos, of how amorality became morality, of how human beings came into existence and came to accept the burden of moral responsibility and sacrifice placed upon them. Myths provide paradigms and structures for living; they present mysteries which put people into direct contact with the powerful forces of the cosmos.

Every aspect of Northwest Coast life was imbued with myth and with ceremony—the representation of myth through motion. The display of a family's or individual's myths, of mythically bestowed treasures, rights, statuses, and wealth, and the portrayal of a group's ancestral heritage, were inextricable parts of every social occasion. No meal began without the recital of a myth or sacred song, no feast could be held without the ritual acknowledgment of the beneficence of the animals upon which one was dependent, no change in status could occur without the revalidation of the myths about how that status came to exist. The moral person, in telling the myths of his family's past, indicated that he had accepted the burden of that past.

The celebration of the glory of a clan's mytho-historic heritage can be found everywhere in Northwest Coast life. Every object of ritual importance—canoes, boxes, bowls, houses, poles, chairs, clothing, spoons, bracelets—is decorated with images of the clan's mythic ancestors, with depictions of incidents in the clan's history, with images of the cosmos and of man's place within it. In some tribes, even people's bodies were tattooed with images of the clan's ancestral spirit-beings. These images, called crests by anthropologists, were symbols of the beings from whom a clan traced its origin and the origin of its possessions.

Any object which had been decorated with a crest was imbued with the vital forces of the spirit world and was considered to be alive. The spirits could act through these objects; these objects acted as pathways for power to travel from the spirit world to the human world. Because of the power they possessed and controlled, these objects were important parts of rituals and were used to contain and direct power in the ritual.

The right to wear or display these crests, to perform rituals relating to them, and even to pronounce their names, was a highly valued prerogative. Many of these images, as befits an image that deals with the transformation of the mythic world into the modern world, display symbols of change and transformation, mingling human and animal forms in ways which show that the two are manifestations of each other, locked in an inextricable mesh of social relations and ritual responsibilities, of shared identities and destinies. Through the display of crests, Northwest Coast ceremonies provided for the expansion of the self and the group beyond their social boundaries and in doing so linked humans to each other and to the vital forces of the cosmos. Rituals demonstrate the place and purpose of human action in the universe as a whole. Rituals make opposites equivalent: a local house becomes the entire universe, a human becomes a cosmic being, the past of myth becomes manifest in the rituals of the present.

This expansion of the self and the group to equivalence with the cosmos is achieved by the close identification of individuals with their ancestors and with the spirit-beings whom they portray in dance and embody in this world. In Northwest Coast thought, a person is only one component of a complex being which consists of that person's body, the person's sacred name, a spirit-being's body, and a composite soul shared by human and spirit-being together. The sharing of a single soul enables a human to manifest his spirit self simply by changing his visage and the appearance of his body. In order to become a spirit-being, then, a person merely brings the cosmic power of the spirits into his house and then puts on a mask depicting the spirit-being. Then, with the ordered poetry of speech and dance, he carves out of space and time the ordered beauty of the cosmos.

The shared representations of self and transformation are an important aspect of Northwest Coast crest design. Depictions of an animal or spirit-being show the human soul residing in the being's chest, or between the ears as if it were a frontlet (a forehead mask). Indeed, humans wore frontlets on ritual occasions when they were not to be transformed into a spirit-being but still needed to represent the nascent spirit component of their rank. The boxes in which treasures were stored often show images of transformation and the mingled identities of spirit-beings and humans. This constant representation of transformation is not surprising once we realize that these items were meant to recapitulate myths and that myths are about transformations.

The shared identities and transformations of the self which are so essential a part of Northwest Coast thought and ritual are depicted in several ways. On totem poles and house posts, which recapitulate key myths of a clan's past, transformations may be represented merely by a linear progression of images, or by a complex interweaving of the bodily parts of the different figures as they change from one to another. Some tribes used mechanical masks that can be opened and closed to conceal or reveal the altered identities of a single being (fig. 74).

Transformation is frequently shown by depicting different aspects of a single identity on the opposite sides of an object. For example, a Haida box shows the spirit-being Cirrus Clouds on one face of the box and the spirit-being Eagle on the other. The shared human soul of the two spirits is shown in both its spirit

Figure 74 *A Kwakiutl mechanical transformation mask, partially open. The mask depicts the head of a raven, flying scavenger, inside that of a wolf, a land-based predator. An image of the wolf, painted in relief, is visible on the inside of the outer case.*

form, located beneath the mouths of the spirit-beings, and its human form, represented in profile to either side of the faces of the two spirit-beings. On the sides of this box, the Bear crest of the clan is represented in its two forms as well, first as animal and then as human.

The way in which symbolic oppositions are obviated through ritual is well shown by this Haida box (fig. 75). Cirrus Clouds and Eagle are opposite to each other in that Cirrus Clouds are the prevalent clouds of the Northwest Coast summer, and Eagle, who flies in cumulus clouds, is the lord of the winter sky. Eagle and Cirrus Clouds stand in mutual opposition to Bear, who is a land creature most active in the summer, and to humans, who are land creatures whose rituals are more frequent in the winter. All these oppositions, these separate identities, are linked into a single coherent entity, all their differences obviated and combined into a box for the storing of powerful sacred objects.

Another way in which transformation of the self is shown is through the static depiction of the very moment of equilibrium between the two components of the self. One of the most striking examples of this type of image is found on a frontlet on which the human identity of Eagle is seen emerging from the bird's chest at the same moment as Eagle is losing his avian identity (fig. 76). Eagle's face has already become humanoid, and the beaky avian component of the self is represented as a tongue about to be pulled into Eagle's mouth. As the wearer of this frontlet moved and danced, firelight reflecting off the haliotis shells surrounding the image threw different parts of the image into shadow or light so that it would seem constantly to change.

Perhaps the most cogent image of transformation occurs on the Raven rattle (fig. 77). Here we see Raven carrying a dead man toward the afterlife on his back. The man's vital force, seen as a red bridge like a tongue, has been cap-

Figure 75 *Storage chest, Haida, Skedans, Queen Charlotte Islands, British Columbia. Large chests were used to store family valuables such as masks, coppers, Chilkat blankets, and whistles and rattles. Carved and painted with family emblems, chests like this one were handed down from generation to generation. Because the corners of this chest are dovetailed (not a native joining technique), we may speculate that a Chinese carpenter did the initial construction work.*

tured by a frog, a symbol of life, which is itself being captured by a crane, the symbol of death. In the Raven's beak is a small red object representing both the sun, which was Raven's gift to mankind, and the man's soul, which is man's reciprocal gift to the spirits. On the belly of Raven is the face of the shared soul of Raven and mankind, its beak recurved into its own mouth in a cogent symbol of the cycle of reincarnation. The use of the Raven rattle in ritual not only reaffirms mankind's covenant with Raven, but through its intertwined images of life, death, and the cycle of rebirth, the rattle directs these vast forces in a specific cyclic pattern of transformation.

One of the most important images of the autocosmic self in Northwest Coast ritual is found in coppers. These plaques were one of the most treasured of ritual possessions, and their exchange, sale, and sometimes destruction at potlatches were events of the greatest significance. Through their symbolism, coppers link man to the entire universe. Their shape recapitulates that of the body and soul of a being, making equivalent the body of the chief, the body politic of his clan, and the bodies and souls of all the animals which the clan has captured. The color of the copper symbolizes the red of salmon flesh on which mankind survives; the menstrual blood which is a mother's first gift to her unborn children; the color of the sun, which was Raven's first gift to mankind; and the fire by which man both cooks his food as the myths require him to and burns his wealth and his corpses so that they become food for the spirit-beings.

The chief was the representative of his house, and his person was the nexus by which the many varied components, both spirit and human, which comprise his own and his group's identity, became united. The way in which this was

***Figure* 76** *A chief's frontlet, probably Haida but collected among the Kwakiutl, showing the instant of transformation when all the component identities of a single being are in equilibrium.*

***Figure* 77** *Raven rattle, Haida, Masset, Queen Charlotte Islands, British Columbia. This rattle was used by chiefs and high-ranking members of the community to punctuate their speech and actions. Most dancers of the northern group (Tlingit, Haida, Tsimshian) held the rattles upside down (with the Raven's breast up) lest they come to life and fly away, as a legendary Raven rattle once did.*

achieved in ritual was evidenced by the chiefs' ceremonial costumes. Every piece of a chief's clothing and adornment—from frontlet or crest hat, downward through facial painting, jewelry, yokes and collars, robes and tunics, kilts and leggings—might be decorated with a crest design. The vertical serialization of these images turned the chief into a living analogue of a totem pole, encapsulating his and his clan's ancestral heritage. At ceremonials, where the chief stood as symbol of his house, the carved speaker's staff he held, which symbolized his authority, was analogous to the house's totem pole, from which the house derived its authority.

One item of chief's costume—the Chilkat Tlingit blanket (fig. 78), a ceremonial robe adopted by many other Northwest Coast tribes—provides perhaps the clearest example of the portrayal of the chief as avatar of both the human and spirit components of a single identity. These blankets show, in highly stylized form, the image of a crest animal as if it were on a box, and as if the four sides and lid of the box had been flattened into a single plane. A person wearing such a blanket became analogous to a treasure stored in a box. The sharing of a single soul by both crest animal and human was indicated by placing the image of the blanket's soul—seen as a humanoid face in the center of the blanket, which represented the lid of the box—over the place in the human chest where the human soul resides. When a chief wearing a Chilkat blanket is seen from the front, then, we see his social, human self, with his nascent spirit identity shown by the image on his frontlet or crest hat; from the chief's rear we see only his supernatural alter ego, which has its human identity depicted as a frontlet between its ears. Thus, as a chief wearing such a blanket moves and turns, he is continually being transformed before our eyes.

Through transformation the participants in the Northwest Coast ritual became more than just individuals, and the dimensions of their actions transcended the limitations of everyday space and time. Each chief became the representative of his house and his house's spiritual authority, linked to the ancestral past by costume and to cosmic forces by paraphernalia such as Raven rattles and speaker's staffs. The careful placement of hosts and guests on mats around the room reproduced the geographical distribution of the world's villages—the social map recapitulating the cosmic map. The ceremonial house itself stood for the universe as a whole, its various rooms differentiating the various parts of the world, its vertical beams representing the axis mundi which links the human realm to the spirit realm, its great horizontal beam standing for the vault of the sky and the Milky Way. Thus, once the universe was contracted to the size of the ceremonial house whose boundaries had been expanded until they were coterminous with the entire universe, the actions of distribution that occurred at feasts recapitulated the process of distribution at a cosmic level.

In short, then, the potlatch was not, as it has so often been described, just a prestige contest. Analysis of the details of potlatches shows, on the evidence of the emphasis on protocol and the careful enactment of myths and dances, that the structure of potlatches and feasts was intended to recapitulate the structure of the universe as a whole. The moral person, in telling the myths of his family's past and in distributing the wealth of which he was merely temporary custo-

Figure 78 *Chilkat blanket, Tlingit, Alaska. The Chilkat blanket was part of Northwest Coast ceremonial costume. It takes its name from the Tlingit subgroup responsible for its popularization through trade. For Haida and Tlingit peoples, a complete outfit on ceremonial occasions included tunic, apron, and leggings, often woven in the Chilkat style, as well as frontlet, clan hat, and Raven rattle or staff. The blanket was worn around the shoulders.*

dian, indicated that he had accepted the burden of that past, the burden of the covenant which says that he must dance, sing the sacred songs, give away his material possessions and even, ultimately, his very life for the benefit of other beings. The moral person dedicated his life, in some ways sacrificed himself— through his wealth, which was the symbol of his self—for the benefit of others, just as animals sacrificed themselves for the benefit of mankind. Northwest Coast ceremonies celebrated the relevance of the past to the actions of the present; they linked the political and social structure of the group to the innermost spiritual values of the members of the group, especially that of self-sacrifice, as expressed and refracted through cosmology; and they presented, in a cohesive poetic statement, the universal conflicts and dilemmas of human life and the nature and purpose of human existence.

Chamula Carnival: The "Soul" of Celebration

Priscilla Rachun Linn

With verve and zest the Tzotzil-speaking Maya Indians of San Juan Chamula commemorate a turbulent history in their yearly pre-Lenten carnival celebration.* The Chamula ritually and symbolically re-create an energetic martial atmosphere of wars, rebellions, and conquests. These upheavals have scarred the lives of their ancestors and remain vividly alive in the rich oral tradition of the Chamula, who have survived for centuries as corn farmers in the central highlands of Chiapas, Mexico.

Despite the apparent focus on social strife and disorder, Chamula Carnival does not grant its religious celebrants—members of a volunteer hierarchy who change office each year—the license and freedom often associated with carnivals in other cultures. Traditionally carnivals celebrate disorder and create an accepted time to run riot. Citizens who are usually responsible ridicule one another and gleefully or maliciously shatter social decorum. While certain elements of disorder do emerge in Chamula Carnival, I believe another theme prevails: the struggle the Chamula undergo to create order in the face of both social and personal disruption. The disruption forms one element of this struggle, and the attempt to balance forces out of control, another. I will show here that the struggles dramatized in carnival, one of which has been illustrated in the *Celebration: A World of Art and Ritual* exhibition at the Smithsonian Institution's Renwick Gallery, reflect the very struggles the Chamula face in controlling their passionate souls so that they may survive in peace and health.

---

* I would like to thank the Doherty Foundation for Latin American Studies for a grant awarded in 1970–71, and the Harvard Chiapas Project for a grant in 1972, which made this fieldwork possible. I would also like to thank Professor Evon Z. Vogt, leader of the Harvard Chiapas Project, for making facilities available during the course of this study and for his generous guidance and support throughout all phases of this research.

Carnival, or, The Festival of the Games

The Chamula call carnival *Tahimoltik*, or "The Festival of the Games," with the name bearing connotations of competition and play.

As a religious event, carnival celebrates the young warriorlike Christ of Chamula myth, who fled in a deadly game from pursuit by evil demons. They finally captured and killed him on a cross by thrusting a lance into his side. In Chamula myth and in Catholic teaching, Christ died to rise up again later. Similarly, the Chamula have repeatedly resurrected a cultural identity throughout violent periods of war and death.

As a political commemoration, carnival links this divine passion of Christ to major historical disorders, such as Cortés's conquest of Mexico in 1524; the French intervention of 1861–67; the Caste War of Chiapas, an Indian revolt which the Chamula began in 1867 and ended with Ladino (mestizoized Mexican) suppression in 1870; the nineteenth-century fight over boundaries between Chiapas and Guatemala; and the Mexican Revolution of 1910 and 1917 (Bricker, 1973:84–85).

The symbols of war appear throughout the ritual and the verbal games of carnival, but never lead to chaos or tumultuous disruption during this celebration. For example, the Town Crier of Chamula loudly proclaims the themes of war and conquest during the fiesta. In this proclamation, which remains the same year after year, three "cavaliers" (who are historically either conquerors or soldiers) journey from Mexico City to San Cristobal de las Casas (the Ladino town closest to Chamula) bearing symbols of military conquest—flags, drums, trumpets, fireworks, cannons, fifes, and bugles. These objects figure prominently in carnival today. The cavaliers bring a Ladina consort with them and have sex with her in the woods, then return eating foods with strong sexual connotations—toffee, sweet squash, and blood sausage. Although the proclamation sends the ritual celebrants off and running at set intervals throughout the fiesta, as if in military attack, its effect brings humor rather than fear to its audience, for it ridicules Ladino lust and impropriety. By placing the social disorder caused by their conquerors in a humorous context, the Chamula win an unspoken triumph in a struggle with their adversaries, for the Indians demonstrate their conqueror's clear moral depravity.

Other examples of their attempt to balance disruptive forces appear in military themes which surface in representations of their ritual personnel, their sacred objects, and their ceremonial activity, often gamelike in its exuberance.

A large cast of characters participates in a complex series of rituals which must be logistically coordinated and arranged. The men sponsoring this (and all other festivals) in English are called "cargo holders," a name deriving from the Spanish word *cargo,* meaning burden. Among many indigenous groups in Mexico and Guatemala—not only in Chamula—cargo holders bear the burden of a year's service to their village, either in a religious or a political office. Cargo holders gain prestige from these offices according to the political power of their office or the amount of money they spend, especially when celebrating festivals. The major cargo holders of carnival, called "Passions" and "Flowers" in Tzotzil (fig. 79), must use up a vast amount of their savings, the equivalent of thousands

Figure 79 *Passion's costume, San Juan, Chamula, Chiapas, Mexico. This costume is worn by an outgoing religious office holder called the Standard Bearer of the Passion (Alferez Pasion) during carnival. An incoming Standard Bearer of the Passion wears a dark tunic.*

of dollars, hence they gain the greatest prestige among religious cargo holders of Chamula.

Passions and Flowers, though never called divine in themselves, serve as Christ's guardians and corporal representatives. A female impersonator, acting as Nana Marina Corcorina, Cortés's mistress, and the Ladina in the Town Crier's proclamation, wearing a specially woven blouse over traditional male ceremonial attire, accompanies one of the Passions. Passions and onlookers joke with "her," emphasizing "her" shameless ways. The Passions run with "her" in the plaza of the ceremonial center, not haphazardly, however, but in a set path whenever the proclamation triggers their flight. Since the Chamula almost never run in everyday life, this in itself is an unusual act, a reversal of normal movement. It is balanced, however, by its performance in a context of order and sequence which the Passions with their sexually disorderly Ladina mistress do not disrupt if possible.

While flags, fireworks, drums, trumpets, and so forth, mentioned in the Town Crier's proclamation, fill the air with discordant noise and show vividly against the blue sky of carnival's dry season, perhaps the most striking military object is found in the Chamula presentation of Christ. Instead of a plaster, wood, and cloth image which cargo holders and their ritual specialists tend in other saints'-day celebrations, in carnival, Christ and the Virgin Mary take the form of weapons. These deities appear as sacred silver lance tips, the same kind of lances which killed Christ in Chamula myth. They fit by means of a socket at their base to the end of wooden flagpoles about 2½ meters long. The attached flag becomes "clothes" for the lance tip, with its floral pattern signifying divinity. Sacred as well are the red, green, and sometimes yellow ribbons attached to the base of the lance tip when fastened to the pole. The Passion, when running and dancing with the flags and lance tips, enables Christ to reenact the games played shortly before His death. Thus the Chamula, in their struggle to overcome violence, transform a destructive implement into an object of extreme divinity.

A strong indication of another struggle to balance order and disorder emerges in the figure of the Monkey (fig. 80). One set of Monkeys assists the Passions and Flowers with their many chores and responsibilities. Monkeys in part derive their names from their conical, beribboned hats made of monkey fur. In contrast to the other ritual celebrants of carnival who appear in tradi-

Figure 80 *San Juan, Chamula, Chiapas, Mexico: Monkeys, fully decked in carnival regalia, run bearing flags as part of their ritual obligations during this emotionally charged festival.*

tional ceremonial attire, Monkeys dress like the French grenadiers of the 1861–67 French intervention. They act as military policemen and keep order for the cargo holders. When necessary, they hit uncooperative troublemakers with a dried bull penis stretched over a wire. These Monkeys also serve food and drink during the elaborate ritual meals the cargo holders provide.

"Free Monkeys," unattached to the religious sponsors of the fiesta but sporting the same costumes as the "Soldier Monkeys," freely carouse in the plaza and marketplace. They get drunk; they sing, dance, and play musical instruments in small bands; they pester folks. The Free Monkeys may be likened to the demons who, according to Chamula myth, killed Christ. I would like to stress here, though, that the Free Monkeys do not participate in the religious ritual of carnival. Instead they symbolize the threat of disorder, which Christ's death brought in myth, and wars brought in history, to Chamula. Yet even these rowdy characters must show respect for the cargo holders. They, too, may feel the sting of a bull penis rod when they become too disruptive to the celebrations.

Militaristic Ritual of Carnival

Passions and Monkeys—their costumes displayed in the Smithsonian Institution *Celebration* exhibit—are the most prominent leaders of the militaristic ritual of carnival which reflects the Chamulas' struggle to survive as a people. One of these rituals, the Bell Dance, is performed from Saturday to Ash Wednesday of carnival by male religious office holders and their male helpers. These dancers circle one at a time around clay kettledrums wrapped in rope netting which hereditary ceremonial drummers lightly thump. Each dancer takes a turn to carry the flagpoles with a sacred lance tip attached, while wearing a jaguar skin trailing down the back of his head to which sheep bells have been sewn. An embracer lifts each performer skyward at the end of his turn, as if to lift the sacred lance in imitation of Christ's resurrection to heaven. Then he slips the jaguar skin onto the next performer's head. Some Chamula have said that the jaguar defended Christ when demons chased Him. Bricker, in her historical analysis, likens each performer wearing the jaguar skin to a soldier defending God, and aptly translates this in her own words as the "Dance of the Warriors" (1973: 112).

Two other dramatically warlike events occur in carnival and merit special attention here. The first, a staged fight with dried horse dung, recalls the war between Mexico and Guatemala, and the second is a rite of purification by running through fire—a rite that is presented in the *Celebration* exhibit. Both take place on the second-to-the-last day of the Festival of Games, while the run through fire is a climax of the gamelike testing which occurs throughout carnival. The horse-dung fight takes place shortly before the run through fire, as youths form two opposing lines, one representing Mexican Carrancistas, the other, Guatemalan Pinedistas. The youths pelt each other vigorously with the dried horse dung, but the "war" ends in a draw after three forays, with each side winning once by overtaking the other. It is significant to note that the battle does not end in a free-for-all but follows prescribed rules.

Figure 81 *San Juan, Chamula, Chiapas, Mexico: These shoes were sold to Indians of San Andres Larrainzar, Chiapas. High-backed sandals signify past or present holders of political or religious office in the highlands of Chiapas.*

Likewise, the run through fire follows its own ceremonial order. Shortly after noontime, the Passions and Monkeys, bearing flags both with and without sacred lance tips on their staffs, run through burning thatch which young boys strew on the plaza in front of the church. If a runner has gravely sinned, he will be punished by falling into the flames which lick his sandaled feet (fig. 81). This happened to a Monkey in 1972, who luckily emerged unscathed from his tumble, while the others continued to lope past him. A fall can be caused by Passions and Monkeys carelessly jostling one another but may only be blamed on a runner's own lack of coordination. Runners must follow each other in a set sequence, finishing the course even if they momentarily stumble.

Carnival and Disorder

While it may appear from these accounts that the militarylike ritual of the cargo holders and their helpers does not give way to high-jinks and ritualized verbal attacks on a performer's personal foibles, as in some carnivals throughout the world, social disruption may indeed take place during carnival. When it does, the gods send rain as a sign of their displeasure, and the political officials punish the religious official who has shirked his duty by throwing him (and sometimes his wife and other guilty helpers) in jail.

It is the personal failure of the religious office holder, a representative to the gods for the other Chamula, which troubles the members of this community most during carnival. During the Festival of the Games, gods put humans to the test of meeting the most extravagant divine demands. The Passions and Flowers, especially, must uphold the highest standards of generosity, etiquette, purity, foresight, and self-control, while at the same time enacting the ritual which is linked to the traumatic disruptions of war, rebellion, and conquest. During the five days of carnival, as incoming and outgoing office holders, they must cheerfully and without reserve provide three costly ritual meals of beef, salt, chili, tamales, tortillas, coffee, sweet rolls, sweet water, and cane liquor to all their male and female helpers, as well as to assembled onlookers (fig. 82). The outgoing Passions must sacrifice a bull, entailing great financial outlay, and offer its meat during these ritual meals. (It is the penis of this bull which usually forms one of the bull penis rods for a Monkey.) They must feed and provide cane liquor for their helpers so that no complaints of stinginess arise. They must not fight with other religious cargo holders or any other person while they are cel-

Figure 82 *Chamula, Chiapas, Mexico: A Passion, center, flanked by four Monkeys and his ritual advisor in white poncho to his right, stands behind the large banquet table. On either side of the table stand bottles of rum and purificatory pine needles, ready for distribution to the ritual specialists in honor of the gods. Behind the table, sacred flags are fastened to a cross. They, too, will be "fed" with the smoke of incense.*

ebrating, no matter what grievances arise. They, their wives, and their helpers must remain sexually pure, keep their appearance clean (shown in the cleanliness of the costumes displayed in the *Celebration* exhibit), and provide copious, pure offerings of candles and incense to the images of the deities entrusted to their care.

The gods put not only the cargo holder's virtue to a test, but also his stamina. Beginning weeks before the actual festival, activity continues day and night with hardly a rest. Cargo holders groggily fulfill their ceremonial requirements, exhausted and seemingly asleep, keeping up this pace until each returns to his house in an outlying hamlet and a more normal life.

Due to these excessive demands, the cargo holder, his wife, and his respected adviser cannot always maintain order among themselves and their helpers. If the cargo holder does maintain order among his helpers he delights the gods, who will in turn bestow blessings on his community. If he fails, however, and often he does, the stern and punitive gods send drought, famine, illness, and hardship—for they have little tolerance for human weakness and folly. The ceremonial leaders engage in more than a ritualized military struggle; they wage an earnest battle to counteract the negative traits which may surface in what the Chamula regard as a very weak human nature. These traits, when unchecked, threaten the very livelihood of the community that the cargo holders serve.

Carnival and Chamula Souls

In the same way that the cargo holder must control his negative traits to protect his community, individual Chamula struggle to control their negative disruptive traits. These negative traits may threaten a person's very life and health. Though the Chamula may appease their deities through fiestas and sacred offerings, they can never repay their gods for having created them in the first place. The Chamula compound their unworthiness by eliminating bodily wastes and consciously sinning. The Chamula state that humans are wasteful, dirty, selfish, or liars; they are disrespectful of the deities' needs; they have illicit sexual relations; and in many other ways they disgust the gods with their human frailty.

This frailty is also reflected in the Chamula perception of the human soul. While interpretation of soul activity varies greatly among the Chamula, all acknowledge the possession of two kinds of souls. One soul, an internal soul, is generally thought to exist at the tip of the tongue. It gives the Chamula their power to speak and to reason, to be eloquent and to state their defense either before gods or humans when the need arises. It stays in the body when a person is conscious, but leaves when someone is asleep, drunk, in sexual climax, or dying.

The other soul is a wild animal spirit companion—a beast or bird such as a jaguar, coyote, hawk, weasel, raccoon, opossum, or coatamundi (to mention the ones most commonly listed by the Chamula)—which lives in the mountains under the protection of the earth lords and the soul's patron saint, Saint Jerome. Animals possessing five toes on their paws instead of four are recognizable as soul animals. The animal soul represents the passionate, physical side of humans. These creatures eat, fight, copulate, and die. When an animal spirit companion dies, its human counterpart dies; when wounded, its human counterpart falls ill. There is always a struggle to contain and control the lusts and passions of one's animal soul if it is too strong; to protect it if it is too weak.

The Chamula do not approve of violence among humans, yet it occurs either in verbal or physical disputes. These disputes signal that animal souls are fighting in the spirit realm. In the human realm, such fights lead to accusations of witchcraft, if misfortune or illness befalls one of the disputants. When illness strikes, people appeal to the beneficent gods to seek revenge on animal souls out of control, and to protect their own violated animal. Hence the Chamula must struggle to force their tongue soul to guide reason and to restore social equilibrium when animal-soul passions have skewed human relations and cast the disruptive evil of witchcraft over the land.

The Festival of the Games vibrantly presents Chamula's historic struggles to survive as an independent culture through the dramatization of ritual battles by cargo holders and other celebrants with military aspect. We see that the ritual battles (like the real battles) do not destroy the Chamula, for these people maintain a strong sense of order even when portraying chaos. Carnival presents, as well, Christ's mythic struggle as a savior, through the ritual use of the lance heads. Though the Passions run with the sacred lances as if pursued by demons, the lances emerge divine, always touched with extreme reverence and raised to heaven in the Bell Dance, just as Christ rose to heaven upon His resurrection.

Finally, the Festival of the Games presents the struggle of the individual cargo holder to present the reason of the tongue soul before the gods instead of the violent passions of the animal soul.

In the same way that the tongue soul preserves and protects a Chamula, so carnival has the potential to preserve the good will of the gods and to protect the Chamula from divine punishment. In the same way, however, that the animal soul disrupts and destroys, so carnival has the potential to disrupt social relations and destroy beneficial divine blessings.

The struggles of carnival parallel the struggles of the two kinds of human soul. In a metaphoric sense this crucial celebration becomes a soul for its community. In the same way that the soul both protects and endangers an individual, carnival protects and endangers the Chamula. This festival embodies on ritual and ceremonial levels the struggle each human must encounter to balance the opposing forces of a restless versus a reasoned and reasoning soul. It should not be surprising that this festival, touching the very essence of the Chamula conflict on its most personal level, has become the most significant celebration for a community in which festivals often gladden the heart and spiritually renew an indomitable culture's will to survive.

Bibliography

Bricker, Victoria Reifler
    1973   *Ritual Humor in Highland Chiapas.* Austin and London: University of Texas Press.

Gossen, Gary H.
    1974   *Chamulas in the World of the Sun.* Cambridge, Mass.: Harvard University Press.

Linn, Priscilla Rachun
    1976   "The Religious Office Holders in Chamula: A Study of Gods, Rituals, and Sacrifice." Ph.D. dissertation, Oxford University, England.

Pozas, Ricardo A.
    1959   *Chamula, un pueblo indio de los altos de Chiapas.* Memorias del Instituto Nacional Indigenista 8. Mexico.
    1962   *Juan the Chamula: An Ethnological Re-Creation of the Life of a Mexican Indian.* 1948. Reprint edition. Berkeley: University of California Press.

Vogt, Evon Z.
    1976   *Tortillas for the Gods: A Symbolic Analysis of Zinacanteco Rituals.* Cambridge, Mass.: Harvard University Press.

Wilson, George Carter
    1972   *A Green Tree and a Dry Tree.* New York: Macmillan.
    1974   *Crazy February: Death and Life in the Mayan Highlands of Mexico.* 1966. Reprint edition. Berkeley: University of California Press.

4

See *Figure 83.*

Religious Celebrations

Victor and Edith Turner

In defining "religion," we should trace the word back, through Old French, to the Latin *religio,* for it has been nurtured in a specific cultural tradition, that of Western Europe. We find that, according to Cassell's *New Latin Dictionary, religio* means: "Strict observance of religious ceremonial, moral scruples, conscientiousness, an object of worship, a holy thing or place, the worship of a particular deity, and a bond between man and the gods." Cicero derived the word from *relegere,* "to gather up again" or "to go over again in thought or speech." But many authorities today would derive it from *religāre,* which means "to bind fast." *Religio* was adopted by the Catholic Church to mean a system of faith in and worship of a divine power and also the recognition of a divine being to whom worship is due. By the twelfth century it came to denote the monastic state of life bound by vows and a rule. In most of these usages religion is clearly regarded as: (1) *social,* connecting human beings with deities and one another; (2) *public,* involving public practices as well as beliefs; and (3) *systematic,* representing an ensemble of beliefs, sentiments, and practices which have for their object invisible and intangible beings or powers which a human group recognizes as superior, on which it depends, and with which it can enter or has entered into relation, either by interior worship (prayer, meditation) or by exterior, "liturgical" acts. Such an extended definition would apply to the tenets and usages both of the simpler and more complex cultures in regard to transhuman powers and entities.

Anthropologists usually call religious practices "ritual." To celebrate is to perform ritual publicly and formally, though sometimes "the public" may consist of no more than members of a single family. Rituals celebrate or commemorate transhuman powers which, though invisible, are regarded by believers as the first and final causes of natural and cultural phenomena.

The study of ritual took a great step forward when, in 1909, the French folk-lorist Arnold van Gennep wrote his epoch-making book, *Les Rites de Passage,* the importance of which scholars have hardly begun to grasp. Van Gennep first grouped together all rituals "that accompany transitions from one situation to another and from one cosmic or social world to another" (p. 13). Then he divided these "rites of passage," or transitional rites, into three phases: *separation, margin* (or *limen,* denoting "threshold" in Latin), and *reaggregation,* for which he also uses the terms "preliminal," "liminal," and "postliminal." The first phase (of separation) comprises symbolic action signifying the detachment of the individual or group from an earlier fixed point in the social structure or from a set of cultural conditions, or both. Thus in boys' initiation rites in preindustrial societies, the boy is often forcibly removed from his mother and from her domain (hut, hearth, kitchen) and removed to a site inhabited only by males. In the third phase (reaggregation or reincorporation) the boy, transformed into a man, is returned to the everyday world in which he will now assume adult responsibilities no longer under the direct authority of his mother. But it is the second phase, "liminality," which is really central to the ritual process (Turner, 1967, 1969, 1974). The first phase clearly demarcates sacred space-time from mundane space-time. Sometimes violent acts (circumcision, knocking out teeth, shaving hair, animal sacrifice) betoken the "death" of the novice from his former sociocultural state. The third phase represents the often exuberant return of the novice to society and the desacralization of the entire situation. Symbols of birth or renewal are frequently displayed in reaggregation rites, which constitute a festive celebration, a triumph of order and vitality over death and indeterminacy. For between separation and reintegration there occurs the liminal stage, a period and area of ambiguity, a sort of social limbo, which has few of the attributes of the sociocultural life that precedes and follows it. In liminality the novice enters a ritual time and space that are betwixt and between those ordered by the categories of past and future mundane social existence. The cultural guidelines of secular conduct are now erased or obscured. Something weird and numinous replaces them. Liminality is better regarded as a process than a state. The liminal process has three major aspects or components, which interpenetrate in practice but may be analytically distinguished. These are (1) the communication of *sacra,* the Latin word for sacred things—we would speak of symbolic objects and actions representing religious mysteries, frequently referring to myths about how the world and society, nature and culture, came into being. Sacra, in fact, refer to the origins and foundations of cosmic order and also to the unformed void or infinite space held to have existed prior to the ordered universe. Sacra may represent both law and freedom, necessity and chaos; (2) the encouragement of ludic recombination—here we have the element of play (Latin *ludus,* "game," "play," "sport," "jest," "joke"), for during liminality ritual participants, as we shall see, are confronted by masks, images, contraptions, costumes, and the like, which represent the playful recombination of cultural traits or constituents in unusual, even bizarre and monstrous configurations unknown to secular experience; (3) the fostering of communitas, a direct, spontaneous, and egalitarian mode of social relationship, as against hierarchical relationships among occupants of structural status-roles.

The liminal phase may be public and open or secret and sequestered. Initiation ritual, whether into full adult status or into an elitist association, tends to segregate novices or "initiates" in forest or mountain retreats, caves, or specially constructed camps and shelters that are protected from profane (hence polluting) intrusion by screens, fences, taboos, and even, at times, by weapons. Public liminality is often the major phase in seasonal or calendrical rituals (planting, first-fruits and harvest rites, change-of-season rites, and those celebrating important points on the sun's ecliptic from northern to southern solstice). There is an interesting difference between sequestered and public liminality: in the former the novices (or "liminaries") are humbled and leveled, stripped of anterior rank or status, to fit them for a higher status or state (boy to man, girl to woman, commoner to headman); in the latter, everyone in the community is a liminary, and no one is elevated in status at the end of the rites. Rites performed at major calendrical terms often portray turnabouts of normal social status: the poor play at being rich, the rich at being poor; kings and nobles are abased and commoners wear the insigna of rule. But these ritual reversals are only part of the story. Just as important are the ways a society finds in these public rituals of depicting, commenting on, and critiquing itself and its social environment. As contrasted with initiation rituals and rituals of the life cycle, these seasonal festivals do not emphasize the symbolism of birth, maturation, death, and rebirth—that is, of linear developments—but rather by many devices (costumes, masks, floats, banners, tableaux, microdramas, and the like) develop a "metalanguage," nonverbal as well as verbal, which enables participants and spectators to realize just how far they have fallen short of or transgressed their own ideal standards, or even, in some kinds of ritual, to call those very ideals into question, especially under conditions of sharp social change. Such rituals are often performed in the centers of cities, in village or town squares, in full view of everyone. By this means, societies renew themselves at the source of festal joy, having purified themselves through collective self-criticism and jocund reflexivity.

Since this book has its origin in an exhibition of celebratory objects culled from museum collections, it should be noted that virtually all of the objects in the exhibit were once components in one or other of the phases of the ritual process as analyzed above. They owe their character not only to the idiosyncrasy of the cultural tradition forming their original context but also to their function within the tripartite, transformative process. Some of the most evocative, enigmatic, bizarre, and fantastic objects are those associated with liminal activities. Let us then consider in more detail the three features of liminality mentioned above: communication of the sacra, ludic recombination, and communitas.

Communication of the Sacra.   The heart of the liminal matter is in this communication. Through it in active ritual systems it is believed that those undergoing the rites will change their nature, be transformed from one kind of human being to another. In liminality, instruction is given by ritual specialists or cognoscenti that converts potential understanding into real gnosis. There is a return to first principles and a stocktaking of the basic cultural inventory. Often there is a display of sacred objects, sometimes, though more rarely than has usually been stated, direct instruction in ethics and correct behavior, and usually a recital of mythical narratives. The eminent classical scholar Jane Harrison divided sacra into three kinds, mostly with reference to initiation rites but applying to some extent to seasonal rituals as well. These are: (1) exhibitions, "what is shown"; (2) actions, "what is done"; and (3) instructions, "what is said."

(1) The *exhibition* of sacra may include evocative instruments or sacred objects, such as relics or images of deities, heroes, ancestors, or saints; sacred drums or flutes, or other musical instruments; or ensembles of ritual symbols, such as Amerindian medicine bundles. In the Lesser Eleusian mysteries of ancient Hellas, for example, the sacra consisted of a bone, top, ball, tambourine, apples, mirror, fan, and woolly fleece. Each of these had multiple meanings, the full range of which was known only to adepts, and the sacra were connected with myths about the agrarian mother-goddess Demeter and her daughter Persephone. In many cultures the sacra include masks, costumes, figurines, effigies, rock paintings, icons, and other depictions and disguises. Not infrequently the objects seem unimpressive and simple to the uninitiated observer. It is in fact their interpretation that is complex, not their outward form, though some sacra may be very elaborate indeed.

(2) Sacra may be *actions,* Greek *dramata* (from *dran,* to do). In liminality, "dramatic" performances may be presented, by ritual specialists or adepts, drawn from episodes in myths or religious epics. Such myths often embody cultural ideals, but often they transcend or transgress conventional morality when portraying the deeds of deities or heroes, the originators of cosmos, nature, and society. Such sacred dramas are often intrinsically connected with dance. Liminal ritual and myth are designed to bring about a restoration of the cosmogonic past when all sensorily perceptible phenomena came into being. Dance is the generative power par excellence, which brings the whole person into communion with the fundamental meanings, values, and goals of a living culture.

(3) The sacra may also be communicated by *instruction*. Adepts and elders teach neophytes the main outlines of the theogony, cosmogony, and mythical history of their societies or cults, usually with reference to the sacra exhibited. Often the most sacred things shown, most sacred dance dramas, form a central cluster of ideas, images, feelings, and rhythmic interactions which constitute a kind of symbolic template or master pattern for the communication of a culture's most cherished beliefs, ideas, values, and sentiments. Sometimes the human body itself, painted, tattooed, or otherwise cosmeticized, becomes the metaphor or model for nature, culture, society, and thought. Its limbs, organs, and processes may be interpreted as the manifestation of invisible faculties such as reason, passion, wisdom, compassion, and so on. In dance these components are energized, representing and periodically reinstigating the dynamics of nature and human society.

Ludic Recombination.   Ludic recombination is the analysis of culture into factors and their free, playful ("ludic") recombination in any and every possible pattern however deviant, grotesque, unconventional, or outrageous. This process is quintessentially liminal, and, in a disconcerting way, makes excellent sense with regard to the new state and status that celebrants or neophytes will enter. In communicating the sacra, ludic recombination comes into play. Such recombination may itself be traditional, as in most preindustrial societies, or it may be spontaneous, as in changing or large-scale, complex societies. For example, in the sacra exhibited in ritual celebrations, particularly in the liminal phase, certain physical and cultural features are often represented as disproportionately large or small. A head or nose or phallus or breasts may be out of proportion, or incongruous forms may be created from components of familiar, culturally defined "reality." These might include "monsters," compounded of elements from human or animal forms; for example, animal-headed gods, or human-headed animals. In solemn, initiatory ritual, such exaggerations or distortions of reality may be regarded as religious mysteries; in the public liminality of joyous seasonal celebrations, they may serve the purposes of caricature, satire, or lampoonery. In both cases they encourage liminaries to ponder. For when elements are withdrawn from their usual settings and recombined in totally unique configurations, such as monsters or dragons, those exposed to them are startled into thinking anew about persons, objects, relationships, social roles, and features of their environment hitherto taken for granted. Previous habits of thought, feeling, and action are disrupted. They are thus forced and encouraged to think about their society, their cosmos, and the powers that generate and sustain these. The cake of custom is broken and reflexive speculation liberated. Liminality is, therefore, potentially, and even in traditional cultures often actually, a realm of primitive hypothesis where there is some freedom to juggle with the factors of existence. When neophytes are being initiated there is clearly a pedagogic or instructional intention behind this seemingly promiscuous intermingling and juxtaposing of the categories of event, experience, and knowledge.

Communitas.   Communitas is, to quote Znaniecki (1936:chap.3), "a bond . . . uniting people over and above any formal social bonds." In communitas there is a direct, total confrontation of human identities which is rather more than the casual camaraderie of ordinary social life. It may be found in the mutual relationships of neophytes in initiation, where communitas is sacred and serious, and in the festal ecstasies of great seasonal celebrations. In many initiations the participants undergo a leveling process. The distinctions of their previous status, sex, dress, and role disappear, and as they share common trials and eat and sleep in common, a group unity is experienced, a kind of generic bond outside the constraints of social structure, akin to Martin Buber's "flowing from I to Thou." Communitas, however, does not merge identities; instead it liberates them from conformity to general norms, so that they experience one another concretely and not in terms of social structural (e.g., legal, political, or bureaucratic) abstractions. Although the participants are stripped of status, their secular powerlessness may be compensated for by sacred power, the power of the weak. Within this situation the total individual is fruitfully "alienated" from the partial *persona,* making room for the possibility of a total (rather than a perspectival) view of the life of society. Attachment to one's fellows, detachment from one's social structure—these form a transient pairing. Pure communitas exists briefly where social structure is not. This is necessarily a transient condition because it does not fit into the orderly sequential operation of day-to-day society. Rather, it tends to ignore, reverse, cut acoss, or occur outside "obligatory" or "necessary" structural relationships. Nevertheless, in most preindustrial societies communitas is not sought as an end in itself but is treated as a means of purifying, redefining, and revitalizing a social structure which is itself regarded as of divine origin and to which no alternative form is proposed.

The rituals we have been discussing, those of the seasonal and life cycles, are usually performed by communities possessing a certain political and legal unity. In other words, a measure of peace and security, based on a shared acceptance of organized force within the group as a sanction against illicit violence, is a prerequisite for their performance. Yet the marginal and ambiguous areas of social life constituted by relationships between premodern polities also have religious and ritual aspects. Relations with strangers, and more markedly with those who are not quite strangers, but with whom, on occasion, one may barter goods, trade, even intermarry, or share a single language, may be conceived of as containing or being regulated by powers of a supernormal magnitude and character, which can be influenced by religiomagical ritual. Warfare, raiding, feuding, and vendettas between neighboring groups in preindustrial societies often become highly ritualized and associated with religious and magical ideas and beliefs. Unlike rituals within political units, rituals linked with warfare treat power as something to be won rather than as the "natural" rhythmical source of the fertility of crops, animals, human beings, and sylvan produce. Such power is often achieved by individuals, not bestowed by the ancestors or gods. Warfare is usually conducted in liminal zones between conflicting groups and has, among other attributes, an initiatory aspect, particularly for young, neophyte warriors, and a renewal aspect for their seniors. Individual prowess and skill tend to be ritualized and are often embodied in ritual objects. An example is available from the Smithsonian exhibition, *Celebration: A World of Art and Ritual*. One of the most celebrated cultures of headhunters in the world is that of the various Jivaro-speaking tribes of Ecuador and Peru, who inhabit many of the rivers forming the headwaters of the Amazon. Among them, warfare is a religious activity and is focused on a belief in a special vital force known as *arutam*, which anthropologists have translated as "soul power." All the objects illustrating this chapter have reference to soul power.[1]

Jivaro Headhunting Celebration

For Jivaro men, to remain alive very much depended on finding and guarding soul power. Children were born without it; no boy was expected to survive puberty who had not had visions manifesting it. But old men, greatly respected, demonstrated their soul power through their mere survival. The man with a powerful soul manifested such desirable traits as honesty, intelligence, energy, and industriousness. Soul power protected one against physical and magical danger. If it disappeared, a man became vulnerable to his foes' treachery in war or magic and soon met his death. Jivaro men used the hallucinogen *Datura* to seek visions of souls who conferred power. Such visions were said to involve an encounter with fierce or monstrous apparitions. If the seeker met his ordeal bravely, an ancestor appeared to him and granted him long life and success at headhunting. The vision quest was a kind of liminal phase removed from mundane space-time. The access of soul power following the vision induced feelings of bellicosity and confidence, soon followed by the organization of headhunting parties against hostile Jivaro tribes (which, nevertheless, might contain kin and relatives by marriage).

Warfare was connected with soul power, for head-taking enabled warriors to renew their soul power; without taking heads, they would die themselves as their power slowly faded. For the soul met in vision did not reside permanently in the human body. Before going on a raid men had to confess their visions to each other. Confession caused the soul to leave the body and return to the spirit world as a strong wind. Only the power of the soul, literally "a wasting asset," remained to protect each combatant. It was believed that men who died on a raid had already lost their power without realizing it. Taking a head gave one the right to use *Datura* again on returning home and thus acquire a new soul. A new vision not only gained a new soul but also retained magical control over the old soul, released before battle. In effect, if men did not go on raids every few years, their souls were believed to wander at night, thus exposing them to hostile bewitching shamans. Since many men met violent ends, each was thought to have a highly dangerous avenging ghost. This ghost, known as *muisak,* if it were not dealt with by appropriate ritual means, might kill the head-taker or one of his close kinsfolk by changing into deadly snakes or falling trees, or by entering machetes and guns to cause fatal, seemingly self-inflicted "accidents."

Many people have heard of the "shrunken heads" (*tsantsa*) prepared by Jivaro from decapitated foes. Few realize that the technical work of boning, skinning, and preserving the head was accompanied by elaborate ritual which was directed at transforming the power of the dead enemy's malevolent, avenging soul into a socially positive power, enabling not only the slayer but also his fellow raiders to renew the beneficent soul power, the *arutam,* which, unrenewed, was only too liable to leak away.

Several days after its return with shrunken heads, the war party celebrated the first of three victory feasts. These might be described as "rites of reaggregation"—the entire headhunting expedition might perhaps be regarded as a "liminal period," containing ordeals, mysteries, ritual, and the emergence of communitas in the raiding party. During the feast, known as *numpen,* the victors ritually purified themselves, and the heads, of the pollution of killing. The celebrants symbolically controlled the avenging ghost's power by having the slayer impart it to two of his female kin as he held the *tsantsa* aloft. Since women hardly ever attained soul power, and never went headhunting, their exposure to the head endowed them with magical power which enhanced their ability to perform traditional female tasks. This rite was repeated in the other two victory celebrations. If the ritual was properly performed the vengeful soul could no longer injure the victor. The feasts that followed, *suamak* and *napin,* were much more elaborate. Great economic activity surrounded the preparations. Between 150 and 200 guests were housed and fed—a large number for so scanty a population. The large quantities of food and manioc beer consumed were both source and symbol of joy and well-being. These two feasts contained rites of intensification. Values, rules, goals, and sentiments which ordered the religious and social universe of the Jivaro were revivified. Communitas was the norm, though quarrels sometimes arose and fighting took place—for people bring their conflicts with them to mass gatherings as well as their desire to express fellow-feeling. In Jivaro culture fights were attributed to the vengeful enemy ghost, but these were promptly resolved to thwart its purpose of harming the victors. The head-taker won great prestige through these feasts; not only was witness borne to his augmented soul power, but he was also hailed as a generous host concerned with the entertainment and welfare of his kith and kin.

The rituals of the headhunting process may be seen as instruments for the transformation of "wild," dangerous, and alien power into "domestic," life-enhancing, "in-group" energy. They also indicated at any given time the degree of repute or standing possessed by any given male; no statuses were permanent, all were in flux, delicately in tune with changing environmental circumstances.

The Jivaro celebratory objects shown in this chapter are symbols, each having multiple meanings. Most of them represent aspects of soul power and refer to ritual stages of its acquisition and possession. But ritual, including celebratory, objects are usually more than mere signs or indicators of religious powers and ideas: they are instruments, even embodiments of such invisible efficacies. At the triumphal feasts, each member of the war party, after grooming himself and applying body paint, adorned himself with objects of display, including those shown here. The warriors used their ornaments to reveal to the community the power of their soul, parade their current status and prestige, and frankly attract women. (Medals have similar functions in Western society but are not usually thought to have intrinsic magical effectiveness.) The strongest souls were known as the Powerful Ones (*kakaram*), warriors who repeatedly slew enemies and so earned the right to the most elaborate adornments. Only the Powerful Ones might drape the collar ornament on their shoulders, for the bones in it bespoke the bravery of the wearer (fig. 83). They were leg bones of the *tayo* bird, hunted in caves haunted by jaguars and dangerous jaguar spirits. The ancestor who appeared to a man under the influence of *Datura* often took the form of a jaguar or the mighty anaconda serpent. Many trips had to be made to the caves to complete a single ornament. These same soul-power-conferring creatures were represented also by jaguar tooth necklaces and snakeskin armbands.

The *etsemat* headwrap also related to the acquisition of soul power. When a boy passed through his puberty rites, he began to tie up his loose, long hair with this band (fig. 84). Later, when he captured heads, he carried the trophy by means of this band slung over his shoulder. Jivaro, in fact, attributed great

Figure 83 Collar ornament, Jivaro, Ecuador.

Figure 84 Headwrap, Jivaro, Ecuador.

Figure 85 Feathered headdress, Jivaro, Ecuador.

Figure 86 Wooden comb, Jivaro, Ecuador.

strength and vitality to their hair, "the visible seat of the soul," according to the anthropologist R. Karsten. Hair grooming was a ritual act, involving, in addition to the headdress (fig. 85), headwrap, and dorsal head ornaments, the palmwood comb (fig. 86). Belts of human hair also adorned warriors. The prospective wearer cut the hair from a deceased enemy, wove or glued it into a belt, then held a small feast to consecrate its power before wearing it in public on cere-monial occasions. To declare that he had arrived at man's estate, a boy hunted a tree sloth in the forest, then shrank its head as though it had been a human enemy's. His father then sponsored one or two feasts for his son. During these feasts the celebrants gave the sloth's head the same ritual treatment as a similar human trophy. The lethargy of the sloth, far from being a negative symbol, as in the West, betokened the creature's great longevity, thus making it an admirable substitute for a human, since, as we have seen, the older the man, the more his soul power. If a slain enemy was found to be a kinsman of a member of the raiding party, his head was not taken. Instead, a sloth's head was substituted and treated ritually as if it were a man's. With the feasting and ritual, the victor earned the same power as if the head had been a human victim's. Other adorn-ments and celebratory objects illustrated in this chapter in a sense owe their existence to the complex of beliefs about soul power. To use metaphorical lan-guage, they have been "charged" or "magnetized" by this power, both generic and personal, which ebbs and flows in accordance with the individual's experi-ence in headhunting, vision quests, ritual, and social life. They can also be re-garded, in the terms discussed above, as "liminal sacra," to be exhibited, com-municated, and acted upon, in such a way as to inscribe in the Jivaro consciousness knowledge of the system of meanings and values that gives shape, relevance, and joy to their lives of struggle and difficulty in the moun-tainous forest lands they so turbulently inhabit. The "liminoid" element of ma-nipulation and innovation is clearly present, too, for collections of Jivaro objects show considerable range in the style and intensity of effort behind their con-struction.

Revitalization Movements:
The Ghost Dance and its Liminal Sacra

History itself has sometimes generated religious phenomena approximating those found in liminal periods. This happens during epochs of marked cultural change and its accompanying personal psychological stress. Anthony Wallace sees such epochs as providing conditions for the emergence of "revitalization movements," "deliberate, organized, conscious efforts by the members of a so-ciety to construct a more satisfying culture" (Wallace, 1968:75–79). Often such movements (also known as "nativistic and revivalistic movements") seek to revi-talize a traditional institution, while endeavoring to eliminate alien persons, cus-toms, values, even material culture from the experience of those undergoing painful change. When powerful invaders and colonizers exert economic pres-sure and political force on indigenous groups of simpler material culture, who have no means of sustained military defense, revitalistic movements tend to take on a religious character. Many of the features found in liminal and liminoid situations come to dominate the new religion, drawing sustenance from many hitherto separate tribal traditions. Elements of the alien culture are frequently borrowed and synthesized with confluent autochthonous symbols, myths, beliefs, and rituals. Ludic recombination of old and new cultural components rapidly takes place. Traditional shamans become new prophets. Their dreams and visions in trance and ecstatic dance become new myths, and these are dramatized in new rituals, some of which become institutionalized. Existential communitas seizes the first converts and the new, rapidly improvised "message," cosmology, world-view, and round of rituals spread to embrace in a religious community many scattered groups whose only previous bond was a like fate, a shared oppression.

James Mooney's classic study of the Ghost Dance (1896) describes such a revitalization process.[2] Its liminal character is obvious. It was a mixture of native and Christian elements, simultaneously looking back to the glorious Indian past and to a hoped-for future when the buffalo would return, beloved ancestors would come back to life, and the White Man would disappear. Its prophet, even Messiah, was a Paiute Indian, Wovoka or Jack Wilson, who preached a nonviolent code of peace, honesty, kindness, and a return to old ways, by dancing the Ghost Dance. Though it was fundamentally a pacific, spiritual movement, it was developed by the Sioux into a more militant version, no doubt in response to the oppressive conditions in the Pine Ridge reservation. It was here at Wounded Knee, in December 1890, that the infamous massacre took place during Ghost Dance meetings. One man's communitas is another man's "insurrection"!

Though practices varied from tribe to tribe, the Sioux dance was not atypical. According to Mooney, leaders fasted for a day before the dance, purified themselves in a sweat lodge, and had their faces and bodies painted by a medicine man. Next the dancers were robed in the sacred ghost shirt. The dance usually began about noon, when all joined in a circle around a small tree (fig. 87). A woman shot off four sacred arrows, retrieved them, and hung them in the tree, with the bow, a wheel, gaming sticks, and a staff. These sacra were all derived from visions. All then sat in a circle, singing, while they ate sacred food. Afterwards, the assembly rose, danced in a circle, faster and faster, until trance was induced. This mode of vertiginous arousal of an altered state of consciousness is found in many cultures, for example, among the dervishes (Persian *därvish*), Muslim ascetics who sought to achieve collective ecstasy through whirling dances and the chanting of religious formulas. When they came out of trance, participants (like the Amerindian Jivaro) told one another of their experiences in the spirit world, and dancing resumed. No musical instruments were used to accompany the songs, which, along with the trance, were the core of the dance. Unlike calendrical rituals in more stable societies, Ghost Dance meetings were held irregularly. At one period they lasted for four days. For a time the Sioux danced only on Sundays, but as their situation became more desperate, they danced more frequently. Ghost dancing gradually declined during the nineties, but it left a legacy of shared symbols, songs, and attitudes toward the world which have continued to influence Pan-Indianism in the present century.

Figure 87   *Hide painting of the Ghost Dance, Southern Cheyenne, Oklahoma. Note details: Cheyenne women wear braids, Arapaho women unplaited hair; performers induce a hypnotic trance by waving handkerchiefs; the medicine man (a figure standing to one side) helps a man who has stretched out a blue handkerchief toward him to enter the spirit world.*

Mooney gives us some information about the meanings of these sacra. "The design and color of the paint applied to the forehead, face, and cheeks of the dancers varied with the individual, being frequently determined by a previous trance vision of the subject, but circles, crescents, and crosses representing respectively the sun, the moon, and the morning star, were always favorite figures" (1896:68). Mooney presents a Sioux interpretation of sacra in a text written in the Teton Dakota dialect by George Sword, an Oglala Sioux Indian, and translated by an Indian for his friend, Miss Emma C. Sickels. Of the ghost shirts George Sword said:

> They paint the white muslins they made holy shirts and dresses of with blue across the back, and alongside of this is a line of yellow paint. . . . A picture of an eagle is made on the back of all the shirts and dresses. On the shoulders and on the sleeves they tied eagle feathers. They said that the bullets will not go through these shirts and dresses, so they all have those dresses for war [fig. 88]. . . . The ghost dancers all have to wear eagle feather on head. With this feather any man would be made crazy [i.e., enter trance] fan with this feather. In the ghost dance no one is allow to wear anything made of any metal, except the guns made of metal is carry by some of the dancers. When they come from ghosts or after recovery from craziness [come out of trance], they brought meat from the ghosts or from

Figure 88   *Ghost Dance shirt, Southern Arapaho, Oklahoma.*

the supposed messiah. They also brought water, fire, and wind with which to kill all the whites or Indians who will help the chief of the whites. They made. sweat house and made holes in the middle of the sweat house where they say the water will come out of these holes. . . . (p.42)

Mooney believed (p.34) that the ghost shirt may have been suggested by the Mormon "endowment robe," a seamless garment of white muslin adorned with symbolic figures. The Mormons regarded the Indians as the Lamanites of their own sacred writings and received many Indians into their church, investing them with the endowment robe. In any event, George Sword's text reveals how traditional themes and symbolic motifs were juxtaposed and combined with elements drawn from their experience of the whites—guns, "bullet-proof" shirts, etc., with the eagle, a sacred bird in Sioux religion, regarded as a messenger of the departed dead and mentioned in many myths. In the Ghost Dance it is the eagle spirit who bears those who have "died" in trance to the messiah and the ancestral ghosts. The Ghost Dance is, like most liminal processes, a symbolic restoration or reenactment of the creative or generative past when creation was, so to speak, new-minted and unpolluted. Its sacra, including the signs of traditional games (wheel, sticks, often shinny sticks), stand for a timeless time, when the ancestors and the living play together in happiness, where buffalo are abundant, and the painful present, brought on them by the whites, has been "washed" or "blown" or "burned" away by the natural forces of water, wind, and fire.

Clearly, these accounts suggest that there are many similarities between revitalization (or "millenarian") movements, such as the Ghost Dance, and rites of passage, such as puberty or funerary rituals. This may be because both deal with transition and liminality. Millenarian movements arise in historical periods when the society as a whole, or major groups in it, are in a transitional, liminal state. Major religions, such as Christianity and Islam and the Bhakti movements in Hinduism, seem to have begun as revitalization movements. Much of the mythology and symbolism of such movements has actually been borrowed from those of traditional *rites de passage*. But a circular process seems to be involved here, for successful revitalization movements tend to become institutionalized and to reestablish orderly cycles of life-crisis celebrations and a liturgical year with feasts and fasts which, though containing much of the prophetic message of charismatic founders, nevertheless become increasingly associated with the seasonal or calendrical round. Historical *limina* (betwixt-and-between periods) may provide propitious conditions for the birth of religions, stable epochs for their routinized continuance. At their genesis the liminal experiences transgress traditional liturgical and theological boundaries. Later, new ritual channels are grooved and the new experiences, crystallized in myths and symbols, become the content of ordered liminality. Pilgrimages to sacred shrines and places become acceptable substitutes for millenarian impulses and largely satisfy aspirations to communitas and liminal experience (instruction through sacra and ludic recombination).

American Catholic and Protestant Religious Celebrations

Two articles in this section on "Religious Celebrations," "Brothers and Neighbors: The Celebration of Community in Penitente Villages," by Marta Weigle and Thomas R. Lyons, and "Word, Song, and Motion: Instruments of Celebration among Protestant Radicals in Early Nineteenth-Century America," by Daniel W. Patterson, concern themselves respectively with ritual modes associated with "marginal," "radical," or "pioneer" groups (to use the authors' terms) of Catholics and Protestants. As far as displayable objects are concerned, Catholic cultures tend to be richer than Protestant ones. This is due to the important role of visual imagery in the former and auditory imagery in the latter. As Patterson writes of radical Protestant groups in America: "The Bible [was their] 'only rule of faith and practice.' This led them toward a word-centered worship. Their art forms were not painting or sculpture, not material objects, but oratory (prayer, testimony, and especially sermon) and song (congregational hymn and spiritual song). Since these worshipers also stressed some form of experiential religion, they had a third, even less recognized expressive mode: gesture, dance, patterned movement through space. Given the evanescence of sound and motion, our record of the dominant expressive forms of early nineteenth-century American Protestantism is necessarily very imperfect." This should be contrasted with Weigle's and Lyons' account of Good Friday afternoon as celebrated by "The Brothers of Our Father Jesus, commonly (and pejoratively) known as Penitentes, men of Hispanic descent who still live in or have migrated from the rural communities of northern New Mexico and Southern Colorado." Weigle and Lyons write: "[There was] a penitential procession in which one of the two Brothers dragged a death cart and a simulated crucifixion. Death is depicted as a black-robed or skeletal female figure, commonly called Dona Sebastiana, who brandishes a wooden hatchet or drawn bow and arrow."

Since "the Protestant Ethic" came to dominate early American, indeed Colonial, culture, and later fused with eighteenth-century "Enlightenment" notions which stressed the primacy of "Reason," it is perhaps not surprising that the celebratory tradition in the United States came to focus on human beings rather than things and that the objects used (fireworks, decorations for floats, streamers, flower pieces, paper costumes, etc.) tend to be ephemeral and for the most part are discarded after being used once or twice. Europe "aux anciens parapets," with its "idols," "graven images," its religious and political hierarchies, its lingering feudal relationships, its overt class and semi-caste structures, was the "Babylon," the "Egypt," to be abandoned and forgotten, and any of its tokens and reminders, such as statues of saints or effigies, were to be held not in reverence but contempt. A new "cleaner and greener land" was to be the pure, natural context of a new democratic beginning, "under God" alone. The Old World was to be repudiated. Of course, this "iconoclastic" (in the sense of "image-breaking") attitude was not shared by the millions of European and Latin American Catholics who arrived later. But the mainstream American paradigm had already been set: public celebrations emphasized song, music, patterned movement through space, at the expense of sacred images and portable shrines. Nevertheless, great visual shows and pageants, ebulliently endowed with "a surplus of signifiers," like the Mardi Gras of New Orleans and the recent burgeoning of Trinidadian carnivals in major American cities, represent the continuing vigor of originally Catholic celebratory traditions.

The essays on radical Protestants (especially the Shakers) and the "Penitentes" sharply bring out this contrast between celebratory processes that stress sacred "things" and those that focus on the moral, philosophical, and religious worth of "persons," an opposition which forms one of the pervasive themes of the Smithsonian's exhibition. Let us call celebrants who attribute a special quality to the visually perceptible vehicles of cultural, especially religious, meaning used in ritual, "iconophiles," that is, "lovers of images." Then let us call those who oppose the use of images or "idols," "aniconic"—or in their actively proselytizing role, "iconoclastic," that is, destructive of religious images. Iconophiles stress the signifier (visual image) over the signified ("meaning[s]") in relating them; iconoclasts regard the visual signifier as unnecessary, even obstructive, sometimes "diabolic." Iconophilic religions—the majority in our Smithsonian sample—often develop complex and elaborate systems of ritual; symbols tend to be mainly nonverbal and interpreted by myths bound up with the seasonal calendar or with the creation or origination of the world. Iconoclastic religions are often concerned with radical reform and seek to purify the "underlying religious meaning" by erasing the iconic "vehicles," which they regard as "idols" interposed between believers and truths enunciated or lived by religious founders and primary expounders. Verbal exegesis; development of literacy in order to read and ponder on "the Word"; emphasis on "the Spirit" ("Which quickeneth and giveth Life"), on inward conversion rather than public initiation, on healing through prayer and touch, on "sacred speech with heightened tonal and rhythmic patterning" (*see* Patterson, "Word, Song, and Motion"), and on "a rich choreography of postures and gestures": these characteristics tend to be linked with the destruction or abandonment of visual iconic symbols. Iconic symbols are often signs and centers of traditional groups, based on kinship, neighbor-hood, or feudal ties of homage and fealty. Stress on the word often accompanies the emergence of the notion of the individual-in-general rather than the cor-porate group as the main unit of ethics and judgment. In the religious domain, major forms of mediation, such as priesthood, sacraments, and set prayers, are replaced by private devotions, the downgrading of ceremonial objects, a direct relationship to deity, and ministers who preach the Word under inspiration from the Spirit. The traditional corporate group is replaced by voluntary associ-ation, forming a religious community of "saved" individual souls. Patterson shows how these "aniconic" modes of worship found supreme expression in the radical Protestantism of the American Shakers and Methodists. Their concern was with "becoming." Their services "sought to induce and to structure a trans-formation of the personality and to create a sacred community. Word, song, and motion served them by both inciting this change and expressing it." The Catho-lic Penitentes did not lack for word, song, or motion, but these were, so to speak, scripted by rubric and ordered by custom. They did not abound in "spontaneous testimony" nor generate "a continuous flow of ... distinctive new songs (which) originated in inspired states," as did the Shakers. Yet the Peni-tentes' "stylized dramatizations" of scriptural events evoked powerful feelings. Here, of course, celebratory objects were much in evidence. Weigle and Lyons write:

> The popular *Encuentro* ... the meeting between Jesus and His Mother on the way to Calvary, is usually enacted during the late morning of Good Fri-day. Women with or without family ties to the Brotherhood process from one direction carrying a black-robed image of the Virgin, usually Our Lady of Sorrows. Brothers come from their *morada* (meeting-house or chapel) bearing various standards and holy images, chief among them a nearly life-sized *Cristo,* robed in purple or red with hands bound. When the two groups meet there are recitations and hymns recounting the Passion. At the appropriate time, the figures of Mother and Son are brought close together in a symbolic final embrace. It is a period of intense emotion, especially for women participants and onlookers, many of whom recall sons lost un-timely, especially in war. Before the images are returned to the *morada,* most observers come forward to adore and kiss the garments of the *santos* (sacred images) and the border of the standards.

A common thread can be seen to run through the four examples of religious celebration discussed: Jivaro headhunting celebration, the Plains Indians' Ghost Dance, Protestant meetings, and Catholic Holy Week solemn celebrations. All recognize a transhuman controlling power that may be either personal or im-personal. In societies or contexts in which such power is regarded as imper-sonal, anthropologists customarily describe it as *magic,* and those who manipu-late the power are magicians. Wherever power is personalized, as Deity, gods, spirits, demons, genii, ancestral shades, ghosts, or the like, anthropologists speak of *religion*. By this definition, the celebrations we have considered contain both magical and religious procedures. The four rituals are concerned with danger, either subjective or objective. For Patterson's article is partly about the danger of "death and hell" from which the poor sinner must be saved by the pouring of "convicting power" into his heart. The radical Protestants' meetings celebrated the saving efficacy of the Bible as "the only rule of faith and practice," and their joy was proportionate to their dread of damnation. The danger inherent in Jivaro headhunting is obvious, and the ritual sublimation of the fear of it formed an essential strand in the tribal cultural pattern. The Ghost Dance complex was a "last stand" response to the agonizing danger of total culture-loss. The New Mexican Catholics who took part in or watched the vivid dramatizations of Christ's Passion, Via Dolorosa, and Resurrection reexperienced the sufferings and dangers of their own lives, buffeted as they felt themselves to be by the World, the Flesh, and the Devil. By compassion for Christ's Passion they sought a remedy and a source of sanctifying grace. Deity, danger, protection, salvation seem then to be ingredients of a wide range of religious celebrations. Yet we should let Ronald Grimes ("The Lifeblood of Public Ritual," below) have the last word here on the nature of celebration—and his formulation applies particularly well to religious celebration:

> Celebrations . . . are not practice for some more real kind of action, say, pragmatic or economic action, nor are they sublimations for some remembered or more desirable action. In a celebratory moment the ritual action is a deed in which the symbols do not merely point, mean, or recall but embody fully and concretely all that is necessary for the moment . . . a public celebration is a rope bridge of knotted symbols strung across an abyss. We make our crossings hoping the chasm will echo our festive sounds for a moment, as the bridge begins to sway from the rhythms of our dance.

When we see celebratory objects unknotted from their place in the saving rope or watch films of rites, let us restore these symbols in our imagination to the contexts of impassioned experience in which they truly belong.

Notes

1. Research on Jivaro religion was conducted by Dr. Priscilla Linn of the Smithsonian Institution. We are indebted to her for her careful review of the relevant literature, cited in the bibliography for this chapter.

2. We are grateful to Dr. Ira Jacknis, of the Smithsonian Institution, for his research on Ghost Dance materials in the possession of the National Museum of Natural History.

Bibliography

Gennep, Arnold van
  1960   *The Rites of Passage*. 1909. Reprint edition. London: Routledge and Kegan
              Paul.
Harner, M. J.
  1972   *The Jivaro*. Garden City, N.Y.: Doubleday/Natural History.
Karsten, R.
  1935   *The Head-Hunters of Western Amazonas: The Life and Culture of the Jibaro
              Indians of Eastern Ecuador and Peru*. Societas Scientiarum Fennica, Com-
              mentationes Humanarum Litterarum, vol. VII, pp. 1–598.
Mooney, James
  1896   *The Ghost-Dance Religion and the Sioux Outbreak of 1890*. U.S. Bureau of
              American Ethnology, *Fourteenth Annual Report, 1892–93*. Washington, D.C.:
              Smithsonian Institution.
Stirling, M. W.
  1938   *Historical and Ethnographical Material on the Jivaro Indians*. Bureau of
              American Ethnology, Bulletin 117. Washington, D.C.: Smithsonian Institution.
Turner, Victor
  1967   *The Forest of Symbols: Aspects of Ndembu Ritual*. Ithaca: Cornell University
              Press.
  1969   *The Ritual Process: Structure and Anti-Structure*. Chicago: Aldine.
  1974   *Dramas, Fields, and Metaphors: Symbolic Action in Human Society*. Ithaca:
              Cornell University Press.
Wallace, Anthony F. C.
  1968   "Nativism and Revivalism." In *International Encyclopedia of the Social Sci-
              ences*, vol. 11, pp. 75–79. New York: Macmillan and the Free Press.
Znaniecki, F.
  1936   *The Method of Sociology*. New York: Farrar and Rinehart.

Word, Song, and Motion: Instruments of Celebration among Protestant Radicals in Early Nineteenth-Century America

Daniel W. Patterson

O n an evening late in the 1790s, one burdened American sinner made his way home from a Baptist meeting where the saints had, to no avail, striven mightily with him. His spiritual condition was desperate. For six weeks he had carried a sore weight within his breast and had prayed continually that God would "pour convicting power" into his heart "till it burst asunder like the marsh-mud before the cannon ball." On this night, suddenly, in the middle of the road, a "hot flash like lightning" struck through his neck and shoulders into his heart. It drove out, he later said, "the sore lump, and every weight" about him and left him with his hands stretched, "as light as nothing," on his tiptoes, "expecting every step to leave the earth, and step into the air." His happiness was "truly unspeakable." He hurried home to testify "what great things the Lord had done" for him, fell to "skipping across the floor, singing psalms, and hymns," and then lay down "in perfect peace, and death and hell were far removed" (Bates, n.d., pp. 28–29).

The world of the early American Protestant radical had not only its private rejoicings but also its communal celebrations—its Baptist communion-and-foot-washing Sundays and river baptizings (fig. 89), its Methodist revivals and love feasts, its interdenominational camp meetings and singing conventions. Outsiders usually saw this, however, as a sour world, and devoid of art. Even the Shakers, who now have a reputation for aesthetic sensitivity, did not strike their contemporaries so. The critic John Sullivan Dwight thought their songs "the very plainest, baldest thing that could be called music" (1847:157). British gentlemen likened their dances to the frenzies of the "howling dervishes of Bagdad" (Buckingham, 1841:62) or to the caperings of "penguins in procession" (Vigne, 1832:261). Inspecting the Shaker village at Mount Lebanon, New York, Charles Dickens saw only grim, factorylike buildings and grim, wooden old

Figure 89   *An eighteenth-century river baptism near Philadelphia. From Morgan Edwards,* Materials Toward a History of the Baptists in Pennsylvania, *1770.*

Shakers and "felt about as much sympathy for them, and as much interest in them, as if they had been so many figureheads of ships" (1842:214).

Radical Protestantism has rarely enjoyed a good press. In the nineteenth century its reputation was partly the victim of Victorian sensibility, for Anglo-American sectarians and revivalists had little taste for overstuffed elegance. They did not, however, cultivate even homely arts like those practiced in the same years in New Mexican villages or in German settlements in Pennsylvania. They carved and painted no santos for display in chapels and processions, illuminated no certificates to commemorate births and baptisms.

Anglo-American Protestants did not celebrate, as others did, with material objects. One reason is that in the earlier years of the Republic the sectarian and revivalist fervor burned hottest in the recently settled back country. New settlers who wore clothes "mostly made of the deer's skin," whose bedsteads were formed of "forks driven into the ground and poles laid on these," who rocked their children in a sugar-trough or pack-saddle cradle, had little room for concern with the creation of implements for rituals (Finley, 1855:70). They did not even have halls large enough to gather in. They were not, however, wholly indifferent to aesthetic effects. They felt the impressiveness of the natural surroundings in which they set their camp meetings. "The purple curtain of night fell over the earth from the darkening sky," wrote one western minister:

> God's golden fire flashed out in heaven, and men below kindled their watch-fires. The encampment, a village of snowy tents, was illuminated with a brilliancy that caused every leaf to shine and sparkle as if all the trees were burnished with phosphorescent flame. It was like a theater. It was a

> theater in the open air, on the green sward, beneath the starry blue, in-
> comparably more picturesque and gorgeous than any stage scenery. . . .
> (Finley, 1855:321–22)

But if their material circumstances constrained these revivalists, their outlook
was also shaped by a long resentment of the upper class. They disliked the trappings that symbolized its privileges. The early Methodist circuit-rider Peter Cartwright fired "the grape-shot of truth" against "*rings,* ruffles, and all kind of ornamental dress" (1856:190). It delighted him to see "those proud young
gentlemen and young ladies, dressed in their silks, jewelry, and prunella, from
top to toe," seized, despite themselves, by the holy jerks: "The first jerk or so,
you would see their fine bonnets, caps, and combs fly" (1856:48–49). Like fashionable dress, the pews of elegant churches signified wealth and status. Their
use, the Methodist charged, "goes to exclude the poor, contravenes the Divine
law, and prevents the realization of that blessedness that God has provided for
the poor" (1856:481). These egalitarian Protestants adopted plain dress for their
costume and functionalism for their architectural style. They barred the creation
of any elaborate appurtenances of worship—"ornamented pulpits, pewed and
cushioned seats, organs, and almost all kinds of instruments"—that would
"make a vain show and gratify pampered pride" (Cartwright, 1856:235).

Most such groups grounded their objections upon the Bible as "the only rule
of faith and practice." This led them toward a word-centered worship. Their art
forms were not painting or sculpture, not material objects, but oratory (prayer,

Figure 90 *Camp meeting.*

testimony, and especially sermon) and song (congregational hymn and spiritual song). Since these worshipers also stressed some form of experiential religion, they had a third, even less recognized expressive mode: gesture, dance, patterned movement through space. Given the evanescence of sound and motion, our record of the dominant expressive forms of early nineteenth-century American Protestantism is necessarily very imperfect.

Their song survives to us more richly than their spoken word. As an oral tradition, early Baptist hymnody persists among conservative white congregations in scattered localities, principally in the Appalachians, and more widely among rural blacks, but usually in richly modified forms (*see* Sutton, 1977). The Methodists, a group that submitted more readily to centralized direction by educated leaders, long ago abandoned their traditional song. But the texts of their camp-meeting and revival songs had contemporary publication in scores of small songsters. To a limited extent the tunes of these and other denominations found their way into print. A thousand melodies, perhaps even two thousand—they have never been accurately numbered—survive in songbooks published for northern revivals or for southern and midwestern singing schools, or after the Civil War for fundraising campaigns of black colleges.

The singing-school books—normally oblong "end-openers" printed in a "shape-note" system that facilitated sight reading of their music—are the principal and most distinctive surviving artifacts of this religious movement. Issued from such publishing centers as Cincinnati and Philadelphia, or from local presses in places like Harrisonburg, Virginia, or Pumpkintown, East Tennessee, they were compiled by home-taught rural musicians and in turn sold by the hundreds of thousands to a rural market. A half dozen of these anthologies continue in use in southern singing conventions, still in print a century to a century and a half after their first publication.

Musically—and sometimes even textually, as the following example shows—this repertory of religious song is one of the most impressive achievements in the full range of the American folk arts:

"Negro Hymn of the Judgment Day"

Don't you see the chariot riding on the clouds?
The wheels in the fire how they roll, how they roll!
    O that morning you'll hear a mighty roaring,
    That'll be the earth a-burning,
    When the Heavens fly away.

Don't you hear the trumpets blowing for the dead?
Don't you hear the bones, how they shake, how they shake!
    O that morning, etc.

Don't you see the graves they open and the dead arising?
And the bones in the fire, how they burn, how they burn!
    O that morning, etc.

Don't you see the eyes through the lids how they stare?
And the living worms, how they gnaw, how they gnaw!
    O that morning, etc.

Don't you see the king a-coming on the clouds?
See the nail prints in his hands, how they shine, how they shine!
   O that morning, etc.

Don't you see His robes a-flowing on the light?
And His head and His hair white as snow, white as snow!
   O that morning, etc.[1]

The written record does not comparably preserve any oral-sermon texts from the early nineteenth century, but it does hold accounts that intimate their art and power. One of the fullest is James B. Finley's description of the oratory of the Methodist circuit rider Peter Cartwright. This famous western preacher began one sermon, says Finley:

> with a loud and beautifully-modulated tone, in a voice that rolled on the serene night air like successive peals of grand thunder. . . . For the first ten minutes his remarks, being preparatory, were commonplace and uninteresting; but then, all of a sudden, his face reddened, his eye brightened, his gestures grew animated as the waftures of a fierce torch, and his whole countenance changed into an expression of inimitable humor; and now his wild, waggish, peculiar eloquence poured forth like a mountain torrent. Glancing arrows, with shafts of ridicule, *bon mots,* puns, and side-splitting anecdotes sparkled, flashed, and flew like hail till the vast auditory was convulsed with laughter. . . . This continued thirty minutes, while the orator painted the folly of the sinner, which was his theme. . . . then he commenced to change, not all at once, but gradually, as the wind of a thundercloud. His features lost their comical tinge of pleasantry; his voice grew first earnest, and then solemn, and soon wailed out in the tones of deepest pathos; his eyes were shorn of their mild light, and yielded streams of tears, as the fountain of the hill yielded water. The effect was indescribable, and the rebound of feeling beyond all revelation. He descanted on the horrors of hell, till every shuddering face was turned downward, as if expecting to see the solid globe rent asunder, and the fathomless, fiery gulf yawn from beneath. . . . Again he changed the theme; sketched the joys of a righteous death—its faith, its hope, its winged raptures, and what beautiful angels attended the spirit to its starry home—with such force, great and evident belief, that all eyes were turned toward heaven, as the entire congregation started to their feet, as if to hail the vision of angels at which the finger of the preacher seemed to be pointed, elevated as it was on high to the full length of his arm. He then made a call for mourners into the altar, and five hundred, many of them till that night infidels, rushed forward. . . . (Finley, 1855:323–25)

Accounts of the ex-slave preacher John Jasper of Virginia come somewhat closer to capturing the imagery and style of the oral delivery. In a sermon about the ascension of the prophet Elijah, we are told, Jasper:

> standing off like one apart from the scene, described it so thrillingly that everything was as plain as open day. To the people, the prophet was actually and visibly going away. They saw him quit the earth, saw him rise above the mountain tops, sweeping grandly over the vast fields of space,

and finally saw him as he passed the moon and stars. Then something happened. In the fraction of a second Jasper was transmuted into Elijah and was actually in the chariot and singing with extraordinary power the old chorus: "Going up to heaven in a chariot of fire." The scene was overmastering! For a time I thought that Jasper was the real Elijah, and my distinct feeling was that the song which he sang could be heard around the world. (Hatcher, 1908:69)

But even if these accounts gave full and accurate texts of the sermons preached by Cartwright and Jasper, they would still not suggest the full complexity of their art, if we may judge by the performance practices of their twentieth-century descendants. These preachers deliver a sermon not in a common speaking manner, but as sacred speech with heightened tonal and rhythmic patterning. Not until the twentieth century would their art be recognized for what it is: the dramatic performance of a chanted lyrical poem, extemporaneously composed, and delivered during the periodic celebrations of radical Protestant communities.[2]

The kinesic dimension of these ceremonies is hinted at in references to Cartwright's uplifted finger or Jasper's taking a position at one side of his pulpit to describe Elijah's flight. In the performances of their modern successors we see a rich choreography of postures and gestures, of movements around the pulpit and out into the congregation, and in some denominations, of the congregation's responsive, ecstatic seizures. But even in early depictions we also discern larger symbolic uses of sacred space in the worship service. The Methodists, to take one example, built for their camp meetings an elevated preaching stand from which to deliver God's word. At the foot of this they placed the mourners' bench, and they centered this arena at the heart of the encampment. In Dickson D. Bruce's reading of the services (1974:86–87, 132–33), they opened with seating that symbolized religious and social distinctions: the preacher elevated and apart, the men and women on separate sides of the congregation, the blacks segregated. When the sermon had its intended effect, the convicted sinners separated from the saints, rushing forward to the mourner's space. But then the divisions dissolved. The preacher descended, exhorters came forward, and male and female and even blacks and children mingled, united in a democratic gospel.

The early American Protestant radicals expressed their religious experience, then, not in ceremonial objects so much as in motion, word, and song. This practice cut across denominational, regional, and ethnic lines, for it was carried by the Second Great Awakening, a "nationalizing force," as Donald Mathews called it, that "enveloped the whole country" and created "a common world of experience," not through a strong national organization but through "strong local churches that shared values and norms" (1969:42–43).

Even a group as marginal and deviant as the Shakers would display, despite appearances to the contrary, an affinity for these same expressive forms. The Shakers did, it is true, produce a body of inspired drawings and paintings. They wore a uniform but hardly grim costume of butternut or gray or blue. They built tasteful meetinghouses with slim, tapering handrails and walls and woodwork painted a symbolic white and blue. Their written records show that they even introduced ceremonial objects into the worship service: drawings; symbolic black, red, and white sheets that mediums went through the assembly, waving; and "a tin cylindrical box, covered with cloth and leather," upon which one brother beat with a "small stick with a stuffed ball upon one end" to punctuate prophetic declarations (Avery, n.d.:147–57).

Rightly understood, however, all these exceptions prove the rule. The symbolic cloths and the drum had use in but a single Shaker meeting. The meetinghouse architecture is simply the ultimate refinement of dedicated craftsmanship working within the functionalist aesthetic that Shakers shared with other Protestant groups. Shaker costume was unadorned plain dress (fig. 91), conservatively retained after it had passed from fashion in the outside world. The Shakers themselves paid little attention to their inspired drawings (figs. 92 and 93). Their letters and journals scarcely mention them, and never with any recognition that they formed a distinct genre of spiritual gift. Few Shakers, in fact, ever exercised this gift. Those who did were mainly a handful of young women in two communities, working sporadically during a period of only fifteen years.[3]

Where the Shakers most paralleled the other groups was in the emphasis they gave to word, song, and motion. Preaching took a subordinate role in their worship, but they encouraged spontaneous testimony and, at certain moments in their history, prophetic utterance. No group surpassed them in the cultivation of song. They might sing as many as eighteen pieces in a single service and had many specialized genres of religious songs. Most of their songs originated in

Figure 91 *A Shaker outdoor service on the Holy Hill of Zion, Harvard, Massachusetts, about 1845. Shakers sometimes held services in their orchards when the trees bloomed. From David Lamson,* Two Years Among the Shakers, *1848.*

Figures 92, 93 *One of a set of "hearts of blessing" given to members attending a Shaker meeting in 1844. Sister Polly Reed was the inspired "instrument" who made them. Recipients thought of these as sacred texts rather than as drawings.*

inspired states (fig. 94), and for a century and a quarter the Shakers had a continuous flow of these distinctive new songs. Their surviving song manuscripts hold some eight to ten thousand spirituals; their full repertory must actually have been far larger. The Shakers also elaborated gesture and motion into distinctive arts. They choreographed and memorized pantomimes to underscore the meaning of many of their song texts and performed them as group rituals. They made sacred dances and marches central to their worship services, devising over the years more than thirty of these exercises (*see* Patterson, 1979).

These dances had their origin in the emotional intensity of Shakerism in the early years of the faith. The new converts, like other American revivalists, broke into spontaneous bodily manifestations of their joy in salvation. These motions the Shaker leaders regularized for periodic performance by the united congregation. They marshalled biblical precedents in support of the resulting religious dances, but their goal was actually to use dance to unite the assembly and raise it into life and power (fig. 95). Toward the close of a Shaker meeting, says one account, "they would sing quick songs and the people would dance, each like a living spark, as David danced before the Ark." And in this quick dance "would almost always come the inspiration, and heavenly gifts" (Mace, 1896).

These Shaker dances imply a last reason for the indifference of the Protestant radicals to the creation of ceremonial implements. The material object best symbolizes a state of being; the Shaker's concern was instead with the process of becoming. Shakerism was a progressive faith—its members' perfectionism was grounded on a belief in continuing revelation. They explicitly symbolized this view in one group of their physical exercises, the marches. The marching song will almost always mention going, traveling, moving, marching toward Heaven. As squads of Believers circled the meeting hall in the marches, they enacted a

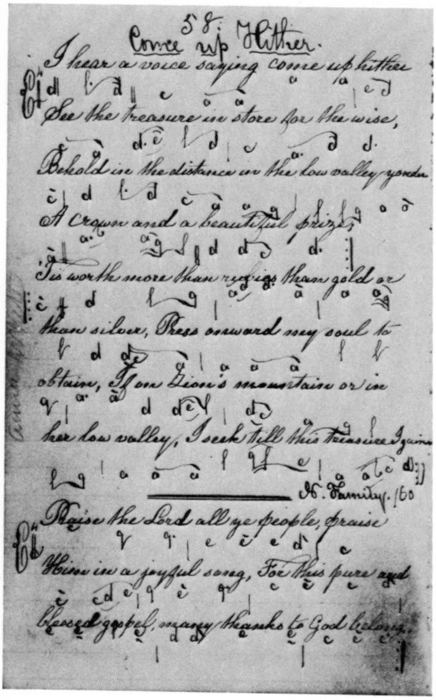

Figure 94 *A page from a Shaker song manuscript in "lettered" notation.*

Figure 95 *A Shaker circular march in the meetinghouse at Mount Lebanon, New York. From* Frank Leslie's Popular Monthly, *December 1885.*

Pilgrim's Progress. In a related ritual called the "Narrow Path" the members symbolized and encouraged an inward progress by slowly and carefully walking a thin line, setting the heel of one foot before the toes of the other, reading the while from an *invisible* book entitled "Spiritual Reflections." The only Shaker drawing to attempt to depict any of these exercises shows a straight and narrow path running across eight sheets of a scroll. Dangers and implements of torture surround the path—pincers, stones, serpents, racks, spears—but at the far right, on the last sheet, flowers and fruit trees spring up beside the path, and it enters the Walls of Zion, where Shiny Angels stand guard. Within the path, however, no pilgrim toils. It stands completely empty, and not, I think, because the Shakers thought all men had abandoned the cause of virtue. The Shaker artist wanted not a static picture of a pilgrim and a path, but an actual enactment of the spiritual journey. She gave the task to the eye of every viewer.

The concern of Shaker or Methodist, then, was with becoming. Their religious services sought to induce and to structure a transformation of the personality and to create a sacred community. Word, song, and motion served them by both inciting this change and expressing it. However such groups may differ in doctrine or practice, one may nevertheless discern in them these underlying means and aims, uniting the entire radical wing of early American Protestantism.

Notes

1. From *The Journal of American Folklore* 9 (1896):210. The original makes a fumbling and inconsistent attempt to capture the pronunciation and grammatical usage of a black singer; I have regularized the text here for readability.

2. In *The Art of the American Folk Preacher* (1970), Bruce A. Rosenberg explores the rhythmic and formulaic elements of the improvised "spiritual" sermons of contemporary black preachers. The tonal dimension of these sermons, the denominational and racial and regional variations within the tradition, and other facets await serious study.

3. I establish the dating and authorship of most of the surviving inspired Shaker artworks and reproduce ones not already known to the public through Edward D. Andrews's *Visions of the Heavenly Sphere: A Study of Shaker Religious Art* (1969) in a forthcoming monograph, *Gift Drawing and Gift Song: A Study of Two Forms of Shaker Inspiration* (Sabbathday Lake, Me.: The United Society of Shakers, 1982).

Bibliography

Andrews, Edward D.
    1969   *Visions of the Heavenly Sphere: A Study of Shaker Religious Art.* Charlottesville: University Press of Virginia.

Avery, Giles G.
N.D.   "Historical Scetches or a Record of Remarkable events With Remarks & Il-
            lustrations Kept by Giles B. Avery." Library of Congress, Papers of the Shak-
            ers, No. 53.
Bates, Issachar
N.D.   "A Sketch of the Life and Experience of Issachar Bates Sen. Transcribed
            from a Manuscript Copy belonging to the Church at Enfield N.H. By M. E.
            H." Vol. I. Emma B. King Library, Shaker Museum, Old Chatham, N.Y.
Bruce, Dickson D.
1974   *And They All Sang Hallelujah: Plain-Folk Camp-Meeting Religion, 1800–
            1845.* Knoxville: University of Tennessee Press.
Buckingham, J. S.
1841   *America, Historical, Statistic, and Descriptive.* Vol. I. New York.
Cartwright, Peter
1856   *Autobiography of Peter Cartwright, the Backwoods Preacher.* Edited by W. P.
            Strickland. New York.
Dickens, Charles
1842   *American Notes for General Circulation.* Vol. II. London.
Dwight, John Sullivan
1847   "The Shakers at New Lebanon." *The Harbinger* 5 (Aug. 14).
Finley, Rev. James B.
1855   *Autobiography of Rev. James B. Finley; or, Pioneer Life in the West.* Edited by
            W. P. Strickland. Cincinnati.
Hatcher, William E.
1908   *John Jasper, the Unmatched Negro Philosopher and Preacher.* New York.
Mace, Aurelia
1896   *Commonplace Book of Aurelia Mace.* Entry for 7 Apr. The Shaker Library,
            United Society of Shakers, Sabbathday Lake, Me.
Mathews, Donald
1969   "The Second Great Awakening as an Organizing Process, 1780–1830: An Hy-
            pothesis." *American Quarterly* 21 (Spring):23–43.
'Negro Hymn of the Judgment Day"
1896   *Journal of American Folklore* 9:210.
Patterson, Daniel W.
1979   *The Shaker Spiritual.* Princeton: Princeton University Press.
Rosenberg, Bruce A.
1970   *The Art of the American Folk Preacher.* New York: Oxford University Press.
Sutton, Brett
1977   "In the Good Old Way: Primitive Baptist Traditions." *Southern Exposure* 5
            (Summer-Fall):97–104.
Vigne, Godfrey T.
1832   *Six Months in America.* Vol. II. London.

Brothers and Neighbors: The Celebration of Community in Penitente Villages

Marta Weigle
Thomas R. Lyons

Por ser mi divina luz	By this Divine Light,
¡Ay! Jesús de l'alma mia	O Jesus of my soul,
Llevando en mi compania	I take in my brotherhood
A nuestro Padre Jesús.	Our Father Jesus.
Escuchen bien, pecadores,	Listen well, sinners,
Los esclavos de Jesús,	All ye slaves of Jesus,
Cumplan con el juramento	And comply with your oath
De nuestro Padre Jesús.	To our Father Jesus.

Initial stanzas of an alabado *or hymn transcribed and translated from a* Penitente Brother's *cuaderno or copybook by poet Alice Corbin Henderson in the 1930s.*[1]

The Brothers of Our Father Jesus, commonly (and pejoratively) known as Penitentes, are generally men of Hispanic descent who still live in or have migrated from the rural communities of northern New Mexico and southern Colorado.[2] Today a recognized, incorporated lay religious society of the Roman Catholic Church, this Brotherhood, or Pious Confraternity, evolved in what was a remote, inadequately ministered frontier province of New Spain during the late eighteenth and early nineteenth centuries. Throughout the Mexican (1821–48) and U. S. Territorial (1850–1912) periods, localized groups of Brothers, eventually known as *moradas* (a term applied both to the chapter and its meetingplace), contributed substantially to the physical, social, and spiritual welfare of pioneer Hispano communities in the northern Rio Grande Valley and beyond. Such local associations, many of which now belong to larger, formally structured *concilios* or councils, also helped to preserve the New Mexican Spanish language, folklore, and traditional Hispanic customs, celebrations, and rituals in an increasingly Anglo-dominated society. Although their strength has diminished markedly during the twentieth century, some one hundred *moradas,* mostly in New Mexico and Colorado, continue to sponsor pious observances, especially during Holy Week, and to provide, insofar as possible with very limited means, year-round mutual aid for members and unobtrusive charitable acts for neighbors within the immediate community.

Faith, exalted by its very simplicity, Hope of Salvation, through the imitation of Christ's suffering, and Charity unlimited toward their fellowman—these form the Trinity governing the 'Penitente' cult of Taos county, New Mexico.

A 1936 statement by Reyes N. Martínez, a sympathetic nonmember observer of his Arroyo Hondo neighbors who were Brothers of Our Father Jesus.[3]

To become a Brother, the initiate must devote himself to the Passion of Jesus and commit himself to lead a simple, selfless, and exemplary Christian life. He is expected to remain a practicing Roman Catholic and to maintain a good relationship with his wife and family. Men join the Brotherhood for a variety of reasons: because their fathers and grandfathers were members;[4] because they vowed to do so if certain adverse conditions like personal or family sickness, injury, or peril were alleviated; because religious and philosophical convictions compelled such a commitment; because they desired prestige or fellowship; and so on. Although all Brothers are considered equal with respect to the divine, various elected temporal officers, sometimes called *Hermanos de Luz* or Brothers of Light, govern the *morada,* supervise its rituals, and organize its charities. The highest position is that of *Hermano Mayor* or Elder Brother, and such a man is almost always a trusted, capable leader within the confraternity.

In those days when a man's harvest was ready he did not say to his neighbor, 'Come, help me.' His neighbor watched the field of his neighbor, and he knew when it was time to go and help. He did not have to be asked. . . . That is the way it should be. A man should help his neighbor without being asked.

Former Brother Cleofes Vigil of San Cristobal, New Mexico, during an interview in the late 1960s.[5]

The tangible benefits of Brotherhood membership include monetary aid and timely donations of food, labor, and vigils for the sick or incapacitated. Sometimes members are required to subscribe to insurance plans to cover burial expenses, but more frequently *moradas* act as effective, informal burial societies working with or without the priest and/or undertaker in conducting the wake, funeral, and interment. All such fraternal mutual-aid benefits are extended to nonmembers on request. As anthropologist Paul Kutsche and student Dennis Gallegos have recently reported: "Requests are rarely made by non-Catholics, but such a request is likely to be honored. '*Somos todos hijos de Dios*' ('We are all the sons of God whatever sect we belong to') is a folk saying which covers this attitude."[6]

Although there certainly were and are tensions between Brothers and nonmember neighbors, community life seems to have been, and in some places still is, enhanced by the presence of an active, functioning *morada*. Besides serving as an informal court, a welfare agency, and a burial society, the *morada* also provides the setting and personnel for both joyous and solemn community celebrations. Chief among these in traditional Hispano village culture are feast days and Holy Week observances.

The *mayordomo* who had been named at the previous feast day took charge of naming the people who were to help clean the church. The statues were brought down from their niches, dusted, dressed in new tunics, and set back in their places. Not only the church was cleaned but every house in the village was whitewashed inside, and smoothly plastered outside. . . .

When everything was in readiness, down to colorful silk dresses, people from the neighboring villages rode and walked into town to take part in the *fiesta,* which started on the eve with the usual religious ceremony of vespers.

Bonfires lit the path for the procession that came out of the Church and moved around the *plaza* in the twilight. The men standing around the bonfire poured gunpowder on an old anvil, placed a heavy rock on top, and with the red-hot point of an iron rod touched the powder. This resounding salute to the patron saint added a staccato to the beat of the drum and the gay ringing of the bell, which a man, ascending to the roof by a ladder, struck with a rock in each hand.

The next day, after the morning services, the choir and friends were invited to bountiful feasts by the *mayordomo,* who stood at the door as the people poured out of the church. . . .

In the afternoon different sports were held. The *Matachines* dance was given sometimes in the open *plaza* square; starting from there the dancers went up the *cordilleras,* dancing in the patios at different homes. . . .

I remember the dancer's fantastic costumes: purple shirts trimmed in pink, green ones in yellow—all in bright, contrasting colors. Bunches of bright-colored ribbons hung down their backs from the fancy, bishoplike caps; jewels, laces, and fringes covered their faces. Gay silk handkerchiefs floated from their shoulders and waists. This costume made a wave of color as each dancer took his turn, and with a stamping step to the tune of the one fiddle danced in and out around the single file of dancers, facing forward in two lines. Each participant held stiffly in one hand a fanlike wooden *palma* made of gaily painted sticks. . . .

The villages, usually dark and quiet at night, were now lighted and lively, for the *mayordomo* was giving a dance, the closing event of the *fiesta.* . . .

The *sala,* where the dance was given, was illuminated by candles placed on *arañas,* two crossed sticks hanging from the ceiling. Between dances, the mud floor was sprinkled with water to keep the dust down. . . .

The musicians, a fiddler and a guitar player, sat on chairs placed on top of a table at the head of the hall. Against the two side walls sat the chaperons and the *abuelitas* cuddling sleeping babies under their black shawls and puffing at their cigarettes. The whole family, from the grandparents to the wee baby, attended the dance.

Cleofas M. Jaramillo's recollections of "la funcion *(feast day)" in Arroyo Hondo, New Mexico, around the turn of the century.*[7]

Feast days traditionally celebrated varied from village to village, but most communities observed Corpus Christi (usually in June), St. John's Day (June 24), St. James's Day (July 25), St. Anne's Day (July 26), various of the Twelve Days of Christmas, and the all-important village patron saint's day with vespers, mass, processions, *bailes* (dances), sporting contests, gambling, special foods, and general merrymaking. Everyone participated to transform the mundane on such special occasions. As Jaramillo recalls, villagers, *santos* (holy images and statues, usually of wood—*see* fig. 96) and buildings were cleaned and gaily attired. Her account of daytime dancing and sports and nighttime vespers and *bailes* points out the celebration's happy contrast to the usual sobriety of workaday occupations and the dark, silent sequestration for all but evildoers at night. Sociability is intensified within this highly charged, specially demarcated atmosphere. Under the watchful eye of musicians, *bastoneros* appointed to keep order, and old grandmothers, the very "stuff" of village social life is displayed in the packed dance halls where rivalries and courtships frequently lead to impromptu singing and dancing contests as well as to fights.

Such fiestas were everyone's province. Individual Brothers helped share administrative and financial responsibilities and participated fully, but they were not formally involved as an organization. The *morada* itself sometimes served as the *depósito* or repository for village *santos;* from the *depósito* the *santos* would be carried on feast days to an open-air altar, or a location where they might be honored by all-night vigils. It was only on feast days for the *morada's* patron saint that the Brothers bore sole responsibility for the joyous occasion, which resembled the usual fiesta pattern of combined sacred and secular elements.

Brothers at Villanueva, New Mexico, observe the Day of the Triumph of the Holy Cross on September 14 or thereabouts (*see* figs. 97–103). Friends and neighbors are invited to celebrate with them in the afternoon, and preparations start early in the day. There is much socializing. Leavetaking is often marked by *abrazos,* embraces, between Brothers and departing neighbors.

It is important for this or any *morada* to honor its patron and to be properly blessed and annually renewed, because during Holy Week it becomes the center for the most solemn celebrations of both the Christian and village year.

Figure 96 *The Virgin in her somber attire.*

Figures 97–103 *Penitentes observing the Day of the Triumph of the Holy Cross, Villanueva, New Mexico.*

Figure 97 *Food is prepared by women* auxiliardoras *or auxiliaries, while the Brothers set up the outdoor stations of the cross and an altar table.*

Figure 98 *The procession begins about 3:00 P.M., when the Brothers emerge from their* morada *carrying their standard. (Note the school bus which has brought some people, including a large group of children, to the service.)*

Figure 99 *Worshipers kneel at the first station of the cross.*

Figure 100 *The procession proceeds to subsequent stations, with the priest at the end of the line.*

Figure 101   *When the priest participates, he says Mass. The* Hermano Mayor *also delivers a short sermon.*

> You know this, that many people come up here to this *morada* in the Holy Weeks. We pray the *estacions* of the Cross. . . . Now, well, in the Holy Week we got some ladies that belongs to the Society, too, and that lady they'll help us here make the food, because we stay here three days, saying the stations every day, and pray until midnight. And we eat all together in here. This is like a retreatment, but we just pray and that's all we do in here, do our penance in this *morada* here. All the *Hermanos* gets together for three days. . . . Every year we'll invite people from our vicinity, our neighbors, and to come over and say the stations with us. That comes about three o'clock. . . . And we start from here from the *morada*, and go to the *Calvario* and come back.
>
> Hermano Mayor *Jacobo Rodríguez, interviewed inside his* morada *on November 26, 1978.*

During Holy Week, the *morada* (the name means "dwelling place") becomes a literal home for the Brothers in retreat there, usually from Tuesday evening through Friday night or Saturday morning, and a symbolic home for the community. Men from different families gather together as one family, while neighbors bring food and make formalized *visitas* or visits to them. In turn, Brothers pray for their benefactors and welcome those who wish to worship with them in lay devotions such as the stations of the crosss, dramatic tableaux and readings commemorating selected aspects of the Passion, and *Tinieblas* or Tenebrae ceremonies.

Figure 102 *If no priest participates, the* Hermano Mayor *delivers his sermon and prayers are offered.*

Figure 103 *The procession returns to the* morada *and there is a short prayer service inside the chapel.*

Cleofas M. Jaramillo recalls that in Arroyo Hondo, New Mexico, "on Monday and Tuesday of Holy Week the conical adobe ovens [*hornos*] were seen smoking throughout the three villages, while the week's supply of bread and *panocha* [thick, sweet pudding made from sprouted wheat flour] was being baked." Meat was forbidden, but:

> There was a great deal of exchanging done of *charolitas*—dishes—at noon on both Holy Thursday and Good Friday. Neighbors and friends were seen carrying back and forth small bowls filled with *panocha, capirotada* [bread pudding], *torrejas con chile* [egg fritters with chile], or whatever other nice dish they had prepared. This exchange of special dishes went on in every small village during Holy Week.[8]

The Brothers were part of this communal network. Sometimes their wives and families prepared their food; sometimes *mayordomos* were appointed or volunteered to oversee these special repasts. Always, cooks vied with one another to prepare notably delectable and ample offerings.

Quien da luz en esta casa?	Who gives light in this house?
Jesus.	Jesus.
Quien la llena de alegria?	Who fills it with gladness?
Maria.	Mary.
Quien la conserva la fe?	Who preserves its faith?
Jose.	Joseph.
Luego bien claro se ve	Then it is clearly seen
Quiero alcanzar el perdon	I want to attain forgiveness
Teniendo en mi corazon	Carrying in my heart
A Jesus Maria y Jose . . .	Jesus, Mary, and Joseph . . .

Opening lines of a common prayer formula recited by both Brothers and visitors to the morada, *sometimes as a dialogue between those inside and those seeking entrance. The full prayer is recited as one approaches the door and may be continued until one reaches the* oratorio *altar.*[9]

Most *moradas* are simple, unobtrusive structures with at least two rooms plus a storage area or loft. One room, usually the only one heated, serves for meeting, eating, and sleeping, while the other is an *oratorio* or chapel. *Hermano Mayor* Jacobo Rodríguez describes the objects in his *morada's* chapel thus:

> This item I call him the *matraca*. When the *Hermanos* are resting the *Hermano Mayor* comes in here and call them with this thing. Then the *Hermanos* comes in and start praying. This item here I call him the *cuerda*. These are one of the materials that whip Christ. This one here I call him the *vela*. This is one of the materials where the face of Christ stamped on it. This one here I call him a *disciplina*. This is one of the items that the *jorjinas* whip Christ when they crucify him. All these items I keep in here in the *morada* to remind what they use when they crucify Jesus.[10]

Orlando Sena, a Brother from Sena, New Mexico, tells what he and his fellow members do during their retreat:

Well ... the prayers that we prays are rosary, and we pray for the ... dead, and we pray for the cripple, we pray for the blind, and we pray for a lot of people to help, so that God will help them out, and to have good intentions and all that. So, that's what we do. And I hope that some other young people will get interested, and will join with us in the Brotherhood. And that's all we do ... all we do is just pray for, for our people so God will help them, and keep them in good health.[11]

Brothers in retreat at their *morada* may receive a number of visitors, including *Hermanos* from other *moradas* and neighbors, who bring gifts of candles and money in exchange for prayers Brothers recite for all their deceased within memory. Many of these visitors were (and are) women. Writing of Córdova, New Mexico, in the 1920s and 1930s, Lorin W. Brown noted that:

Some women make these pilgrimages in their bare feet. ... Sometimes a woman will come to the lodge on her knees for the last thirty or forty feet and ask for bread, in God's name. A Brother will come to the door and give her a crust of dry bread and a cup of sagebrush tea, bitter as gall. The woman's dead relatives are then mentioned in petitions the Brethren address to God or some saint for the repose of their souls.[12]

Brown was a young man in his late teens when his mother, Taos native Cassandra Martínez de Brown (later López), became a schoolteacher in Córdova. He recalls:

It was my mother's custom to pay a personal visit to the *morada* during the evening of Holy Wednesday. I was with her on one of these occasions. ...

After the prayer service, we received thanks for our offerings of candles and money. We returned thanks to them for their intercessions for our departed ones. Courteously escorted through the door, we stepped out into the dusk. There, close to our path, three figures, masked and scourging themselves, paid a remarkable tribute to a woman they revered and respected, and for whom they chose this supreme recognition of her worth as neighbor, mentor, and friend.

I think that this demonstration was more noteworthy in that my mother was a Protestant, a fact known to all but discounted entirely in the esteem they held for her. I was greatly awed and moved. ...[13]

Here is a profound reciprocity indeed, and it persists today, albeit expressed through less physically severe forms of self-mortification.

Oracion:	Prayer:
Adoremos a este Cristo y bendicenos, que por tu santa cruz y pasion y muerte redimiste al mundo y a mi pecador. Amen.	Let us adore this Christ and bless ourselves that by the merits of Thy cross and passion and death Thou redeemed the world and me a sinner. Amen.

Note: This short prayer is said at the end of the recital at each station, people kissing the ground as they rise to walk to the next station.

Cantico:	Hymn:
Los inmensos dolores de	The immense sufferings of
Jesus Soverano.	Sovereign Jesus.
Repuesta:	Answer:
Lloren los corazones de	Cry hearts of all Christians,
cristianos, por la pasion	for the passion
y muerte de nuestro Senor.	and death of our Lord.

Note: This short hymn is sung as people walk from one station to the other.

Mrs. Alcaria R. Medina of Arroyo Hondo recited these words to Reyes N. Martínez in the late 1930s.[14]

During Holy Week, space outside the *morada* is considered no less sacred than the altar within. The symbolic home then becomes the center from which processions to shrines, graveyards or *camposantos,* sites marked by one or three large crosses and called *Calvarios,* local chapels, and churches, in effect weave a sacred network around and about the community. For a time, everyone lives within this periodically sacralized sanctuary.

Holy Week activities are the responsibility of the *Hermano Mayor.* He orchestrates both private and public observances according to local tradition, present circumstance and resources, personal requests from Brothers, and his own sense of appropriate solemnity. In general, penitential processions, which *formerly* included self-flagellants and cross-bearers, are more private, while stations of the cross and readings/tableaux evoking the Passion are more central and public, and continue so today.

Like other chapels and Catholic churches, most *moradas* have indoor stations of the cross affixed to their *oratorio* walls. During Holy Week, Brothers also set up outdoor *estaciones* using small wooden crosses. The large cross in front of the *morada* generally serves as the first station, and one several hundred yards distant, designated as the *Calvario,* is the fourteenth and final station in this lay devotion. Both neighbors and Brothers recite the Way of the Cross together periodically throughout Holy Week.

The popular *Encuentro* or Encounter, a stylized dramatization of the fourth station, the meeting between Jesus and His Mother on the way to Calvary, is usually enacted during late morning of Good Friday. Women with or without family ties to the Brotherhood process from one direction carrying a black-robed image of the Virgin, usually Our Lady of Sorrows. Brothers come from their *morada* bearing various standards and holy images, chief among them a nearly life-sized *Cristo,* robed in purple or red with hands bound, and usually known as *Nuestro Padre Jesús Nazareno,* Our Father Jesus Nazarite. When the two groups meet there are recitations and hymns recounting the Passion. At the appropriate time, the figures of Mother and Son are brought close together in a symbolic final embrace. It is a period of intense emotion, especially for women participants and onlookers, many of whom recall sons lost untimely, especially in war. Before the images are returned to the *morada,* most observers come forward to adore and kiss the garments of the *santos* and the border of the standards.

Ya la cruz carga Mi Nazareno. ¡Ay, que mis culpas son aquel peso!	Now the cross is borne by the Nazarene. Oh, and to think this burden was caused by sin.
Tres veces postra el duro leño en tierra al hijo del Padre Eterno.	Three times the heavy burden causes Him to stoop. Oh, Son of the Eternal Father!
Su amable madre encuentra tierno y queda herido de ambos el pecho.	His beloved mother tenderly He encounters and doubly the wounds augment in His breast.
Mujer Piadosa le ofrece un lienzo y el rostro santo recibe de premio.	A Pious woman a cloth to Him offers and the stamp of the Holy Countenance she receives as a reward.
A los que lloran por sus tormentos que lloren manda por sí y duedos.	Let those who weep for their sins dedicate their tears to His followers for love of Him.

Part of a long albado *copied from two different* cuadernos—*one belonging to* Rezador *(Prayer Leader) Tranquilino Lujan of Cerro Gordo Street, Santa Fe, and one to* Hermano Mayor *Octaviano Sandoval of Sapello, New Mexico. Aurora Lucero-White collected, combined, and translated the texts in the early 1930s.*[15]

Good Friday afternoon is marked by special observances. In the past, these included a penitential procession in which one or two Brothers dragged a death cart and a simulated crucifixion. Death is depicted as a black-robed or skeletal female figure, commonly called *Doña Sebastiana,* who brandishes a wooden hatchet (fig. 104) or drawn bow and arrow (fig. 105). Persistent legends tell how an accidental jolt of her cart (which has fixed wheels and was sometimes filled with stones to increase the severity of the penance when the horsehair rope cut more deeply across the Brother's bare chest) caused the arrow's release, killing either a bystander or the penitent Brother himself. Such beliefs and *memento mori* served as vivid reminders of mortality. Death was in no sense sought or worshiped, but "a 'good death' (*buena muerte,* one in the state of grace leading to entrance into heaven) was a favor fervently to be prayed for."[16] Anthropologist George Mills has suggested that in their *moradas* and processions, Brothers powerfully juxtaposed the two types of death—Christian death, symbolized by crosses and crucifixes, and "unprepared-for" death, sym-

Figure 104 *Death in her coffin. Note that she carries a hatchet in this representation.*

bolized by *Sebastiana* in her crude New Mexican ox-cart—in a wall *nicho* or niche, on the altar, or beside the door.[17]

In this century, the simulated crucifixion, in which a black-hooded, white-shrouded Brother was briefly bound to a cross during a short meditation or sermon on the last words or an appropriate song or prayer, has been replaced by no less effective expressions. Wooden *santos,* some with articulated limbs, are used throughout. Even if human actors take roles in a quasi-Passion play, the dramatic tableaux are in no sense literal enactments either of scripture or Way of the Cross devotions.

One such "dramatic reading" takes place on Good Friday afternoon in the vicinity of Ranchos de Taos, New Mexico. Writer Blanche C. Grant straightforwardly recounted the rites she witnessed there shortly after World War I:

> In front of the half square which the building makes, was run a rope, supporting a sheet curtain, which did not hide from view the workers who

Figure 105 *Figure of Death in a cart, New Mexico. A cart, covered with black cloth and painted with skeletons and white crosses, is drawn by black buffaloes and bears the figure of Death, carrying a bow and arrow.*

brought out of the *morada* and placed in position, a black cross, about seven feet high. On this they hung an old wooden figure of the Christ about the waist of which fluttered two aprons, pink beneath and white on top. On the head was the crown of thorns which was secured by corn-colored ribbon caught under the wooden beard. By his side stood a bare-footed centurion, dressed in white and wearing over his cross-marked fore-head, a colored turban into which was thrust a tiny American flag. He carried a spear, a pole topped with an old bayonet, with which he struck the figure in the side at the proper time in the reading. Again, this was the only effort at dramatization during the whole "play" which is in reality a service.

When the reading was done, the figure was tenderly lifted from the cross and carried to the shrine of Mary—an image placed on a table nearby covered with white oil-cloth. It was carried past the three little girls, all in black, save for orange-blossom wreathes over their flowing hair. They held a long cloth on which were three impressions of the thorn-crowned Christ head. Then the wooden figure of the Crucified One was laid in a coffin lined with artificial flowers and decorated on the outside with strips of white embroidery which, against the black, suggested carving. When the peaked rooflike top was closed, the men lifted the coffin. Out from the *morada* came a young man who carried a crucifix on his shoulder. He led the whole procession. He ... wore a regulation khaki army overcoat. Behind the coffin, held high on the shoulders of the bearers, followed and well-nigh staggered, the fellows who had been inside the church and on whose bleeding backs we had heard the swish of the lash fall during the service. They wore their coats and bandaged their heads with colored kerchiefs. We followed after, stopped too at the cross and then watched the procession turn and wind its way back to their *morada,* singing as they went.[18]

Except for the flagellants inside, the "service" she describes is remarkably similar to those reported in intervening decades,[19] and it continues so today.

A series of photographs taken at San Mateo, New Mexico, in 1925, show community and Brotherhood participation in a more elaborate sort of Passion play. Historian Dorothy Woodward, who corresponded with eyewitness Harriet Mayfield, summarized the events depicted:

Issuing from the *morada,* the *Pitero* [flute player], whose music was weird and penetrating, began to play. Three young girls, in white confirmation robes, led the march going forward on their knees. Each one carried a platter on which there were a crown of thorns, a hammer, and a reed, some of the instruments of the Passion. ... Following them were St. Veronica and the three Marys. The Christus, bound and weary from the blows of the crowd, was brought out of the *morada* by the Roman soldiers. They placed on his shoulder a heavy cross the weight of which bent him down. He took his place in the procession and was followed by more Penitentes carrying an image of Christ also in bonds. They marched from the *morada* up the canyon and back to the *morada.* ...[20]

Whatever the form of solemn celebration, the Crucifixion is central to Christian faith. Raising the cross, whether literally or symbolically, reconsecrates and reaffirms the local community and recalls the redemption of the world. It is critically important that every believer be allowed to participate in this supreme mystery. As Jesuit scholar Thomas J. Steele astutely observes of all such "passion plays," whether Brotherhood-sponsored or not:

Despite the disastrous character of the death of the God-man as it is viewed objectively, the event (when viewed subjectively as the redemption of Christians for their sins) calls for involvement not just for individuals but for a whole village of persons who have their main identification on the village level. ... The important thing is that one has become involved, has helped, whether as actor or as singing and praying member of the congregation, to perform the cosmogonic event of the Christian world.[21]

This applies to Brothers as well. They too participate and help make possible this participation, especially in communities without a resident priest. Holy

Week observances are thus not only rituals of spiritual transformation for religious individuals but also important expressions of communion and community. They reconfirm basic interpersonal ties which make continued existence both possible and significant.

Companeros, pues nos convidan	Companions, we are invited
Los angeles y serafines,	By angels and seraphims,
Vamos en su compania	Let us, in their company,
Un alabado cantando.	Sing a hymn of praise.
Dadme una muerte feliz,	Give me a happy death
Hombre, Dios, Jesus Sagrado,	Man, God, Jesus sacred.
Dadme una muerte feliz,	Give me a happy death,
Madre mia del Rosario.	My mother of the rosary.

The opening stanzas of an alabado, *"A la Madre del Rosario," "To Our Mother of the Rosary"), sung by Brothers in Arroyo Hondo, New Mexico.*[22]

A lengthy rosary service led by one or more Brothers generally precedes *Las Tinieblas,* the so-called earthquake or Tenebrae service of Good Friday night. This is the Brothers' last public ritual during Holy Week. Together with most villagers and often a fair number of outsiders, they gather in the church or *morada* for a devotion similar to the official Church ritual which commemorates the chaos following Jesus' death.

At the beginning of *Tinieblas,* the only light comes from thirteen to seventeen candles in a triangular white standing candelabrum, a special black *tenebrario* holder, or on the altar. Each candle or pair of candles, which symbolize the desertion of the apostles, is extinguished following the singing of an *alabado* verse. Lorin W. Brown describes what happens when the last light, representing the dead Lord, is removed or covered:

> Suddenly, a voice calls out *"Ave Maria,"* whereupon a deafening tumult breaks out. It is the clapping of hands added to the clattering racket of the *matracas* in the hands of the Brethren. When the noise dies down, someone is heard saying: *"Un sudario en el nombre de Dios por l'alma del difunto Jose."* ("A prayer for the repose of the soul of the deceased Jose, in the name of God.")
>
> A subdued murmur is heard as most of the assembly join in the semi-whispered response to the request. Another name is called out, and the request is complied with. Perhaps three or more requests for prayers are called out and complied with when the same voice again calls out *"Ave Maria,"* and the clapping of hands is resumed with the accompanying sounds as before . . . [including] the rattling of heavy chains.[23]

The alternating cacophony and prayer lasts nearly an hour before the single remaining light is returned and the others relit from it. If held in a church, the Brothers leave first, facing the altar and walking backward until out of the door. If at a *morada,* nonmembers depart immediately.

The *Tinieblas* is a dramatic highpoint in the village year. Families and neighbors literally huddle together in the din-filled, disorienting darkness—in the midst of chaos. At the same time, they symbolically take a stand in the face of this disintegration and are, in a sense, "heartened." In calling out the names of their beloved departed, they vividly recall the human history and foundations of their community. Thus, although apparently the antithesis of the crowded, brightly lit *baile* hall, the darkened church or *morada* is no less a place for the celebration of enduring human ties.

Perhaps most important in the tumult and prayer of the *Tinieblas,* both Brothers and neighbors fulfill the charge given by the deceased in this popular funeral hymn:

Adios por ultima vez	Good-by for the last time,
Que me ven sobre la tierra	Those who see me on this earth,
Me echan a la sepultura	Place me in the sepulcher
Que es la casa verdadera.	Which is truly my house.
Adios todos los presentes	Good-by, all those present,
Que me van a acompañar,	All who accompany me,
Rezen algun sudario	Pray a *sudario*
Para poder alcanzar.	In order to overtake me.
Adios todos mis proximos,	Good-by, all my neighbors,
Toditos en general,	All, all in general,
Encomienden mi alma a Dios,	Commend my soul to God,
No me vayan a olvidar.	And do not forget me.
Fin-Fin-Amen	The End-Amen[24]

Notes

1. Alice Corbin Henderson, *Brothers of Light: The Penitentes of the Southwest* (1937:86, 87). According to Henderson, this "small *Penitente* copy-book, much worn from use ... includes nineteen songs; one of these recounting the whole story of Christ's life and Resurrection, has one hundred and forty stanzas" (p. 85). A slightly different version of the Spanish text is in Juan B. Rael, *The New Mexican 'Alabado'* (1951:33–34, 140). This particular *alabado* is not included in John Donald Robb's pioneer collection, *Hispanic Folk Music of New Mexico and the Southwest: A Self-Portrait of a People* (1980), but Robb does reproduce two illustrated, handwritten pages from a Brother's small notebook or *cuaderno* (p. 619).

2. For a reliable history and description of the Brotherhood, see Marta Weigle, *Brothers of Light, Brothers of Blood: The Penitentes of the Southwest* (1976), and her companion compilation of some 1,200 sources, *A Penitente Bibliography* (1976). Most notes in this paper will cite only more recent works. For example, for further historical background on the villages and the Brotherhood, see appropriate chapters on New Mexico social history in Oakah L. Jones, Jr., *Los Paisanos: Spanish Settlers on the Northern Frontier of New Spain* (1979).

3. Reyes N. Martínez, "Early Settlements, Folkways of Northern Taos County," last line of

a three-page ms. dated February 29, 1936, in the files of the New Mexico Federal Writer's Project, History Library, Museum of New Mexico, Santa Fe [hereafter designated FWP-MNM]. Martínez was a young field writer on the Project at the time, and he submitted a number of manuscripts describing Brotherhood rites and beliefs from a non-member neighbor's perspective.

4. Orlando Sena of Sena, New Mexico, paid tribute to his father in an interview with Thomas R. Lyons on November 19, 1978. When asked whether he had always wanted to be a Brother, Sena replied: "Well, I, I always pretend to be one until I was up to be the age to come in as a Brother. My, my father was, was a Brother for I think fifty years in the *morada*. So he told me one day ... do you wanna be in my place because I'm gonna die. You know, he was old and I told him sure. And I went and I became a Brother and I got so much faiths on it ... I think I will never get outta it till I die the same way as my Dad did ... And that's why I, I'm asking the young ones to come on and join us because it's one of the greatest things in the world for a man to be ... and I really thank my Dad for making me become a member of the Society of the Brotherhood. And I think that's, that's a great thing and I have to appreciate that to my Dad."

5. As reported by Stan Steiner in his contemporary portrait of *La Raza: The Mexican Americans* (1970:4). Vigil is a rancher, poet, and singer who has recorded two albums of hymns for Taos Recordings and Publications, Taos, New Mexico 87571: "New Mexican Alabados" (TRP-3, 1961), and "*Buenos días, paloma blanca:* Five Alabados of Northern New Mexico" (TRP-122, n.d.).

6. Paul Kutsche and Dennis Gallegos, "Community Functions of the *Cofradía de Nuestro Padre Jesús Nazareno*" (1979:92). According to the first note, Kutsche provided "some of the field data," while Gallegos, then of Jemez Valley High School and "a native of a Northern New Mexican village, provided the bulk of the field data" (p. 98).

7. Cleofas M. Jaramillo, *Shadows of the Past (Sombras del pasado)* (1941; reprint 1972:48–49, 50–51). For photos, musical transcriptions, and a brief discussion of *Matachines* dances, see Robb, *Hispanic Folk Music* (1980:741–80). Jaramillo is Reyes N. Martínez's sister. For pictures of their village and its religious settings, see Robert L. Shalkop, *Arroyo Hondo: The Folk Art of a New Mexican Village* (1969). For more on feast days there and elsewhere, see Juan B. Rael, "New Mexican Spanish Feasts" (1942:83–90).

8. Jaramillo (1972:67); also noted in Kutsche and Gallegos (1972:94). For more on native Hispanic foods and their association with various celebrations, including Lent and wakes, see Fabiola Cabeza de Baca Gilbert, *The Good Life: New Mexican Food* (1949:37–43).

9. Reyes N. Martínez, "Oraciones: Prayers," second page of a ms. dated April 10, 1940, in the FWP-MNM. (Note that *no* diacritical marks appear on the original typescript.)

10. Jacobo Rodríguez (whose New Mexico village will not be identified), interview with Thomas R. Lyons, November 26, 1978.

11. Interview of November 19, 1978.

12. Lorenzo de Córdova [pseud. for Lorin W. Brown], *Echoes of the Flute* (1972:41–42). This is part of an undated ms., "Lent in Córdova," which Brown wrote while a field writer with the New Mexico Federal Writers' Project. The bulk of Brown's FWP contributions, most of which deal with Taos and Córdova, are collected and documented in Lorin W. Brown with Charles L. Briggs and Marta Weigle, *Hispano Folklife of New Mexico: The Lorin W. Brown Federal Writers' Project Manuscripts* (1978).

13. Lorenzo de Córdova (1972:33–34), part of a 1971 essay entitled "Echoes of the Flute." For more on Brown's mother, see Briggs and Weigle (1978), and for more on Córdova, including Brown and his family, and *santos*, see Charles L. Briggs, *The Wood Carvers of Córdova, New Mexico: Social Dimensions of an Artistic "Revival"* (1980).

14. Martínez, "Oraciones" (1940:3–4). (Again, no diacritical marks on the original typescript.) Also see Reginald Fisher, ed., *The Way of the Cross: A New Mexico Version* (1958).

15. Aurora Lucero-White with Ina Sizer Cassidy, "The Penitentes of New Mexico," p. 22 of a ms. dated August 31, 1936, in the FWP-MNM. A slightly different version of the Spanish text is in Rael, *New Mexican 'Alabado'* (1951:47, 142).

16. Thomas J. Steele, S. J., *Santos and Saints: Essays and Handbook* (1974:90). Also see his more recent article, "The Death Cart: Its Place among the Santos of New Mexico" (1979:1–14).

17. George Mills, *Kachinas and Saints: A Contrast in Style and Culture* (1953), unpaginated exhibition catalogue. Also see Marta Weigle, "Ghostly Flagellants and Doña Sebastiana: Two Legends of the Penitente Brotherhood" (1977:135–47).

18. Blanche C. Grant, *Taos Today* (1925:30–31).

19. Chief among these eyewitness accounts are: Mary Austin, "Native Drama in Our Southwest" (1927:437–40); Fred M. Mazzrella, "The Penitentes" (1954:10–11); Harold Nelson Ottaway, "The *Penitente Moradas* of the Taos, New Mexico, Area" (1975).

20. Dorothy Woodward, "The Penitentes of New Mexico" (1935:235). This seminal work has been reprinted with a foreword by Myra Ellen Jenkins in *The Penitentes of New Mexico* (1974). Harriet Mayfield's description and two of her eight photographs appeared in the *Los Angeles Sunday Times* (May 31, 1925) under the title "Devout People Enact Sacred Drama Every Year in Quaint Town."

21. Thomas J. Steele, S.J., "The Spanish Passion Play in New Mexico and Colorado" (1978:256).

22. Reyes N. Martínez, "A La Madre Del Rosario: To the Mother of the Rosary," unidentified ms. in the FWP-MNM. (Again, no diacritical marks in the original typescript.) The note reads: "This hymn is sung by the members of the Penitente fraternity in ceremonies held at their lodge, during Lent." A slightly different version of the Spanish text is in Rael, *New Mexican 'Alabado'* (1951:130).

23. Lorenzo de Córdova, *Echoes of the Flute* (1972:43).

24. Henderson, *Brothers of Light* (1937:106, 107). A slightly different version of the Spanish text is in Rael, *New Mexican 'Alabado'* (1951:135). Also see the section on the *despedimento,* a song of farewell in which the deceased speaks in the first person, in Robb, *Hispanic Folk Music* (1980:710–16).

Bibliography

Austin, Mary
1927   "Native Drama in Our Southwest." *Nation* 124:437–40.
Briggs, Charles L.
1980   *The Wood Carvers of Córdova, New Mexico: Social Dimensions of an Artistic "Revival."* Knoxville: University of Tennessee Press.
Brown, Lorin W., with Charles L. Briggs and Marta Weigle
1978   *Hispano Folklife of New Mexico: The Lorin W. Brown Federal Writers' Project Manuscripts.* Albuquerque: University of New Mexico Press.
Córdova, Lorenzo de
1972   *Echoes of the Flute.* Santa Fe, New Mexico: Ancient City Press.
Fisher, Reginald, ed.
1958   *The Way of the Cross: A New Mexico Version.* School of American Research Publication. Santa Fe, New Mexico: Graphic Printing.
Gilbert, Fabiola Cabeza de Baca
1949   *The Good Life: New Mexican Food.* Sante Fe, New Mexico: San Vincente Foundation.
Grant, Blanche C.
1925   *Taos Today.* Taos, New Mexico: By the author.
Henderson, Alice Corbin
1937   *Brothers of Light: The Penitentes of the Southwest.* New York: Harcourt, Brace.
Jaramillo, Cleofas M.
1972   *Shadows of the Past (Sombras del Pasado).* 1941. Reprint. Santa Fe, New Mexico: Ancient City Press.
Jones, Oakah L., Jr.
1979   *Los Paisanos: Spanish Settlers on the Northern Frontier of New Spain.* Norman: University of Oklahoma Press.
Kutsche, Paul, and Gallegos, Dennis
1979   "Community Functions of the *Cofradía de Nuestro Padre Jesú Nazareno.*" In *The Survival of Spanish American Villages,* edited by Paul Kutsche. Colorado College Studies, No. 15 (Spring), pp. 91–98.
Lucero-White, Aurora, and Cassidy, Ina Sizer
1936   "The Penitentes of New Mexico." Manuscript dated Aug. 31, *New Mexico Federal Writers' Project,* History Library, Museum of New Mexico, Santa Fe.
Martinez, Reyes N.
1936   "Early Settlements, Folkways of Northern Taos County." Manuscript dated Feb. 29, *New Mexico Federal Writers' Project,* History Library, Museum of New Mexico, Santa Fe.
1940   "Oraciones: Prayers." Manuscript dated Apr. 10, *New Mexico Federal Writers' Project,* History Library, Museum of New Mexico, Santa Fe.

N.D. "A La Madre Del Rosario: To the Mother of the Rosary." Manuscript, *New Mexico Federal Writers' Project*, History Library, Museum of New Mexico, Santa Fe.

Mayfield, Harriet
1925 "Devout People Enact Sacred Drama Every Year in Quaint Town." *Los Angeles Sunday Times,* May 31.

Mazzulla, Fred M.
1954 "The Penitentes." *Empire: Magazine of the Denver Post,* Apr. 11.

Mills, George
1953 *Kachinas and Saints: A Contrast in Style and Culture.* Colorado Springs, Colorado: Taylor Museum of the Colorado Springs Fine Arts Center.

Ottaway, Harold Nelson
1975 "The *Penitente Moradas* of the Taos, New Mexico Area." Ph.D. dissertation, University of Oklahoma.

Rael, Juan B.
1942 "New Mexican Spanish Feasts." *California Folklore Quarterly* 1:83–90.
1951 *The New Mexican 'Alabado.'* Transcription of music by Eleanor Hague. *Stanford University Publications in Language and Literature,* vol. IX, no. 3.

Robb, John Donald
1980 *Hispanic Folk Music of New Mexico and the Southwest: A Self-Portrait of a People.* Norman: University of Oklahoma Press.

Shalkop, Robert L.
1969 *Arroyo Hondo: The Folk Art of a New Mexican Village.* Colorado Springs, Colorado: Taylor Museum of the Colorado Springs Fine Arts Center.

Steele, Thomas J., S.J.
1974 *Santos and Saints: Essays and Handbook.* Albuquerque, N.M.: Calvin Horn.
1978 "The Spanish Passion Play in New Mexico and Colorado." *New Mexico Historical Review* 53:239–59.
1979 "The Death Cart: Its Place among the Santos of New Mexico." *Colorado Magazine* LV/1:1–14.

Steiner, Stan
1970 *La Raza: The Mexican Americans.* New York: Harper and Row.

Weigle, Marta
1976 *Brothers of Light, Brothers of Blood: The Penitentes of the Southwest.* Albuquerque: University of New Mexico Press.
1976 *A Penitente Bibliography.* Albuquerque: University of New Mexico Press.
1977 "Ghostly Flagellants and Doña Sebastiana: Two Legends of the Penitente Brotherhood." *Western Folklore* 36:135–47.

Woodward, Dorothy
1974 *The Penitentes of New Mexico.* Ph.D. dissertation, Yale University, 1935. New York: Arno Press.

5

See *Figure 111*.

Sociation and Sociability in Political Celebrations

John J. MacAloon

King, they reject thee,
King, they hate thee.

Play like tides of the sea,
You Inexplicable, Great Mountain.
Our Bull.

Swazi Incwala chants

Among the many ritual types falling under the rubric of "political and civic celebrations" are rites that celebrate a rise in status, such as the festivities of kingship. Of these, the most famous example in anthropological literature is the Incwala ceremony of the southern African Swazi people, documented by Hilda Kuper (1947) and subsequently reinterpreted by Max Gluckman (1963:119–36), Victor Turner (1967:108–10), and others. The rite has received so much attention because it exhibits in quintessential form structural features, symbolic motifs, and performative patterns that recur in the political ceremonies of many peoples.

Incwala takes place at the summer solstice, marking the emergence of the new year from the dying old one, and it is full of lunar symbolism as well. The celebration of the first-fruits of the harvest, the presence of supernatural and ancestral beings, and the sacrifice of ritually selected animals further join the cosmological and natural orders with the social order undergoing transition in the inauguration of its new lion-king.

Through much of the ritual, the king is secreted away in a sacred enclosure—an aspect of liminal symbolism common to initiation rites everywhere—attended only by priests who treat him with powerful medicines. Complicated rites of reversal attend the reappearance of the king before his subjects when the moon is full. In the very moments of his elevation, the king is brought low, "divested," as Turner puts it, "of all the outward attributes, the 'accidents,' of his kingship and . . . reduced to its substance, the 'earth' and 'darkness' " (1967:110). He is first naked, save for a prepuce-cover, then costumed as a wild monster, sliced open and bled by the sharp grass that "adorns" him as he dances crazily, wild with pain and rage. In dance, chant, and gesture, discrete groups of subjects alternately pity and lament for him; taunt, vilify, and revile him; and extol his strength and triumph. As Gluckman wrote of Kuper's description:

> One can feel the acting out of the powerful tensions which make up national life—king and state against people, people against king and state; king allied with commoners against his rival brother-princes, commoners allied with princes against the king; the relation of the king to his mother and his own queens; and the nation united against internal enemies and external foes, and in a struggle for a living with nature. (1963:125)

Gluckman understood the oscillation between expressions of rebellion and solidarity within the rite as part and parcel of one another. While the ceremony "is not a simple mass assertion of unity," it does "defend the kingship against the king" and depends on "the acceptance of the established order as right and good." Gluckman stressed that "the dramatic, symbolic acting of social relations in their ambivalence is believed to achieve unity and prosperity" (1963:125–27, 129). In his commentary, Turner argued that the regeneration of the "normal structured order of the Swazi kingdom" depends upon the "social antistructure" of the ritual's liminal phase for its affective and moral efficacy (1967:110).

Along with unity and rebellion, structure and antistructure, there is another dialectical opposition present here, one less clearly understood, that between solemnity and festivity. Not only is the final phase of Incwala one of communal feasting and revelry (another common pattern); not only is one of the rites a period of ritual work for the king in the queen-mother's garden, described by the Swazi by a term for "working with little energy, with play and dawdling"; but among the related Zulu at any rate, the whole first-fruits ceremony is called "playing with the king." The entire rite, engaging the most sacred, serious, and socially consequential features of Swazi life, is a celebration possessing an irreducibly ludic aspect.

Rank, Leadership, and Conspicuous Creation

These oppositions are encoded in remarkable objects, complex and symbolic in form, which are used dynamically in their appropriate settings. In many other celebrations (especially those illustrated in the *Celebration* exhibition), the same kinds of opposition can be found.[1] Several objects are the insignia of chiefs or other civic and political notables: garments or ornaments whose rare or laboriously produced materials, unusual quantity or workmanship, or ritual transformation from mundane items into prestige-bearing *sacra* symbolically distinguish the leader from his subjects, persons of higher from those of lower rank or accomplishment. Yet in an equal variety of ways, each is also a highly charged emblem of the ties that bind together leader and led, the high and the low, in a common social world.

The extraordinary Hawaiian *'ahu 'ula,* a cape of intricately woven and tied feathers (fig. 106) could be worn only by important chiefs. Yellow feathers were rarest and the most difficult to collect. The number of feathers, together with the overall size of the garment, indicated the relative status of the chief who owned and wore it on ceremonial occasions. Yet, in its making, the *'ahu 'ula* came to embody the interdependency as much as the social distance between the various ranks. Male commoners trapped the birds and commoner women wove the bast foundation, while craftsmen-priests alone could tie the feathers into the design. The symbolism of solidarity and interdependence (and, presumably, of dominance and hostility as well) between the social ranks was given even more patent expression in the aristocrat's walrus-tooth pendant suspended from a braid of human commoners' hair.

Often the "same" object of prestige has very different connotations in different social systems. The Maori, too, wove delicate and intricate feather cloaks, but in this politically acephalous and socially egalitarian society, the cape was imbued with no ascriptive power of rank but with the personal power, or *mana,* of the individual who owned it and of the succession of individuals who

Figure 106 Feather cape, Hawaii, eastern Polynesia.

handed it down—power won through particular deeds and experiences. Yet here, too, the object embodied not only the special prestige of its owner but ultimate community ties as well. *Mana,* for the Maori, is the most significant force in the common social universe and is available to almost anyone who cares to pursue it. The Maori cape, like the experiences it stores and enshrines, embodies the puzzle of *mana* that has bedeviled the understanding of Western scholars since the turn of the century. In societies like the Maori, *mana,* is at once the diffuse and general ground of cultural structure and, at the same time, the most focal, particularized epitome of it.

Like the Hawaiians, Fijian Islanders are organized into chiefdoms (though less centralized ones); like the Maori, there is no class of substances forbidden to all but high-ranking persons. Here prestige objects like the *tapa* cloth breechclout (fig. 107) are marked by quantity and size, not material. Every Fijian man wears a breachclout, but the chief's may be hundreds of feet long, worn draped about him on ceremonial occasions. Wealth in *tapa* cloth, worn or rolled up, is an index of power and status, but *tapa* itself is an everyday item.

Often ritual context controls the messages delivered by conspicuous objects. Among many Central African peoples, utilitarian need has bred a class of objects used to flick away flies and other insect pests. Whisks made from dried elephant tails (fig. 108), because of the beast's size and power, are typically associated with chiefs and other male elders. Yet in the final phase of the *Nkang'a* puberty ceremony of the Ndembu people, the newly initiated girl carries such a whisk

Figure 107 *A Fijian noble dressed in swaths of* tapa *cloth. Drawing by Theodor Kleinschmidts, 1877.*

Figure 108 *Elephant-tail fly whisk,
probably from the Northern Congo Basin.*

in a double act of inversion and usurpation. The powers of a low female are
likened to those of a male chief in a statement asserting the opposition and
unification of the powers of the strong and weak.[2]

In the modern West, power, prestige goods, and monetary wealth are so
closely identified that they have readily been confused with one another elsewhere. Whether of rare and tabooed material like Hawaiian *oo* and *i'iwi* feathers, or commonplace and unrestricted like Fijian *tapa;* whether accumulated
and stored "as such" like Yurok dentalia shells, or woven into costumes like the
feathers of a Guaraní outfit (fig. 109), such goods have often been mistaken for
the functional equivalents of currency by Westerners; at the same time their embodiment of solidarity and interconnection has been ignored in favor of their
representation of stratification and domination. To take but one example, generations of American observers mistook the dentalia shell complex of the Yurok
Indians of Northern California for a wealth quest in our sense and even on occasion referred to them as "primitive capitalists." In truth, accumulation of dentalia by high men and families is understood by the Yurok to mark and accompany success in esoteric religious practice rather than economic success in
entrepreneurial acquisition.[3]

In some small-scale societies, financial assets may be joined with political and
religious qualification in the selection of persons for office. However, instead of
a means of consolidating and augmenting wealth (as is generally the case with
us), office-holding in institutional complexes like the "cargo" system among
Mexican and Guatemalan peoples entails the spending of such assets in fulfilling
the office-holder's responsibilities. In the cargo system, the creation of transient
status hierarchies (fig. 110) helps prevent the development of class hierarchies
by leveling income and wealth.

Figure 109 *Guaraní chieftain's feathered headdress, Guaraní, Paraguay, or Brazil.*

Figure 110 *Cargo-holder's house model, Mexico (?). This model, made by an unknown artist, depicts a scene of religious or political officeholders from the region of Lake Atitlan, Guatemala. The Indians depicted are probably Chakchiquiel-speakers.*

Figure 111   Wooden clan hat, Haida,
Skidegate, Queen Charlotte Islands,
British Columbia.

The famous institution of the potlatch among such Northwest Coast Indian groups as the Kwakiutl and the Haida (*see* Stanley Walens's essay in this volume) also involved, in the short run at least, not the hoarding but the giving away of wealth in exchange for social position. But the potlatch differs in many respects from the cargo complex: the former involves elaborately formal gift-giving of prestige goods, while the latter requires the routine financing of celebrations with food or food-derived commodities; in the former, the giver gains a more permanent and heritable rank, while in the latter he wins temporary and non-heritable power and status.

There were several kinds of traditional potlatch, but the largest involved the installation and confirmation of persons acceding to positions as heads of ranked clans, ranked lineages within clans, or ranked houses within lineages. The ceremony asserted the rank of the receivers as well as the givers, for gifts were distributed according to a minutely scrutinized order of precedence. Indeed the whole performance proclaimed the principles of rank and reciprocity which generated the social order. The preconditions of these principles are group identity and membership, and the potlatch asserted these strongly—from the items of crest art laboriously created (and not given away) by the potlatch-givers to the regalia of hosts and guests alike. To mention but one item included in the exhibit: the marvelous Haida clan hat (fig. 111), beneath which an agitated human face would peer out at the present, twinned with the imperturbable and trans-temporal gaze of the bear above, seems to proclaim *sumus ursi, ergo sum,* "We are bears, therefore I am." To the extent that a civic or political celebration engages a society in a total encounter with and transformation of itself, it will contain regenerative markers of the whole range of identities of those who compose it, as the potlatch demonstrates in its every aspect.

The objects briefly discussed here and those in the rest of the exhibition collection are all "conspicuous creations," devices for mobilizing, attracting, focusing, and ordering attention. Whether through their materials, iconography, tabooed condition, form of display, aesthetic quality, or combinations of these, such objects remind the participants of and add to the conspicuousness of the occasions for which they are created, conferred, exchanged, and displayed. As these examples have shown, such objects emblemize both social differentiation and conflict, and unity and solidarity. In the rites of differentiation in which these objects are "performers," there is no greater commonality of experience than the conspicuously shared intensity of attention created. This seems a small thing, readily taken for granted, until one pauses to realize that attention is, perhaps, the most precious human good. It is tautological to say that transitions of the greatest practical consequence for a people's normative life, drawing them briefly into the novelty, freedom, and terror of antistructure, and mobilizing them in all their manifold identities, are likely to provoke their most intense attention. To say that such rites will not succeed without so attracting their attention is not tautological in the least.

The Play of Politics

But why should the Haida have elaborated such a complex form as the potlatch to proclaim what is obvious to every Haida and which every other social act asserts: corporate identity, rank, and reciprocity? Clifford Geertz asked this same question of the Balinese cockfight and recognized in its answer signals of play (1973). In English language and culture, we are accustomed to categorizing cockfights as play, tacitly recognizing a more general relation between form and material analyzed by Georg Simmel:

> This complete turnover, from the determination of the forms by the materials of life to the determination of its materials by forms that have become supreme values, is perhaps most extensively at work in the numerous phenomena that we lump together under the category of *play*. Actual forces, needs, impulses of life produce the forms of our behavior that are suitable for play. These forms, however, become independent contents and stimuli within play itself or, rather, *as* play. (1950:42)

In political and other rites that instrumentally maintain and regenerate social systems, "actual forces, needs, impulses of life" remain directly present and central, and to describe such performances as "games" pure and simple is to commit a category error whose roots will be indicated below. Nevertheless, the rules which govern their instrumental action may in certain modes and moments of the rite become hyperelaborated and in others become "supreme values" in which formal representation of material interests dominates those material interests themselves. In the potlatch, this ludic element appears under a double aspect as tense, gamelike contest in the focal exchanges, and as festivity in the dancing, singing, feasting, and drinking which surround, permeate, orchestrate, and punctuate the performance process. These latter also concern themselves with identity, rank, and reciprocity, but in a way at once more incorporative, aesthetically distant, and psychologically proximate, through the refocusing of heightened collective attention on style, form, and good feeling. These two aspects of play are intimately related in sociopolitical rites such as potlatch, cargo, and *Incwala*. As Huizinga realized in the most important sentence in his manifesto *Homo Ludens,* all play either "represents a contest or becomes a contest for the best representation of something" (1955:13). When *Incwala* is described generically as "playing with the king," this hidden unity is recognized.

We in the West typically fail to recognize such unity because of our tendency to separate the "core" of the rite, its "serious business," from what we take to be the peripheral "carrying on," "letting loose," and "screwing around" that accompany it. But the phrases "mere enjoyment," "just having fun," "mere licentiousness" are rarely known in other cultures and, where known, are infrequently apposite in ritual contexts like the ones described here. In these cultures, pleasure is not in itself a guilt-ridden thing; there are gods who play, and kings, chiefs, and cargo-holders have as a central feature of their "duties" to make the people feel good. For hierarch and subject alike, these performances must not only make the obligatory world of stratification, domination, and leadership desirable, but make the desirable world of shared good feeling obligatory. If people feel good at rites of installation and confirmation of leaders, a fine augury for the future course of the leader's tenure and rule has been achieved. In this respect, the festive component of these celebrations is just as instrumental as their "business end"; indeed, it is the same end, conducted more thoroughly as play.

In our culture, we tend to take "feeling good" as a fact of individual psychology. We see it in contradistinction to, or at the expense of, being with and for others in that construction of society out of contending interests, duties, and purposes that Simmel called "sociation." But this opposition is a false one, as Simmel points out:

> All these sociations are also characterized, precisely, by a feeling, among their members, of being sociated and by the satisfaction derived from this. Sociates feel that the formation of a society as such is a value; they are driven toward this form of existence. In fact, it sometimes is only this drive itself that suggests the concrete contents of a particular sociation. (1950:42–43)

Simmel called this discrete sociological drive "sociability," the autonomous or "play-form of sociation." Interior relationships between the antinomies we have been exploring—hierarchy and equality, social structure and antistructure, solemnity and festivity—are revealed in the properties of sociability in a way that throws additional light on political and civic rites. These performances are supreme acts of sociation, using differentiated rules, roles, and ranks to answer to sober, ineluctable material interests. Yet they depend just as fully for their efficacy on the generation of sociability, which is, according to Simmel, ludic and democratic in nature.

> Equality . . . results from the elimination of both the wholly personal and
> the wholly objective, that is, from the elimination of the very material of
> sociation from which it is freed when it takes the form of sociability. Yet
> the democracy of sociability even among social equals [much less among
> superiors and subordinates] is only something *played*. Sociability, if one
> will, creates an ideal sociological world in which the pleasure of the indi-
> vidual is closely tied up with the pleasure of the others. In principle, no-
> body can find satisfaction here if it has been at the cost of diametrically
> opposed feelings which the others may have. (Simmel, 1950:47–48)

Corporate satisfaction is a goal of political rites, but it would be a great mistake
to collapse the whole of them into sociability. In *Incwala,* as we have seen,
"diametrically opposed feelings" take center stage in certain phases of the performance, not accidentally those of most determined sociation under the sway
of objective societal constraints. But in other phases of the rite, sociability reigns
supreme, whether in the purer modes of festing, feasting, and revelry or in
mixed forms such as the Swazi's "dawdling work" for the king in his mother's
gardens. Where rank and status are among the preeminent properties of the
social field, sociability can never take over political performances entirely. But it
must be richly present and may even lend its tone to the whole, for sociability,
not the "wholly objective or the wholly personal," is everywhere the original
grounding of social strucure. Thus the Swazi, in the very act of making a king
and surrendering to his authority, rightly understand that they are "playing with
him" in the double sense of the phrase.

Modern Political Celebrations

Several key differences between modern political rites and those of small-scale
societies have been pointed out by sociologists and anthropologists. The themes
of humility and leveling at the moment of elevation and differentiation are present in modern rites, but in different symbolic forms (*see* Richard Dorson's essay in this volume), and organized rites of rebellion as normative ritual phases
are rare. For example, at American presidential inaugurations, it is customary
for the president-elect in his speech and demeanor to emphasize his common
citizenship and equality with those assembled to raise him up to the highest
political status. Indeed, throughout the rite, democratic symbols take precedence over hierarchical ones. But it is simply inconceivable that, say, in the moments just before the oath-taking, the members of Congress should rise to chant
insults at the president-elect, or that the inaugural parade should be halted by a
group of citizens reviling a president who has shed his morning coat for the
tattered rags of the urban poor.

To be sure, hostile performances sometimes take place, for example the
"Counter-Inauguration" staged by the antiwar movement in 1968. It featured a
boycott of the official capital ceremonies, their replacement by protest speeches
and the swearing-in of a squealing pig, then a march to intercept the official
parade, whereupon obscenities were chanted and rocks and eggs were hurled
at the president's limousine. But the language we use to describe these—"pro-

tests," "boycotts," "alternatives," staged by "dissenting" or "criminal" "fringe groups" and "subversive elements"—shows that we conceive of them as evanescent phenomena linked to transient situations. They are not regular occurrences thought to be necessary and efficacious for the normative rite, the "acting of conflict [which] achieves a blessing—social unity." Gluckman's explanation of this contrast is broadly accepted:

> Modern political ceremonies may not take this form because our social order itself is questioned. . . . There are tensions between too many diverse political and other groups in our society to be dramatized simply, and, paradoxically, because of the very fragmentation of our social relationships we do not have as well-developed or as frequent rituals which involve the appearance of persons according to their social roles. . . . Our monarch reigns, but does not rule, and though Swazi and Zulu kings perforce acted through, and were constrained by, officials, they ruled as well as reigned. In our society, the parliamentary system and local government provide two among many secular mechanisms to express opposition overtly. (1963:126, 135)

Gluckman's particular contrast here is to England, but it is truer still of the United States. Our president neither rules nor reigns, but "governs" and "leads," terms whose constitutional and practical content is continuously under dispute; the press, still more of an adversary than in England, is but one of the other notable "mechanisms to express opposition"; and the scale of the nation, not to speak of its further multiplicity and fragmentation of social ties, is greater.

These social structural constraints have their correlates in national symbology. As Durkheim pointed out, the collective representations arrayed to evoke and create unity in pluralistic, organically solidary societies are necessarily more abstract. From the generic God of what Robert Bellah calls "the American civil religion" (1967), summoned to witness the inaugural oath-taking, to the ceremony's repeated appeals to vague concepts like "liberty," "justice," and "progress," the ritual symbols are little likely, or unpredictably likely, to seize the intense attention of the majority of Americans by incorporating the rich particularities of the lives they live.

In our society of relative material plenty, conspicuous consumption tends to be a more notable accompaniment of political ceremonies than conspicuous creation. Nonetheless, remarkable material objects are often made on these occasions and may represent attempts by individuals or groups to attach their lives more fully to political ceremonies than the conduct and symbolism of the ceremonies themselves allow. The *Celebration* exhibition contains two objects associated with inaugurations. The first is a quilt, laboriously stitched by one or more rural women and composed of multicolored ribbons from the inauguration of President Harrison in 1841. The second is a silver gilt ewer, commissioned from Tiffany's by the citizens of Washington and presented to President Lincoln at his inauguration in 1861. Both of these are, as we say, "commemorative" objects, material embodiments of and testimonies to the attention certain citizens gave to these events, and attempts to fix them in memory. But they testify as well to the social distances between their makers and givers and the political ceremony itself. Moreover, we do not classify them as ritual, or even political, objects, but rather as items of folk and luxury-craft "art," with some political "overtones."

This reflects what Ralph Nicholas has called our culture's "deconstruction of the arch," our conception of politics, religion, social relations, art, commerce, and the rest as separable and separate domains, related to be sure, but never fully merging in experience.[4] The effects of this cultural structure on the organization of cultural performances have been richly explored by Victor Turner (1969; 1974:53–92). Ritual has fissioned into a multitude of performance *taxa*—church ceremonies, theater, commercial fairs, art exhibitions, sports, musical concerts, and the like—each serving particular social groups or constituting serial moments in the lives of individuals with multiple group ties. We perceive that performances of one kind have consequences of another kind, for example, the political implications of theater; but rarely is the whole made whole again within discrete performances. Those few occasions in which the entire nation's identity and destiny are condensed in single performances—V-E Day or President Kennedy's funeral—are typically related to severe crises, centered on the absolute themes of life and death and (happily) irregular and conditioned entirely by traumatic historical circumstances. Sometimes such crises do generate ongoing political rites conducted in many locales and centered on ultimate concerns. But, as the Memorial Day ceremonies analysed by W. Lloyd Warner (1959) show, these too are dependent upon rapidly changing historical events: Vietnam put an end to an already waning Memorial Day tradition.

Those ongoing, large-scale civic performances that do regularly incorporate domains of experience otherwise thought separate are not typically celebrations of national identity but of identities that are regional (rodeo), local (New Orleans Mardis Gras, Philadelphia Mummer's Parade, Santa Fé Festival—*see* Ronald Grimes's essay in this volume), ethnic (Chicago's St. Patrick's Day), or racial ("Juneteenth" emancipation celebrations—*see* William Wiggins's essay in this volume). In each of these celebrations, national symbols are arrayed, and the performance comments, implicitly or explicitly, on the structural conflicts between national and subnational allegiances and identities. Indeed, Juneteenth can be understood as a rite of rebellion from the official history of American emancipation—a rite that exists in splendid isolation from, and not a valued segment within, the July 4th celebrations of the white majority, celebrations themselves so optional and variable that they no longer bind.

The Politics of Play

A feature shared by the civic performances just mentioned suggests a dimension of modern celebrations little described and still less understood by social scientists. In all of these events, the dominant motif is play and the dominant motive is sociability. In them, our cultural suspicion of "mere enjoyment" (pointed out earlier in the context of Western misunderstandings of non-Western rites) is suspended. In such performances, instrumental political action is not just penetrated by, it is submerged in general and consensual good feeling. In our national political performances, properly so-called, the situation is different, more complicated, and reveals an anxious ambivalence about the relationship between politics and play, social stratification and sociability.

Observers from more rigidly hierarchical societies have long noticed a distinctive ludic element in the political rites of democratic peoples. As early as the 1820s, visiting French aristocrats described English elections as "carnivals," "spectacles," "saturnalia" (Ethel Jones, 1930:195). Europeans today remain amazed and horrified at the carnival atmosphere of American political conventions, with their tooting horns, outlandishly costumed delegates, and incongruous invocations of state football teams prior to delivering votes to would-be leaders of the nation.

Conventions and elections are our most normative, regular, and consequential political performances, yet the same polarization between sobriety and inversive play is found in evanescent political movements. The split in the 1960s antiwar movement between the Quakers and Catholic left on the one side and the Yippies on the other (made most provocatively plain at the 1968 Counter-Inauguration mentioned earlier), and the opposition between the old left and such groups as the *situationistes* in the Paris uprising later that year (an opposition condensed in the slogan scrawled on the Sorbonne wall, "Je suis Marxiste, tendence Groucho") are but two examples. Moreover, this division has a long history, harking back through surrealist and dadaist prototypes after World War I to charivari and carnival protest "traditions" in late medieval and early modern Europe (Natalie Davis, 1975; LeRoy Ladurie, 1979).

Yet for all the regularity and historical pedigree of the ludic, both within normative performances and in the protest movements directed against them, we, as a people, pretend not to notice it. When outsiders point to the exaggerated ludicity of our political rites, we gloss over it in embarrassed and worried silence, or else take to the opposite, and equally nervous, extreme of asserting that "politics is all a show anyway." We seem no more able to acknowledge the appropriateness of play and sociability in such contexts than to openly proclaim that we elect our leaders to make us feel good. Our speech, no less than our behavior, betrays our profound ambivalence and confusion. Nowhere else is what I call "the complex of 'mere's' " such a common item in everyday speech as it is in the United States: "mere symbols," "mere rhetoric," "mere show," "mere enjoyment," "mere politics," "mere play," and (under a variety of more familar terms) "mere sociability."

The other notable member of this set is "mere games." If political ceremonies are often "mere shows" to us, politics itself—still that most serious of things in a nation begun as a radical political experiment—is commonly and contemptuously referred to as "playing political games." There is yet another layer to this cultural puzzle. No people on earth is more unabashedly devoted to games, in the forms of school and mass spectator sports. From our presidents to our pundits, we borrow, without batting an eye, many of our metaphors for political leadership, cooperation, and style from the domain of sport.

Some have been led, therefore, to assert that events like the Super Bowl, World Series, and Rose Bowl have emerged as the principal rites of American civil religion. Their exceptional importance in national life cannot be doubted, but in the present forms at least, they cannot aspire to such status. Still more thoroughly than the local, regional, and racial celebrations discussed earlier, they attempt to confine political representations to the periphery, their dramatization of subnational corporate identities is weaker still, and they reaggregate fewer of the performative genres split off from one another over time. However, fitting all of these performances together into one mosaic reveals a hidden cultural program. In all of them, we seize upon occasions of relatively purer sociability, consensually framed as play (contest, festival, or both), and attempt to solve, or at least to escape from, our terrible confusion about the relationship between, in Simmel's phrases, the world of objective political and social constraints and the subjective world of personal enjoyment and autonomy. But this "strategy" seems to offer no satisfying exit, no substitute for a real integration of sociability and sociation, playful form and ineluctable content. The proof of this lies in the way we either resent those "spoilsports" who point out the social contents of our sport spectacles, or else resignedly shrug assent to them, saying yes, it's all exploitation and big business. These responses are but inverted parallels of those we give to whoever forces us to notice the carnivalesque characistics of our political conventions and inaugurations. These and national sports events are but mirror images of one another, and other civic performances that more neatly and less ambivalently integrate the realms of sociation and sociability cannot seem to rise, even when the mass media take an interest, above restricted thresholds of attention.

Are there no examples, then, of particular, ongoing performances on a national scale to which we might look to observe these sociocultural conundrums working themselves through in more auspicious forms? The Olympic Games are clearly one such example, though here I can only outline this general claim, the detailed arguments for which are to be found elsewhere (MacAloon, 1981; and forthcoming).

Social scientists have long understood that feelings of solidarity can be generated not only by an intense revelation of the interdependency of contending populations *within* a wider social unit, but also through a shared encounter with external rivals and opponents *without*. At their broadest level, the Olympics are a performative and ideological appeal to the highest identity of "humankindness," condensed in evocative symbols of world community (Olympic flag, medals, hymn, five-ringed logo, flame, and the rest), and evidenced by such golden moments of sociality as the Games sometimes create. But at a more structurally resonant level, they are ludic competitions between nations. In them, the "whole United States" understands itself to be taking on other whole nations, indeed the whole world of other nations. Our most consensual national symbols are arrayed on the playing fields of each "New Olympia": flag, anthem, initials, uniforms. The only other "structural" identity officially and normatively marked in Olympic performances is that of the individual, iconically represented by the athlete's body. The whole realm of social identities intermediate between the individual and the nation receives no explicit representation (though in breached Olympic performances precisely these are asserted). Yet in spite of, or rather because of, these constraints that performatively subsume a multitude of individuals into a "nation," and generate a context of common striving, we are freed to attend in a variety of ways to our other identities. From the composition of the United States team to the incredible density of popular commentary from every quarter on its and its rivals' performances, we attend as rich and poor; male and female; young and old; urban and rural; black, white, yellow, and red; Protestant, Jewish, and Catholic; western, eastern, and southern; Italian-, Hispanic-, Polish-, and Japanese- . . . Americans.

This performative structure, the prepotent historical conceit of the ancient Games and the accrued history of the modern ones, the wealth of oral folklore and literary motifs that the Games pick up, the need for popular ethnography of the others with whom Americans are increasingly conscious of sharing a world, and the intrinsic interest for us of high-level sport—all help account for the unrivaled demography of attention to the Olympics every four years. But just as significant is the rejoining of the genres of game, rite, festival, and spectacle in the Olympics, producing not a return to the arch of life in small-scale societies, but a new ramified performance system appropriate to large-scale pluralistic ones. This performance system leads a multitude into betaking themselves together outside of their daily routines, enthralling themselves with "the conquest of the useless," witnessing athletes' transformations of *themselves* into conspicuous creations, and crowning these otherwise rather ordinary fellow citizens as heroes and kings.

Because they are voluntary and their focal performances are sports, because of their simplified and dramatic ("autonomous" in Simmel's language) representations of social relations and the experiences of sociability that they provide to athletes and fans alike, we frame the Games overall as play. But for many years now, Americans have either groused about their "corruption by politics" when we've shown poorly, or else happily suggested that they demonstrate the superiority of our political institutions when we do well. More is involved here than poor sportsmanship, garden-variety chauvinism, or irrational contradiction. It is the same cultural inability to configure the relationship between play and politics traced earlier in national political rites. In the context of the Olympics at any rate, there are signs of a change. If opinion polls, newspaper editorials, and diplomatic conversation be any evidence, it took the Carter administration less than two weeks to convince the American people that, short of dropping a bomb or sending an army, boycotting the Moscow Olympics was the most severe political step that could be taken against the Soviets for the Afghanistan invasion. It took so little time to get the message across because we already knew. We are coming to realize consciously what much of the rest of the world, especially the socialist states, have known and proclaimed for a long time: that international sport is politics conducted as sociability.

How abiding and generalizable these developments may turn out to be is difficult to judge. The Games are magnificently self-contained and neither belong to nor are controlled by any one people. For these and other reasons, they can never substitute for national political rites, properly speaking, and limits are placed on how thoroughly any one nation can read back from them to its own cultural structure. Still, on the evidence of the Games, Americans may have begun to divine more broadly that play, in several of its forms, is politics, and politics play, in the sense that the two may constitute one another in the selfsame moment. This is a process enshrined in political rites elsewhere, as we have seen, and if changes are to come in our own national political celebrations, they are surely to incorporate this dimension. The alternative is to stand pat in the prolaptic relations between sociation and sociability that presently mark our conceptions and performances. Social structural constraints make this outcome more likely, but it will not help us live easily in the new domestic world that is forming about us.

Notes

1. The discussion of exhibition objects that follows owes much to the research of staff members of the Smithsonian Institution, and I gratefully acknowledge their contributions.

2. Victor and Edith Turner, personal communication, 1980.

3. Thomas Buckley, personal communication, 1977.

4. Ralph Nicholas, personal communication, 1978.

Bibliography

Bellah, Robert
  1967   "Civil Religion in America." *Daedalus* 96.
Davis, Natalie Z.
  1975   *Society and Culture in Early Modern France.* Stanford: Stanford University Press.
Geertz, Clifford
  1973   "Deep Play: Notes on the Balinese Cockfight." *The Interpretation of Cultures.* New York: Basic Books.
Gluckman, Max
  1963   *Order and Rebellion in Tribal Africa.* London: Cohen and West.
Huizinga, Johan
  1955   *Homo Ludens.* Boston: Beacon.
Jones, Ethel
  1930   *Les Voyageurs Français en Angleterre de 1815 à 1830.* Paris: Boccard.
Kuper, Hilda
  1947   *An African Aristocracy.* Oxford: Oxford University Press.
Ladurie, LeRoy
  1979   *Carnival in Romans.* New York: Braziller.

MacAloon, John J.
   1981   *This Great Symbol: Pierre de Coubertin and the Origins of the Modern Olympic Games.* Chicago: University of Chicago Press.
   1983   "Olympic Games and the Theory of Spectacle in Modern Society." In *Rite, Drama, Festival, Spectacle: Rehearsals Toward a Theory of Cultural Performances,* edited by John J. MacAloon. Philadelphia: Institute for the Study of Human Issues (in press).

Simmel, Georg
   1950   *The Sociology of Georg Simmel.* Translated and edited by Kurt H. Wolff. New York: Free Press.

Turner, Victor
   1967   *The Forest of Symbols.* Ithaca: Cornell University Press.
   1969   *The Ritual Process.* Chicago: Aldine.
   1974   "Liminal to Liminoid in Play, Flow, and Ritual." *Rice University Studies* 60: 53–92.

Warner, Lloyd W.
   1959   *The Living and the Dead: A Study of the Symbolic Life of Americans.* New Haven: Yale University Press.

The Lifeblood of Public Ritual: Fiestas and Public Exploration Projects

Ronald L. Grimes

Public ritual is identical with neither civil religion (Bellah, 1974) nor secular ritual (Moore and Myerhoff, 1977), since it may involve symbols less official, more regional, or more ethnic than the former and more sacred or ecclesiastical than the latter. "Public ritual" (Grimes, 1976:43) is a more inclusive category capable of including most examples of civil and secular ritual. Public ritual is distinguished by its interstitial position on the threshold between open and closed groups—by its aim to tend the gate which swings in toward those who are ritual initiators and outward toward ritual strangers.

Two contrasting examples of public ritual are the Fiesta of Sante Fe, New Mexico, and the Public Exploration Projects (PEPs) in Ontario, Canada. The fiesta, held annually since 1712 for several days in November, is a citywide celebration, attended by tourists, who typically outnumber the population of the city of Santa Fe. It is a collage of parades, pageantry, processions, plays, proclamations, raffles, masses, dancing, singing, melodrama, drinking, crownings, knightings, fashion shows, competitions, art displays, fighting, blessings, ambling, and sales. Although the fiesta has moments of symbolic inversion (Babcock, 1978:13–33) and spontaneous communitas (Turner, 1969:132), its dominant ethos is better described as ritual "superstructuring." Government and tourism, the city's dominant industries, provide civil and economic symbols which pervade the fiesta but do not determine its ideological center. Ethnic, civic, and ecclesiastical symbols such as the De Vargas figure, the fiesta queen, and the Marian statue La Conquistadora, are the core symbols. The fiesta occurs in a tri-ethnic city inhabited largely by Hispano Catholics, Anglo Protestants, and some indigenous people, particularly Pueblos, Navahos, and a few Apaches. The historical roots of the fiesta lie in the mythico-historical story of the Virgin's inspiring Don Diego de Vargas to reconquer without bloodshed in 1692 the village of Sante Fe after the Tano people had driven the Spaniards back to El Paso in 1680.

Public celebrations which differ from the fiesta in all but the most essential respects are the Public Exploration Projects (cf. Grimes, 1978) conducted by Actor's Lab of Toronto. Actor's Lab is a theater research ensemble, founded in 1972, whose performances and paratheatrical projects are markedly ritualistic in tone. As their former name, Le Théâtre de l'Homme, suggests, they aspire to a "theater of humanity"—to an archetypal, cross-cultural, transhistorical theater. Whereas the fiesta revels in regionalism, ethnicity, history, and civic display, the PEPs, first held in 1976, are marked by ideological universalism, ahistoricism, natural settings, and open or sequestered spaces.

The Lab is strongly influenced by the Polish Theatre Laboratory and its founder-director, Jerzy Grotowski. The PEP's basic ethos is "parashamanistic" (cf. Grimes, 1979a:19), and Lab people want to *initiate* the public into its explorations, while fiesta organizers want to *introduce* fiesta spirit into the public arena. Much hinges on this distinction between introducing and initiating. The Lab intends to create spaces and animate interactions so that its half-dozen or so members can meet fully—without name, status, or pretense—strangers who are invited to the PEPs.

Although the writing, directing, and acting at Actor's Lab are done by Canadians, its performances are not typically about Canadian or regional themes, despite the close connection of the PEPs and the Canadian bush of northern Ontario. The emphasis in performances and projects alike is on elemental symbols such as pieces of cloth, candles, stumps, water, earth, stone, and fire. While the geographical center of the fiesta is the central city plaza, the Lab often takes participants to natural settings, as the title of one of its projects, "Theatre Wilderness," implies. PEPs can include, for example, silent walks, nonverbal sound, dancing, searching, waiting, stalking, resting, and so on. The tone is that of vision quest, rite of passage, and shamanlike attendance to embodied actions arising from the unconscious. PEPs sometimes bear titles such as "Night of Vigil," "Night of Wanderings," and "Night of the Song of Myself."

Celebrations transpire in the ambiance of varying kinds of ritual strategies. Two such strategies are the "superstructuring" and the "deconstructing" of ordinary interaction ritual (Goffman, 1967). Deconstruction is a mode of negation, of symbolic stripping. Superstructuring, on the other hand, is a form of symbolic amplification. If we take as a baseline the gestures, postures, rhythms, dress, and other symbols of everyday living, ritual deconstruction drops below the line of habitual decorum before it rises in dialectical fashion to the immediacy of celebration. Superstructuring, on the other hand, ascends positively by augumenting everyday life to produce a ritual hyperbole.

Since we usually think that celebration is a collective way of ritually ascending, we often are blind to the underbelly of festivity, even though demons, devils, and monsters may blatantly haunt public celebrations in masked costume. We are apt to overlook the downward movement of festive rituals, since we think of them stereotypically as consisting only of fun, happiness, sport, play, and extroversion. We imagine that celebration can arise only by amplifying or inverting the gray routine of humdrum, workaday ordinariness. We are also prone to treat as celebrations only those events that are open to the general public, so we seldom think of celebrations as bringing in an invited public. When the word "celebration" is invoked, we conjure up images of revelrous noise, floats, tall puppets, loud music, long speeches, much drinking, bawdy behavior, and gross masks. In short, we identify celebration with its expansive, superstructuring form.

But celebration is not necessarily upward- or outward-moving nor positively related to everyday behavior. Celebration may be an inversion of such behavior, but regarding it as such does not answer the question whether a specific celebration turns ordinary action right-side-up or upside-down. Superstructuring a celebration means magnifying and turning a culture's good, virtuous, proper side to public view. Deconstructing a celebration means turning the public view toward the under, down, dark, unstructured, or emergent side of culture.

Rituals are not only embedded in social processes, they also process actors, things, spaces, and times. Furthermore, they are in process; they develop and decline. So one should not too quickly summarize the essence of some type of ritual (say, celebration) without noting these three distinguishable kinds of ritually significant processes: the social processes *surrounding* ritual; the work of processing which a ritual *does*; and the process of change which a ritual *undergoes*. My concern here is to illustrate the work of ritual processing which the fiesta performs by superstructuring and the PEPs perform by deconstructing. Both the Fiesta Council and Actor's Lab engender not only ritual processes but related dramatic ones as well, so I will offer an interpretation of the fiesta's "Entrada Pageant," as well as the Lab's production of *Blood Wedding*. My processual interpretation employs a framework which I have articulated more fully elsewhere (Grimes, 1979b) and which distinguishes several moments or layers of any ritual: ritualization, decorum, ceremony, liturgy, and celebration.

The Fiesta as Ritual Superstructure

The fiesta begins with a decorous phase. Decorum is a ritual mode of civility, politeness, and neighborliness, most obvious in everyday, face-to-face interaction. Decorum is ritual in the sense of habitual hellos, goodbyes, and handshakes; also in the less visible sense of preconscious stylizations of gesture and social space. Many examples of it appear in the fiesta: variety shows, style shows, concerts, audiences with fiesta royalty, formal banquets, and indoor balls. Decorous actions are scattered throughout the festival but dominate the initial phase by providing the first major fiesta symbol, the fiesta queen. On the opening day of fiesta her crowning and enthronement are the most ritually elevated daytime events. Even though they are coupled with the knighting of the De Vargas figure (fig. 112), these events are usually regarded as the fiesta queen's in the same way that weddings are sometimes felt to be in some special way the bride's.

The second major fiesta symbol to appear is Zozobra (fig. 113), a giant puppet of Old Man Gloom, who is burned atop a high hill after dark on the first day. The burning is a celebrative rite, which many regard as the true, or popular, beginning of the fiesta. Celebration is that kind of ritual moment which occurs toward the play end of the work/play continuum. Celebration is immediate,

Figure 112 *De Vargas (center) and his staff on the set of the "Entrada Pageant."*

Figure 113 *Zozobra, the Fiesta Queen (center), and the Fiesta Council President (right).*

momentary, comparatively free of pragmatic goal-orientation; it is relatively expressive, "useless," and free of heavy ideology. For this reason specifically celebrative actions are often experienced by fiesta participants as pagan or profane. Other fiesta activities which evoke a celebrative sensibility are carnival rides, parade clowns, street dancing, foods purchased at booths, a children's costume and pet parade, and an iconoclastic melodrama.

The spectrum of fiesta participation is broadest in decorous and celebrative events. It is narrowest in the liturgical phases, epitomized by the Marian image La Conquistadora ("The Conqueress") and the solemn pontifical fiesta mass which is enacted in a Hispanic, mariachi idiom. Liturgical rites are those which constitute the intentional work of a people in an effort to symbolize ultimacy and transcend the naturally-socially constructed world. The liturgical layers of the Santa Fe Fiesta are ecclesiastical, specifically Roman Catholic. Masses, publically displayed *retablos* (flat paintings) of saints (fig. 114), and processions—particularly the candlelight procession to the Cross of the Martyrs (Franciscans killed in the native revolt of 1680)—bear the liturgical weight of the fiesta.

The fiesta's ritual strategy is to "superstructure" a link between Catholic liturgical and Hispanic ceremonial symbols. Ceremony consists of power negotiations in ritual form. Usually it involves official, political, tribal, or ethnic groups. Its ethos is rhetorical and imperative, which contrasts with the stylized friendliness of decorum. Ceremonial gestures are bids for authority, prestige, recognition, and control, usually on an intergroup level. The key ceremonial symbol of

Figure 114 A retablo *of Santa Barbara on the Santa Fe Plaza.*

the fiesta is the Hispano male elected to play the role of Don Diego de Vargas in the "Entrada Pageant." This ceremonial drama provides the rationale for having a fiesta at all, and the determinative scene from the pageant is clearly of a negotiating tone.

De Vargas, with his soldiers and Franciscan priests, approaches the villa of Santa Fe on horseback. The year is 1692. The dramatic action is now occurring on soil not far from the spot on which the original *entrada* (formal entrance) occurred three hundred years ago. The native people who drove the Spaniards out in 1680 still hold the city. When the Tano Indians (played by Hispanic actors, since native people presently refuse to play the parts) resist De Vargas's entry, he persists. The hero takes a gamble, requiring faith and courage, the narrator reminds us. He removes his armor but has placed himself under the guidance of La Conquistadora, the conquering Virgin. He is still the symbolic head of genealogies for many modern descendants of the conquistadors. And thus he enters the city, unprotected. With sheer boldness, friendly confidence, and daring faith he intimidates the natives into surrendering and complying with a ritual submission to the Spanish king and God. Then the play concludes by implying that the fiesta itself is the happy result of this conquest of violence itself. What is not dramatized in the pageant is De Vargas's *Journal* account of how he cut off the village's water supply and had to lead a bloody reconquest a year later.

Liturgical actions precede, follow, and permeate the pageant, marking it as the fiesta's ritual apex. The pageant is a dramatic superstructure, erected on ritual bedrock. The play amplifies the city's history, transforming it into a chartering tableau. It elevates a diachronic moment in Santa Fe's history into a synchronic paradigm for modeling the conditions under which festivity can occur. Everything happening before and after this performance occurs in the wake of De Vargas's definitive penetration into the spatial heart and soul of the city, the Santa Fe Plaza.

A comparatively unemphasized layer of ritual processes in the fiesta consists of action not deliberately structured and arising from primary psychobiological roots. "Ritualization" consists of gestures which some might regard as instinctive, mindless, accidental, irrelevant, or unconscious. Ritualization is preintentional symbolic action. It differs from celebration inasmuch as the latter is postintentional, presupposing a suspension of work, goals, and deliberate action. Ritualization processes are difficult to disentangle from decorous and celebrative ones, but examples of actions in which ritualization clearly increases are drinking, gorging, erotic behavior, fighting, smoking, browsing, joshing, some of the moblike qualities which follow the burning of Zozobra, and the spontaneous actions that arise in the children's parade. In these, value and intention, as well as meaning, must be inferred from what seems to happen spontaneously or idiosyncratically, but nevertheless repetitively. Ritualization is cultivated during the fiesta mainly through overeating and -drinking, though the decorum of fiesta-going requires that people complain about the excesses, hide the fighting, and turn an indulgent eye away from erotic encounter. Ritualization is practiced but rhetorically treated as crude and unnecessary.

PEPs as Ritual Deconstruction

If I interpret the PEPs in terms of the same ritual processes, their ritual inten-
tionality does not appear so expansive and upward. PEPs deconstruct ordinary
behavior. Their object is to unravel or un-jam habitual ways of perceiving the
world. Their goal is not liturgically buttressed ceremony but ceremonially pro-
voked ritualization. Ritualization, not ceremony, is their principal process, so
their movement is one of deconstructing the chronology of history and the decorum of the larger society.

A project begins with ceremonial gestures which establish who is an insider
and outsider, who is in authority, and what some of the rules are. People are
invited to participate; sometimes they sign up and pay for their participation.
With the shutting of the first door the invited public begins a rapid, initiatory
stripping away of gestural habits in order to approach transient communitas.
People are told not to talk, especially about what is transpiring. Conversation is
discouraged. Performing or actor-training exercise is prohibited. And mystifica-
tion of leadership, a sure sign of ceremonial process, is strong at the beginning.
People feel apprehensive, unsure, afraid, inhibited. Doors are closed, or cities
are left behind. Lights are dimmed; explanations are withheld. Leaders are
sometimes not explicitly identified, so participants privately speculate and cov-
ertly search for authority. People watch and listen expectantly, never quite
knowing when they will eat, sleep, interact, or have free time. Sometimes they
are told that the Lab will not teach any positive technique but only help remove
blocks and clichéd actions. The question informing the ceremonial phase is:
What is the minimal structure, language, and leadership necessary for self, other
persons, and Otherness to emerge and meet?

Ceremonial rites facilitating such an exploration consist of Lab members' having covert meetings and discussions among themselves, setting up or choosing
locations, subtly animating what seem open or undirected actions, providing objects for participants to work with, and sometimes overtly directing action. Part
of the Lab's ceremonial agenda is to keep leadership in low profile to facilitate
nonhierarchical interaction. But hierarchy is needed, of course, to enforce egalitarian processes, so the Lab maintains the status and prerogatives of director-
ship.

Ceremonial actions by Lab members aim to facilitate ritualization processes
which arise from the untamed, uncultured depths. The Lab refers to actions
which court these processes as "the work" or "studies." In its freest form the
work is undirected action in an empty or open space in which one or more
persons go with whatever emerges from inside or among them. What emerges
is a source of animating power, an undefined "it." "It" can connote the unconscious, the sacred, rhythm, or the unpremeditated.

Ritualization processes are, of course, hard to describe or isolate. They are
better understood as a special quality of action rather than special actions.
Outsiders might see them as animallike, crazy, aimless, demonic, drifty, or ridic-
ulous. But insiders experience them as a flowing surge of animate energy,
sometimes foggy, sometimes crystal clear, but always moving, literally and meta-

phorically. As soon as one can name a specific action by having worked through it, it is already leaving the zone of the work.

The object of every PEP is to help participants peel away bodily and emotional acculturation so this primordial sense of animate responsiveness to the internal and external environment can emerge. So ritual criticism offered by Lab people takes the form of locating nameable or typed actions and urging participants to break through them to actions they cannot name. Any action identifiable as having been learned from psychophysical disciplines such as actor training, martial arts, physical education, and movement arts such as dance or mime, draws criticism. The resultant atmosphere can be mysteriously simple or astonishingly full of undertow.

Walking, dancing, and, occasionally, eating are typical celebratory rituals in Public Exploration Projects. Celebration in this context is attentive ordinariness. Lab members seem to feel that one reaches this kind of quietly powerful simplicity only by going through the chaos of ritualization and its attendant explosiveness. So celebrations are actional afterglow in the PEPs. When the ritualization work fails, the celebrative gestures have the aura of a hangover. When the ritualization-to-celebration bridging is successful, one celebrates with no special celebrative apparatus—no costumes, games, rides or revelry—just the immediacy of attentive walking, eating, or some ordinary action. Only if a final meal is served does anything like extraordinary, corporate festivity arise.

When a PEP ends, Lab members must face their profession, that of performing. Other participants return to acting or some other job. Decorum is barely visible at the end of a project. A few names and addresses are exchanged. Politeness returns, leaving people feeling strangely false. Watches are put on; schedules are restored. Most participants experience considerable culture shock and dislocation; their own culture seems foreign. Its stylizations are too obvious. Leaving the bonding of communitas is a rite of separation and reincorporation at once. One is quite aware of "putting on" the face necessary just to walk down a sidewalk, make a phone call, catch a bus, or try to eat a meal with one's family without being a stranger.

The difficulty faced by Lab members subsequent to ritualization work in PEPs or studies is how to value performing after searching for and teaching nonperforming. Sometimes they deny that they are performing at all. They do not pretend to be someone else; they reveal themselves, they say. The intention to reveal rather than conceal is declared by both PEP participants and Lab members; the difficulty and desirability of doing so arises on both sidewalk and stage.

Lab performances are, I would suggest, liturgical, not in the sense that they contain ecclesiastical rites, but in the sense that they are "good works," necessary but insufficient ways of remembering and anticipating moments of graceful breakthrough. Peformances are structures for preserving moments of flowing ritualization, but the very act of preserving demands the reintroduction of theatrical decorum, no matter how intimately revealing a performance may be. The problem against which Lab people perpetually struggle is that preserved immediacy can itself easily become a musclebound habit, in which case archetype slips embarrassingly into stereotype.

In my estimation the richest example of a Lab play is its adaptation of García Lorca's *Blood Wedding* (fig. 115). It is a drama containing a ritual, as is the "Entrada Pageant." A scene which compares provocatively with De Vargas's entrance into the village of Santa Fe is the prenuptial village scene.

Dancing breaks out. The energy is high; the air is full of leaping. The costumes, elaborate by Lab standards, only minimally suggest Spain. This could be Anyvillage, Anywhere. The groom and his competitor mockingly display their rivalry as if the display itself might stem the need for violence. Soon the village idiot, played by the Lab's artistic director, becomes the focus of attention. He seems both to determine the action and to be the toy with which others play. He is teased and tantalized. Sexuality and violence are played at, as if they have no power to disrupt the collective joy of the villagers. The determination to celebrate seems at once to preclude violence and to prepare and foreshadow it.

Audience members who see the performance often comment that they wish they could have joined the festivities at this moment. Such sentiments, of course, miss an essential point of the play, namely, that participation in the wedding celebration implies complicity in the ritualized dance of murder which climaxes the play, leaving in its aftermath tragically isolated women and two dead men wrapped arm in arm, virtual brothers in death.

The Lifeblood of Public Ritual

"Violence," says René Girard, "is the heart and secret soul of the sacred" (1972:31). Religion, he argues, consists of the ways we try to defend ourselves against the contamination of violence, which spreads with the dynamism of a plague. Ritual can be a means of substituting "good" or "pure" violence for this polluting kind. A sacrificial crisis occurs when these rites are neglected or break their containers and the distinction between contained and free-floating revenge disappears. In such a crisis, what Girard calls "violent mimesis" (p. 47) sets in and the resemblances between combatants grow. Hero and villain look increasingly alike.

Girard tells the terrible half of an important truth. Public festivity can contain the lifeblood of a group, city, or culture, and if it does, such festivity simultaneously and symbolically makes of the many, one blood, and spills symbolic blood in doing so. I will venture to say that every celebration is in some sense an *entrada* and a blood wedding. Every attempt at public celebration is a paradox of tragic isolation and festive integration. Every celebration makes us symbolic kinspeople and enforces our separation. Every celebration is an inspired, bloodless reconquest and a bloody act of cutting off a waterflow.

Fiesta participants speak of the De Vargas figure and the fiesta queen as if they were symbolically husband and wife, even though no ritual marries them. Ethnicity is wed in sentiment to civicality. But this "marriage" is never ritually consummated, so the reconquest continues to happen. And in *Blood Wedding* the wedding between bride and groom cannot be completed with fidelity. Instead, rivals become brothers in blood.

Because *Blood Wedding* is constructed out of the psychosocial lives of Lab

Figure 115 *Bride and groom in* Blood Wedding.

members, and the Entrada is constructed out of the historico-civic lives of Santa Feans, neither drama is merely aesthetic or formalistic. Neither situation permits the luxury of speaking with impunity about making bonds or spilling "blood." Both dramas are active attempts to effect or negotiate the lifeblood of the people involved. The rituals and their attendant plays not only illustrate or reflect upon living situations; they also transform, and in uncanny ways foreshadow, what happens among the participants. The rituals work. Because they work, they are dangerous. But they work because they transpire in the danger zones of culture.

Celebration rises as a bubble in a cauldron of public ritual. Rituals are the lifeblood of culture. They circulate and keep in process what is immensely destructive if spilled in society at large and left exposed to dry. Rituals, like blood, must be contained and must flow or they signify death as surely as they signify life. They float on the surface of crisis and rift. What if the dark chaos unleashed by the Lab's ritualization work corrodes group integration, precipitates hasty or faithless marriages, or reduces directors to wordless idiots? What if the fiesta's ceremonial display of a bloodless, military reconquest only perpetuates an ongoing cultural reconquest? And what if those of us who witness and interpret celebrations are implicated by complicity and become voyeurs or parasites, unable either to face our own shedding of blood or to make ritual kin?

Celebratory moments are the most fragile in a ritual. Ritualization and ceremony are the most powerful or dangerous elements; liturgy and decorum, the safest and most stable. Is it claiming too much to suggest that all ritual aspires to celebration? In the celebratory moment, form and dynamic, spontaneity and structure, are not mutually opposing alternatives. Of course, not every ritual which aims to become celebratory should be called a celebration. The celebratory motive is "fictive" (Kliever, 1979) or ludic (Huizinga, 1955). It is a magnet for cultural creativity and ritual subjunctivity (Turner, 1979). In the very moment that Santa Feans "reconquer, not Indians, but violence itself," they have created a ritual "fiction." Fiction is not the same as lying or wishful thinking, because a fiction draws culture into its wake. Its object is not merely to reflect the cultural status quo but to transform it in a moment of specially concentrated time. Such a moment can quickly be dragged back into the ambiance of the social system or even co-opted by other ritual processes such as ceremonial ones. The Lab's aspiration "to meet without hiding or pretense," like the Fiesta Council's goal of conquering violence itself, is a creative ritual fiction—a form made, not just to mirror the conflictive, violent social situations from which it is born, but also to deny aspects of those situations and emphasize others. Rituals and dramas can be either a substitute for, or prelude to, the actions they symbolize. Celebration is that ritual moment in which such enactments actually effect what they symbolize. They are not practice for some more real kind of action, say, pragmatic or economic action, nor are they sublimations for some remembered or more desirable action. In a celebratory moment the ritual action is a deed in which the symbols do not merely point, mean, or recall but embody fully and concretely all that is necessary for the moment.

If celebration is understood in this way, it functions as a goal and criterion. So we need to judge to what extent fiestas, projects, and other public rituals are creative fictive deeds, not just the semblances of deeds. To do so we would have to decide whether the repetition of such ritual actions means that they have not quite accomplished what they signify. Classical psychoanalysis would have us regard ritual repetition as compulsive. But I propose another suggestion. Even when rituals are culturally creative and for a moment accomplish what they signify, entropy is a fundamental law, and therefore whatever is achieved ritually begins to erode in the very moment of its success. Therefore we repeatedly pay the high cost of spilled symbolic blood as we await receptively the moment in which a celebration can make of us one blood. A public celebration is a rope bridge of knotted symbols strung across an abyss. We make our crossings hoping the chasm will echo our festive sounds for a moment, as the bridge begins to sway from the rhythms of our dance.

Bibliography

Babcock, Barbara A., ed.
  1978   *The Reversible World: Symbolic Inversion in Art and Society.* Ithaca, N.Y.:
            Cornell University.
Bellah, Robert
  1974   "Civil Religion in America." In *American Civil Religion*, edited by Russell E.
            Richey and Donald G. Jones. New York: Harper and Row.
Girard, René
  1972   *La Violence et le Sacré.* Paris: B. Grasset.

Grimes, Ronald L.
.1976   *Symbol and Conquest: Public Ritual and Drama in Santa Fe.* Ithaca, N.Y.: Cornell University.
1978   "The Rituals of Walking and Flying: Public Participatory Events at Actor's Lab." *The Drama Review* 22/4:77–82.
1979a   "The Actor's Lab: The Ritual Roots of Human Action." *Canadian Theatre Review* 22:9–19.
1979b   "Modes of Ritual Necessity." *Worship* 53/2:126–41.
Goffman, Erving
1967   *Interaction Ritual: Essays on Face-to-Face Behavior.* Garden City, N.J.: Doubleday.
Huizinga, Johann
1955   *Homo Ludens: A Study of the Play Element in Culture.* Boston: Beacon.
Kliever, Lonnie D.
1979   "Fictive Religion: Rhetoric and Play." Paper presented to the American Academy of Religion's annual meeting, New York City.
Moore, Sally F., and Myerhoff, Barbara G., eds.
1977   *Secular Ritual.* Amsterdam: Van Gorcum.
Turner, Victor
1969   *The Ritual Process: Structure and Anti-Structure.* Chicago: Aldine.
1979   "Dramatic Ritual/Ritual Drama: Performance and Reflexive Anthropology." *The Kenyon Review,* n.s. 1/3:80–93.

"They Closed the Town Up, Man!": Reflections on the Civic and Political Dimensions of Juneteenth

William H. Wiggins, Jr.

Juneteenth is an Emancipation celebration which commemorates the freeing of slaves in east Texas and western Louisiana. It began on June 19, 1865, when General Gordon Granger landed at "Madagosca Bay"[1] near Galveston, Texas, and "spread the news around" that slavery was over ("Juneteenth . . .," 1951:30). As late as the 1940s, Blacks in such neighboring Louisiana towns as Port Allen and Lake Charles chartered excursion trains to Galveston on June 19th:

> It was something that they felt very strongly about. Because I know I can remember older people saying 'Well, I'm going this year because it may be my last.' And I went such and such a time before. It was something they really held dear.[2]

The celebration later became an important item of "cultural baggage" carried by Louisiana and Texas Blacks who migrated north into Arkansas and Oklahoma after Reconstruction and west to California during the Dust Bowl era of the 1930s, and World War II.

Juneteenth is classified as a secular celebration because the rituals performed on this day are borrowed from the traditions of July 4th; there are parades with bands and floats, picnics, dances, baseball games, and other types of games and sports (fig. 116)—as opposed to rituals originating from Black church services.

The morning parade is one item borrowed and fashioned to the Afro-American theme of freedom. The line of march has included smart-stepping brass bands, pretty "prancing horses," local orders of Masons, Shriners, Knight Templars, and other fraternal organizations, resplendent in their parade dress. However, the theme of freedom is ever-present. Often the floats depict the historical fight of Afro-Americans for freedom. And there are symbols and slogans in

Figure 116 *A Juneteenth bull-riding contest.*

abundance, too (fig. 117). One placard carried the slogan: "Fourteen slaves brought here in 1619." In some parades axes are carried to symbolize death to the slaveowner, and torches are carried in others to symbolize hard-earned freedom. But the most effective symbol used to be the ex-slaves who were

Figure 117 *A Juneteenth parade in Anderson, Texas.*

placed at the end of the march. And in Brenham, Texas, the Black citizens called their elected parade queen "The Goddess of Liberty" (Wiggins, 1975:47).

Juneteenth celebrants come from all political and civic segments of the Black American community. The celebrating throngs have been described as not being

> of all one type. They were all types. You had sweet Lucys. You have those, you know, who are fairly intelligent. You have those who are intelligent. And you have . . . hippies. You have all types of people out there. And the ages from I'd say from one month to ninety [years].[3]

No other celebration comes close to matching Juneteenth's appeal among Black Americans who trace their roots back into Louisiana and Texas slavery.

Juneteenth is a persistent regional metaphor of the Black American experience. Its myriad rituals, beliefs, legends, and symbols all center on the Black American community's long and as yet unresolved struggle to wield meaningful political power and to be accorded civic respectability. The outside social status accorded southwestern Blacks has caused them to look upon Juneteenth as "their" day. One celebrant recalled:

> Well, at that time we used to ask why they celebrated that day and our parents would always tell us 'This was the day that the Negroes was supposed to celebrate: the 19th of June.' And I never did know definitely why, but I knew that they would always say that was "our day" and that the 4th of July was for the white folks.[4]

However, in the final analysis, Juneteenth does not polarize Black and white Americans. Rather it has become an annual cultural observance primarily devoted to civic affairs. For Black citizens it serves as a yearly reminder that their slave heritage is not a badge of shame and inferiority. As one celebrant aptly put it:

> I have never felt that we should stop telling our children and letting them know about the 19th of June, and about our people as slaves. I don't think you should be ashamed of it, because it's true. And I think they should know about it because these that are growing up now are not going to know anything of what our people went through.[5]

This dual theme of the survival and termination of slavery takes numerous symbolic and ritualized forms within the Juneteenth celebration.

Celebrants create and tell legends which explain the origin of Juneteenth:

> How Juneteenth got started . . . is legendary in nature. However, my eighty-six-year-old father swears it is the truth; that an ex-Union soldier (Negro) rode a mule given him by Abraham Lincoln, Yessuh, all the way to that section of the country. And when he got to Oklahoma, he informed the slaves that they were free. From there he went to Arkansas and Texas. It was on the nineteenth of June when he arrived in Oklahoma. My father

swears it, and he says if his father was still alive, he would do the same swearing without batting his eye. Many of the old-timers are with him one hundred percent.[6]

This etiological legend takes the mule out of slavery's cotton fields and tethers him in Washington, D.C., the nation's capital and issuance site of the Emancipation Proclamation. His owner is no longer an oppressive slave master, but President Abraham Lincoln, the great emancipator. Both the mule and the slave are socially elevated from their shared roles of servile toil. The mule no longer pulls a plow or wagon; now he proudly carries a Black messenger of freedom. By the same token, the messenger breaks his silent acceptance of slavery by loudly proclaiming the message of freedom. Thus, in this Juneteenth legend, the mule and the slave, twin symbols of American slavery, are recast as symbols of Emancipation.

Personal dress and grooming have long been a popular means of expressing Juneteenth celebrants' social equality with their town's white citizens. One celebrant expressed those sentiments this way:

> You know as near as I can remember, the 19th of June was just a second Christmas . . . everything . . . is especially set aside for that day. Even bought your new shoes, your new clothes, and dressed up, your hair cut, everything, you know. You went all out, really.[7]

This Juneteenth dress code has slave origins and is observed by Black emancipation celebrants in other parts of the country. As early as 1651, Massachusetts's legislators passed a law condemning "men and women of meane condition" for wearing the clothing of "persons of greater estates, or more liberal education" (Nash, 1970:6). And after Denmark Vesey's revolt some colonies passed legislation restricting the dress of slaves (Genovese, 1974:559). There are numerous accounts of newly freed slaves celebrating their freedom by shedding their rags and dressing up in the fine attire of their masters. A recently emancipated Virginia coachman marked his change in social status by dressing in his master's clothing (Franklin, 1968:226). One Confederate diary noted that emancipated "Negro women, dressed in their gaudiest array, carried bouquets to the Yankees" (Chestnut, 1949:536). The following interesting statement graphically indicates the ex-slaves' association of dress styles with an elevated social status:

> July 4th—Saturday I was ill in bed with one of my worst headaches, but I came down when callers arrived. They talked of Negroes who flocked to the Yankees and showed them where the silver valuables were hid by the white people; *ladies' maids were dressing themselves in the mistress's gowns before their very faces and walking out.* (Chestnut, 1949:544; italics added)

Today's well-dressed Juneteenth celebrants are in this same tradition. In the second half of this century it has been noted that some southern white communities still exert negative social pressure on Black males who refuse to wear work clothes on weekdays. These brave souls, who, Jack Schwartz argues, are merely trying to "raise self-esteem, and status symbolization, and cushion the traumatic effects of a subordinate position" (1963:224–31), are labeled "smart niggers" by some of their fellow white citizens (Lewis, 1955:54).

The "Afro" or "natural" hairstyle worn by many contemporary celebrants of Juneteenth also symbolizes a mass Black rejection of their second-class citizenship status (D. Llorens, 1967:239–44). Several American scholars have discussed the class and psychological dynamics associated with the texture of Black hair. For a long time it was desirable to have straight or "good" hair as opposed to crinkly or "bad" hair (Cleaver, 1973:9–21; *see also* Lewis, 1955:56–66; and King and Ogunbizi, 1963:65–71). The "Afro" worn by Juneteenth celebrants affirms the growing acceptance of "natural" hair texture instead of hair that has been chemically processed and straightened. A former process-wearer put it well:

> The process was more or less propaganda and made many men feel that unless they wore their hair processed they didn't look good; that if they didn't have straight hair they were inferior. The newer generation doesn't feel inferior just because its hair isn't straight. (Llorens, 1967:143)

Juneteenth celebrants also demonstrated their rise from slavery to social parity with their white neighbors in the preparation and ingestion of special foods. On Juneteenth you

> really set aside that day for special cooking. You didn't eat the same thing you know, like everybody. That day you had special food: barbecue beef, mutton, pork. Everything that is especially set aside for that day.[8]

The annual barbecue ritual serves as a reminder of the slavery endured by Afro-American slaves. The smell of a gutted hog slowly barbecuing over white-hot hickory ashes links each year's Juneteenth celebrants with their slave ancestors: they are experiencing the same aroma that slaves and newly emancipated Blacks did earlier. It can be further noted that the barbecue pit serves as a fitting symbol of the slave's servitude and also of their emancipation from bondage. Juneteenth celebrants praise the "pit barbecue." One celebration cook apologized for not barbecuing "the old way [where] you used to dig a hole and have a pit."[9] Making this simple hole in the ground is an annual reenactment of the precise way that slaves and the first celebrants of emancipation barbecued their meat.[10] Is it any wonder that "pit" and not "southern" is the adjective primarily used by Afro-American barbecue merchants in such northern cities as Indianapolis, Chicago, and Cleveland? And some barbecue merchants would rather go out of business than alter their slave-originated pit method of cooking to meet current sanitation standards (Zobel, 1977:61).

Juneteenth speakers annually reassure their audiences that they are American citizens. The need for such an annual reminder is clearly evident in this frustrated outburst made by a minister after a stirring Juneteenth sermon: "I'm not a citizen of this country. My home is in glory."[11] Liberal doses of patriotism and racial progress are the cure that Juneteenth speakers have traditionally given their audiences. As one celebrant remembered:

They would mention that he [the Black American] always obeyed all the laws. And he fought in all the battles and that nobody can point their finger at him for being a traitor. I've heard that and ... I can recall that in this note there would be his attainments. And how he hasn't reflected anything but credit on himself since being free.[12]

In addition to securing inspiring speakers, the local Juneteenth Committee would promote civic pride in their communities by: sending out the date to community members who had moved away; planning, cooking, and serving the annual meal; and organizing the celebrants into teams to clean up the community "cemetery"[13] and "countryside."[14] This group of Black citizens would start

meeting just about, ooooh, let's say the first or second week in May and we'd run about three or four meetings and you'd have all your money and everybody would have seen everybody and by the time the 19th of June come, well, you should have all your plans ready. And all you have to do is go buy your meat and you got your prices on it and your wood to cook it with and that was normally it.[15]

Two of the committee's activities, the morning parade and afternoon baseball game, have been successful means of improving race relations between the Black and white citizens in the Southwest. The parades through the downtown area force the white citizens to see the various civic, religious, and social organizations that exist in their town's Black community. The receiving of a parade permit keeps alive in the Juneteenth celebrants a sense of citizenship in the town (fig. 118). And the mingling of Black and white citizens along the parade route also gives the Black citizens a feeling of civic self-worth.

But it has been the Juneteenth baseball games that have done the most to improve race relations in the small towns of Texas, Louisiana, Arkansas, and Oklahoma. It is hard to fully appreciate the uniting effect that these games had on the Black and white citizens of these area hamlets. No business was transacted on Juneteenth. One old baseball star bragged:

And that day that we had that 19th of June, they closed the town up, man! They closed the bank up. They closed the bank up, the stores up, and come down [to the baseball game].[16]

And another celebrant remembered integrated baseball games on the 19th of June:

Now you take out there at Cheek [Oklahoma]. Now every time we had a picnic, we had a white community out there too. Generally you had a baseball game. Now the first integration I saw long years [ago], we used to play white boys out there in Cheek, way back there. Negro boys used to play the white boys outta Cheek all the time.[17]

The social significance of these Juneteenth baseball games is underscored by the fact that baseball is the sports metaphor for American culture. Jacques Bar-

Figure 118 *Juneteenth committee members preparing a float.*

zun argues that "whoever wants to know the heart and mind of America had better learn baseball" (1978:9). And President Herbert Hoover once said: "Next to religion, baseball has furnished a greater impact on American life than any other institution" (quoted in Barzun, 1978:9).

Our cultural calendar reflects baseball's impact. American springs are marked by major league spring training, and the president or some other elected official or national figure throws out the first ball at the opening game of the season. Like the Japanese emperor's planting of the first rice shoot in May, the president's ritualistic first pitch in April also signals the beginning of the American planting season. And, by the same token, the World Series, which is often referred to as "the fall classic," is in essence a national cultural harvest festival. The crops that were planted in the spring and cultivated during the warm summer months have now been harvested, and the nation has time to play and rejoice over the harvest before the chilling winds of winter drive Americans indoors.

American English is heavily sprinkled with baseball nomenclature. For example, "major league" and "big leagues" are synonymous with the best in our society. A successful broadway play is a "smash hit." In the affairs of the heart, a spurned American boy might say "I can't get to first base with her" or "I struck out." Our military brass often refers to the "home base" of operations. An American criminal is often said to have run "afoul" of the law. Unreasonable financial demands are considered to be "out of the ball park," while conversely a reasonable price is "a ball-park figure." A successful person is often described as an individual who has "cleaned up," in the fashion of baseball's "clean-up hitter." An ill-advised project has "three strikes" against it. Americans take "a rain check" on invitations they cannot accept. And a novice in any field of work is often called a "rookie." Perhaps the clearest indication of baseball's influence on American speech is the fact that the simple phrase "ball game" on a Juneteenth program conveys the idea of baseball to black and white celebrants alike.

Juneteenth's exciting baseball games and colorful parades often received positive news coverage in local newspapers. As one celebrant said:

> Oh yeah, they used to cover it. . . . The paper, take for instance *The Banner Press* here, we used to call it *The Brenham Daily Banner Press*. It give good coverage on it. 'Bout the only time you see anything for a Negro that wasn't that he stole something was on the 19th of June.[18]

But celebrants of Juneteenth have never been totally satisfied with these various unofficial recognitions of their celebrations. There has always been a very strong political side to Juneteenth celebrations. Local candidates for public office are remembered as having helped, sponsored, and spoken at past celebrations:

> Yes, they would invite the candidates out to speak like they used to. And the primary now comes off now in August, now. But it used to be in June and they'd have the candidates. All the candidates would come out and speak. And, generally . . . the candidates would give beef. The man running for sheriff or judge or something, he'd give them the beef. And another one would give the bread and they'd cook it and have a celebration.[19]

This political activity often bore fruit. In one east Texas town a mayor who had sponsored post-Juneteenth observances saw to it that electricity, street lights, sewer lines, and indoor toilets were made available to the Black voters before he left office.[20] And "black and white" Juneteenth buttons were worn by Atlanta, Georgia, civil-rights marchers during the early 1960s.[21]

Refusing to work on June 19th is the most politica! of all Juneteenth rituals. It speaks to the heart of the issue. For if slavery is "forced labor," what better way to register your individual rejection of the system than by simply refusing to work? Stories like the following narrative are still told by some Juneteenth celebrants:

> I have a friend—I wish she were here to tell you—her uncle or grand-daddy or something was seemingly on his way . . . seemingly his boss or master had sent him some place to get a load of flour or something and he was on his way back when he met a white man and he told him "Well,

you're free now." He said "Sure enough. Do you mean that?" He said "Yes. You're free." Said he said "Thank you." Said he got out and left the wagon right there. (Laughter) Said he didn't even complete his journey to carry it back. He said "I'm free. I'm not going any further." She tells that. I don't know if that's true or not, but she was telling that the other day. But I don't know if that's true or not.[22]

A popular boast is: "My daddy said he wouldn't ask a mule to move if it was sitting in his lap on the 19th of June."[23]

Since emancipation, a wide range of Blacks have adhered to the ritual of not working on June 19th. Sharecroppers were given the day off.

My great-great grandfather told me stories of the 19th and how they did him. And how sometimes Negroes were supposed to be picking cotton and the boss man was always talking about "Well, tomorrow's your day. So I won't be looking for you tomorrow." They always gave them this day off, regardless of when it came. They always gave them this day off. They never had to worry. They always knew they had this holiday coming.[24]

But factory workers did not always get the day off. One celebrant noted the differences in agricultural and industrial jobs as far as observing the 19th of June was concerned:

You see most all of them people was farmers, so they could lay their crops aside a couple of days and go. But you can't do that on a job. . . . And no kidding, I have seen guys lose their jobs for taking off for the 19th of June. I've actually seen it happen. They lost their job. The man would tell 'em "Well, by God, if you don't work the 19th of June . . . don't come back. . . . Get your time!"[25]

And college students at Jarvis Christian College[26] and Prairie View A and M College[27] were excused from classes on the 19th of June.

This quasi-holiday status of Juneteenth eventually spawned the sentiment to make this day in June a legal holiday. One Juneteenth speaker told his audience:

And may I stop here and say that many of the Black peoples today feel that we should not celebrate or should not work toward a legal holiday for the deliverance of a Black man from slavery. [But] many of us Black folks today feel that this is wrong. That we should set aside and work toward a legal holiday.[28]

And a celebrant concurred with this sentiment by arguing that Juneteenth "should be a red spot on the calendar and really took aside for."[29]

In the decade of the 1970s, Juneteenth legislation was introduced into the Texas state legislature. In 1972, two Black congressmen, Zan Holmes of Dallas and Curtis Graves of Houston, introduced a resolution which recognized "Juneteenth as an annual, though unofficial, 'holiday of significance to all Texans and, particularly, to the blacks of Texas, for whom this date symbolizes freedom from slavery' " ("Austin Wire," 1972:10). And in 1979, Black State Representative Al Edwards introduced a bill to make Juneteenth an official Texas holiday and it passed (" 'Juneteenth' Day . . .," 1979:8). Through this political action, Representative Edwards assures the "end of the old traditions when Blacks had to sneak off their jobs to celebrate the day" (ibid.). Representative Edwards also feels that his recently signed legislation will allow "Blacks and other Texans to take pride in Black culture. . . ." (ibid.).

This recently passed Juneteenth law will have significant, immediate, and future civic and political implications for southwestern Black Americans. Representative Edwards's Juneteenth legislation elevates this one-hundred-and-twenty-five-year-old informal freedom festival from being primarily a "jollification," "wang dang doodle," "function," "hoe down," "good times," or "nigger day"[30] that only had significance for Blacks, to an official Texas holiday which must be recognized by all citizens of the Lone Star State. In short, Juneteenth can no longer be viewed by outsiders as a "nigger day" or its Black celebrants as "niggers." The passage of this bill finally gives official status to the underlying tradition of all the past Juneteenth celebrations, i.e., affirming Blacks' right to first-class citizenship and attempting to improve their sociopolitical condition through the American political process. The Edwards bill gives encouragement for future civic and political struggles, because, beginning on June 19, 1980, white Texans are required by law, not because of some paternal largess, to "close the town down!"

Notes

1. Interview: Mr. Willie Hygh, Karnack, Texas, 16 June 1972.

2. Interview: Mrs. Effie Lewis, Detroit, Mich., 10 Aug. 1972.

3. Interview: Mrs. C. A. Nelson, Milano, Texas, 19 June 1972.

4. Interview: Mrs. Ellie Fisher, Little Rock, Ark., 12 Nov. 1980.

5. Interview: Mrs. Katherine Burton, Hawkins, Texas, 14 Nov. 1972.

6. Personal communication from Mr. Haywood Hygh, Jr., Compton, Cal., n.d.

7. Interview: Mr. Paul Darby, Austin, Texas, 15 Nov. 1972.

8. Ibid.

9. Interview: Mr. Lovelady, Rockdale, Texas, 19 June 1972.

10. *See* Douglass (1963:797). Thirty-five years after Douglass made his statement, sponsors of a September 22d Emancipation Celebration advertised that "a feature of the day

will be an old-fashioned barbecue of beef, pork, mutton, and chicken" ("City News in Brief" [1898:4]).

11. Interview: Reverend Smith, Rockdale, Texas, 19 June 1972.

12. Interview: Mrs. E. B. Tollette, Little Rock, Ark., 19 Sept. 1973.

13. Interview: Mrs. Florence Hygh, Rockdale, Texas, 15 June 1972.

14. Interview: Mr. J. E. Reaves, Tyler, Texas, 13 Nov. 1972.

15. Interview: Mr. Paul Darby, Austin, Texas, 15 Nov. 1972.

16. Interview: Mr. Judson Henry, Hawkins, Texas, 14 Nov. 1972.

17. Interview: Mr. Marzee Douglas, Ardmore, Okla., 21 June 1972.

18. Interview: Mr. Booker T. Washington Hogan, Breham, Texas, 15 Nov. 1972.

19. Interview: Mr. Marzee Douglas, Ardmore, Okla., 21 June 1972.

20. Interview: Mr. Booker T. Washington Hogan, Breham, Texas, 15 Nov. 1972.

21. Interview: Mrs. Elizabeth Hodge, Hawkins, Texas, 13 Nov. 1972.

22. Interview: Mrs. Lillian Crisp, Ardmore, Okla., 21 June 1972.

23. Personal communication from Ms. Bess Lomax-Hawes, Washington, D.C., n.d. This image also appears in "Big Bill" Broonzy's "Plough-hand Blues":
"I wouldn't tell a mule to get up, Lord,
   if he'd sit down in my lap.
I wouldn't tell a mule to get up, Lord,
   if he'd set down in my lap.
Now I declare I'm through ploughin'
   Oooh Lord, that's what killed my ol' grand pap."
See Nicholas (1973:49).

24. Interview: Mr. William H. Ammons, Tyler, Texas, 12 Nov. 1972.

25. Interview: Mr. Paul Darby, Austin, Texas, 15 Nov. 1972.

26. Interview: Dr. Martin Edwards, Tyler, Texas, 13 Nov. 1972.

27. Interview: Dr. Joseph J. Grimes, Tyler, Texas, 13 Nov. 1972.

28. Transcription: Reverend Kelly Williams, Rockdale, Texas, 18 June 1972.

29. Interview: Mr. Paul Darby, Austin, Texas, 15 Nov. 1972.

30. "Nigger day" is defined as "a loggers' name for Saturday" (see Adams, 1974:206). Mississippi's May 8th and Florida's May 22d Emancipation Day observances were also referred to as "nigger day" by some of the celebrants I interviewed.

Bibliography

Adams, Ramon F.
  1974   *Western Words: A Dictionary of the American West.* Norman: University of Oklahoma.
"Austin Wire: Juneteenth Recognized by House."
  1972   *Dallas Morning News,* 10 June, p. 10.
Barzun, Jacques
  1978   "Sports World Coming out of the Closets." *The Herald-Telephone,* 20 Mar., p. 9.
Chesnut, Mary Boykin
  1949   *A Diary From Dixie.* Edited by Ben Ames Williams. Cambridge, Mass.: Riverside Press.
"City News in Brief."
  1898   *The Illinois Record,* 17 Sept., p. 4.
Cleaver, Eldridge
  1973   "As Crinkly as Yours." In *Mother Wit from the Laughing Barrel: Readings in the Interpretations of Afro-American Folklore,* edited by Alan Dundes. Englewood Cliffs, N.J.: Prentice Hall.
Douglass, Frederick
  1963   "Rejoicing Over the Proclamation." *Douglass' Monthly* V (Feb.):797.
Franklin, John Hope
  1968   *From Slavery to Freedom: A History of Negro Americans.* New York: Alfred A. Knopf.
Genovese, Eugene
  1974   *Roll, Jordan, Roll: The World the Slaves Made.* New York: Pantheon.
" 'Juneteenth' Day Becomes State Holiday in Texas."
  1979   *Jet,* vol. 56, no. 18 (July 19), p.8.
"Juneteenth: Texas Carries on Tradition of Emancipation Holiday with Amusement Park Celebration."
  1951   *Ebony,* June, p. 30.
King, H. H., and Ogunbizi, T.
  1963   "Should Negro Women Straighten Their Hair? Two Points of View—American, African." *Negro Digest,* Aug., pp. 65–71.
Lewis, Hylan
  1955   *Blackways of Kent.* Chapel Hill: University of North Carolina Press.
Llorens, D.
  1967   "Natural Hair: New Symbol of Race Pride." *Ebony,* Dec., pp. 239–44.
Nash, Gary B.
  1970   *Class and Society in Early America.* Englewood Cliffs, N.J.: Prentice Hall.
Nicholas, A. X., ed.
  1973   *Woke Up This Mornin': Poetry of the Blues.* New York: Bantam Books.
Schwartz, Jack
  1963   "Men's Clothing and the Negro." *Phylon* xxiv (Fall):224–31.
Wiggins, William H., Jr.
  1975   " 'Lift Every Voice': A Study of Afro-American Emancipation Celebrations." In *Discovering Afro-America,* edited by R. D. Abrahams and John F. Szwed. Leiden: Brill.
Zobel, Kathleen
  1977   "Hog Heaven: Barbecue in the South." *Southern Exposure* V (Summer and Fall):61.

Postscript

I n organizing the *Celebration* exhibition, the Smithsonian Institution has
undertaken the most difficult task a museum can be faced with. It has at-
tempted to take the unconscious and make it conscious; to take the material object and show its symbolic or spiritual meaning; to take ephemeral material and put it in a permanent scholarly context; to take objects from diverse
and unfamiliar cultures and communicate their meaning to an American audience; and, perhaps most difficult of all, to take objects from American culture
that are familiar to their users and show how they carry symbolic meanings similar to the exotic objects collected from apparently unrelated cultures.

Even with the help of the catalogue and this book, the attentive American visitor to the exhibit may have difficulty receiving the message that is being sent.
While all humans share common assumptions concerning the world in which
they live, the American of 1982 is perhaps least in touch with the roots of his
celebratory behavior. The linkage between, say, the Washington Cherry Blossom
Festival and rituals of fertility, fecundity, and renewal in other cultures can be
only dimly recognized, as Roger Abrahams points out in his essay. American festivals are neither dominated nor controlled by the forces of nature that shape
many of the world's festivals. That the Washington Cherry Blossom Festival is
scheduled in advance and takes place on the appointed days whether or not the
cherry blossoms are early or late suggests this fact.

Ritual and ceremony continue to exist in American life, but they are often
shaped by forces external to the "folk": for example, by commercial or governmental considerations. Observers are quick to perceive the commercial implications behind American rituals, and Daniel Boorstin has even coined a phrase,
"pseudo-event," to describe the screen of distortion and manipulation that modern man must penetrate to get to the real event.

Many observers question the validity of the term "folk" in its application to the American scene. That term, particularly outside the United States, has often referred to cultural survivals of the past, the traditions—sometimes belittled but more often exalted—of a contemporary industrial society's premodern past. The term "folk culture" has usually been distinguished from "tribal culture" through the division between colonial powers and the areas of the world they colonized. The contrasting terms continue to reflect their association with white and non-white worlds, or more generally between cultural survivals in highly industrialized societies as contrasted with those survivals, or sometimes dominant traditions, in "third world" cultures undergoing various forms of modernization or industrialization. But America, or rather the United States of America, never had a feudal past in the European sense, as Louis Hartz and others have pointed out, and for a variety of reasons and with a variety of exceptions, leaped onto the world stage as a nation created by an act of will rather than by tradition, a "novus ordo seclorum" as the inscription on the truncated pyramid on the U.S. one-dollar bill proclaims. The fact that few Americans understand this fundamental national symbol reinforces the point made concerning the tenuous character of American folk traditions. Although many European-derived folk traditions survived in America from colonial times and continue today (increasingly recognized and encouraged by such events as the Smithsonian Festival of American Folklife), and although many Native American (Indian) tribal traditions survived, evolved, and flourish today, the folk traditions associated with the European-derived American population groups have been transformed by rapid changes in technology; by "Americanization" of newly arriving immigrants; by the decline of religious belief; and by improvements in medicine and public health (which have obviated the need for many of the propitiatory aspects of traditional ceremonies).

This cultural transformation has drained some American celebratory events of their initial meaning and added new meanings consistent with the secular, secure, and "mass culture" character of contemporary American life. Instead of being crucial to the existence of the folk, American celebrations are sometimes merely incidental and entertaining epiphenomena. Indeed, as Richard Dorson points out in his essay: "We must reckon with the deplorable *lack* in the United States of festive occasions." And, as Barbara Myerhoff adds, American festive occasions are more often celebrations of an individual's birth, marriage, divorce, or death, rather than communal recognitions of the importance of *communitas* in present-day life.

An extreme (and therefore instructive) example of the distinction between U.S. and non-U.S. folk festivals is the Turtle Festival at Churubusco in Indiana. Although not discussed in this book, Richard Dorson has elsewhere described how the festival arose from the belief of a local farmer that there was a huge turtle in the local lake. Draining the lake to discover the turtle, the farmer discovered the falsity of the belief. But the incident stimulated the community to celebrate annually the "giant turtle" of Churubusco.

As Dorson has pointed out, if such a festival arose in some other part of the world, it would undoubtedly express the *belief* of the community in the real existence of the turtle; in the United States the celebration reflects the community's good-natured nonbelief. The celebration, while it can legitimately be seen as a folk festival, is more reflective of American mass culture, with all its skeptical, hedonistic, and commercial overtones.

Although there is no evidence of any society surviving without ritual, as Myerhoff points out, it is perhaps harder for Americans in 1982 to *understand* the symbolic and unconscious meaning of their own and others' rituals than to *engage* in ritualistic behavior at home and *enjoy* observing ritualistic behavior abroad. Will the *Celebration* exhibition make the American visitor conscious of the rituals he shares with other humans around the world? Although the introductory section is optimistically entitled "Objects Speak," the objects do not speak their underlying meaning directly. Will the American, who demonstrates emotionally that his flag is more than a piece of colored cloth when he reveres or reviles it, understand that the other objects in the exhibition have similar emotional connotations and symbolic implications in the cultures in which they are embedded? This is the museological challenge that the Smithsonian hopes to meet: to take the "divine *detritus,* the holy or beautiful images and artifacts bequeathed to us by celebration, whether exalted or frenetic" (as Victor Turner so eloquently puts it), and make the material residue convey its emotional and symbolic meaning to a different audience in another time, place, and context.

Whether the Smithsonian succeeds or not will be determined by how effectively the visitor is led along the path of comprehension to enlightenment. Education is a process of leading, as the word's Latin origin suggests. The achievement, the understanding, must ultimately come from the one being led, not from the one leading. It is possible for the visitor to go out the same door wherein he came none the wiser and perhaps burdened with more misconceptions than he had when he started. But if the visitor is led by the exhibit to a greater conceptual and emotional understanding of himself and others, rather than being merely stimulated by bizarre customs and exotic objects, then the Smithsonian will have performed the role given it by its founder, James Smithson, to aid in "the increase and diffusion of knowledge among men."

Wilcomb E. Washburn
Director, Office of American Studies
Smithsonian Institution

About the Contributors

Roger D. Abrahams

Roger D. Abrahams, Kenan Professor of Anthropology and Humanities at Scripps and Pitzer Colleges, has had long research interests in festivals and other public performances. Most of his writings have focused on Afro-American folklore and culture, beginning with his *Deep Down in the Jungle ... Negro Narrative Folklore from the Streets of Philadelphia* (1964); Anglo-American balladry; children's lore; and, most recently, folklore theory. Books of his soon to be published include *After Africa* (with John Szwed), *The Man of Words in the West Indies, Folktales of the Black World*, and *Events: A Poetics of Everyday Life*. He has served as President of the American Folklore Society and has been a member of the Smithsonian Folklife Advisory Council.

Barbara A. Babcock

Barbara A. Babcock is Associate Professor of English at the University of Arizona. She received her B.A. in Comparative Literature from Northwestern University, and her M.A. and Ph.D. in Comparative Literature from the University of Chicago, where she was also a Special Fellow in Anthropology. She has taught at the University of Texas (1972–78), been a Weatherhead Fellow at the School of American Research (1977–78), and Member of the School of Social Science at the Institute for Advanced Study (1979–80). Her principal research interests are narrative theory, modes of reflexivity and inversion (especially Pueblo ritual clowning), and ethnoaesthetics and folk art. Her publications include: "The Novel and the Carnival World" (1974); " 'A Tolerated Margin of Mess': The Trickster and his Tales Re-considered" (1975); "The Story in the Story: Metanarration in Folk Narrative" (1976); "Liberty's a Whore: Inversions, Marginalia, and

Picaresque Narrative" in *The Reversible World: Essays in Symbolic Inversion* (1978), which she also edited; "Too Many, Too Few: Ritual Modes of Signification" (1978); "Ritual Undress and the Comedy of Self and Other: Bandelier's *The Delight Makers*" (1980); "Reflexivity: Definitions and Discriminations" in *Signs about Signs: The Semiotics of Self-Reference* (1980), which she also edited; and " 'Arrange Me into Disorder': Fragments and Reflections on Ritual Clowning" (1981).

J. C. Crocker

J. C. Crocker was educated at Duke University, the Université de Paris, and Harvard University. As part of the Harvard Central Brazil Project he carried out research among the Bororo Indians of Mato Grosso, Brazil, and he has published numerous papers on this society. He has taught at Duke University, New York University, Université de Paris-X (Nanterre), and he is now Professor of Anthropology at the University of Virginia. His current research interests include ethnicity in complex societies, structural aspects of popular culture, and critical relationships between anthropology and the humanities.

William H. Crocker

William H. Crocker, currently Associate Curator of South American Ethnology at the Smithsonian Institution, took his degrees in anthropology at Stanford University and the University of Wisconsin, Madison. He first went to the Ramkokamekra-Canela in 1957 to commence a re-study of an earlier monograph, *The Eastern Timbira,* written about these same people by Curt Nimuendiju, who lived with them in the 1930s. Crocker has returned to the Canela ten times in twenty-two years and spent sixty-four months with them. One of his specialties, besides studying long-term processes of change, is the analysis of the numerous and lengthy Canela festivals, all of which he has seen several times.

Richard M. Dorson

Richard M. Dorson was Distinguished Professor of History and Folklore and Director of the Folklore Institute at Indiana University. He was also a member of the Smithsonian Council and of the Smithsonian Folklife Advisory Council. His publications include *Jonathan Draws the Long Bow, Bloodstoppers and Bearwalkers,* and *Land of the Millrats.* Professor Dorson died on September 11, 1981.

Ronald L. Grimes

Ronald L. Grimes is Associate Professor of Religion and Culture at Wilfrid Laurier University, Waterloo, Ontario, Canada, where he teaches religion and the arts, as well as ritual studies. He is the author of *The Divine Imagination,* a book on the major prophecies of William Blake, and *Symbol and Conquest,* a book on public ritual and drama in Santa Fe, New Mexico. Recently he has written a number of articles on ritual and theater. He is Chairperson of the Ritual Studies Consultation of the American Academy of Religion.

Barbara Kirshenblatt-Gimblett

Barbara Kirshenblatt-Gimblett received her Ph.D. in Folklore from Indiana University in 1972. She has served on the faculties of the University of Texas, University of Pennsylvania, Columbia University, and most recently, New York University, where she chairs the Department of Performance Studies. She is a Research Associate at the YIVO Institute for Jewish Research. Her publications include *Speech Play: Research and Resources for Studying Linguistic Creativity* (1976); *Image Before My Eyes: A Photographic History of Jewish Life in Poland 1864–1939* (1977), with Lucjan Dobroszycki; and *Fabric of Jewish Life: Textiles from The Jewish Museum Collection* (1977), with Cissy Grossman. Her most recent book, *Ashkenaz: Essays in Jewish Folklore and Culture,* will be published by the University of Pennyslvania Press.

Priscilla Rachun Linn

Priscilla Rachun Linn, Smithsonian Post-Doctoral Fellow for 1981, holds a D. Phil. from Oxford University, England. In 1970 she joined the Harvard Chiapas Project upon the invitation of Professor Evon Z. Vogt, and she conducted fieldwork in San Juan Chamula, Chiapas, financed by a Doherty Foundation Grant in Latin American Studies. Between 1979 and 1981, she researched Latin American objects, coordinated research, and wrote labels for the *Celebration: A World of Art and Ritual* exhibit. Currently she is editing for publication her Oxford B. Litt. thesis, "A Structural Study of Ritual Transvestism," and her D. Phil. thesis, "The Religious Office Holders in Chamula." Married to Johannes F. Linn, economist, she is the mother of two children, "Pepi," aged 7, and Natasha, aged 3.

Thomas R. Lyons

Thomas R. Lyons is an archaeologist specializing in the application of earth-oriented spacecraft and aircraft digital data and photographic imagery to the analysis of historic and prehistoric cultural resources. He received his doctorate from the University of New Mexico and is Chief of the Remote Sensing Division, a joint National Park Service/University of New Mexico operation. Current projects include a publication series on remote sensory applications research; a cultural ecology study of Catalonia, Spain; and field investigations of the "Penitentes" of northern New Mexico and southern Colorado. He lives in Albuquerque, New Mexico.

John J. MacAloon

John J. MacAloon took his advanced degrees with the Committee on Social Thought at the University of Chicago. His research interests include the social anthropology of the nation-state, international cultural performances, and nineteenth-century social history. He is the author of *This Great Symbol: Pierre de Coubertin and the Origins of the Modern Olympic Games* and editor of *Rite, Drama, Festival, Spectacle: Rehearsals Toward a Theory of Cultural Performances*. He is presently Assistant Professor, Social Sciences Collegiate Division, and Associated Faculty, Committee on Social Thought, the University of Chicago.

Barbara Myerhoff

Barbara Gay Myerhoff was born in Cleveland, Ohio, and educated at the University of Chicago and the University of California at Los Angeles, where she received her doctorate in 1968. She is currently Professor of Anthropology and was formerly Chairperson at the University of Southern California. She has been a research associate at the Andrus Gerontology Center, University of Southern California, and in 1958 she received a Woodrow Wilson Fellowship. She has done fieldwork in South Central Mexico and in various parts of California. She is author of *Peyote Hunt: The Sacred Journey of the Huichol Indians* (1974) and *Number Our Days* (1978). She is co-editor, with Sally Falk Moore, of *Symbol and Politics in Communal Ideology: Cases and Questions* (1975) and *Secular Ritual: Form and Meanings* (1977). In 1977, with Lynne Littman, she won an Academy Award for the documentary film, *Number Our Days*.

Daniel W. Patterson

Daniel W. Patterson heads the Curriculum in Folklore at the University of North Carolina at Chapel Hill. He is a native of the state and studied at Duke University and the university where he now teaches. He is the author of *The Shaker Spiritual* and is currently preparing an edition of American nineteenth-century tunebook spirituals and a study of early Presbyterian gravestone iconography in the South.

Richard Schechner

Richard Schechner is Professor of Performance Studies at New York University's School of the Arts and has been Director of The Performance Group. Dr. Schechner's books include *Public Domain, Environmental Theater, Essays on Performance Theory*, and, as editor, with Mary Schuman, *Ritual, Play, and Performance: Readings in the Social Sciences/Theatre*. He has done fieldwork in India, Japan, and New Guinea.

Edith Turner

Edith Turner was born in England and obtained her master's degree from the University of Virginia. She has done much fieldwork with her husband, Victor Turner, and is co-author with him of *Image and Pilgrimage in Christian Culture* (1977). She has been co-editor of *Primavera* literary magazine.

Victor Turner

Victor Turner was born in Scotland and obtained his doctorate from the University of Manchester in 1955. He has served as Chairman of the Committee on Social Thought at the University of Chicago and is now the William R. Kenan, Jr., Professor of Anthropology at the University of Virginia. He has done fieldwork in Zambia, Uganda, Mexico, Ireland, Italy, France, Japan, and Brazil. He is the author of *The Forest of Symbols* (1967), *The Drums of Affliction* (1968), *The Ritual Process* (1969), *Dramas, Fields, and Metaphors* (1974), *Process, Performance, and Pilgrimage* (1980), and other monographs, and, with Edith Turner, *Image and Pilgrimage* (1977).

Stanley Walens

Stanley Walens, Assistant Professor of Anthropology at the University of Virginia, has specialized in the study of North American Indian ritual. He is author of *Feasting with Cannibals,* a monograph on Kwakiutl religion and cosmology.

Marta Weigle

Marta Weigle is a folklorist whose primary research interests lie in the Southwest, particularly New Mexico, where she has lived intermittently since 1961, and permanently since 1970. She received her doctorate from the University of Pennsylvania and is now an Associate Professor of Anthropology and English at the University of New Mexico, Albuquerque. Her present projects include an NEH-sponsored study of "Governmental Support of the Arts in New Mexico, 1933–43," a book on the Santa Fe and Taos writers' colonies, and a book on women and/in mythology. She lives in Santa Fe.

William H. Wiggins, Jr.

William H. Wiggins, Jr., is Associate Professor in the Afro-American Studies Department at Indiana University. He is a minister in the Christian Methodist Episcopal Church, having served as Chaplain at Lane College in Jackson, Tennessee, and at Texas College in Tyler, Texas. He has been a Rockefeller Fellow, doing research out of which this study emerged.

Index

Page numbers in *italics* refer to illustrations.

Photographic Credits

References are to figure numbers.

Raymond Adams: 94
American Museum of Natural History: 72–74
Thor Anderson: 80, 82
Baessler Archive, Museum für Völkerkunde: 107
Brooklyn Museum: 76
William H. Crocker: 56–62
Linda Dégh: 7
Ronald L. Grimes: 113–115
Michel Huet: 67
Institute for the Study of Human Issues, Philadelphia, Pa.: 12, 13
Jewish Museum: 52–55
Martin Karcher: 26, 27, 30
Hilda Kuper: 8, 9
R. Lambert: 31, 32
Library Company of Philadelphia: 89
Library of Congress: 24, 90
Thomas R. Lyons: 96–103, 104
R.K. McCord; Glenn Short: 17
Museum of the American Indian, Heye Foundation; George E. Pepper: 15
Museum of International Folk Art; Glenn Short: 18
Barbara Myerhoff: 50
National Archives: 70
New York Public Library: 92, 93
New York Times Pictures; Chester Higgins, Jr.: 71
Princeton Museum of Natural History; J. Bradley Babcock: 16
Sangeet Natak Akademi, New Delhi: 33
Richard Schechner: 29, 34, 35
School of American Research; Glenn Short: 14
Glenn Short: 19
Andrei Simic: 42, 47–49
Robert J. Smith: 6
Smithsonian Institution; Kim Nielsen: 2, 3, 5, 10, 11, 21–23, 36, 46, 68, 69, 75, 77, 78–79, 81, 106, 109; Jeffrey Ploskonka: 1, 25, 44, 45, 63, 64, 108, 111
William C. Sturtevant: 38–41
Suzanne Szasz: cover, 20
Victor Turner: 37
Wendy Watriss–Fred Baldwin: 116–118